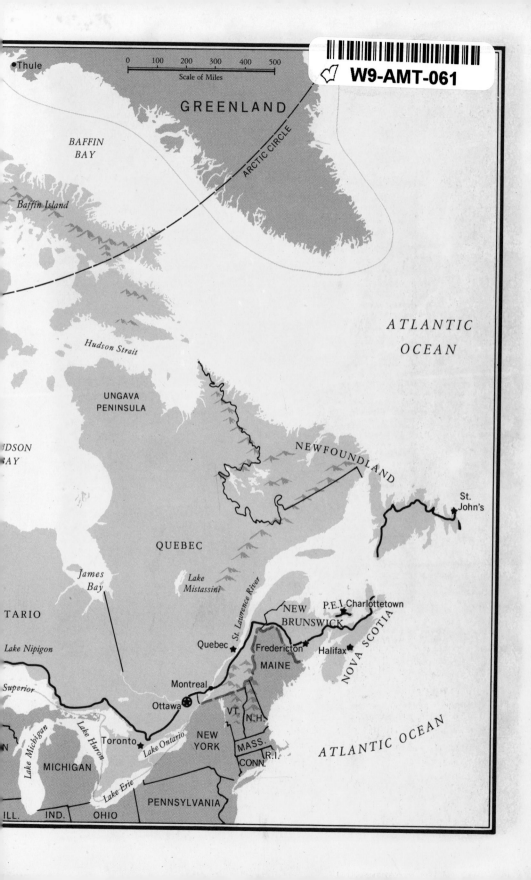

Thule

GREENLAND

BAFFIN
BAY

ARCTIC CIRCLE

Baffin Island

Hudson Strait

UNGAVA
PENINSULA

ATLANTIC
OCEAN

JDSON
BAY

NEWFOUNDLAND

QUEBEC

St. John's

James
Bay

Lake
Mistassini

St. Lawrence River

P.E.I. Charlottetown

NEW
BRUNSWICK

TARIO

Lake Nipigon

Quebec

Fredericton

Halifax

NOVA SCOTIA

Superior

Montreal

MAINE

Ottawa

VT.

N.H.

ATLANTIC OCEAN

Lake Michigan

Lake Huron

Toronto

Lake Ontario

NEW
YORK

MASS.

R.I.

CONN.

MICHIGAN

Lake Erie

PENNSYLVANIA

ILL.

IND.

OHIO

Scale of Miles

0   100   200   300   400   500

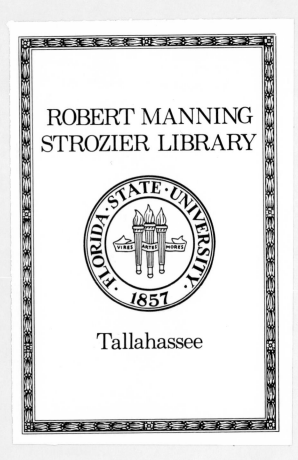

PORTRAIT OF
Canada

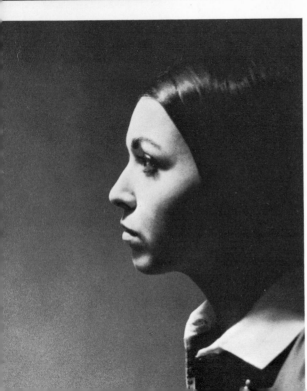

C Portrait of ANADA

by JAY and AUDREY WALZ

Photographs by John de Visser

A NEW YORK TIMES BOOK

American Heritage Press

NEW YORK

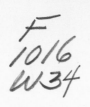

For all readers living south of
That Peaceful Border who have never
heard a Canadian say, *"Some of my*
best friends are Americans."

BOOK DESIGN *by Jos. Trautwein*

MAPS BY FRANCIS & SHAW, INC.

Copyright © 1970 by The New York Times Company.
All rights reserved.
Published by American Heritage Press, a subsidiary of McGraw-Hill, Inc.
Published in Canada by Fitzhenry & Whiteside.

Library of Congress Catalog Card Number: 77-111657
07-068090-6

Contents

c. 1000 The Norsemen build a large settlement in Newfoundland. (Excavations conducted since 1960 seem to prove this theory.)

1497 John Cabot, a Venetian navigator sailing under the English flag, reaches the shores of Newfoundland on St. John's Bay and claims the island for the British crown.

1534 Jacques Cartier plants on a Gaspé promontory the first French flag on North American soil.

1576–78 Sir Martin Frobisher, searching for the Northwest Passage, discovers and explores Baffin Island and Baffin Bay.

1605 Samuel de Champlain establishes the first French settlement in the New World at what is now Port Royal, Nova Scotia.

1608 Champlain founds Quebec City on the heights overlooking the St. Lawrence River.

1610 Henry Hudson, in his fourth quest for the Northwest Passage, discovers Hudson Bay, giving Britain her claim to the region. A mutinous crew sets him, his young son, and seven men adrift in a small boat, never to be seen again.

1670 King Charles II charters "The Governor and Company of Adventurers of England trading into Hudson's Bay," making the company sole owners of Rupert's Land, which eventually includes all of northwest Canada.

1713 Following the War of the Spanish Succession, the Treaty of Utrecht gives England mainland Nova Scotia, while France retains nearby Cape Breton Island.

On Cape Breton France begins building the fortress of Louisbourg, the largest in North America. It takes more than twenty years and serves as a base from which French privateers raid New England shipping.

1745 Provincial American forces capture Louisbourg, which Britain returns to France in 1748.

1749 To placate New Englanders, indignant over the return of Louisbourg, the British establish a military base at Halifax, Nova Scotia.

1750's The British expel thousands of French-speaking Acadians from their homes on the best farmlands and in the coastal villages of Nova Scotia.

1758 The British capture Louisbourg and raze it. They encourage the migration of New England colonists to lands vacated by the Acadians.

1759 General James Wolfe of England defeats General Louis Joseph Montcalm of France on the Plains of Abraham at Quebec City on September 13. Both generals are fatally wounded in the battle.

1763 Under the Treaty of Paris all of French North America becomes British territory.

1774 The Parliament of England adopts the Quebec Act, which guarantees French Québecois the right to speak French and to worship as Roman Catholics. French civil law is kept in force in the colony.

1775 After the outbreak of the American Revolution, American troops from New England and New York occupy Montreal and most of Quebec, abetted at first by Quebec farmers. The Americans fail to take the Citadel at Quebec City.

1776 The occupation forces retreat hastily when large numbers of British reinforcements arrive at Quebec City in the spring.

The Revolutionary War precipitates the exodus to Canada of forty thousand Loyalists.

1778 Captain James Cook, aboard the *Resolution,* puts in at Vancouver Island.

1788 John Meares, English merchant, establishes a trading post on Vancouver Island at Nootka Sound.

1789 Alexander Mackenzie, a Scottish explorer and fur trader, discovers the river that bears his name, following it to its mouth on the Arctic Ocean.

1791 Under the Constitutional Act, the British Parliament gives a measure of self-government to the central area of Canada and establishes two provinces there, Lower Canada (Quebec) and Upper Canada (Ontario), so called because it is up the St. Lawrence River.

1792 Captain George Vancouver explores and surveys the northwest coast of North America, circumnavigating the island now named for him.

1793 Mackenzie reaches the Pacific coast, completing the first overland journey across North America north of Mexico.

1797 David Thompson, fur trader, explorer, and self-trained cartographer, begins a series of journeys through the Canadian west, mapping the country so accurately by 1811 that much of his map is accepted today.

1808 Simon Fraser travels the length of the Fraser River.

1812 War between the United States and Great Britain is fought on Canadian soil and on the Great Lakes, but no territory changes hands.

1818 Following the Napoleonic Wars, British naval officers, inspired by Sir John Barrow, turn to Arctic exploration. The heroic work of Sir John Franklin, Sir John Ross, Sir William Edward Parry, and others begins to define Canada's Arctic coastline.

1837 Louis Joseph Papineau, leader of the French-Canadian Reform Party in Lower Canada, fires the *patriotes* to open rebellion against British authority. The revolt is put down by British regulars and English Canadian volunteers.

William Lyon Mackenzie, Scottish-born editor, political leader, and insurgent, tries to seize Toronto in an abortive rebellion against Upper Canada's governing clique. Later attempts by sympathetic Americans to "free Canada" are driven back.

1840 Lower and Upper Canada are reunited by the British Parliament. The two provinces do not work well in tandem, and some other form of union is sought.

1845 Sir John Franklin, with the *Erebus* and the *Terror,* sets off on still another search for the Northwest Passage.

1846 The United States and Great Britain agree to establish the western border at the 49th parallel, settling a long and bitter dispute in which the United States pressed for "Fifty-four Forty or Fight" and Britain claimed the Oregon Territory.

1848 When nothing is heard of Franklin or his ships after three years, the British Navy sends a relief expedition, the first of forty search parties in the next eleven years, which amass extensive geographic information on the Canadian Arctic. Evidence is finally found that all 129 of Franklin's men died of privation.

1864 A conference of delegates from Ontario, Quebec, Nova Scotia, New Brunswick, and Prince Edward Island meets at Charlottetown to discuss uniting in a confederation of Canada. Plans are furthered at a Quebec conference later in the year.

1865 Canadians, long antislavery, are sympathetic to the North in the American Civil War, and at least ten thousand men from Nova Scotia alone are volunteers in the Union Army, but the British government has been largely pro-Confederate, and the Canadian government regards the victorious Union Army with uneasiness.

1866 Fenian (Irish Republican) Civil War veterans strike at Britain by invading Canada at several points, with small success. On retreating across the United States border, they are arrested and disbanded by American authorities.

1867 The British Parliament approves the British North American Act joining Ontario, Quebec, Nova Scotia, and New Brunswick into Confederation as a Dominion of the British Empire.

1870 The Hudson's Bay Company's domain of Rupert's Land and Northwestern Territory, at the urging of the British government, is transferred to the new Confederation, which pays the company 300,000 pounds. Although the Bay keeps choice lands and mineral rights, this is a bigger bargain than the Louisiana Purchase.

The Province of Manitoba is formed after the first métis rebellion, led by Louis Riel, is put down without bloodshed by imperial and Canadian troops.

1871 On condition that she be given a rail link with the rest of Canada, British Columbia joins the Confederation.

Construction is begun on the transcontinental Canadian Pacific Railway.

1873 Prince Edward Island joins the Confederation.

1885 Canadian troops put down a second métis rebellion farther west, in land that will become Saskatchewan. This time the métis fight hard, and when they are finally overwhelmed, Riel is captured, convicted of treason, and hanged.

The last spike is driven at Craigellachie, British Columbia, and the Canadian Pacific Railway is completed after fourteen years' effort.

1903 The vexing question of the boundary between Canada and Alaska is finally settled by the Alaska Boundary Commission, consisting of three Americans and three representatives of British-Canadian interests. An Englishman votes with the Americans, and the Yukon loses its warm-water outlets.

1905 Saskatchewan and Alberta become the eighth and ninth provinces of Canada.

1926 An Imperial Conference in London declares that Great Britain and the Dominions are "autonomous communities within the British Empire, equal in status, in no way subordinate one to another in any aspect of their domestic or external affairs, though united by a common allegiance to the Crown, and freely associated as members of the British Commonwealth of Nations."

1931 The Statute of Westminster further clarifies Canada's autonomous position by removing remaining legal inequalities between Canada and the British government.

1940–42 On June 23 the Royal Canadian Mounted Police schooner *St. Roch,* Sergeant Henry Larsen commanding, leaves Vancouver on her west-to-east voyage through the Northwest Passage. On October 11, 1942, after two winters in the polar ice, the *St. Roch* reaches Halifax.

1944 Traversing the Passage from east to west this time, the *St. Roch* reaches Vancouver only eighty-six days after she left Halifax and is the first vessel to travel the Northwest Passage in both directions.

1949 Newfoundland, a British colony for more than three hundred years, becomes the tenth and latest province of Canada.

1959 The St. Lawrence Seaway, a joint undertaking of Canada and the United States to open the Great Lakes to ocean traffic, is inaugurated on June 26 at Eisenhower Locks near Cornwall, Ontario, with Queen Elizabeth II and President Eisenhower attending the ceremonies.

1967 Canada marks her first century in Confederation with a year-long celebration, opening scores of parks, museums, and auditoriums and welcoming fifty million visitors to her first world's fair, Expo 67, at Montreal.

The Big Land

"Canada is really not so much a country as it

is a geographical expression."

Left, the magnificent Rockies of western Canada. Above, a
priest approaches a large Ukrainian church in Manitoba.

The church is the dominant structure in this French village on the Gaspé Peninsula.

Canada's foremost tourist, Pierre Elliott Trudeau, campaigned for the office of prime minister by urging his countrymen to join him in a "great adventure of discovery."

"The important thing," he kept insisting, "is that Canadians are beginning to realize for the first time that this country is a fabulous place."

Mr. Trudeau, an inveterate traveler, had swum the Bosporus, trekked through the Arabian Desert, and crossed the Himalayas—only to find his "great adventure" at home. And if Canadians are beginning to experience the excitement of their land, then outsiders, too, are beginning to sense the stirrings above North America's 49th parallel.

Thousands caught glimpses of this excitement at Expo 67, where Canadian pavilions, both federal and provincial, were among the most original and where Canadian-made films displayed breakthroughs in cinematic techniques that have since been used in American films and on American TV. Perhaps what these visitors saw surprised them. This wasn't the Canada most of them had encountered at the quiet lake resorts to which they had gone for a spot of fishing. This was unknown country.

For anyone who wants to explore the Big Land in a big way, the longest continuous highway in the world beckons. It is the Trans-Canada, spanning five thousand miles across the top half of a continent and completed in time for the country's centennial celebration in 1967. An American driver starting at St. John's in the Province of Newfoundland, the highway's eastern terminus, will discover at once that Canada really is a foreign country. The brightly colored little houses spilling down steep hillsides or perched high atop cliffs overlooking a raging sea are like nothing in New England or elsewhere in this hemisphere. The many languages spoken on the waterfront also make the traveler feel he is farther from home than he thought. And when he does hear English, he's hard put to identify the accent. Is it Irish, or Devon English, or a bit of both with a little Shakespearean thrown in? If he still thinks, as many Americans do, that Canada is simply a northern extension of the United States, except for the royal crowns on highway markers, the Newfoundland stretch of the Trans-Canada should jolt him out of that notion. He may be pulled up short, as we were, by a flock of sheep dozing on the sunny highway. Our horn barely disturbed them, though one elderly ewe did raise a reproving head.

We had seen dozens of flocks grazing on the hillsides of Turkey and Jordan, but that was the extent of our acquaintance with the species. Happily we saw a man with a stick swing up the highway. The shepherd at last. But he simply stood there regarding us.

"Can you move your sheep off the highway, please? We have to catch the ferry."

Slowly he surveyed the flock. "They're none of mine," he said finally. Then walking up to the car, he inspected us at length, too. "You in a hurry?" We nodded. "Foreigners," he said, nodding in turn.

A pastoral scene on the shores of Newfoundland's Conception Bay

He meant "off-islanders." Americans and people from the rest of Canada and other odd places are all considered "foreign." Off-islanders are frequently in a hurry. True Newfoundlanders pay no attention to time.

"There'll be someone along."

"But when?"

From around a clump of trees another native sauntered, stopping halfway to the road to consider the situation. Then he whistled, and a dog bounded up from a totally different direction. Man and dog hustled the sheep off the road. "There you are," the first Newfoundlander said, gesturing us ahead as though he were personally awarding us the freedom of the highway. The second man also graciously waved us on.

We caught the ferry to Nova Scotia, having allowed ourselves at the beginning of our journey the extra time that Newfoundlanders had advised, being wise in the ways of their fellows.

Newfoundland suggests the wild west coast of Ireland, while the Province of Nova Scotia lives up to its name by being indeed a New Scotland, although perhaps a little softer than the old and with an unexpectedly French fishing village here and there. But the Trans-Canada at once puts a tourist in the most Scottish spot west of the Hebrides,

Cape Breton Island. He begins to pass an infinity of rocky coves, shrouded in mist on a gray day, the pines providing dark accents. High on his right looms a mountain. Is it his imagination or is there a distant skirl of bagpipes? He rolls down his window and realizes he actually is hearing "Over the Water to Skye." There's a school of Scottish arts and crafts not far off the road, and it may be part of its annual festival he is catching on the wind.

He probably won't escape the province without hearing the pipes again. An extraordinary number of Nova Scotians seem to play them, and of these, a great many are teen-age girls who in a different environment might be drum majorettes or flower children. They're mini-skirted, but the skirts are kilts.

The sea is always with the traveler until he pushes on into the next province, New Brunswick, where the landscape is suddenly pastoral as he follows the Saint John River valley on his way toward Quebec. He passes the longest covered bridge in the world—everything in the Big Land, even an antiquated bridge, is big—and at a gas station he hears French spoken. But these speakers, he is told, are Acadians, not Québecois. The only Acadians he has heard of are in Longfellow's *Evangeline*. They aren't just a poet's fancy, he learns, but a good proportion of the population of New Brunswick, descendants of the early French settlers, including some of those who were driven out of Nova Scotia by the British in the 1750's.

Soon the motorist is swinging along the south shore of the St. Lawrence in the Province of Quebec, traveling through an extension of the Gaspé country, a region of small French villages, one of which, St. Jean Port Joli, seems to be inhabited entirely by woodcarvers.

A bevy of beauties swirl in a mountain meadow on Nova Scotia's Cape Breton Island.

At Lévis he must make a decision. From here to Montreal the Trans-Canada is a fast superhighway, crossing level lowlands, ignoring towns, and offering little of interest. We would recommend that he cross the St. Lawrence to Quebec City instead, coming up under the frowning heights of that citadel of New France. Wandering afoot through the largely restored old sections of both the Lower and Upper towns, he will feel he is not only in another country but in another age. When he can finally pull himself away, there's only one road to Montreal—Route 2 along the north shore of the St. Lawrence.

In winter or summer this winding route has its charms. We followed it in the other direction—from Montreal to Quebec City—on our way to the latter's famous Winter Carnival and delighted in spotting seventeenth-century farmhouses, their steeply pitched roofs heavy with snow. At Ste. Anne de la Pérade we happened on the annual ice-fishing festival, when two thousand gaily painted ice-fishing huts create a second village on the river. There was also a dance floor built over the ice, where young and old in bright winter dress were stomping away. The carnival air of Ste. Anne almost distracted us from the bigger carnival ahead. Both carnivals are movable feasts. That at Ste. Anne de la Pérade can occur any time between the end of December and the middle of February—whenever the tomcod arrive to spawn. Only then does the word go out. "The fish don't follow the calendar," one Québecois said. But ice fishermen follow the fish and arrive by the thousands. The Winter Carnival at Quebec City, however, is really a Mardi gras, a pre-Lenten festivity whose dates are governed by the date on which Easter falls in a given year.

Throughout Quebec an enormous church dominates each village the traveler passes. These grandiose structures seem out of all proportion to the small villages, even allowing for the fact that farmers from the countryside come to Mass on Sunday. Despite all the changes wrought in the province by the "Quiet Revolution" that began in 1960, the Catholic Church is still the heart of rural Quebec. When the traveler finally reaches the small towns of Canada's prairies, he'll find other towering structures dominating the landscape—the grain elevators. In the prairies, by contrast, the churches are small and varied, and many sects are represented.

Even before he reaches Montreal a percipient tourist will realize that he has been in three different "countries," although he has just begun his transcontinental trip. Newfoundland is one, a highly individualistic island still attached only loosely to Canada. The Maritime Provinces of Nova Scotia, New Brunswick, and Prince Edward Island constitute another "country," all three sharing qualities that unite them in much the same way that the New England states form an entity within the United States. (Prince Edward Island can still be reached only by ferry; the Trans-Canada Highway perforce by-passes it.) Quebec is the only province that actually calls itself a "nation"—a French nation, of course—and it does so loudly.

The most strident of the separatists are to be found in Montreal, where two-thirds of the population is French-speaking, while the wealth of that lively metropolis is largely controlled by the third whose first language is English. This has made for a volatile situation—and for the occasional use of such devices as plastic bombs. The visiting American shopper may be coldly instructed by a salesgirl to *"Parlez français, s'il vous plait."* Once he explains that he is, unfortunately, a unilingual American, she will consent to wait on him in the English she speaks fluently, but visiting Canadians are not always treated as kindly.

French Canadians complain that they can't even "work in French" in their own biggest city, and when they visit Toronto, they are asked sharply, "Can't you speak English?" The traveler on the Trans-Canada, once he has crossed the Ontario border on his way to Ottawa, will roll through a succession of small towns named Alfred, Plantagenet, Clarence, and Cumberland. There's Wendover, too, and the traveler will begin to think he has crossed the channel between France and England. But just when he has decided that Ontario is *the* really English province, he'll find that the American influence seems to be changing the very character of the landscape. In fact, Ontario is neither English nor American but in its way the very essence of what Americans think of as "Canadian."

Beyond the "Queen Province" lie two more countries: the prairie provinces of Manitoba, Saskatchewan, and Alberta with their "wall-to-wall wheat" under wind-tossed clouds in a big sky; and at the end of the road, British Columbia, which used to be very British indeed, but has lately been responding so strongly to Columbia's influence that its

18

separatists think B.C. should become the fifty-first American state.

There are, then, six "countries" in Canada, and to the north of them two vast territories, the Yukon and the Northwest, domains of ice and snow and untapped resources. But that's not the end of the internal divisions that characterize Canada. Along the northwest border of Quebec are farm communities where everyone speaks English. In Ontario there are towns almost wholly French. In parts of the prairies every farmer in sight is bilingual in English and Ukrainian—yet just a few miles away there may be a solidly Icelandic settlement.

This tells the tourist something basic about the Big Land. Canada is not a melting pot like the United States, where people of many cultures have blended to create a society that is clearly American. Canada is a mosaic built up of many cultural bits and pieces, each retaining a distinct identity. This form of development has, in fact, created a major problem for Canadians, the problem of a national identity. "What," they have been asking themselves in scores of books, magazine articles, and newspaper editorials, "really is a Canadian?"

Is he a Toronto banker sipping a sherry in his very British club? A prairie farmer on his way to his Ukrainian Orthodox Church with its onion dome? A Calgary oilman in his American Stetson? A West Coast Japanese technician driving to a spanking-new factory? The Toronto banker, because of the scope of his interests, may have a national approach to Canada's problem of identity, but the others will probably concentrate on local concerns.

This divisiveness has tended to weaken the federal government at Ottawa while allowing the provincial governments to grow stronger and more truculent. More than one provincial premier, in fact, has insisted on being addressed as "Prime Minister," though only the head of the federal government is traditionally accorded that title. The separatist attitude in Quebec has been widely publicized in the United States, but other provinces have been nearly as ready to go their own way if not given it within Canada's Confederation. The centennial celebration in 1967 may have braked that trend somewhat, but only time and the influence of Canada's strongly federalist Prime Minister Trudeau will tell.

Confederation came hard to Canada. It began in 1867, but Newfoundland, the latest comer, joined only in 1949. Yet there were settlements in Canada before the *Mayflower* anchored off Massachusetts. Why the long delay before the Canada we know emerged as a country?

"Geography, chiefly," some Canadian authorities will tell you. "Even today Canada is really not so much a country as it is a geographical expression."

Canada's sheer size has been the major problem right up to recent times. The vast land that spreads across the top half of the North American continent is, in fact, the second largest country in the world, exceeded in area only by the Soviet Union. The forty-eight contiguous American states could be stowed into Canada, together with all of Western Europe including the British Isles, and there would still be land left over.

What's more, Canada's southern and more habitable region is divided into sections by huge natural barriers. Our traveler on the Trans-Canada Highway has already encountered two of them: the Gulf of St. Lawrence, which he crossed on leaving Newfoundland, and the St. Lawrence River itself, too wide to be bridged for most of its length. When he reaches western Ontario, north of lakes Huron and Superior, he will encounter a third great barrier, although it won't hinder him today as it did the early pioneers. This is an eight-hundred-mile stretch of rock, water, and muskeg (deep bog), which once separated eastern Canada from its great prairies. The builders of Canada's first transcontinental railroad, the Canadian Pacific, had to blast through the rock so frequently that they erected dynamite factories along the way. Then they used the broken rock as fill in the muskeg.

Not until the railroad pushed into Canada's west with connecting lines coming up from the United States could the prairies really be opened for settlement. Until then a farmer's sources of supply were impossibly distant. When the first contingent of Mounties trekked west ahead of the railroad to keep order among the trappers, Indians, and American whiskey peddlers, their horses dropped from exhaustion along the way.

The prairies are the country that hoboes in Canada call the "Big Lonely." From the Lake of the Woods to the Rockies, from Kenora in Ontario to Calgary in Alberta, almost the only breaks on the horizon today for a thousand miles are the grain elevators, five thousand of them, painted in bright colors—turquoise or even salmon pink with a yellow roof—to enliven the landscape.

Overhead arches what Canadians regard as the biggest sky in the world. The sky over the Russian steppes is probably just as big and clear, but the Canadian steppes are closer to home for an American tourist, who will be surprised to find many small Slavic towns there. At the turn of the century there was a mass migration to these plains by sturdy settlers in sheepskin coats—most of them Ukrainians, who have jealously preserved their culture. So have the Croats and Serbians and Magyars who settled in clusters. More pieces in the Canadian mosaic.

The great plains roll right up to the Rockies, which provide a painted backdrop for Calgary. From here the Trans-Canada offers the tourist some of the world's most magnificent scenery, particularly on the stretch beyond Lake Louise where the highway crosses the Rockies at Rogers Pass and pushes on through range after range to reach the Fraser River gorge in British Columbia.

This is much more rugged country than anything south of the border, and for decades it seemed an impassible barrier between the rest of the country and the English settlements on Canada's western coast. The people there had come in by sea or up from what is now the state of Washington, and most had settled not on the mainland but on Vancouver Island. British North America little concerned them.

The easterners who dreamed of a continent-wide Canada could persuade British Columbia to join the Confederation only by promising them a railroad connection with the rest of the country. The genius, money, sweat, and political turmoil that went into the building of the Canadian Pacific are known only to Canadians. Now it has grown into one of the two greatest railroad systems in the world. What's the other? The Canadian National, of course.

Today a traveler can cross Canada by plane or by the longest continuous highway in the world or by transcontinental train. For sightseeing, we ourselves are torn between the rails and the highway. They follow much the same route, so the actual sights will be largely the same but the experiences will differ. As railroad buffs we would recommend the excitement of one of the last great train trips left in a changing world. As people interested in Canada we would go by car. With a car you can stop to investigate.

On our first trip we stopped between Calgary and Vancouver at Kamloops, British Columbia, a modern cow town and a rock-hunter's paradise. We acquired a handsome slab of rock and an interesting bit of Canadian background. We were told of the English outpost there in which up until the First World War the citizens rode to the hunt in pink coats, tallyhoing after wolves. When the war began, the hunters returned to England, and most of them were killed. For a while they had been another piece in the mosaic.

A short way beyond Kamloops the Trans-Canada tourist will come to the Fraser River canyon, the incredible gorge the river cuts in its turbulent course. Wherever the highway allows, pull off and take a look—and try to imagine that you are paddling your way through that wild water bordered by sheer cliffs. The passage down the Fraser has been described as one of the "most difficult exploration trips on record," and you can believe it. In 1808 Simon Fraser and twenty-three companions did it somehow—Fraser, however, was disappointed: he thought he was on the Columbia River when he started, and finding he had explored the wrong river, he angrily refused a knighthood for his effort.

In a country as big as Canada Fraser was not the first to go astray. Alexander Mackenzie did it notably. In the 1780's he was a young fur trader working out of Montreal, pushing farther and farther west in pursuit of the pelts that made men rich. The farther he traveled for profit, the more he became obsessed with an idea that had no money in it. He was determined to be the first white man to reach the Pacific by an overland route.

In 1789, while trading around Great Slave Lake, well north of what is now the Province of Alberta, he discovered a broad river that flowed west. This, he decided, would carry him to the coast, and with a few Indians and voyageurs he set out. He knew nothing of navigation. The only figuring he had ever done was in a Montreal counting house. When the river veered north as well as west, he had no instruments to tell him where he was going. Look on a map at the river that today is called the Mackenzie, and you will see why he was confused. He named it "Disappointment River" when it took him fifteen hundred miles by canoe to the "Hyperborean Sea," as he called it. We know it as the Arctic Ocean.

That his discovery and exploration of one of the world's great rivers would make his name immortal never occurred to Mackenzie. He would not settle for one ocean when he was bent on reaching another. After two years he managed to get himself to London, where he studied astronomy and navigation and bought a set of proper instruments. Thus equipped, he returned to Canada and the fur trade.

He built a fort miles west of any existing trading post, at the fork of the Peace and Smoky rivers in what is now northern Alberta. In May, 1793, he pushed off with another Scotsman, six French Canadians, and two Indian hunters to work his way through the maze of mountains to land's end in the west. Even today, with every foot of the way mapped, the trip is a nightmare. Towering canyons twist this way and that; rapids, falls, and whirlpools make every yard a struggle. At one portage Mackenzie and his men carried the canoe and supplies over sheer mountain face. Naturally the men wanted to turn back, but their determined leader drove them on.

The terrain along the way was too rugged even for Indian tribes to have settled there. After grinding weeks the men finally reached Indian country, where warriors threatened from a riverbank. Alone and unarmed, Mackenzie went to meet them. Before they parted, his new friends told him of bad Indians to the west, and the bad Indians warned him of worse Indians farther on.

When he finally reached the Pacific, Mackenzie met Indians who had already learned to hate white men. "Macubah," they said, had come in a great canoe and fired on them. Mackenzie reached the Pacific on July 22, 1793, and we now know that Captain George Vancouver—Macubah—had arrived in a British ship about seven weeks earlier. Mackenzie himself never fired a gun. Instead he shot the sun with his new instruments and painted on a rock an inscription commemorating the conclusion of his journey "from Canada, by land."

It would be eleven years before Lewis and Clark would even begin their expedition across the North American continent, and they would have official encouragement and funds. One young Scotsman, who would later become Sir Alexander Mackenzie—you can see his portrait by Sir Thomas Lawrence in the National Gallery at Ottawa—had beaten them to it.

Although Mackenzie and other epic characters managed to get

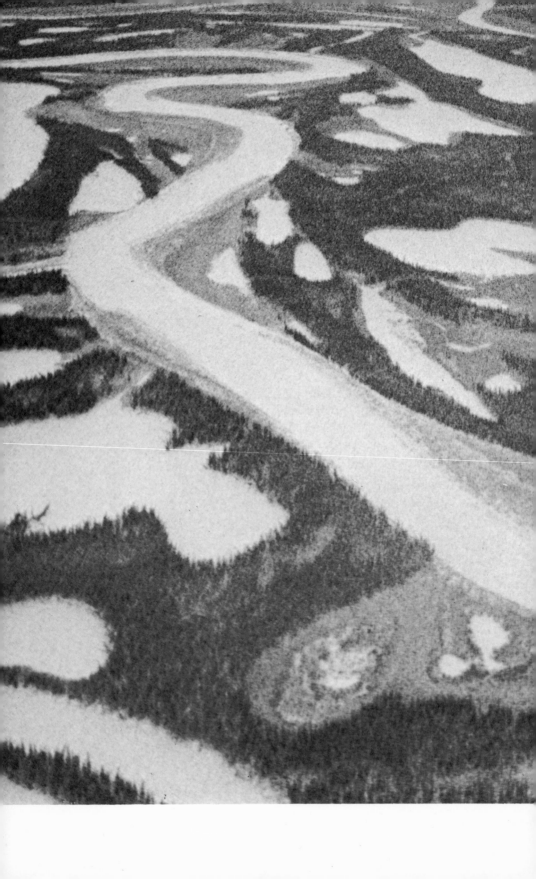

his abstract pattern of curves and free-form shapes is actually an
rial view of the Mackenzie River delta near the Arctic.

around a difficult country, most settlers in Canada stayed put. Even until fairly recent times they lived in communities that were isolated except for an often distant railroad connection. Not until the development of modern means of communication and transportation—radio, television, the automobile, and the airplane—did they feel the impact of other cultures, but by then the mosaic pattern was well established. Even today in British Columbia, where far-out modern houses cling to the mountainsides around Vancouver and some of the best people indulge in pot, the sedate English influence persists. So tourists as well as little old ladies can enjoy afternoon tea in the lobby of the famed Empress Hotel at Victoria, watch a cricket match, and in the library of the capital view a bonnet worn by the good Queen herself.

This diversity, while it lasts, makes the Big Land that much more interesting for the tourist, and the driver on the Trans-Canada will sense the differences as he crosses from province to province. But with modern communications the American influence is becoming all pervasive, to the alarm of those Canadians who want to see a Canadian identity develop.

It has hardly had time to do so. Only since 1931 has Canada been a fully sovereign state, and it was 1947 before a Canadian had any legal existence as such. Today, while his basic national status is "Canadian citizen," he is still a British subject, a fact that annoys some Québecois. Canadians had just begun to shake off the tenuous British influence when the full force of modern America was upon them.

In most places at which the traveler in Canada today decides to stop, he can pull into an American-style motel, park among cars of familiar make, pick up his favorite soft drink and magazine, and tune in many of America's TV programs. Canada has developed the longest television circuit in the world, extending through seven time zones, but 47 per cent of the shows telecast by the nationally owned Canadian Broadcasting Corporation in 1969–70 were American. In Canada the American influence has penetrated even rural Quebec, where on a country storefront the tourist will see the same metal advertising sign for Coca-Cola that he sees everywhere in the United States, with only the language changed. It now reads "Ça ravigote" ("It refreshes").

Again geography provides the explanation. For the vast majority of

Canadians, the United States border is never very far away. Despite the country's total size, every one of its cities and most of its towns have grown up in a continental ribbon that is not more than four hundred miles wide at most and occasionally narrows to one hundred miles. This ribbon hugs the American border as closely as the inhabited area of Egypt does the Nile. North lies a wilderness of infinite riches, but modern Canadians have proved reluctant to pioneer the north—even the near north that is part of the provinces, not of the territories. Because the whole huge country has only twenty million inhabitants, there is still plenty of room and a comfortable standard of living to be had on the southern fringe, so there they stay.

If they want the freedom of the wilderness for a weekend of fishing or hunting or boating, it is within easy drive of high-rise apartment buildings. Everywhere there are lakes beyond counting—in some areas more lakes than people. Canada boasts one third of the fresh water in the world, nearly three hundred thousand square miles of it, and it really is fresh. In the north most of the lakes are so clear that their bottoms can be seen from a low-flying plane.

The country's great rivers are already yielding billions of kilowatts of electric power, 157 billion in a recent count. But for most of their length no power stations are in view. Instead, surging water pours through silent forests.

One river that astonished us by its size when we arrived in Canada was the Ottawa. There it was in all its broad magnificence, the *grande rivière* of the voyageurs, the path over which many of the early explorers had traveled on their way west—the west not just of Canada but of the United States as well. And we had never heard of it. We were somewhat consoled to read in *The Rivers of Canada* by the distinguished Canadian writer Hugh MacLennan that it is unknown in some of its aspects to Canadians, too. No one, for instance, has yet determined the river's exact length, although it is officially given as around seven hundred miles. But there are those who think it rises from a series of smaller lakes to the east of its official source. It forms the boundary between Ontario and Quebec from Lake Timiskaming to the St. Lawrence, and MacLennan points out the strong contrasts between one bank and the other. On the Ontario side are broad farms set in rolling hills covered with an abundance of hardwood trees. On the Quebec side are wild pine forests where wolves howl in the moonlight less than 125 miles from Canada's capital.

The nation's inexhaustible resources of water may one day provide an invaluable export. For politicians, however, the idea is too new to accept. They declare emotionally that Canada will never sell her "God-given heritage" of water, although why her oil, minerals, metals, and trees are not also part of that heritage they never explain. Both Canadian and American engineers have advanced tremendous though dissimilar plans for the utilization of the country's water resources to benefit the entire continent, and something like them may one day come about. But in Canada's current nationalistic mood, those are fighting words.

The forests are certainly being utilized. The Big Land today leads the world in the production of newsprint. You would see why if you flew 1,700 miles west from eastern Quebec to Lake Winnipeg, made a 300-mile jog north, and then flew west again for 1,300 miles to reach the Pacific Coast. All the way you would pass over nearly solid forest cover, broken in the east by lakes and in the west by mountain peaks thrusting above the tree line. On such a flight you would pass over most, but not all, of Canada's billion acres of woods. The huge timber industry, tremendous forest fires (sometimes water-bombed from big planes), and windfall have not made a dent in them. Of course, the big lumber companies do reforest, largely to get improved growth, but forestry experts say there are now 241 million acres of young growth restocked not by man but simply by nature.

The flight, in short, would give you a glimpse of the great northern wilderness that is the last frontier of adventure on this continent. Part of it lies, as we said, within the boundaries of Canada's provinces, part in her Northwest Territories. Not long ago it was virtually a private preserve for those who could afford to be flown in on fishing and hunting safaris costing five hundred to a thousand dollars a week. Today we tourists are pushing on up there.

At one time the only permanent inhabitants of the north were trappers and guides, Indians, and farther up, Eskimos. There were also a few prospectors, Mounties, and Hudson's Bay Company men, prototypes of colorful characters in American movies of the twenties and thirties. To the irritation of Canadians, Americans tend to think the north is still like that.

There is, in fact, a scattering of towns right across the northern provincial areas, although they are still few and far apart. There are lumbering and newsprint-manufacturing towns, and more importantly, mining towns. Every year Canada is discovering more great caches of minerals and ores and bigger deposits of oil. The petroleum reserves under part of Alberta alone are estimated to be greater than those of Kuwait, hitherto considered the richest. The Big Land now leads the world in the production of nickel, platinum, and zinc; is second in production of cadmium, cobalt, gypsum, and uranium; and is third in gold, titanium, and aluminum; and much of that wealth comes out of the north. So there are rail lines into the far country, scheduled air services, bush-plane flights—and roads.

At several points in eastern Ontario a driver can swing off the Trans-Canada, get onto Ontario Route 11, and heading almost directly north for several hundred miles, arrive at the small bush town of Cochrane, where Route 11 turns northwest. Here, in one recent year alone, ten thousand tourists stowed their cars and boarded trains of the Ontario Northland Railway to chug on up to Moosonee on James Bay, an enormous arm of Hudson Bay.

There are Sunday, Wednesday, and Friday all-passenger excursion trains to Moosonee during July and August, but otherwise the Polar Bear Express is a freight train with coaches in the rear. It travels north on Monday, Wednesday, and Friday; south on Tuesday, Thursday, and Saturday. Officially it makes only eight stops, but actually it halts wherever it is flagged down or has to drop off freight, which is addressed to a milepost. At scheduled stops Indian kids pile aboard, headed for the snack bar to buy ice cream. The train is their diesel-powered Good Humor wagon.

After they arrive in Moosonee many visitors want to press still farther north—people get the fever—and now the Province of Ontario is granting their wish. The Minister of Lands and Forests recently announced that a seven-thousand-square-mile area fronting on both James and Hudson bays has become Ontario's first "primitive" provincial park. It will be called Polar Bear Park for a very good reason: it contains Ontario's largest concentration of polar bears. The park also contains bearded seals, walrus, arctic foxes, colonies of snow geese

and blue geese, and two to three hundred caribou. In addition it is a breeding ground for ptarmigan, although the area is not within the Arctic Circle. Hunting is prohibited; it's all strictly for viewing, and there is plenty to see. An American traveler would have to fly to Kenya to photograph as many exotic animals in their natural habitat. Presently the only access to the park is by chartered plane from Moosonee, but officials hope that hovercraft will shortly provide a practical way in for more tourists. Visitors who fish there now rely on local outfitters to fly them and all their necessary camping equipment

*The Trans-Canada Highway cuts through rock of the Pre-Cambrian
Shield on the north shore of Lake Superior.*

to wilderness waters at a stiff price.

There's another exciting new approach to the north that few Americans drive because of the distances involved. That's the Mackenzie Highway, opened for its full length of 625 miles in 1961. It starts in western Canada just beyond Peace River, Alberta, a town that is itself 600 miles above the American border.

Nowhere does the Canadian north have more sweep and loveliness than along the Mackenzie route, which is, in fact, just a broad gravel road. But the traveler who reaches its terminus, Yellowknife, the new

31

capital of the Northwest Territories, had better not disparage the "Highway." To the people who live there it's a modern miracle, their first all-weather connection with the outside world. (Even bush planes can't take off for days on end during some of the winter weather they have up there. But in summer temperatures range from 50 to 70 degrees or even 80 degrees.)

Nowhere along the "Highway" is there a motel. However, campgrounds, cooking facilities, and shelters are well distributed. Canadians are inveterate campers, so this suits them perfectly. They are also avid fishermen. When we drive off to some event—say a park opening or a political rally—without fishing tackle, our building superintendent can't believe his eyes. Whatever our destination he knows a lake nearby that is noted for a certain type of fish.

Near Yellowknife amateurs have been known to haul a 14-pound trout out of Great Slave Lake, even though their attention was focused partly on the tremendous silence around them and partly on the deep shadow that the five-hundred-foot-high red cliffs cast on the still water.

In Yellowknife itself, however, it won't be quiet. The capital does have hotels, but a visitor shouldn't plan on sleeping much if he arrives in summer. That's the season with twenty hours of daylight, and most of the townspeople stay up to enjoy it. Children play ball at midnight, and in July the men play in a round-the-clock golf marathon.

For the true adventurer, the trouble with exploring this part of the north is the number of people he will encounter along the way: the helping hands at campsites; the camera fans who crowd his view of rushing Alexandra Falls near Enterprise; those ball-playing kids at Yellowknife. Here he is, two thousand miles north in a vast underpopulated country, and there are friendly people everywhere.

But a determined man can get away from it all in Canada. A pair of Toronto honeymooners spent two and a half weeks canoeing through an area of the wilderness without seeing a soul. At the end of that time they met two men who were there by appointment. They were expert guides hired to help ferry the newlyweds' canoe through a rapids. Until then the honeymooners had shared a solitude that both felt had heightened their perception of the beauty around them.

They had started from Glacier Lake to travel 250 miles down the South Nahanni, one of Canada's last great wilderness rivers. For sixty years it has also been a mystery river because two headless bodies were found on its banks in 1908; how and why they got there has never been explained. The ghoulish old story didn't inhibit the honeymooners; it simply assured them that they would have the place to themselves.

Below Glacier Lake the river is enlarged by melted ice and snow from the mountains around it, widening and hurrying on its way until it plunges 316 feet at Virginia Falls, 120 miles from the lake. (Niagara Falls at its highest point drops only 167 feet.) The honeymooners, although impressed by the falls, were even more impressed by the canyons that the river has cut through the mountains for the next eighty miles. There are three of them, ranging in length from twelve to twenty miles, with walls that rise as high as 3,500 feet. It was at one of these canyons that the couple had to have their canoe ferried, because the river rushes through it in a dangerous rapids. Here they stopped to spend a week as the guests of a trapper who has worked the river for a quarter of a century. He left them largely to themselves while he went about his own business in the wilderness, although they probably enjoyed his company after their many days of solitude.

There are other wonders along the South Nahanni, including a hot spring that warms the water to 98 degrees, and one day this area may become as popular with tourists as Niagara Falls is today.

A distinguished new Canadian, Austrian by birth, says that where he comes from, Canada is pronounced "Keine dah," which means "nobody there." Well, hardly anybody, with only twenty million people in a country of Canada's staggering size. So for anyone anxious to get away from it all, the Big Land has a special charm in today's teeming world.

Skiers at Garibaldi Park, British Columbia

2 Winter Landscape

"Nature still wins even at this stage of a go-go century."

*Untimely warm spells sometimes melt the ice sculptures
at Quebec City's winter gala.*

Friends of ours from Virginia not long ago decided to see Canada
in all its winter splendor, and to see it thoroughly. So in January, 1969,
they took a transcontinental train from Montreal to Vancouver. They
also rode the train on their way back east "to see by daylight everything we had missed at night on our way west." They were four hours
late pulling into Montreal but otherwise experienced no inconvenience.
"It was just beautiful the whole way!"

Undeniably the Virginians saw a fair amount of Canada, but happily
they never felt it. Their train stopped, for example, in Edmonton,
Alberta, but a look around the station would hardly reveal what the

city's people were experiencing during that grim January. The temperature there averaged nearly 20 degrees below zero for the month, dropping on the twenty-sixth day of killing cold to 39 degrees below. The cold was aggravated by driving winds. Meteorologists can calculate exactly the degree of aggravation that winds impose, and this "wind-chill factor" at times made the actual cold in Edmonton equal to 60 degrees below.

Winter nights are longer in Canada than they are to the south, and the combination of cold and darkness takes its toll of the human spirit. An Edmonton psychiatrist found that as the cold persisted, people were becoming uneasy, nervous, and irritable, a state common to Arctic explorers of the past when they wintered near the Pole. But it takes record lows to faze Canadians. They are a hardy people addicted to tall tales of the winters they have seen.

Canadian artists, particularly the painters, reflect this obsession with the northern winter. The summer visitor can therefore get some idea of life during the colder months by visiting any of the galleries that feature collections of Canadian paintings: the National Gallery at Ottawa, the provincial galleries at Quebec City and Toronto, the Art Gallery of Hamilton, and notably, the McMichael Conservation Collection of Art at Kleinburg, Ontario, a short drive north of Toronto.

Except for Cornelius Krieghoff's happy habitants, bundled up and busy in the throes of winter, most Canadian snowscapes show no people at all, or at most, one lonely figure. Krieghoff was not really a Canadian but rather a German painter who came to Quebec in the nineteenth century and found that the life of French-Canadian farmers, particularly when the snow was piled high, was ideal subject matter for the picturesque scenes so popular in Europe. One painting that more truly reflects the Canadian attitude hangs in the National Gallery at Ottawa. It is by the noted contemporary Quebec artist Jean-Paul Lemieux. Titled *Night Visitor,* it shows in the foreground a looming figure—indistinct in the darkness, but evidently a tall man in a long heavy coat and fur hat—beyond whom, across a bright expanse of snow, a tiny train is vanishing into the far distance. No one has come to meet the visitor; there is no sign of a town anywhere near. Did he climb down from the train at some whistle stop in the northern solitude? Canada's immense space, pervading cold, and mysterious nights are in that picture. Another painting by Lemieux, this one privately owned, is called simply *Road in Winter* and is a study of a rutted logging track wandering off into the snow-deep bush.

"And once again, as in so much Canadian art whether in print, in paint or on film, the typical subject is a winter landscape without figures," the Canadian critic Philip Stratford once observed. He was reviewing the work of two young Quebec poets. Of *Boreal* by Yves Préfontaine, Stratford wrote: "He is still haunted by the terrifying Boreal, god of cold and Nordic void," and the images in his poetic landscapes "are our images: upwrenched frozen roots, phantom trees, scarred soil, sleet, snow, stone and wind." And in two recent Canadian short stories, critic Peter Buitenhuis pointed out, "the cruel force of the Prairie winter takes its grim toll of the characters' emotions and even of their lives."

Its winter mantle has always been a burden on Canada's shoulders. The French court was at one point so horrified by tales of winter's hardship in Canada that it seriously considered trading its whole North American empire for a West Indies island noted for its rum. The British were great colonizers, but their settlement of Canada was slow. It took economic desperation (as in the case of Scottish crofters who had lost their lands) or religious fervor (in the case of the Mennonites) to drive people to the New Siberia. When, at the turn of this century, Canada launched a campaign to attract immigrants from Europe, Germany officially protested "the attempt to lure our fellow countrymen to this desert subarctic region."

No official protest could dam the human tide flowing into Canada at that time, although the economic survival of not only the individual farmer in the west but indeed of Canada as a continental nation was in doubt. The only practical crop on the vast prairies was wheat, but no strain of wheat then known could survive the early killing frosts of the region, which also suffers from a late spring. At Regina, Saskatchewan, the temperature is above freezing for only five months of the year. A hardy, quick-ripening variety of wheat was desperately needed.

The man who finally discovered the famous Marquis strain and was knighted for his efforts was Sir Charles E. Saunders, as unlikely a hero of the wheat fields as can be imagined. He was interested not in cereals but in music and poetry, and although he was an Ontarian of English stock, his only published work was in French—*Essais et Vers*. But his father, William Saunders, was a passionate horticulturist who established the experimental farm now within the borders of Ottawa.

Will Saunders trained his children in plant breeding long before any agricultural college taught the technique. Wheat was one of his passions, and in an endless search for a hardy variety he and his dragooned children crossed Canadian wheat with species imported from Russia and from India's Himalayan Mountains. His sons once said that they bred at least seven hundred strains themselves. When Charles escaped from the farm to teach music at women's colleges and write music columns for the newspapers, his father summarily brought him back by having him appointed Dominion Cerealist.

Somewhere among the hundreds of strains the Saunders family had grown was the answer to Canada's need, but which variety was it? A technical problem delayed the answer for ten years: wheat could not be milled in small lots.

It was Charles who found a short cut. He simply popped a few grains of each experimental strain into his mouth and chewed them. The resulting color and degree of glueyness indicated the kind of bread a particular strain would make. Charles chewed his way through a hundred batches before he came on a single stack in a neglected corner of the farm. It was labeled "Markham," but Charles changed that to the more elegant and French "Marquis"; this was the strain from which he developed others, Ruby, Garnet, and Reward, all adapted to the difficult climate of the west.

Life was hard in the early days, not just on the prairie frontier, but also in the settled east. Houses were barely heated. Roads and streets were not cleared, and a man often had to shovel his childrens' path to school before struggling off to his shop. Horsecars were not heated in the cities, and passengers burrowed their feet into the deep straw that covered the floor. In a snug sleigh with a hot brick at his feet and a buffalo robe for cover, a man could keep warm, but immigrants couldn't afford private sleighs.

A few of the early country churches still have buggy sheds in which horses were sheltered during the lengthy sermons. There were mangers for feeding them, too, on fodder hauled along to church by the congregation. As in northern Maine, barns were often an extension of the farmhouse, so a man could get to his stock without having to negotiate a fifteen-foot snowdrift in the morning. Snowshoes were as common as boots today; men traveled miles on them. In the cities snowshoeing was a favorite winter pastime because the sport permitted a beau to touch a belle's ankle while gallantly lashing a snowshoe to her foot. The racquetlike footgear had originally been worn by Canadian prairie Indians while hunting buffalo after a big snow.

Canadians learned early that the best way to confront their climate was to make sport of it. A freeze-up of the St. Lawrence River once meant that a series of ice bridges would link villages on the opposite shores. The inhabitants traveled back and forth to trade, to visit kinsmen they saw only in winter, or to celebrate Christmas and other holy days. The advent of the icebreaker put an end to this winter neighborliness.

There was at least one miracle associated with the freeze-up. At Cap de la Madeleine the curé, wondering how he could transport stone across the St. Lawrence for the church he was building, appealed to the Virgin. Almost immediately an intense cold spell provided an ice bridge to solve his problem. In gratitude for the miracle he dedicated the church to his Lady.

Immigrants who survived in this land of ice liked to send back pictures of themselves posed in snowy landscapes. William Notman of Montreal, Canada's pioneer photographer, obliged by shooting them in a blizzard that he created by spraying his glass plates with Chinese white. He also employed solid blocks of ice as props in his studio, which was cold enough to make their use practical! And for every Victorian picture of people playing croquet or picnicking, there must have been two of laughing young people at a toboggan party, the amusement considered most Canadian.

Today, of course, ice hockey is the national sport, and on television every Saturday night in winter is "Hockey Night in Canada." What Babe Ruth once stood for in the United States, Bobby Hull, Canadian star of the Chicago Black Hawks, represented in Canada. Even for non-Canadians it was a thrill to see the big blond from Ontario surge down the ice like a locomotive, slapping the puck straight for the net at a lethal speed. Hockey arenas in the United States are beginning to be almost as crowded as those in Canada, but in Boston or Los Angeles tickets are more readily available than they are in Canada, where Toronto's Maple Leaf Gardens and Montreal's Forum have for years had every seat sold out in advance of the hockey season. Seats are often handed down from father to son.

Most Canadian children learn to skate before they start school. Once they become accustomed to their skates, boys start hitting makeshift pucks around, much as American kids bat balls in vacant lots. But in the cities and towns these "skinny" sessions on creeks and ponds have given way to organized play on well-tended indoor ice surfaces. The extent of this Little League hockey in Canada is illustrated by the number of small-boy teams in just one Ottawa neighborhood: the Nepean Hockey Association operates eighty-one teams comprising thirteen hundred boys supervised by an army of adults acting as coaches, timekeepers, referees, and so on. A mother may complain bitterly when she has to pay forty dollars to outfit her seven-year-old for hockey, until she reads of some unsupervised youngster who was killed when a puck hit his unhelmeted head.

As a participant sport in Canada figure skating is said to be second only to hockey. That's hard to believe when a visitor views the crowded ski slopes on a good weekend, but it may be that figure skaters in the prairie provinces, where ski slopes are few, swell the total.

As for skiers, as many as twenty-five thousand will turn out on a winter Sunday on the slopes just across the river from Ottawa—skiers of all ages, the tots trotting off to peewee classes. The very young peep rosy-cheeked out of prams on runners or are strapped like papooses onto their mothers' backs. On the ski slopes north of Montreal, Vancouver, and Quebec City as many Americans as Canadians may show up on a good weekend.

Coming up fast both as a participant and a spectator sport is snowmobiling, popularly known as ski-dooing, since the Ski-Doo, the original Canadian machine, was the first snowmobile. There are one hundred thousand of them already in use in Ontario alone, and they are equally popular in the other provinces. Throughout Ontario snowmobiling is permitted on roads and trails in most provincial parks, with special trails provided in three of them. Local councils or service clubs sponsor races, and there are banked racing tracks in several towns. Races are sanctioned by the Ontario Snowmobiling Federation, which

lays down rules and allots points.

In 1969 the International Snowmobile Meet was held in January at Mosport Park, Canada's only Grand Prix racetrack. The park is in the little village of Orono, fifty miles east of Toronto, and during two days of bright sunshine with low temperatures and glare ice, the village saw plenty of excitement. Strong winds added to the chill factor, which the masked and mufflered racers increased by their own speeds. Eleven of them wound up in the hospital with injuries, but the survivors went on to race again at Oshawa, Ontario, in February. Amateur snowmobilers who ventured onto Ontario highways in 1970 were not so lucky.

Snowmobile racers take off at Beauséjour, Manitoba.

Fifteen were killed, usually in collisions with motor vehicles, while fatalities in hunting, a sport involving seven hundred thousand people, average only ten to twelve a year.

Many snowmobilers are sedate family men who take up the sport when age and added responsibility dampen their enthusiasm for skiing. Old ski clothes are not, however, adequate for this new sport, which requires a warmly padded jump suit. When former Prime Minister Lester B. Pearson retired in 1968, one group of supporters presented him and his wife with the latest in ski-doo suits.

Inevitably the snowmobile was invented by a Canadian, Joseph-

Armand Bombardier of Valcourt, Quebec, who intended it for fast, reliable transportation in the far north. The early commercial model that appeared in 1959 was snapped up by trappers, doctors, missionaries, and geologists, who found it more economical and easier to handle than a team of huskies. The machine is now part of the Arctic way of life, but today most snowmobiles are used for fun.

Such a development is common in Canada, where many practices once done of necessity have become sports—ice fishing, for instance. As we saw at Ste. Anne de la Pérade, ice-fishing grounds sprout across Canada in winter. Bruce West, columnist for the Toronto *Globe and Mail,* has described life in such a village of portable huts, where a "stalwart band of patient sufferers . . . huddle in substandard housing, trying desperately to keep warm with the aid of small propane heaters and such painkillers and cold-chasers as our poor cupboards provide. Some of the more robust members of our dauntless clan sit right out in the open, exposed to winter's fury, peering hopefully down a hole in the ice, like a persevering polar bear waiting for a seal."

On "good" weekends the flow of traffic from centers of population to ski slopes, ice-fishing grounds, and winter resorts approaches the massive summer traffic to cottages, camps, and summer resorts. But with heavy snow, sleet, or intense cold all the brave outdoorsmen vanish, and the landscape is again solitary.

The toboggan and luge slopes are abandoned (luge rhymes with rouge and is a fast one-man sled). Middle-aged curling teams stay home from their indoor rinks. (Curling, brought to Canada by the Scots, consists of "throwing" a stone weighing thirty-five to thirty-eight pounds along a level stretch of ice toward a mark forty-two yards away, while teammates in tam-o'-shanters sweep its path frantically with brooms. Surprisingly the rivalries it generates are intense.) If the snow is too heavy, winter carnivals may be canceled, or at least postponed, as Banff's was in January, 1969.

Considering the hazards a winter carnival faces, it's amazing that Quebec City's has gone off year after year with great éclat. A thaw is even more disastrous than a cold spell to such an enterprise. It melts down the ice sculptures that annually decorate the Château Frontenac's outdoor skating rink. It erodes the battlements of the castle built of ice blocks in the center of historic Place d'Armes. It makes a joke of

Barrel jumping on skates at Quebec's winter carnival

the otherwise exciting canoe race through the ice floes of the St. Lawrence and ruins the ski slopes. Of course, a thaw improves matters for
the girls posed on floats in the big parades, and the bands do better
than in bitter weather, when trumpets freeze up and the mouthpieces
of instruments may freeze to the players' lips.

Survival skills of the past provide the entertainment at a very different sort of carnival, the Northern Manitoba Trappers' Festival. In
1969 it was staged at The Pas, some 350 miles northwest of Winnipeg
by air. The main attraction, as it has been since the 1920's, was the
"dog derby," the 150-mile World Championship Sled Dog Race.
Countless times in Canada's past, men's lives have depended on making that distance in record time—and not over a set course. The trappers at the festival also demonstrated the tricks of boiling tea with
snow over an open fire and cooking bannocks (oatmeal hot cakes)
without stove or pan. Modern flourishes were the power toboggan
races, street dancing, and the crowning of Miss Fur Queen.

The hardy Canadians may have made winter fun on weekends, but
they know from experience that their climate is really no laughing

*Dog-sled races are still popular at carnivals, although sleds are
rapidly giving way to snowmobiles in the North.*

matter. The sheer effort it takes them to get to work day after winter day is hard for Americans to appreciate.

From late November to mid April the snow mounts. Only at a few northernmost points in the United States does it pile up to the depths found across Canada to British Columbia. Actually not much more snow falls on well-settled Canada than on the United States north of the Mason-Dixon line, but the greater cold in Canada keeps it from melting away, and each snowfall adds to the accumulation. Washington, D.C., has about the same mean annual snowfall as Churchill, Manitoba, but the American capital's average temperature for January is above freezing, while the Manitoba town's is 17 degrees below zero. Buffalo, New York, experiences as much snow as Montreal, but its January temperature is ten degrees warmer.

Temperature figures do not tell the whole winter story. There are those blasting northern winds. Winnipeg, Manitoba's capital, which boasts it is the coldest metropolis in America, has a mean annual snowfall of 49.4 inches, only an inch more than falls regularly on Milwaukee, Wisconsin. Winnipeg's daily low average in January is −8.6

degrees, but combined with its *average* winds of 12 mph, the chill factor the city ordinarily experiences is −31 degrees. Milwaukee basks in a January average of 31 degrees above, with breezes Canadians would call "light and variable."

We might as well quote at this point a limerick attributed to Rudyard Kipling, who toured Canada early in this century.

> *There was an old man of Quebec,*
> *Who was buried in snow to his neck.*
> *When asked, "Are you friz?"*
> *He replied, "Yes, I is,*
> *But we don't call this cold in Quebec."*

The Canadian cold can take snow that was beaten into slush by rush-hour traffic and turn it an hour later into an iron-hard plating of rutted ice, a treacherous undercoating for the night's snowfall. Those winds can do more than increase the chill. After a moderate snowfall, say three to four inches, the winds can start up in earnest and create a blizzard, even though not another flake has fallen. At 40 mph the winds can and do blow a few inches of snow into drifts fifteen feet deep. Visibility is reduced to zero. The great open spaces created by freeways and airfields are particularly vulnerable to this kind of attack.

Canada knows from experience that the white stuff is too dangerous to leave lying around on highways and airports. In the Big Land snow removal is big business, with the municipal, provincial, and federal governments all involved in the expensive job of plowing it up and hauling it away by the millions of tons. In paintings done a decade ago the solitary vehicle on a snowy road was a distant sleigh; today on any main road at night that vehicle is apt to be a mammoth orange snowplow, a flashing light rotating on its cab as it pursues its slow way. Apartment dwellers in Canadian cities are not surprised upon wakening in the small hours of a winter night to see a familiar scene in the street below: a plow and a cluster of trucks harvesting the city's crop of snow. In Canadian cities the snow removal begins as soon as there's an inch of snow on the ground. There is none of the delay until a snowfall is over that causes such tie-ups in large American centers.

The statistics of the operation are astounding. Local and national governments expect to spend $100 million annually to plow, blow, sweep, or melt snow off highways and streets. As for airport costs, each winter the Department of Transportation removes about three million tons of snow from Montreal Airport, a big and busy 138-acre establishment. The bill there is $300,000. For the 115 airports administered by the department, Ottawa spends $15 million a year.

In 1968 the city of Montreal budgeted $9 million for clearing the expected one hundred inches of snow from its 1,000 miles of streets and 1,500 miles of sidewalks. Ottawa, with its much smaller population and area, spent $1.75 million getting rid of eighty inches of snow in 1967; its city administration figures that a heavy snowfall costs $300,000 to remove. Toronto for some reason—perhaps because of Lake Ontario—gets less snow than either Montreal or Ottawa. Yet it regularly employs 450 men to remove snow from city streets, and during a heavy snowfall 1,000 men are transferred from refuse collecting to snow gathering.

The equipment used ranges from scooter-sized plows and blowers for sidewalks to five-ton behemoths that will load a truck in forty-five seconds. In addition most cities use spreading vehicles that put down a mixture of sand and salt to melt snow and prevent icing. But the salt in the mix has a corrosive effect on automobiles, and its use has drawn severe criticism. The federal government has been experimenting with a chemical compound called urea (used in fertilizers) that seems to do a better job, but as its cost is several times that of salt, few cities use it. Add the effect of the salt splashed on cars, women's boots, and men's coats to Canada's winter costs. A visitor wanting a look at the old days might go to Saint John, New Brunswick, where at last report horse-drawn plows were still being used.

The winter traveler arriving at Montreal Airport during a snowfall should hurry to the nearest viewing point to catch the show. It starts with a parade of the elephants: big ponderous plows and snow blowers and steel-bristled sweepers. With this equipment it takes the crew of eighty-five to one hundred men only forty minutes to clear away an inch of snow.

The pattern they follow is now widely used in Canada. First the snow is plowed and swept into low windrows, which the blowers suck up and throw in a high arc into the field area. Snow piling up at the edges of a runway in turn creates a snow fence that channels the wind to act as an additional broom for clearing the surface. If storm conditions continue, equipment is rotated from runway to taxiway to apron and back again.

The same big blowers are used on the highways, sending the snow in a high graceful curve into the farmers' fields. A blower in action is almost as impressive as Old Faithful erupting. In the cities blowers obviously won't do. There the stuff must be scooped up.

Each type of landscape presents its problems. To keep the Trans-Canada Highway open across the Rockies, the government employs a snow analyst who often works with army howitzers. At Rogers Pass in Glacier National Park 342 inches of snow falls in an average winter, but in 1953–54 680 inches came down. The highway, which offers some of the most spectacular wintertime scenery in the Canadian west, also crosses seventy-four avalanche sites.

What the analyst does is look for avalanche conditions. When he notes a danger spot, he issues an order to the Royal Canadian Artillery unit on duty nearby. The unit fires an explosive projectile from its howitzers that either brings the snow down in a minimum avalanche, which can easily be cleared off the highway, or settles it safely into cracks and crevices. In 1969–70, however, at some points possible avalanches were bombed down by means of charges dropped from helicopters. This was found to be more precise than the mortar technique, which may be discontinued except in bad flying weather. Of course, not all potential avalanches can be spotted, and to protect highway drivers, nine concrete snowsheds have been built at chronic trouble points.

On their outward side they are solid concrete halfway up. Above that point there are close-set concrete pillars to let in the daylight. The small openings between the pillars came in handy for one couple. As they drove into one tunnel, an avalanche came down, completely blocking the exit ahead. When they turned to backtrack, they discovered a second slide had blocked that exit as well. With their small baby, they could only wait for rescue. It was some time before they were discovered, and still longer before the way out was shoveled clear, but the baby did all right. His bottles were warmed for him by Mounties, who handed them to his mother through the openings between pillars.

Motorists planning to take this route in winter should pick up the booklet "Winter Guide," published by the Department of Northern Affairs in Ottawa, and follow its advice about accepting the guidance of National Park Service officers stationed along the way.

In 1967 the Canadian National and the Canadian Pacific railways spent nine million dollars to keep their trains running close to schedule, even during blizzards. They use chemicals to melt snow from switches and propane-gas heaters to prevent the icing of remote-control switching points, in addition to hundreds of diesel-powered plows and blowers and other equipment. Army howitzers are available to the railroads, too.

In southern Quebec early in 1969 tremendous winds following a heavy snow not only blocked highways but stopped a train bound for Nova Scotia. The train had not yet picked up its diner, so there was no hot food aboard. But the people of a town a few miles away heard of its plight and came out in snowmobiles to pick up the passengers and carry them back to the town, not just for a hot meal, but, as it developed, for the night as well. One elderly woman of Scottish origin, making her first trip since she had landed in Canada decades before, said she hadn't enjoyed herself so much in years. She found the snowmobile ride a special treat.

Early in 1968 a related experience did not amuse twenty-four members of the House of Commons Committee on Transportation. Off to make a study of transportation problems in the Maritimes, they found them without delay. Their chartered aircraft could not land in Charlottetown, Prince Edward Island, their first point of inquiry, because of poor visibility. Taking a train instead, they had to wait hours for the railroad ferry because service was disrupted by pack ice. When they finally reached the island, snow blocked their bus for five hours.

While they were snowbound, a crucial tax bill came to a vote in Parliament, and because of the absence of so many government members, was defeated. Lester Pearson's Liberal Government tottered and almost fell. As a newspaper editorial put it: "Nature still wins even at this stage of a go-go century."

What ice jams on her waters cost Canada is hard to determine, since winter costs for the Canadian Coast Guard aren't separated from general expenditures. To cope with the problem, the Coast Guard maintains ice-operation offices at Sydney, Nova Scotia; Quebec City, Quebec; Trois Rivières in the same province; and Prescott, Ontario.

The coastguardsmen keep a watchful eye on the Gulf of St. Lawrence, the Saguenay River, and the St. Lawrence River itself, which freezes for its whole length above tidewater at Quebec City. For the job, the Coast Guard uses ten heavy icebreakers, eight light icebreakers, and associated vessels.

From late December until well into April the battering-rams of the seas smash their way through the jagged ice of the St. Lawrence to open a channel that will carry the broken ice from upriver out to sea. Because of their size the icebreakers work in the dredged ship channel and by doing so create a path that more ships every year follow to Montreal. If a ship gets frozen in and its situation is positively dangerous (it often isn't), an icebreaker will go to its rescue, but such rescues are not the icebreakers' primary purpose on the St. Lawrence. The Coast Guard's chief responsibility there is to prevent ice jams from piling up and raising the river to flood heights. For all the icebreakers' grinding work, some shore dwellers are occasionally flooded out, particularly in early spring, but this does not happen often. The icebreakers know the places that must be watched in order to keep the ice moving freely downstream.

Passing ships can make trouble for an icebreaker. Most of those sent to Canada in winter are built for ice-clogged waters, and captains conscious of their reinforced hulls sometimes travel the opened channel at too smart a clip. The wash from a ship can snap off a large sheet of shore ice. As this big chunk swings into the channel, it blocks the flow of smaller ice, which quickly consolidates into a jam. Strong winds can have the same effect. At some points floating booms have been laid along the edges of the channel to keep shore ice from moving out.

On the Gulf of the St. Lawrence the icebreakers do much more rescue work. One major task is escorting the ferryboats that run from North Sydney to Port aux Basques, Newfoundland. On one run the giant of the ice-breaking fleet, the big red-hulled *John A. MacDonald* (315 feet long and 15,000 horsepower), chopped eleven vessels out of the ice, including another, smaller Coast Guard icebreaker.

A voyage on the *John A.* is not for the timid. When an ice concentration proves stubborn, the ship rams into it at top speed, her engines shrieking, her hull grinding into the frozen mass. A successful ramming

prays of snow emerge from the powerful snow-removal equipment
sed at Ottawa's Uplands Airport.

usually ends with a loud crack as the ice explodes, but the icebreaker may slide up onto the ice instead and come to a full stop. Then her captain and crew rock the boat; by shifting water ballasts mechanically, they tip her from side to side until she is freed and slides back down off the ice. This very modern vessel carries a helicopter that scouts for her, picking weak points for the captain and warning him of dangerous packing ahead.

Not even in summer does the *John A.* escape her life on ice. From July until October she moves around the Arctic, opening the way for government supply ships, freeing an occasional commercial vessel, making scientific observations, and delivering scientists and their equipment to various northern posts. When the experimental American oil tanker *Manhattan* was negotiating the Northwest Passage from west to east in September, 1969, the *John A.* went to her aid a half dozen times. Three other major icebreakers, the powerful new *St. Laurent,* and *Labrador,* and the *D'Iberville,* share this work. What they learn in the north aids Canada in its war on cold during the "southerly" winter.

Perhaps the most significant step yet taken in coping with the Canadian climate is the creation of the underground city. The largest in the world already exists in Montreal. A smaller one is on the drawing boards at Winnipeg. The visitor roaming Montreal's subterranean realm experiences a chill only if the air conditioning happens to be set too low, and the only snowflakes he'll see will be those used at Christmas to deck the underground shop windows.

A tourist entering Montreal at the Canadian National Railways central station can, if he chooses, live for days without drawing a breath of outdoor air, hot or cold. From the station he can walk to his hotel through glass and cement corridors and thereafter walk or ride (aboard Montreal's colorful subway, the Métro) for miles under the city. In this vast complex he'll find endless streets of shops, theatres, restaurants, and hotel lobbies. Whatever he might want is available, from a haircut or a shoeshine to far-out works of art or the latest in men's suits by Pierre Balmain of Paris. The underground complex will ultimately spread over one hundred acres; the one at New York's Rockefeller Center covers seventeen.

Conceivably, a Canadian employed in one of the connecting skyscrapers and living in one of the high-rise apartments tied into the complex could spend his whole life without going outdoors. He could do his banking, see a doctor, get new glasses, go to a Turkish bath, or take in a movie. If he didn't care to dine in one of the underground city's many unusual restaurants, he could pick up his liquor at the government store and his groceries at one of several supermarkets and go home for the evening. Whatever he needed—furniture, books and periodicals, records—he could buy. There's no exact count of the number of shops, but it has been roughly estimated at five hundred, and they come in all price ranges—as do the restaurants. For exercise he might take up jogging in the early hours.

This hypothetical Canadian would save money on all the things he could dispense with: cars, gas and oil, car repairs, overcoats and raincoats, boots and umbrellas. For an occasional glimpse of the outside world, or a visit with above-ground friends, he could take an elevator to an enclosed rooftop restaurant or bar. Admittedly he would have to leave the place in the end. Montreal's underground city as yet has no cemetery or crematorium.

Out in the big cold world Canadians have sometimes been plagued when it wasn't cold enough. Ten miles from the subarctic port of Churchill is Fort Churchill on Hudson Bay, a converted military base occupied primarily by National Research Council staff, government personnel, and 250 students who attend a vocational school there. In 1968 the freeze-up on the bay was late. This kept the polar bears off the ice, and about two dozen, many of them females with cubs, harassed Fort Churchill that fall.

One bear smashed through a plate-glass window and trapped the district administrator and his wife in their home. (The director and his wife held their bear at bay with brooms and bottles.) Several bears had to be chased away from the post office. Children returning from Sunday school were scattered by bears; one beast turned and slashed a boy's throat before a Mountie running to the rescue could shoot it. (It is illegal for anyone but a Mountie to kill a polar bear except in an officially regulated Eskimo bear hunt.) Everyone must have breathed a relieved sigh when that bit of Canadian landscape was once again cold and solitary.

The
American Occupation

"Here was the headquarters of the American army during
the occupation of Montreal."

ft, the Château de Ramezay, American headquarters in
ntreal in 1775. Above, the death of Richard Montgomery.

*The pastoral Richelieu River, used by some of Montgomery's forces
to travel from Lake Champlain to the St. Lawrence*

THE PLUMP LITTLE American woman with the authoritative manner
had spent most of the week engrossed in the delights of Expo 67.
Tiring finally of the far-out architecture, she decided that a tour of
Old Montreal would provide a happy change. Besides, as the president
of the local historical society at home it was her duty to see what
Canadians were doing about historic preservation. So, with a driver
the hotel doorman had assured her was a knowledgeable fellow, she
set out.

He took her directly to the Château de Ramezay, a squat castlelike
building on Rue Notre Dame. She noticed that it was not kept up as
well as historic sites in the States.

"Here," the driver said with a flourish of his arm, "was the head-quarters of the American army during the occupation of Montreal."

"In 1812?" She couldn't think of any other time that Americans had invaded Canada.

"No, no! They did not get so far in 1812. It was in 1775 that they marched into Montreal and occupied most of Quebec for seven months. Quebec *was* Canada in those days. Beyond," he said as he waved a hand to the west, "there were only a few trappers and soldiers. Come, I will show you where the dais was on which the great Franklin stood to receive the French ladies."

"That was in France," she said firmly.

"First here in Montreal. It was later that he went to France. Look, here is a pass that he signed for a Montreal lady. You see also the signatures of Carroll of Carrollton and another named Samuel Chase."

It was plainly dated "Montreal 11th May 1776" and signed by Franklin, Chase, and Carroll, three men who signed the Declaration of Independence the following July. Whatever were they doing in Canada that May? To cover her confusion, she said accusingly, "That's a Photostat."

"Of course. The original is in the vault. With them was this Carroll's cousin, a Jesuit priest who was not popular with our curés here. Per-haps he came too late. General Burgoyne and his army very soon ar-rived at Quebec City to drive out the Americans."

She had never heard such rigmarole. Everyone knew that Burgoyne had been defeated by the Americans, surrendering at Saratoga with his entire army.

"Franklin was greeted here by General Benedict Arnold, who took the command in Montreal after he was wounded in the leg at Quebec City."

Arnold had been wounded in the leg at Saratoga, she was sure. She had seen the nameless monument there with a boot carved on it. This taxi driver had confused two battles. You really could not depend on local guides. Now he was saying that Franklin had had a printing press installed in the cellar, the first in Montreal. Naturally he had no actual press to show her. People seemed to think that Franklin freighted a printing press along wherever he went. But she was ready to concede that he might have been in Canada. That pass *did* look authentic.

Irritated by the episode, she later did a little research at her local library. To her shock she learned the driver's every word was true, Franklin, Arnold, Burgoyne, and all. Quebec had very nearly become the fourteenth original state.

That early failure to conquer Canada is not stressed much in American textbooks, perhaps because the story has so many elements that could confuse budding patriots. There was George Washington himself planning a major campaign that did not succeed; Benjamin Franklin failing on a diplomatic mission; and Benedict Arnold, of all people, being the only man to emerge from Canada with his reputation enhanced.

Nevertheless, today's visitor to Canada might well look into that first American invasion. Because of it, Quebec has long enjoyed special rights in Canada—rights that some Québecois currently think give the province "special status." Because of it, Canada has developed what some Canadian writers call the national neurosis: a love-hate relationship with her powerful neighbor to the south. Canadians' suspicions of America's intentions toward their country began right there in 1775.

The history-minded traveler to Quebec can retrace the major path of the American invasion through some of the province's loveliest countryside, the Richelieu River valley. Starting near Rouses Point at the New York-Quebec border, Route 9B follows the river most of the way. If the traveler goes by boat, as one group of the invaders did, he can enter the river from Lake Champlain and float serenely past forts that were once fought over and sunny fields where the Americans camped; it is all so peacefully beautiful today that it is hard to imagine guns being fired there. Now only the ringing of the Angelus bell at sunset breaks the silence.

Another arm of the invasion traveled a different route, which for for most of its length can even today be recommended only to the hardy. Benedict Arnold and about eleven hundred sturdy American colonists pushed up the Kennebec River in Maine, crossed to Lake Mégantic in Quebec, and from there traveled up the Chaudière River to the St. Lawrence and Quebec City. From Lake Mégantic to the little town of St. Georges, where the Famine River joins the Chaudière, there is no good road. But from that point on a tourist driving routes 23 and 1 straight up from Boston journeys through the area where Arnold's men stumbled out of the wilderness, starving and in rags, after one of the most harrowing marches in military history.

If they had been opposed at that stage by the habitants, the farmers of the neighborhood—even though the latter were armed only with pitchforks—they could have been beaten. Instead, as they expected, they were taken into warm cottages, fed and clothed, and allowed to regroup for their attack on Quebec City. So far the invasion had proceeded according to plan.

What was behind it all? Why, so early in their struggle with Britain, did the American colonists feel they had to take Canada? Men in the northern colonies especially remembered the horrors of the French and Indian War, when raiders based in Quebec had put many a settlement to the scalping knife or the torch. Washington himself had won his spurs the hard way in that earlier conflict. Wolfe's victory over Montcalm on the Plains of Abraham in 1759 had ended this bloody war, but it had also given the British a base for action against the colonies.

Yet, in 1775 Canada was lightly held. The British had only a handful of regulars there, and the French Canadians were said to be restive under alien rule. Why not persuade them to revolt and join the rebellious American colonies? Meanwhile, those colonies could send up an army to deal with the British regulars before they were reinforced from England.

The reports of French–Canadian restiveness emanated, however, from a dubious source—American merchants and fur traders who had followed the British army into Quebec, expecting to exploit that conquered territory. As Anglo-Saxon Protestants, they reasoned, they would surely be allowed to help themselves to the lands of the French seigneurs and the Catholic Church. They would also dominate the legislature that would be set up and the law courts as well, because under the English code Catholics could not vote, hold office, or practice law. The French Canadians called these men, of whom there were about four hundred, the *Bostonnais,* although many of them were from other areas. By 1765 these *Bostonnais* were bitterly resentful. The course of events in Quebec had not gone their way.

Instead, the British military occupation had hardly disturbed the old French pattern. The seigneurs were officers and gentlemen whom the British command rather liked and whom they left in full possession of their land. To keep everyone happy under a small occupation force, the command likewise left the Church undisturbed. They did replace harsh French criminal laws with the more lenient British system, but the change was generally welcomed.

When a civil governor, James Murray, was finally named, he adopted the same attitude. Furious, the American merchants in Montreal plotted his removal, and they had enough commercial influence in London to accomplish this. But the new governor, Guy Carleton, soon took steps that genuinely outraged not only the *Bostonnais* but also the American colonies in general. Uneasy over his task of holding so large a country with so few men, Carleton persuaded Parliament to confirm the Canadians' rights to their language, their religion, and their civil law. That way, he felt, he could keep them loyal to the British Crown.

The Quebec Act of 1774 was really an astonishing law for Parliament to have enacted at that date. It gave Canadian Catholics the right freely to practice their religion—a right that no English Catholic yet enjoyed. It even allowed the priests to collect their customary tithes from their parishioners, and this at a time when a priest captured in England faced the death penalty.

Among the British themselves the law raised cries of "popery," while among the American colonists the reaction was hysterical. So sober a fellow as Alexander Hamilton said that as a result of the Quebec Act "in time the Inquisition would be burning Protestants at the stake in Boston."

In Philadelphia the delegates to the First Continental Congress included the Quebec Act among the grievances they listed in their 1774 "Address to the People of Great Britain." Parliament, they said, had approved in Quebec "a religion that has deluged your island in blood" and caused other horrors such as "bigotry, persecution, murder and rebellion throughout every part of the world." At the same time they addressed an invitation to the people of Quebec to send delegates to Philadelphia! Perhaps they were counting on poor communications to keep the left hand from knowing what the right was doing.

But the Tories saw to it that copies of the "Address to the People of Great Britain" reached the clergy in Quebec. Naturally such extravagant words were resented, and before a single soldier from the American colonies set foot in the province, the priests were angrily against

The habitants, some of whom are portrayed in Krieghoff's painting Merrymakers, *welcomed the invading Americans.*

them. Nor did the upper-class French Canadians, the noblesse, take kindly to revolutionaries who would doubtless strip them of their land. In addition, Carleton saw to it that men of good family were given militia commissions.

But what of the habitants, the easygoing farmers along the Richelieu, the Chaudière, and the St. Lawrence? They at least listened to the promises American agents made them. Some of these agents were *Bostonnais*, traveling through the countryside ostensibly to buy wheat but actually to stir up the habitants. Some were men sent up from the colonies when the Committee of Safety—an executive committee of the independent Massachusetts Assembly—found that letters and printed broadsides were useless, as most of the Canadian farmers could not read. They took everything written or printed to the curé to be translated as he saw fit.

One trio of American agents made the journey north in the bitter February of 1775; Peleg Sunderland, a weather-beaten hunter; Winthrop Hoyt, who for years had been a captive of the Indians; and John

Brown, the chief agent. Brown, thirty-one, was an attractive young colonial, a graduate of Yale and one-time King's Attorney in New York, who had settled in the Berkshires. He was a member of the Committee of Safety, together with Sam Adams, Dr. Joseph Warren, and John Hancock. When the Americans invaded later in the year, he would have the rank of major. In short, he was a man whom any Daughter of the American Revolution would be glad to claim as an ancestor. But rumors of his arrival at Montreal disturbed "the better classes of people" as much as Che Guevera's appearance in an American town would have done two centuries later.

Brown and others like him moved out into the villages, preaching their politics so effectively that one British officer claimed the habitants were all worked up over that "damned word, 'liberty'."

Liberty for the habitants meant freedom from certain obligations owed to their seigneurs. While they paid only nominal rent for their land, they had to take their grain to the seigneur's mill to be ground, and their lord kept part of the flour. They also had to give him a number of days' labor every year, to build roads and make other improvements on his land. Worst of all, their young men had to serve under the seigneur in the militia when it was called up. In addition, the habitants had to pay a tithe to the local parish. For a while under the British these obligations had been relaxed. But now under the Quebec Act they were the law—or, as the Americans said, "the old tyranny was revived."

Many of the habitants who weren't persuaded by the American agents' promises were frightened by their propaganda. They were told that the barges in the river at Quebec City would be used to carry them into captivity in foreign lands. Carleton was said to have money in his pocket already from the Spaniards who would make them slaves. The British had, after all, exiled the Acadians, so perhaps they really intended to ship off the Québecois. It was possible.

Even more plausible was the story that their young men would be taken to fight Britain's wars in foreign lands. So when Carleton, hearing rumors of an American advance, tried to call up the militia, he stirred up a hornet's nest among the country people. In a small community outside Montreal officials trying to enlist young men were stoned by the women. In the parish of Chicut two seigneurs demanding service from their *renteurs* were taken prisoner. In all of Montreal

Carleton was able to enlist only 120 Canadians, many of them young men of the noblesse. He was bitter over the ingratitude of the country people, most of whom welcomed the Americans with open arms. The habitants sold the Americans badly needed supplies and piloted them across the tricky waters of the St. Lawrence. Two women captured a British scout and delivered him to the American camp.

Washington had warned that the invasion should not be pressed unless the people "cooperate or at least willingly acquiesce." This many of them did, in the beginning. In consequence, the Americans— the larger force from Lake Champlain under General Richard Montgomery, the smaller from Maine under General Arnold—advanced so rapidly that Carleton was nearly captured at Montreal, as several hundred of his men and most of his munitions were. But in a small boat with muffled oars he slid past the American lines, and with his escape down the St. Lawrence to Quebec City the American campaign for Canada was really lost, although Montgomery marching into Montreal in triumph did not realize it.

The visitor to Montreal can stand at the corner of Notre Dame and McGill streets, where the old Récollet Gate in the city's walls once stood, and imagine the Americans swinging in on November 13, 1775. Most of them were wearing red coats "liberated" from the storehouse of Fort St. John on the Richelieu. Few had solid boots. No flag had yet been designed for the American rebels, so some of them carried a plain red banner, while others held aloft a red flag bordered in black. The British jeered at the latter as "a squaw's blanket in mourning for the Boston Massacre." They were a raggle-taggle, undisciplined lot in sharp contrast to the spit-and-polish correctness of both the earlier French and later British forces.

Montgomery himself, however, was a model general, young, handsome, diplomatic. A one-time British officer, he had resigned his commission when he was passed over for promotion and had settled in America, where he married one of the Livingston girls in the colony of New York. When the Livingston clan went over to the rebels, so did Montgomery.

He and Carleton had, in fact, long known each other. In boyhood they had been neighbors in Ireland, where both were members of the Anglo-Irish gentry. They had also served together in the British army.

But one was to be the cause of the death of the other.

Carleton was not only Canada's governor but also her commander in chief. After he reached Quebec City, he prepared to dig in for the winter. If he could hold that citadel until reinforcements arrived in the spring, Canada would still be British. In those days of water transport Quebec City was the key to all Quebec, as Wolfe had realized sixteen years earlier.

Carleton began by expelling from the city anyone sympathetic to the Americans. Every able-bodied man who remained had to do duty on the walls. Sailors from the English ships in the harbor were brought in and drilled. Carleton had only a handful of men, but every one of them could be relied on. Far below, on the river level, Arnold and his small force had already begun the siege, lobbing shot into the town.

Montgomery, once he had Montreal in hand, joined Arnold with re-inforcements. Together they launched a two-pronged assault on New Year's Eve, 1775. The Lower Town, the waterfront, fell easily. Some of Daniel Morgan's rifle corps, Virginia sharpshooters to a man, actually penetrated the Upper Town. But a violent snowstorm blew up, and the weather, as it so often has in Canada, changed history. In the blinding blizzard Arnold's men lost contact with Montgomery's.

Then, as Montgomery led his troops up toward the walls, he was killed by one of the shots fired by the defenders. His body was found the next day only because one arm was thrust up out of the snow. For auld lang syne Carleton gave him an officer's burial, and Americans later hung patriotic engravings of his death on their walls. He was pictured dying like Wolfe in the arms of his men, when in fact his men had fled in confusion to their camp.

Disaster had also struck Arnold's wing of the attack when he was wounded in the leg, and his leaderless men were easily driven back. The Virginians who reached the Upper Town were cut off and taken prisoner. The Americans doggedly continued their siege for dreary months, but never again was Quebec City seriously threatened. That New Year's Eve was the turning point.

General Washington, himself in the midst of a long-range siege of Boston, occupied by British forces under Sir William Howe, could do little to help. The American commander in chief had sixteen thousand raw militia that he was transforming into a trained army while the

Benedict Arnold, who was wounded at Quebec City

British stayed surprisingly inactive. Washington was badly in need of everything but men; arms and ammunition were especially scarce. Cannon had to be dragged all the way from Ticonderoga. For munitions, and even food, he often had to rely on American privateers intercepting British supply ships bound for Boston.

But his army did at last have an official flag, which was unfurled at his Cambridge headquarters on New Year's Day, 1776, only hours after the Quebec defeat. It had thirteen stripes, seven red and six white, as it does today, but the union was the union of the British flag of that day. The colonies had yet to declare their independence.

The Americans' failure to take the Citadel deeply worried their habitant friends. Their uneasiness had in fact been aroused even before the defeat at Quebec City. When he left Montreal, Montgomery had of necessity put the most senior of his subordinates in command, General David Wooster of Connecticut, a blunt old fellow who not only quarreled with his brother officers but cut a ridiculous figure in public. "From his dusty old cocked hat to his coarse boots, he was a back number," an American chronicler has said. That hat, perched on the top of an enormous gray periwig, made the ladies giggle.

Wooster distrusted Canadians, and unwilling to allow the people of Montreal to congregate in large numbers, he decided on the heels of Montgomery's departure to close the Catholic churches, which he called "the mass houses," on Christmas Eve. It was a shock to rich and poor alike to be unable to celebrate the greatest feast of the year. One of the churches Wooster closed can be visited today, the venerable Chapel of Notre Dame de Bonsecours on St. Paul Street near Montreal's old market.

By the middle of January, 1776, Wooster had posted on the church doors an ordinance forbidding anyone to speak against the Continental Congress on penalty of exile from Quebec. This was aimed largely at the priests, who, he wrote, "refuse absolution to all who have shown themselves our friends." But others beside the priests were beginning to speak out critically, and soon forty sledloads of indignant citizens were sent across the ice to Albany. When their friends, many of whom were well disposed to the Americans, protested to the general, he told them he regarded "the whole lot of you as enemies and rascals."

His heavyhandedness was particularly unfortunate in the circumstances. For one thing, the army was melting away. Many of the Americans had enlisted for short terms. As the historian Justin H. Smith has said, the volunteers "had been told that redcoats, papists and savages proposed to come and ravage their homes; and now the redcoats were prisoners, the savages friends, the papists brethren. There was no war."

Why, then, stay to face the Canadian winter, which they considered Arctic? Before Lake Champlain was frozen over, hundreds of them left, marching off in sizable bodies, to the astonishment of the Québecois, who saw soldiers "retreating" when no enemy pursued.

It was, in fact, the worst winter in ten years, cold enough to freeze stones, as the Canadians said. Soldiers on duty actually froze to death at their posts.

But more fell to another enemy. Wooster lost hundreds of his effective men to smallpox, with as many as thirty-seven a day being stricken by it. Pathetic conquerors in unheated barracks, they lay down to die in inadequate clothing, with no blankets over them and no medicine to dull their misery.

The soldiers still on their feet often went unpaid or were paid in "Congress money," paper no one wanted. The French Canadians had seen the French king's paper become worthless after the British conquest. Once bitten, twice shy. They demanded hard money for the few goods they had to sell.

But the American army, from General Wooster on down, had precious little hard money. What they managed to raise—from the richest of the *Bostonnais,* from the pocket of the wealthy General Philip Schuyler, from the distant hard-up Continental Congress, melted away. Wooster depended on the very men he had insulted for the credit he needed.

"Our credit sinks daily," he was soon reporting, and no wonder. Canadians who had accepted promises found that the quartermaster general could not honor the debt. Officers scribbled out IOU's that were not acceptable because they were illegible. If there was a bit of hard cash at hand, the command hoarded it by offering only half the current price for firewood or flour or woolens.

Soon the soldiers began to do what an occupying army always seems to come to: they took what they wanted by stealth or force. It was one thing to see soldiers ransack the seigneur's manor house or steal the curé's watch, but quite another to observe them breaking into a habitant's small winter stock of grain or hauling his cherished cow off to be butchered. Everyone heard of the farmer who, when he insisted on twenty shillings for a load of supplies, had been bayoneted through the throat.

Habitants who in the beginning had taken starving soldiers into their low-ceilinged, smoky cottages and given them a loaf of bread and a pan of warm milk were now taking the chickens in to roost with the family behind barred doors. Many began to hope that with spring the British would come. They always paid.

Instead, more Americans arrived with the first good weather. They came without supplies, without guns and ammunition, many of them eager to finish the conquest of Canada, alarmed lest Quebec City should fall before they reached it. Wooster took numbers of them to reinforce the troops besieging the Citadel, and Arnold replaced him as commander at Montreal. He never stayed where Wooster was if he could help it.

So General Arnold was in Montreal to welcome the small group of eminent Americans when they arrived there on April 29. Since November all the generals—Schuyler, Montgomery, and Arnold—had been urging the Continental Congress to send a commission to expound the ideas of the American Revolution to Canadians. Dilatory as always, Congress did not name the commissioners until February, and not until April 2 could they set off by sloop up the Hudson on a journey that took them twenty-seven days.

They were all distinguished men calculated to influence the thinking of the still hostile "better people." Dr. Franklin already had an international reputation. Samuel Chase, with his flowing locks and steady gaze, presented a stalwart figure. But the member counted on most to sway the noblesse was the aristocratically handsome Charles Carroll of Carrollton, the richest man in America and a Catholic fluent in French. With him went his cousin, Father John Carroll, later the first Archbishop of Baltimore. Abigail Adams thought it a brilliant stroke to include Father John in the mission.

From Albany they had a hard overland journey to Ticonderoga, Franklin's gout plaguing him during the rough ride. At Ticonderoga they boarded a boat for the three-day sail to St. Jean on the Richelieu and drafted a message to Arnold asking that *calèches* be sent to take them to Laprairie, where they could be ferried to the island city of Montreal.

Today, a visitor can ride around Montreal, particularly the park on Mount Royal, by *calèche,* and the carriage driver will be happy to accept American paper money for the fare. But the commissioners that long-ago April were not so fortunate.

They encountered at once the sad state of American credit. No one would carry their express message to Arnold without being paid in silver in advance, and none of the distinguished men had a dollar in hard money on him, not even the richest man in America. Arnold and Wooster were counting heavily on the commissioners bringing up badly needed gold, but all they had was a chestful of the paper that the Québecois detested. Carroll, who had sterling bills of exchange that no one would cash, became in effect a poor man in Montreal. As for Franklin, his being unable to send an express letter was truly ironic: thirteen years earlier at the behest of the English the good doctor had actually set up Quebec's first postal system.

The commissioners stood marooned until one of the *Bostonnais,* a merchant whose exact name is lost to history (it was either McCartney or McCarty), luckily stumbled on them. The sympathetic fellow actually had good money in hand, and he not only sent off a message to Arnold but hired *calèches* for the group himself. That printing press that Franklin was to install in the cellar of the Château de Ramezay was traveling on their heels, in charge of a French printer, Fleury Mesplet. How Mesplet managed to get it to Montreal is not recorded, but printers are an ingenious lot.

Arnold managed to give the arriving commissioners an impressive welcome. There was a salute from the Citadel and an escort of all the "friends of Liberty" that he could dragoon, and at the Château de Ramezay the dais was already erected. After that little went right. The commissioners had come too late.

To give the people a "taste of Liberty," they allowed Wooster's exiles to return and freed from the dungeons of the fort at Chambly (now a tourist attraction) the militia officers who had refused to resign their English commissions. But these people now nursed a bitter grudge. The friends who had given the Americans credit remained unpaid, and even worse, they knew that they faced "the gibbet and confiscations" if the British ever returned.

And the British were coming. At least three thousand of them had already arrived from an unexpected source. Early in March the British in Boston had found to their dismay that Washington had those Ticonderoga guns well entrenched on Dorchester Heights, which commanded all Boston. While American shot dropped into the town, Sir William Howe promptly loaded his troops—the Americans say he had five thousand men, but only three thousand reached Halifax—on all available transport, together with fifteen hundred army wives and children and eleven hundred Loyalist refugees. By March 17 Boston was evacuated, and the Americans could celebrate their first notable victory.

Howe's flotilla sailed to the warm-water port of Halifax in the British colony of Nova Scotia, to the surprise of that small settlement, which was completely overrun. At that time of year Howe's troops could not hope to relieve icebound Quebec. Besides, Howe knew that in spring major reinforcements under General Burgoyne would arrive there. Meanwhile the Crown was uneasy about Nova Scotia itself. The thinly populated colony that had grown up around the naval base at Halifax and the various army fortifications there and elsewhere was too American by half—the half of its citizens who were either of American birth or parentage. These settlers had already shown signs of sympathy with the rebels. The troops would be well employed in keeping these restive colonists down while the Loyalist refugees settled in and changed the character of the population. There was also some fear that Washington and his Continental army might, following their triumph at Boston, march overland to take Nova Scotia. After Arnold's march north such a move seemed more than possible. But Washington did not come, although he did send more ill-equipped troops to Quebec.

On May 6 the first shipload of British reinforcements reached Quebec City, followed quickly by two more. Word came of fifteen ships only forty leagues away. As regiment after regiment of spruce redcoats paraded across the heights above them, the Americans down below, sick and underfed, unarmed and ragged, fled terror-stricken. On their headlong flight they met thousands of fresh arrivals coming

John Hancock issued this poster to urge the habitants t
support the Americans in 1776

72

AUX
HABITANTS
DE LA PROVINCE DU CANADA.

AMIS ET COMPATRIOTES;

Notre Précédente Adresse vous a démontré nos Droits, nos Griefs & les Moyens que nous avons en notre pouvoir, & dont nous sommes autorisés par les Constitutions Britanniques, à faire usage pour maintenir les uns, & obtenir justice des autres.

Nous vous avons aussi expliqué, que votre Liberté, votre Honneur & votre Bonheur, sont essentiellement & nécessairement liés à l'Affaire malheureuse que nous avons été forcé d'entreprendre, pour le soutien de nos Priviléges.

Nous voyons avec joie, combien vous avez été touché, par les remontrances justes & équitables de vos Amis & Compatriotes, qui n'ont d'autres vues que celles de fortifier & d'établir la cause de la Liberté : les services que vous avez déjà rendus à cette cause commune, méritent notre reconnoissance ; & nous sentons l'obligation où nous sommes, de vous rendre le reciproque.

Les meilleures causes sont sujettes aux événements, les contre-temps sont inévitables, tel est le sort de l'humanité ; mais les ames génereuses, qui sont éclairées & échauffées par le feu sacré de la Liberté, ne seront pas découragées par de tels échecs, & surmonteront tous les obstacles qui pourront se trouver entr'eux & l'objet prétieux de leurs vœux.

Nous ne vous laisserons pas exposé à la fureur de vos ennemis & des nôtres ; deux Bataillons ont reçu ordre de marcher au Canada, dont une partie est déjà en route ; on leve six autres Bataillons dans les Colonies unies pour le même service, qui partiront pour votre Province aussi-tôt qu'il sera possible ; & probablement ils arriveront en Canada, avant que les Troupes du Ministere, sous le Général Carleton, puissent recevoir des secours : en outre, nous avons fait expédier les ordres nécessaires pour faire lever deux Bataillons chez vous. Votre assistance pour le soutien & la conservation de la Liberté Amériquaine, nous causera la plus grande satisfaction ; & nous nous flattons que vous saisirez avec zèle & empressement, l'instant favorable de co-opérer au succès d'une entreprise aussi glorieuse. Si des forces plus considérables sont requises, elles vous seront envoyées.

Aprésent, vous devez être convaincus, que rien n'est plus propre à assurer nos intérêts & nos libertés, que de prendre des mésures efficaces, pour combiner nos forces mutuelles, afin que par cette réunion de secours & de conseils, nous puissions éviter les efforts & l'artifice d'un ennemi qui cherche à nous affoiblir en nous divisant ; pour cet effet, nous vous conseillons & vous exhortons, d'établir chez vous des Associations en vos différentes Paroisses, de la même nature que celles qui ont été si salutaires aux Colonies unies ; d'élire des Députés pour former une Assemblée Provinciale chez vous, & que cette Assemblée nomme des Délegués, pour vous représenter en ce Congrès.

Nous nous flattons de toucher à l'heureux moment, de voir disparoître de dessus cette terre, l'Etendard de la Tyrannie, & nous espérons qu'il ne trouvera aucune place en l'Amérique Septentrionale.

Signé au Nom & par l'Ordre du Congrès : JOHN HANCOCK, *Président.*

A Philadelphie, le 24 *Janvier* 1776.

to reinforce them; at one time there were five thousand men stretched along the St. Lawrence, on half rations at best, with meat long gone. All around lay men dying of smallpox, and soon there were English vessels coming up the river, firing as they came. Habitants who had formerly aided the Americans pursued the soldiers with lamentations or curses, fearful of their fate.

Others, anxious to make their peace with the English, led Americans cut off from their boats straight into the arms of the enemy. But Carleton refused to take prisoners. "Let the poor creatures go home and carry with them a tale which will serve His Majesty more effectively than their capture."

It didn't work out that way. Among the men allowed to escape was "Mad Anthony" Wayne, and there were others who would do the King's cause more damage than seemed probable during those May weeks.

At Trois Rivières, on Route 2 midway between Montreal and Quebec City, the Ursuline Convent with a sundial high on one wall is pointed out to the traveler as the place where sick and wounded soldiers were nursed by the Sisters. "For medicines and dressing, the ladies presented a bill for $130, which the officer in charge signed. But it was never paid, you understand? Our local historian has figured that at 6 per cent compounded the United States Government today owes the Ursuline ladies eight million dollars."

At Montreal the commissioners, fearing a British frigate might come to cut off their escape route, departed in some haste, Franklin less than three weeks after his arrival, the others twelve days later. They had accomplished nothing, and Arnold was left to organize the American retreat from the city, which he did admirably. However flawed his character, he was an able soldier.

After the Americans had left, those habitants who had helped them had their cottages burned down or were refused Catholic burial or at best had to stand in public with halters around their necks. Their fellows who had remained neutral, letting the mad English quarrel among themselves, jeered at the sufferers, and never again did the Québecois aid an American military invasion.

It was officially tried again, twice: there was a second Revolutionary War attempt and a major effort during the War of 1812. In 1812 habitants willingly served under their seigneurs in the Battle of Château-guay (across from Montreal) in which the Americans were defeated.

The tourist curious to know what life was like in the Quebec country-side during the American occupation of 1775–76 should visit the pro-vincial museum at Quebec City, which has an extensive collection of genre paintings by Krieghoff, whose work was described in Chapter II. In the years between the American Revolution and Krieghoff's time the habitants had changed very little. They wore the same knitted caps and sashes, drove the same low sledges across the snow. And today, in the Quebec of surging modern development, winter can still produce those horse-drawn sledges with the drivers standing at the reins à la 1775.

One invasion from the States was never turned back, the peaceable invasion. Ideas, inventions, men, and goods have continued to flow northward. It is worth noting that when the French Canadians, in-spired by Louis Joseph Papineau, finally attempted in 1837 to stage a revolt of their own against the British, they were more nearly suc-cessful in Montreal and along the Richelieu, where American ideas had earlier flourished. Today in Montreal the tourist can find not only the latest American paperbacks but also the works of American writers translated into French. And with billions of dollars invested in Que-bec's industry, American credit is good.

A placid scene at Upper Canada Village near the St. Lawrence symbolizes the peace that prevails today on the long border.

4 That Friendly Border

"And we'll go and capture Canada, for we've nothing else to do."

Colonel Allan MacNab, who helped put down the rebellion of 1837–38, bankrupted himself building this mansion in Hamilton, Ontario.

TODAY THE United States and Canada officially hail the broad "undefended border" between the two countries as an example of peaceful coexistence for the rest of the world. Ignoring the 1775–76 fiasco, Americans think that except for a bit of trouble during the War of 1812, the border has always been peaceful, because of America's innate neighborliness.

The average American is surprised to learn that Canadians think it took them a century of stalwart fighting to teach the aggressive Americans to stay on their own side of the line. Ideas were welcomed and capital allowed opportunities, but armed invasion was resisted. Canadian schoolboys of not so long ago voiced that defiance when they recited in ringing tones the words of the national poetess Pauline Johnson:

The Yankee to the south of us
Shall south of us remain.

Nowadays the traveler in Canada can explore certain stretches of the border that once provided an easy approach for military invaders or hotheaded raiders. He might begin by turning off the Montreal-Toronto Highway at Cornwall to follow Ontario Route 2 along the St. Lawrence and the north shore of Lake Ontario as far as Toronto. He'll pass along some lovely island-studded riverscape and through a scattering of peaceful small towns. Along the way are a number of historical markers and more than one historic site. From them he may gain a new perspective on Canadian-American relations.

Viewing its present serenity, it's hard to believe that for nearly a century after 1775 this was one of the most unquiet stretches of water anywhere, with Americans stirring up a variety of troubles. They were discouraged not so much by stalwart Canadians as by British redcoats, as modern Canadian historians firmly tell their countrymen. During times of trouble the defense of what was then British North America depended on the thin red line of Empire.

Part of the shore that was defended is now under water. In order to carry out the St. Lawrence Seaway and Power Projects, eight villages along the river's northern bank were scheduled to be flooded in 1957. Dotting this area were many historic houses and barns, inns and mills, churches and schools. So before 1957 the Ontario Provincial Government decided to move the most interesting or typical to a single location on higher ground.

This was several years before the Egyptians, with international assistance, raised Abu Simbel and moved other ancient temples out of soon-to-be-flooded ground. While Americans heard much about that Egyptian effort, they were told little about the Canadians' modest earlier project. Structures of several periods were transported to the land once farmed by two eighteenth-century Loyalists (Tories to Americans). There a Canadian pioneer village has been re-created, with a lumber mill sawing timber, a cheese factory making Cheddar, a baker shoveling out crusty loaves—it's a bustling little place that even has a stagecoach rattling through it. Situated only a few miles from Morrisburg, Ontario, Upper Canada Village is now open to the public.

Close by is the site, now under water, of the "decisive" Battle of Crysler's Farm, fought on November 11, 1813. There a small band of British regulars turned back a large American force. Near the entrance to Upper Canada Village are a monument to that redcoat victory and a museum that offers the visitor a somewhat confusing sound-and-light account of the battle.

An upstanding Virginia Military Institute cadet taken to see this display was disgusted to learn that the Americans had been sent piece-meal into the battle against redcoats fighting in close order and firing like clockwork. Then he recognized the name of the American com-mander, General James A. Wilkinson.

"That bum! He never was a good soldier or a good American either. He was in that cabal to oust George Washington, and he was involved in Aaron Burr's plot, too!"

Wilkinson had also been, thirty-eight years before the Battle of Crysler's Farm, an officer in the army that occupied Montreal, which doubtless made him an expert on Canada in the eyes of Madison's first secretary of war, William Eustis. Besides, the young republic did not believe in a standing army, so it had few trained officers. Worse than the presence of men like Wilkinson was the absence of trained noncommissioned officers. Without knowledgeable sergeants the in-vading army could not be held together, let alone maneuvered success-fully against the disciplined British. The men broke and ran, and the second American invasion of Montreal (from the west this time) was abandoned.

The truth was that the Americans had expected to win Canada with-out a fight. Only the year before, Secretary of War Eustis had said: "We can take the Canadas without soldiers; we have only to send officers into the provinces, and the people, disaffected towards their own government, will rally round our standard."

Dr. Eustis had been a surgeon during the American Revolution and perhaps was unfamiliar with the 1775–76 fa lure of Canadians to rally round. But Thomas Jefferson himself, through with the Presidency in 1812 and happy as the Sage of Monticello and Madison's chief ad-viser, wrote: "The acquisition of Canada this year, as far as the neigh-borhood of Quebec"—he at least remembered the earlier failure to take Quebec City—"will be a mere matter of marching. . . ."

Both men were expressing an illusion that Americans cherished for decades—the belief that Canadians, given a choice, would prefer American freedom to royal "tyranny." Time and again Americans acted on this notion, and time and again the majority of Canadians rejected it.

In 1812 Canada consisted of Lower Canada (now Quebec) and Upper Canada (Ontario). The Maritime Provinces had separate governments and were not then part of Canada.

Upper Canada, where most of the northern land action of the War of 1812 took place, had been initially settled by refugee Loyalists. Few of them were Tories in the American tradition: wealthy toadies of the British who were opposed to the American Revolution for fear that it would deprive them of property and privilege. The Louckses, for example, on whose land much of Upper Canada Village is laid out, were farmers from the Palatinate in Germany. Loyal to an English king who was also German, John Loucks fought as a sergeant with the British during the American Revolution and was afterward allotted farmland in Ontario. The successive farmhouses the family built—from a primitive log cabin to a much later house of stone—still stand in the village. The Crysler on whose farm the battle was fought spelled his name Kristler originally. He, too, was from the Palatinate, and his descendants' colonnaded mansion is now the village museum. Another loyal German eventually became the proprietor of Cook's Tavern, where the stagecoach stops today. His name had once been Kuch.

Only the French-Robertson House, easily the most distinguished, though not the largest, in Upper Canada Village, was built by people who fit the Tory pattern. Jeremiah French was the largest landowner in Manchester, Vermont. At the outset of the Revolution he joined the King's Royal Regiment of New York, leaving his wife at home to defend his property. But Ira Allan, Ethan's brother, ordered it confiscated.

In 1812 these people and others like them had good reason for resenting the United States. Not only had they been forced to flee the country, but the new government had failed to live up to the treaty ending the Revolutionary War. As few Americans today realize, under that treaty the new United States was required to restore to all refugees their civil rights and confiscated property. But our first government, organized under the Articles of Confederation, had little power over the thirteen original colonies. They flatly refused to act. The resentful refugees were, therefore, hardly ready to rally round the American standard in 1812.

More surprisingly, neither were the non-Tory American settlers in Upper Canada. No, the country was not settled primarily by Loyalists and emigrant English. In 1812 those two groups accounted for only thirty thousand of the inhabitants, while forty-five thousand were nonpolitical Americans who had moved to the north country after the Revolution for a variety of reasons. Most were simply looking for cheap land or for a profitable spot on which to build a sawmill. George Washington and King George III were one to them. When the War of 1812 began, they said nothing and continued to saw wood, letting others lend the regulars a hand. Only when the British command threatened them with expulsion did they do their militia duty.

The militia was used chiefly for dogsbody work: building roads, strengthening fortifications, hauling supplies. Sometimes, decked out in red coats, they made a small force of regulars look larger than it was, thus intimidating, among others, General William Hull, the American commander at Detroit, who surrendered before he was beaten. Militiamen were occasionally used as flanking forces, whose role in every battle was naturally magnified by Canadians. But it was actually the lackluster performance of the American generals that enabled the British to hold Canada with only a small scattered army.

They did more than that. They took back almost all the northern border posts they had surrendered to the Americans in 1796 under Jay's Treaty, from Fort Niagara all the way to Detroit and Michilimackinac beyond. The frontier posts should have been given over to the young United States in 1783, but when England had to reimburse the refugees herself, she decided to keep those profitable centers of Indian trade as long as was comfortably possible.

Only on water were the English in North America decisively defeated in the War of 1812. The greatest maritime power of the day was bested on Lake Erie and again on Lake Champlain by inland fleets the Americans had managed to build in a very short t.me.

It was Oliver Hazard Perry on Lake Erie and Thomas Macdonough on Lake Champlain who kept the Canadian-American border where it is. When peace negotiations to end the War of 1812 began, the English Government, having strongly reinforced its regulars in Canada, had large land grabs in mind. By demanding most of northern Maine, the gap between New Brunswick and Quebec could be bridged tidily. Of course, England would retain the forts she had recaptured and perhaps make the Michigan Territory an Indian buffer state.

The Duke of Wellington, however, sternly advised against making such demands as long as the English in Canada did not control the Great Lakes. So the final treaty left both sides where they had been when the war began. Neither, however, felt quite easy about the Great Lakes, and in 1817 the Rush-Bagot Agreement between England and the United States was signed. It virtually disarmed those waters, allowing each side only four small warships.

Wellington, not trusting treaties, had additional advice to give. The Ontario stretch of the St. Lawrence was exposed to fire from the American shore. A protected passage between Lower and Upper Canada was badly needed. So the Royal Engineers built a bypass, the Rideau Canal, to connect what is now Ottawa with Kingston. Men and supplies from Quebec could travel north on the Ottawa River and then southwest to Kingston via the Rideau River and Canal, whose locks stand today in the shadow of Canada's Parliament buildings.

The logging town of Ottawa grew up around those locks, and no one was more surprised than the citizens of the rough little town when, in 1857, Queen Victoria chose Ottawa as the capital of the Province of Canada. She chose it part y because its location protected it from the Americans! The citizens of Kingston were more than surprised; they were indignant, because they had expected Kingston to be the capital, as it had been for a time in the 1840's.

Kingston was then one of Canada's larger and more distinguished towns. Its architecture is worth viewing today, particularly its courthouse, which is fit to be a capitol. John A. MacDonald, the Father of Confederation and Canada's first prime minister, practiced law there. After the War of 1812 Kingston's defenses were greatly expanded. Even now, its shore bristles with old Martello towers. The town also boasts one of the handsomest Canadian fortifications open to tourists —Fort Henry, built to protect the western terminus of the Rideau Canal. That fort was garrisoned until 1890, but today its "troops" are

college students in period uniforms who stage attractive drills for visitors during the summer.

Along Lake Ontario there are other forts, all currently open to tourists, all associated with Canada's border struggles. There are three in the Niagara area alone—the river was turbulent in more ways than one —but for a change of pace, the visitor might prefer to roam the tree-lined streets of Niagara-on-the Lake. With luck, he might catch the autumn tour of fine old Federal-style houses. They were built to replace earlier homes that were put to torch by retreating American soldiers one December night in 1813. Eighty families were turned out into the snow, and some of their descendants still feel it as keenly as if it had happened yesterday.

At Fort Henry in Kingston, Ontario, students now drill for tourists.

Midway between Niagara-on-the Lake and Niagara Falls on the Niagara Park Commission Driveway stands Queenston, with its monument to General Isaac Brock conspicuous on Queenston Heights. Despite his death during the battle there, his regulars fought on to rout the Americans. Queenston is also the home of Laura Secord, Canada's Paul Revere, a determined little woman who struggled across twenty miles of difficult country to warn the regulars that "the Americans are coming!" As the story goes, she used a cow to camouflage her purpose, driving it ahead of her until she got through the American lines.

She is not without honor in Canada. Across the country there are Laura Secord candy stores. At one time the face on the candy boxes was Laura's own determined middle-aged visage framed by a stiff bonnet, but American influence has subversively transformed Canada's heroine. Currently a misty-eyed maiden, a gentle immigrant from the Old South, purports to be Laura on the candy boxes.

Long before the traveler going west on Route 2 reaches Kingston, he will have seen the truncated remains of a stout windmill near Prescott, Ontario. Neatly whitewashed, it is built of stone wedges that nineteenth-century cannon balls merely drove more firmly into place. The windmill was taller originally, and in one period it served as a lighthouse on the St. Lawrence River. A historical marker states that this is the site of the Battle of the Windmill.

Another skirmish in the War of 1812? No, this battle raged for nearly a week in mid-November, 1838, a quarter of a century later. The Americans who turned the windmill into a fortress from which they withstood a force three times their number were not soldiers but rather foolish idealists and border adventurers who had crossed the river to liberate the Canadians—again. Nine tenths of the people would rise in their support, they had been told—by refugee Canadians.

The Canadians were refugees from a nasty rebellion that had torn Upper Canada apart for nearly a year. What began as a badly needed reform movement was suppressed so ruthlessly that it turned into a badly organized revolt, called by some the Patriot Rebellion, by others the Mackenzie Rebellion because its leader was the little firebrand editor William Lyon Mackenzie.

Mackenzie and his followers had reason to revolt. In those days Upper Canada was governed by a tight little oligarchy, known to its critics as The Family Compact because its most influential members were related by either blood or marriage. The Lieutenant Governor, who had been appointed in London, and his appointive Executive Council could, and did, ignore the elected Assembly. When one Assembly attempted to investigate abuses, the oligarchy sent thugs to the polls next election day. No "reformers" were elected. Young bloods from Compact families smashed Mackenzie's newspaper presses and threw his type into Lake Ontario. Mackenzie himself, however, was repeatedly re-elected to—and just as repeatedly expelled from—the Assembly.

In despair, "the industrial classes" and the farmers, whom the Governor regarded with contempt, decided that only force could aid their cause. In several areas of the province armed skirmishes were fought in 1837, but the rebels, poorly armed and trained and always outnumbered, were everywhere defeated. In Toronto they were scattered by cannon fire in fifteen minutes. Mackenzie fled and managed finally to reach the United States by crossing the Niagara River disguised as an old woman.

Hundreds of others made similar escapes, and their stories and Mackenzie's speeches soon aroused the people of the states along the border, where many thought Canada a "natural extension" of the United States. The American Government remained neutral, but not always effectively so. President Van Buren, faced with a depression at home, wasn't ready to borrow any more trouble.

Nevertheless, Mackenzie and a band of one thousand Canadian refugees and American sympathizers, armed with muskets from the Buffalo arsenal, captured Navy Island, a dab of land on the Canadian side of the Niagara River. There Mackenzie set up a provisional Republic of Canada, issued his own money, and raised his own flag. And there he stayed, his forces supplied daily from the American side of the river by a little American steamer, the *Caroline*.

Unable to dislodge the rebels, the loyalist forces decided to starve them out by destroying the steamer. The plot was concocted at the headquarters of Colonel Allan MacNab of the Canadian militia, and soon sixty men armed with cutlasses were off to seize the vessel. They found her on the American side, but boarded her nevertheless, driving the crew and passengers ashore and killing at least one man, an American. After towing the *Caroline* out into the river, they set her afire and sent her on her way in a blaze that could be seen for miles, her smokestack red-hot but upright to the last.

Men swore long afterward that the *Caroline* went over Niagara Falls while passengers still aboard (none were) extended their arms toward the shore, crying out pitifully. Actually, she seems to have sunk in the rapids, breaking up there. Her bow did go over the Falls, the figurehead later being picked up near Lewiston, New York. The slain American's body was displayed in front of Buffalo's city hall, and American resentment mounted.

But President Van Buren still refused to act like Old Hickory. Instead, when Mackenzie finally retreated from Navy Island to the New

York side, American marshals arrested him for violating the country's neutrality law, and he spent eleven months in jail at Rochester.

MacNab was knighted for his part in the affair and was on his way politically. In 1854 he became premier of Canada, but he lasted for only two years. He would have been shocked if he could have known that Mackenzie's grandson, William Lyon Mackenzie King, would hold the tremendously enlarged office of prime minister for a total of twenty-two years, longer than any man before or since. MacNab's magnificent mansion in Hamilton, Ontario, which he spent his life and too much money creating (he died bankrupt), is today Canada's most successful restoration, a display of lavish early Victorian hard to match north of Natchez, Mississippi.

Meanwhile, however, the flames ignited by the burning *Caroline* spread the rebellion. Americans by the thousands joined secret societies pledged to "liberate" Canada. Not all these Americans were ardent republicans. A good number were men who were attracted during that depression period by Mackenzie's offer of three hundred acres of free land in the "Republic of Canada" to every man who fought for the cause. Not all were men from the states along the border; there were lodges as far south as Missouri. The convention of one of the largest groups, The Hunters, was held in Cleveland. But because the societies were secret, the total number of men involved can only be estimated; figures range from fifteen to two hundred thousand.

Potential invaders of Canada were drilling everywhere in northern New York in 1838, but when they gathered at Ogdensburg on November 11 for the raid on Prescott, there were roughly a thousand men under arms. These were loaded aboard two schooners in the tow of a steamer, which cut them loose on the Canadian side—but not before at least two hundred men had decided to return with the steamer. Further mismanagement of the ships and the invasion plan in general resulted in fewer than two hundred men landing a mile and a half below Prescott, where they dragged their three guns up a steep bank and took up positions near the large six-story windmill. Stone houses and fences nearby lent additional cover, but the men also prudently built a six-foot stone wall on the exposed side of the mill and got their guns in place before the Canadian militia could assemble in force.

Their elected leader was a tall, gentle Polish patriot who had followed his dream of freedom to America. Nils Szoltevcky Von Schoultz, having heard that Canadians lived like Polish serfs, volunteered to free them. Instead, he and his men were encircled by the Canadian militia while both British and American naval vessels patrolled the river, effectively preventing the Hunters from reinforcing the windmill's small garrison. But sharpshooters in the mill successfully held the Canadians at bay from Sunday through Thursday.

On Friday the British regulars decided to put an end to the invasion. With two eighteen-pounders and a howitzer posted strategically on land and a gunboat firing from the river, all out of musket range, the regulars steadily bombarded the mill; another company of regulars, drawn up on either flank and "supported by militia," prevented the invaders from escaping. So those still alive were finally taken, while thousands of Americans lined the opposite shore, watching the unequal fight.

Von Schoultz and nine other men were hanged, with no protest from Van Buren. One hundred and nineteen Americans were deported to Van Diemen's Land (Tasmania), which was then Britain's Devil's Island. Fewer than half of them ever saw home again. Fifty of the men under twenty-one were eventually pardoned and sent back to the United States.

Not even this tragic fiasco ended the movement. There were more incompetent raids—and outrages, too. Under a bully named Bill Johnston, who was little better than a river pirate, a band of Americans boarded the Canadian steamer *Sir Robert Peel*, drove the passengers ashore in their nightclothes, pillaged the cabins in which all had been forced to leave their valuables, helped themselves to twenty thousand pounds of troopers' pay that the ship was carrying, and only then burned her "in revenge for the *Caroline*." Bill Johnston and his gang also robbed the mails at Kingston, all in the name of freedom. In April, 1840, that monument to General Brock was damaged, and in 1841 there was an attempt to blow up the Welland Canal locks. Then it was over, and Bill Johnston is said to have ended his days as a lighthouse-man on the American side of the St. Lawrence.

But the turmoil had cost the British Government two million pounds, enough to make the authorities in England take a long look at the government of Upper Canada. As a result of a report by the Earl of Durham, reforms were eventually put into effect that advanced Canada a good way along the road to Dominion status.

In this period, and for many years afterward, for every refugee who fled from Canada to the States, there were ten Americans who escaped into Canada. They were runaway slaves for whom the cold north country was the last station on the Underground Railway. By 1861 there were thirty thousand free blacks in Canada, but when slavery was ended in the States, the majority must have gone home. A century later the Negro population of Canada was reported to be only thirty-two thousand, including immigrants from the British West Indies. Had the former slaves stayed, their descendants should have been many times that number.

Many who came north in the next invasion did stay on after the excitement was over. They remained to help open up Canada's Far West. Before that happened, however, there would be danger of a war over the boundary, or rather, over the lack of any set boundary from the Rockies to the Pacific.

As late as 1846 such a boundary had not yet been determined. Both the United States and Canada had conflicting claims to the Oregon Country—the region from what was still Russian Alaska all the way south to California. Unable to settle their differences, the United States and Britain had agreed in 1818 to occupy it jointly. In fact, however, they left the territory to the Hudson's Bay Company to administer.

Then, in the 1840's, land-hungry Americans started pushing to the Far West over the Oregon Trail; a trickle of settlers became a flood. Farms and then towns grew up in what are now the states of Washington and Oregon, and the Hudson's Bay factor, with his handful of men, could assert little authority over the hundreds of newcomers, who soon numbered thousands. In characteristically American fashion the settlers established their own governments, enacted their own laws, and clamored for admission to the Union.

In response, James K. Polk ran in the Presidential election of 1844 on the slogan "Fifty-four Forty or Fight!" If elected, he promised, he would take over the Oregon Country all the way up to the Alaskan border. Polk was elected, and a British warship was soon cruising the strait south of Vancouver Island, where the Hudson's Bay Company clung grimly to Fort Victoria. In a short time Polk was ostensibly preparing for war over the Northwest.

In fact, he was more interested in the Southwest than the Northwest, and in 1846 he agreed to a treaty extending the boundary line along the 49th parallel all the way to the Pacific, but swerving south to let Vancouver Island stay British. By so doing, Polk won more land than he had expected to take without a fight—and was free to proceed with a more manageable war, the one against Mexico.

None of the westering Americans had settled in what is now British Columbia. That land was left to the trappers, the traders, and the Indians—until an American prospector found gold in the Fraser River in 1856. When the news reached California, where the Gold Rush of 1849 was on the wane, gold seekers hurried north in anything that floated. They slept in shifts on the decks of steamboats—unless they were paddling their own canoes. In the spring of 1858 twenty thousand of them arrived at Fort Victoria. They were followed by men traveling overland from Oregon, where farmers had left their plows, soldiers had dropped their guns, and coal miners had abandoned their picks.

Without an army or police force the Hudson's Bay factor, James Douglas, nevertheless managed to enforce his regulations. Every vessel, large or small, that entered the Fraser was charged a fee; every miner had to have a license before he panned a shovelful of gravel. Douglas imported Judge Matthew Begbie from England to administer the law; he was a tough, colorful character who settled disputes from his saddle. Matters seemed under control until the Indians, resenting the invasion of the Fraser River country, went on the warpath. The miners organized vigilante committees to punish massacres, and at Yale, head of navigation on the Fraser, they set up a government of their own. Douglas was confronted with the very situation that had defeated his predecessor in the Oregon Country.

But he was in a position to act; there was a visiting British warship in Fort Victoria's harbor, and 156 Royal Engineers had just arrived. Douglas loaded the Engineers, a hundred sailors from the warship, a cannon, and Judge Begbie onto a stern-wheeler and pushed up the Fraser to Yale.

Today the tourist in British Columbia driving along the Fraser River canyon on the Trans-Canada Highway can look down on the turbulent black water that the overloaded little steamboat traveled. The voyage seems more threatening than any imaginable lot of rough miners. So it proved. Their leader, when faced with trained troops and a cannon, promptly surrendered. In fact, he gave a champagne dinner for the men who took him in custody.

Not only did rebellion fade out; so did the gold in the Fraser. Within a year most of the thirty-five thousand men on the river had packed up and gone home. But not all. Douglas would have been happier if four ragged men in particular had followed their fellows. Instead, in the autumn of 1860, they pushed north and east into the mountains, looking for just one more creek that might yield gold, and the night before the first snow they found it, a quarter of a pound in one pan of gravel. That was the start of the Cariboo Gold Rush, which brought men not only from California and Oregon but from the whole world.

The massive influx meant the end of the fur trade, but in its very variety of peoples—hundreds of Chinese came, for instance—there was safety for the British hold on the land. America could hardly claim this lot as settlers. When the gold was gone, the men stayed on to ranch or to work at lumbering far up in the interior of the new colony of British Columbia.

The United States at that time was not in any position to claim new territory. It was in a desperate struggle to preserve what it had—the Union itself. And again an American conflict spilled across the border.

Canada was pro-North because she was antislavery. But Canada was also British North America, and powerful men in England favored the Confederacy. Given a good excuse, they might have been able to engineer the British intervention that the Confederates were urging. Then Canada, willy-nilly, would have been used as a base for a British attack on the United States—unless the United States invaded Canada first. Alarmed, Canada in 1862 mobilized as best she could.

The first "invaders" were peaceable if bothersome. When Lincoln's government instituted a draft, Northern draft dodgers by the thousands poured into Canada. So many came, anxious for work at any pay, that they disrupted the labor market. Other arrivals, in contrast, were the wives of wealthy Southern plantation owners. Such gentlewomen could not be expected to endure wartime privation. Oddly, they often hired as maids former slave women living in Canada.

Other incoming Americans were more dangerous. Confederate purchasing agents were busy in Montreal, some of them buying in-

*The windmill at Prescott, where American invaders took up their
positions in 1838*

formation from Southern spies operating in Canada. A regular traveler between Washington and Montreal was John Surratt, later a figure in the John Wilkes Booth conspiracy. There were also the sixteen Confederates who seized the Northern ship *Chesapeake* between New York City and Portland and headed for Nova Scotia, where they planned to ask for asylum. (A half century earlier the more famous *Chesapeake,* defeated by the British *Shannon* during the War of 1812, had also been taken to Nova Scotia.) Canada returned the Civil War vessel, but managed to lose the Confederate conspirators when asked to extradite them for piracy.

There seem to have been a good number of Confederates waiting when Jacob Thompson, special assistant to Jefferson Davis, arrived at Toronto in July, 1864, to execute certain projects he had in mind. First he planned to eliminate the *Michigan,* the only armed United States vessel on the Great Lakes. To this end Confederate agents seized the Canadian steamer *Philo Parsons,* and took her to Sandusky, Ohio, where the *Michigan* rode in harbor. But in Sandusky a drunken Confederate babbled the whole plot, and the *Philo Parsons* had to retreat in haste to the Canadian side, where those aboard scuttled her. Another project involved sending agents, disguised as delegates, to the Democratic Convention in Chicago. There they would attack Camp Douglas and release its Confederate prisoners. This plot was also discovered.

Despite the goings on in Toronto, Montreal continued to be a center of Confederate conspiracy. Certainly the small group of young and presentable Southerners who moved into St. Albans, Vermont, on October 19, 1864, for a Confederate attack on the northernmost section of the North started thereabouts. They robbed banks of $208,000, stole horses and saddles for their escape, and tried to set fire to the town. At the border they were arrested by Canadian militia, and the loot they were carrying was taken from them. But the Quebec courts restored to the raiders $84,000—all that had been discovered on them —and eventually released every man, declaring that "the transactions in St. Albans, Vermont, were acts of war." A young lieutenant in this raid was also involved in the Chicago fiasco. Apparently there was Confederate traffic between Toronto and Montreal.

The end of the Civil War did not bring peace of mind to the Canadian provinces. Leaders in Upper Canada, particularly John A. MacDonald, the premier, knew that the United States Congress was seething with rage at England. A chief cause of anger was the damage done by Confederate raiders, among them the *Alabama,* built in British shipyards. The United States threatened to claim as much as two billion dollars for the shipping sunk by these raiders. But certain congressmen suggested taking all or part of Canada instead. The United States had the troops to do it, tough veterans who had scorched the Shenandoah Valley with Sheridan, marched through Georgia with Sherman, and brought Lee to surrender in Virginia. Would the Government now simply send the Grand Army of the Republic home, or find other use for it?

Taking a leaf from America's own book, "united we stand," MacDonald and others had been working for a confederation of the provinces. The British Government was sympathetic, but in Canada smaller men, jealous of their local power, blocked the project. Although there could be no united defense, England saw no cause for alarm. Her Government thought America was tired of war after four bloody years.

Not all members of the Grand Army seemed to be so. MacDonald's spies soon reported another unofficial invasion in train. Irishmen in America who belonged to the Fenian Brotherhood proposed, by way of helping Ireland's struggle for freedom, to conquer the nearest English colony, Canada. In 1863 they had written a constitution for a Republic of Canada and named a cabinet to rule it, and now they were drilling troops in several American towns. As they marched they sang:

Many battles have we won, along with the boys in blue,
And we'll go and capture Canada, for we've nothing else to do.

The invasion was set for St. Patrick's Day, 1866, but nothing happened, although MacDonald knew that men were massing on the Maine border, along the St. Lawrence and Niagara frontiers, and in St. Albans, Vermont, where the local authorities understandably did not interfere.

On June 1 two thousand men finally crossed the Niagara River to land near Fort Erie, Ontario. There were no Canadian militiamen within twenty-five miles, but a force equal to the size of the Fenians' soon set out from Port Colborne. The Fenian "General," John J.

O'Neill, and his army met and routed the Canadians at a point called Limestone Ridge, killing nine and wounding thirty-seven. But reinforcements from Buffalo, where eight thousand men had gathered, failed to arrive. O'Neill retreated to Fort Erie, which was defended by a handful of Canadians who were quickly captured, while once again spectators on the American shore cheered. None joined the fight.

That night the marooned army decided to head for home aboard two tugs and two canalboats from the American side. The men had no sooner boarded this flotilla than it was taken in tow by the United States warship *Michigan,* which Thompson, remember, had failed to sink. The United States was belatedly enforcing its neutrality law— "after the invasion of Canada had actually taken place," as Canada's Governor General tartly remarked. Official American action stopped the Fenians at Ogdensburg and other points on the St. Lawrence. More than seven hundred men were arrested. They were, however, soon released, and O'Neill himself was made head of the whole movement. Under his direction on May 25, 1870, eighteen hundred Fenians invaded the Eastern Townships of Quebec, looting and burning before they too retreated for lack of reinforcements—although the frightened militia did not oppose them. At the United States border they were arrested by American troops, and the Fenian War sputtered out.

But the post-Civil War scare given Canada had a good effect. It was apparent that the country, disunited, could not defend itself. The political laggards agreed to confederation, and in 1867 Quebec, Ontario, Nova Scotia, and New Brunswick joined to form Canada. Manitoba entered the Confederation in 1870, British Columbia in 1871, Prince Edward Island in 1873, and the other two prairie provinces in 1905, after they had grown to provincial status.

There was never again an actual armed thrust from the United States, though there were flurries of trouble along the western border. Nothing serious, however, not even when Sitting Bull and a number of his Sioux crossed to Canada after the Custer Massacre. A few Mounties kept that wild horde in hand.

The border between Canada and Alaska, which the United States had purchased from Russia in 1867, was another matter. In 1898 the Klondike Gold Rush dramatized its existence—or nonexistence. When thousands of men crossed Chilkoot Pass into Canada's Yukon, there was talk of collecting duty on the equipment they had purchased in Alaska. But where exactly was the boundary point for customs? As in the Oregon Country, there were conflicting claims by the United States and Canada as to where the border should run.

In 1903 the matter was referred to an arbitration commission, but Theodore Roosevelt, never a man to compromise a dispute, was President. While apparently accepting arbitration, he ordered additional troops to Alaska and made it clear to the British that America would fight for her claim. Not willing to risk war for the sake of more territory for a country she very possibly considered quite big enough, England voted with America on the commission.

Furious at England's "betrayal," Canada decided that she would henceforth determine her own foreign policy. T. R.'s "big stick," wielded across the Alaska border, made Canada declare her independence within the British Commonwealth. Once again an American threat had spurred Canada forward.

History can be curiously neat. In 1938, and again in 1940, two old friends, one of them Mackenzie's grandson, Prime Minister Mackenzie King, the other Theodore Roosevelt's distant cousin, President Franklin Roosevelt, met along that once turbulent St. Lawrence boundary to pledge the mutual defense of Canada and the United States. The first declaration took place when they dedicated the Thousand Islands International Bridge; the second at Ogdensburg, New York, which has been mentioned more than once in this chapter.

"The longest undefended border in the world" is a comparatively modern development. After all they've been through, Canadians have not had much time, as history goes, to outgrow their wariness of American intentions.

5

The Continuing Invasion

"Living next to you is in some ways like

sleeping with an elephant."

ronto's skyscrapers (left) house many American firms.
ove, "Labrador" Smith drives the last spike completing
Canadian Pacific Railway system in November, 1885.

Soon our banners will be streaming,
Soon the eagle will be screaming;
And the lion—see it cowers.
Hurrah boys, the river's ours.

So SANG THE American gold seekers swarming up the Fraser River valley in the 1850's. In those comparatively carefree days the danger to Canada came from Americans bent on taking gold *out*. In the decades since, the threat to Canadian independence has come from Americans bringing gold *in*. Canadians no longer really fear armed attack, although Defense Scheme No. 1—to be called into play the moment United States military forces crossed the border—was a classified document as recently as thirty years ago. It is the continuing, friendly invasion of American investors that has become so worrisome.

Visitors to Bladworth, Saskatchewan, can understand why C. D. Howe, who built hundreds of grain elevators in Canada, is said to have changed the nation's skyline.

The growth of the United States in population, wealth, and power during the last fifty years is staggering from Canada's point of view. There are ten times as many Americans today as there are Canadians. In recent years the whole of Canada's gross national product, the total output of her goods and services, has been about equal only to the annual increase in the gross national product of the United States. American private investors own $30 billion worth of the Canadian economy. They control 28 per cent of Canadian industry, and in certain sectors—manufacturing, mining, oil—the proportions go up to 68 per cent. These are the American absentee owners of Canada. So Canada is frightened by the United States—as frightened as Jonah might have been of the whale if there had been more time to think about it.

There is also a remarkable American physical presence within Canada. Americans have been there for three hundred years. The captain of the *Nonsuch,* the Hudson's Bay Company's first ship to James Bay in 1668, was a mariner from Boston—one Zachariah Gillam. By 1970 an estimated five thousand young Americans had sought Canadian refuge from the draft for military service in Vietnam, and several hundred deserters had fled across the border.

In the centuries between, thousands of Americans have moved north of the border, many to find adventure and jobs, a few simply to escape from the United States. In the aggregate they form a motley group—New England Tories, Pennsylvania Dutch Mennonites, Sitting Bull's Indians, Southern slaves, members of New York's Mafia, draft dodgers from the Civil War onward, railroaders, and industrialists.

The American invasion has at times provided the warp and woof of Canadian history. William Van Horne of Joliet, Illinois, and Clarence Decatur Howe of Waltham, Massachusetts, who both became Canadians, changed, as we shall see, the course of their adopted country.

But, to go back, it was in 1776 that the first surge of American immigration began. The immigrants were Loyalists, colonists who wanted to remain under King George's rule. The first eleven hundred of them, you recall, came into Halifax with Howe. Life in what was to become the United States would have been extremely dangerous for them because of their sympathies. Their descendants, frequently encountered in parts of English Canada today, remember George Washington as the rebel general who summarily hanged more dissenters than has any American leader since.

Some Tories, after reaching the British lines, fought against Washington throughout the Revolution, but with the war lost they had to continue their flight. True colonialists, they were attracted to Canada more often than to the motherland, England. So they emigrated by the thousands to Nova Scotia, New Brunswick, and that new unsettled country, Upper Canada, now Ontario.

English Canadians, loyal to this day to the British monarch, regard their Tory forebears as brave men and women who endured privation and risked death for their principles. Many arrived in Canada with little more than the clothes on their backs. Their first Canadian winter was as hard as the Pilgrims' ordeal at Plymouth.

Settlements sprang up along the fertile banks of the St. Lawrence and the friendly shores of Lake Ontario. The Loyalists, however, were soon outnumbered by "new" Americans pushing out from New England for cheap land or a business location. By 1812 there were forty-five thousand of these apolitical Americans in Ontario alone, as against fifteen thousand Loyalists. Together they outnumbered immigrants from England by at least four to one.

At the end of the eighteenth century an English-speaking province, Ontario, was born to balance the French-speaking province of Quebec, and an attempt to build a nation on the foundation of two languages and two cultures began in earnest. And Americans were in on it.

Manifest Destiny, the ringing call that beckoned thousands of Americans to the Rockies and the Pacific, had no counterpart in Canada. There was no Horace Greeley shouting "Go west, young man."

In Canada the West was only sparsely populated. There were great natural barriers. Instead of an Ohio-Mississippi-Missouri waterway, Canadians faced a great midland wall of Precambrian rock and scrub extending eight hundred miles from around Sudbury, Ontario, over the upper Great Lakes to Kenora, near the border of Manitoba. Only the hardy fur traders and the voyageurs in their canoes attempted to cross it.

Meanwhile, Americans moving west frequently turned north from Minnesota and the Dakotas into the Red River valley in what is now the Province of Manitoba, and from Montana into the great prairie area that became the provinces of Saskatchewan and Alberta. This vast region was then, as it had been since the days of Charles II, the actual property under a royal charter of England's Hudson's Bay Company, whose factors (regional superintendents, one might call them) constituted the *de facto* government of the Canadian West, including the settled areas of British Columbia, where the company ruied for Britain the land it did not own outright. (It was the Hudson's Bay factor, James Douglas, who brought those rowdy American gold seekers into line.) When Canada finally purchased the Hudson's Bay Company holdings, much as Jefferson bought the Louisiana Territory, a survey was made to show the American settlers that they were living north of the United States border. But many were in Canada for keeps, and others came anyway.

Americans have been homesteaders in the Canadian prairies, gold hunters in the Yukon, oil dredgers in Alberta, potash miners in Saskatchewan, and cattle raisers and lumberjacks in British Columbia.

In the five-year period from 1899 to 1904, 159,565 Americans moved into Canada, while only 137,036 settlers came from other countries. From 1910 to 1914 more than 1.2 million immigrants reached Canada from the United States and Britain, nearly three times the number from all other nations.

"The American immigrants," says the government handbook *Canada One-Hundred—1867–1967,* were "mainly experienced farmers with capital and equipment who soon became producers of more wealth and the owners of substantial farms."

Today they and their descendants form a large segment of the Canadian mosaic. It is hard to find them. For the Americans in Canada, just like those at home, tend to melt into the society around them, with the exception of Calgary, where twenty-five thousand "Americans" form virtually an American colony.

Curiously, there is no ethnic classification of American-Canadians, as there is of Canadians who come from Britain, France, Germany, the Ukraine, China, Japan, or other countries. Americans in Canada are just Canadians. This worries those of their countrymen who find the "mosaic" pattern of ethnic distribution more Canadian—and perhaps more manageable—than the mass congealing of the American melting pot.

In no small sense a Canadian's idea of a good American is the tourist who wheels over the border displaying his California or Texas license plates, proceeds to eat heartily and expensively on New York-cut steaks and Southern fried chicken, then departs without losing a particle of his American identity. Some fourteen million such American visitors came and went in 1967, leaving behind 1.4 billion United States dollars to help offset the national trade indebtedness.

American immigrants, however, have been known to outlive a cool reception and to become accepted as great Canadians before they die. Such a man was William Cornelius Van Horne, the Joliet, Illinois, railroader who landed in Winnipeg on New Year's Eve of 1881 to take up his duties as general manager of the Canadian Pacific Railway. It was 40 degrees below zero, but the chill of the station platform was not so cutting as the Winnipeg newspaper editorial that commented on the newcomer's arrival as follows: "Americans have never been popular here in the Red River settlement. We believe that the United States means to grab our Northwest Territories just as they grabbed Oregon in 1846! As loyal, British North Americans we have built our own railroad this far. The Company is wrong to hire a damned, Yankee alien, and Sir John A. Macdonald is wrong to allow it."

Sir John A. Macdonald, Canada's first prime minister, had pushed the railway project in a desperate effort to keep the Manifest Destiny of the United States from taking over Canada. This national purpose, however, did not prevent Macdonald from accepting American capital and an American manager to get the gigantic construction job done.

Van Horne displayed a natural ability to manipulate anything having to do with railroads, from the Morse telegraph key to a stock and bond issue. Out of his headquarters in Winnipeg he worked as engineer, surveyor, construction boss, and explorer. He crossed and recrossed Canada, sometimes on foot, sometimes riding a horse or paddling a canoe, and sometimes pumping a handcar. Whether it was over muskeg, across a mountain pass, or through a canyon cut, rails seemed to roll before Van Horne "automatically as from some mysterious machine," Bruce Hutchison has written. Travelers today may behold the magnitude of the task and the magnificence of what was achieved in no more than five years. All they need to do is board *The Canadian,* which leaves Montreal in midafternoon and reaches Vancouver three days later. The train, traveling the 2,878 miles of Van Horne's daring tracks, negotiates the bluffs of Lake Superior, the Rockies through Banff and Kicking Horse Pass, and the Fraser River canyon, passing through towns with such unbelievable names as Jack Fish, Moose Jaw, Swift Current, Medicine Hat, Kamloops, and Boston Bar.

To bolster capital, Van Horne had to prove the Canadian Pacific Railway's worth. As a start he persuaded settlers and Indians to bring buffalo skeletons to railroad sidings, where he bought them for seven dollars a ton. The C.P.R. hauled the bones east to be ground up profitably for fertilizer.

Van Horne offered to transport Canadian troops from Ontario across the badlands to Saskatchewan to quell the Riel Rebellion. The story of this uprising belongs in another chapter, but Van Horne made good his promise to get soldiers out there in a hurry—eleven days. Although there were stretches of unfinished tracks that had to be covered on foot or by cart, the C.P.R. had proved its worth to national defense. Parliament quickly approved a bill that empowered the government to buy $35 million of C.P.R. bonds. London bankers, convinced that the railroad was there to stay, granted new loans. The C.P.R. was part of Canada.

After the last spike (not gold but "good iron") was driven at Craigellachie in Eagle Pass, British Columbia, Van Horne, attempting a speech, managed fifteen words of understatement: "All I can say is that the work has been well done in every way."

But with the railroad finished, C.P.R., the company, was financially broke. The Canadian Pacific was a fine symbol of national unity, and Prime Minister Macdonald was proud of it. But what use was it? Certainly there were few people to ride the transcontinental trains. There was little freight to be hauled. "Canada," Van Horne remarked, "is doing business on a back street. We must put her on a thoroughfare."

He dedicated the next twenty-five years of his life, until his retirement in 1910, when he was chairman of the board of directors, to making the C.P.R. the mainstay of the Big Land. He built new branches of the system that today covers more than 16,000 miles. He encouraged immigrants to settle on farms to grow crops to fill granaries to fill trains with grain. He was thus the godparent of the multimillion-dollar international wheat sales that support Canada's farm economy. He was also the godparent of Canadian tourism; in order to get passengers on his trains, he built hotels across Canada. What traveler has not heard of the Château Frontenac in Quebec? The Banff Springs Hotel in the Alberta Rockies? Or the Empress at the "end of the line" in Victoria, B.C. (reached only after a ferry trip across the Strait of Georgia to Vancouver Island)?

It is said that Van Horne started out as an American, became a naturalized Canadian, and ended up a subject of the Canadian Pacific. Sir William Cornelius Van Horne, K.C.M.G., died in Montreal in 1915. His private C.P.R. car, the *Saskatchewan,* carried him back home to Joliet, Illinois, for funeral and burial.

In a way, Clarence Decatur Howe, born in Waltham, Massachusetts, picked up where Van Horne had left off. Van Horne's Canadian Pacific Railway had made it possible for the growing of grain to become the great prairie industry. But marketing grain required not only a railroad to ports and population centers but granaries to hold the harvests until the trains could carry them away. Thousands of bins were needed for millions of bushels of wheat, rye, and barley. C. D. Howe arrived on the prairies just in time to fill that need.

Howe graduated from the Massachusetts Institute of Technology in 1907, a depression year. More than a year passed before a job opportunity came his way. Dalhousie University, in Halifax, Nova Scotia, needed a civil-engineering teacher, and Howe decided to "go up to Canada for a couple of years until things get back to normal here."

But Canada got in the Boston Yankee's blood, and he never returned. After five years at Dalhousie he went to Port Arthur, on Lake Superior, to work for the Board of Grain Commissioners. His job was to design grain elevators. Although he had never seen one in his life, ideas came fast. He decided he would like to build some of them himself, and he formed the construction firm of C. D. Howe Company.

Between 1916 and 1935 the firm built most of the grain elevators that visitors see throughout the prairies today. "He was literally to change the skyline of western Canada," wrote a reporter for *Maclean's Magazine*. Howe branched out in the decade before the depression to build bridges, docks, factories, and mills. More than $100 million worth of contracts went through his hands.

His shoulders were broad. His eyes were deep-set and piercing. His voice was biting—"Who's going to stop us?" was a favorite retort to anyone in his way. He was the man "who gets things done"—ruthlessly, if necessary.

By 1936 Howe had made a personal fortune and, at the age of fifty, was thinking of retiring. Instead, the man who "knew nothing of politics" entered politics and became the Liberal party's Member of Parliament from Port Arthur. Prime Minister Mackenzie King made him Minister of Railways and Canals and Minister of Marine. Taking hold fast, Howe united all the transportation agencies into a Department of Transport, then proceeded to take over civil radio and meteorological services. He created the Canadian Broadcasting Corporation. The civil aviation agency became Trans-Canada Airlines, now Air Canada.

In World War II Howe, as Minister of Munitions and Supply, was purchasing agent for more than $10 billion worth of war contracts. In the decade after the war eighteen crown (public) companies, boards, and commissions, from the Atomic Energy Control Board to the Newfoundland Fisheries Board, made their reports to Parliament through Howe.

He was "the architect of modern Canada." He was the biggest executive in the country. Many were sure he would be the first American-born prime minister of Canada.

The crisis and denouement of his career came quickly in 1956. He was so confident that his latest project, the Trans-Canada Pipeline to carry natural gas from Alberta into the United States, would be a tremendous boon to Canada that he drove the bill authorizing it through Parliament under rules of cloture (restricted debate). The Liberal majority passed the measure, but public opinion so resented Howe's tactics that the Liberals were defeated in the general elections the following year. And in Port Arthur Howe lost the seat he had held for twenty years to an obscure schoolteacher. He died in 1960. The thirty-six-inch Trans-Canada Pipeline—extending 2,423 miles from the Alberta-Saskatchewan border to Montreal—was eventually completed and is now an important part of Canada's transportation system.

Since World War II Americans have continued to emigrate to Canada. Eighteen thousand came in 1967. But today it is not the Americans who become Canadians, or even super-Canadians, that trouble Canada. Rather it is the colossal economic invasion that rankles and raises alarms.

George Ball, writing from his experience in the State Department during the early 1960's, says Canada is "fighting a rearguard action against the inevitable—substantial integration [with the United States] which will require for its full realization a progressively expanding area of common political decision."

The average American, always thinking he is the Canadian's closest friend, hardly knows what Mr. Ball is talking about. He has not heard very much about the impact of United States wealth and power on Canada. He has never thought about "integrating" with Canada. Certainly he has never thought that Canada might be annexed, which is what integration would probably lead to. How could the United States annex Canada when it took a couple of generations to bring Alaska and Hawaii into the Union?

But Canadians have thought about it. They know well enough what Mr. Ball is talking about. To them every American move toward closer relations, closer friendship, closer economic cooperation, seems a sinister threat to the nation called Canada.

A 1967 government advisory report on foreign ownership in Canada brought out some startling facts. The United States owns more in Canada than it owns in all of Latin America. More than half of the 743 largest corporations in Canada are U.S.-controlled. Due to the United States investment, foreign ownership in Canada is higher than that in any other developed country, and also higher than that in most underdeveloped countries.

Canada has recently been borrowing nearly one billion dollars of American capital a year. It is this huge inflow of capital that enables Canada to live beyond her means year after year.

The heavy United States investment in Canada makes it possible for—some would say, requires—Canadians to share America's culture. Whether for good or bad, the American invasion brings in American cars, electric appliances, radio and television sets, and the American network shows that go with them. It is said that Canadians know more about the master of *Bonanza's* Ponderosa (Lorne Green is Canadian by birth) than they do about their own prime minister.

Without this "invasion," without the enormous American capital investment, Canada's standard of living, economists agree, would drop almost overnight by at least one third.

Perhaps the first result would be the termination of the costly social welfare programs—old-age pensions, family allowances (baby bonuses), free medical services—of which Canadians are so proud. The system of social welfare in Canada is in many ways superior to that of the United States, but United States capital loans pay for it.

Canadians see a more serious menace from all this. The 1967 government advisory report said that American subsidiaries in Canada acted as an arm of the State Department in Washington. When, the report noted, the United States Government needed to bolster its dollar and its balance of international trade, it called on the big American parent companies to bring home more of the profits from subsidiaries operating abroad. Canadians insist that the American subsidiaries in Canada should plow their profits into the Canadian economy. They resent having the profits flee to the United States—to finance, as they see it, the unpopular war in Vietnam. (The hero of one recent episode in the Canadian-made television serial *McQueen* was an American draft dodger.)

Canadians have resented, too, the U.S. Government order that restricts American subsidiaries abroad, including those in Canada, in trading with Communist countries, such as China and Cuba, whose markets are perfectly acceptable to the Canadian Government. "You should be good corporate citizens of Canada," Canadians keep telling the American managers of American subsidiaries. "Do as we do."

Many Canadians feel that when branch plants tend to follow some of the U.S. regulations affecting their parent firms, a large segment of Canadian industry is hampered by an American political, as well as economic, policy.

There are other complaints: that Canadian branch plants are restricted in their exports in order not to compete with parent firms in the United States, even though Canada needs exports to help her balance of payments; that centralization of research in the parent firms keeps Canadian scientists from jobs they might otherwise have, thus reducing the technical scope of Canadian industry; that Canadians never rise to top management jobs or to the boards of parent firms, where the policy decisions are made.

The resentment today has spread from capital and management to labor. The big industrial unions are all based in the United States. Dock workers at most Ontario, Quebec, and Maritime ports are represented by the International Longshoremen's Association. Most seamen in the Canadian merchant marine are members of the Seafarers' International Union. And most workers in the Canadian automobile plants are members of the United Automobile Workers of America, dominated by locals in Detroit. The Canadian Labor Congress, in fact, is often derisively called a "branch" of the American Federation of Labor and Congress of Industrial Organizations, whose headquarters are in Washington, D.C.

There is also opposition to the growing American "invasion" of Canadian university faculties, which is discussed at greater length in the next chapter.

The way Canadians feel about Americans adds up to a love-hate relationship. The Canadian Smiths don't like the idea of keeping up with the American Joneses, but they really wouldn't live any other way.

"It's fine to live peaceably beside the United States," said one Canadian, "but we don't want it taken for granted that we should act like patriotic Americans all the time. We're not."

Lester B. Pearson, the prime minister who led Canada through her centennial year in 1967, believes his country is just now getting over "a kind of national inferiority complex" that she has suffered for a century and more.

"We moved from British influence to American influence without much feeling of purely national identity in between," he said in an interview on his retirement from office.

"This remains our No. 1 problem. My grandchildren who watch television and read newspapers and magazines learn as much, if not more, about personalities and political figures in the United States than they do about those in Canada.

"The industrial and economic and financial penetration from the south worries me, but less than the penetration of American ideas, of the flow of information about all things American; American thought and entertainment; the American approach to everything."

Or as Prime Minister Trudeau put it: "Living next to you [the United States] is in some ways like sleeping with an elephant. No matter how friendly and even-tempered is the beast . . . one is affected by every twitch and grunt."

Encouraging bilingualism, both Mr. Pearson and Mr. Trudeau have suggested, would be "the best way to establish a Canadian identity separate from the American."

And so it probably would. But getting twenty million Canadians to use both their official languages—English and French—is another great national problem.

6

Academic Assault

"If the trend continues, we Canadians will be a very small minority in a few years."

JAY WALZ

Left, Quebec's venerable Laval University. Above, the quadrangle of Vancouver's new Simon Fraser University.

ONE DAY IN 1963 a battery of bulldozers assaulted a forest-covered mountaintop in Burnaby, British Columbia, five miles east of Vancouver. The bulldozers scalped twelve hundred acres, clearing a plateau for one of the most daring architectural developments in all Canada. It stands there today, white and shining, looking like a new Acropolis designed along the lines of Montreal's Expo 67.

It is, in fact, Simon Fraser University, built at the order of Premier W. A. C. Bennett in two years' time to meet the province's pressing need for more college classrooms. Dr. Gordon M. Shrum, the builder, who later became chancellor, dubbed it "Instant University." Overcoming all problems of material, labor, and expense, he delivered the university to Premier Bennett in time for it to open on schedule in

The University of Toronto's new college at Scarborough is an example of exciting modern design.

September, 1965. To everyone's surprise, Simon Fraser, envisioned as accommodating 1,000 students at first, immediately registered 2,500. The "Instant University" was thus instantly expanded. By 1968 there were 5,500 students on the campus while roaring bulldozers cleared still more trees from the mountainside.

The construction of new universities and the massive expansion of old ones are important features of modern Canada. Among the country's more than four hundred institutions of higher learning there are now at least a score of "Instant Universities" on or near the scale of Simon Fraser. They may be seen from Vancouver all the way east to St. John's, Newfoundland, where Premier J. R. Smallwood tries to provide a free college education for every young man or woman who wants one. He has poured so much money into Memorial University that townsmen say the campus "hatches colleges as a hen hatches chickens." The Premier is also the founder of a very different kind of college in St. John's, the College of Fisheries, Navigation, Marine Engineering, and Electronics, where the island's fishermen are taught to utilize the latest apparatus and techniques.

Many of the new campuses are striking—the work of outstanding young architects with startling ideas. Simon Fraser, designed by Vancouver's Lionel Massey and his associates, has a concourse, a library, cafeterias, a garden mall, a rotunda, classrooms, and offices, all interconnected and virtually under one roof.

Such a design is functional in all kinds of weather. Students arriving in winter by bus or car pull into the underground garage and need never expose themselves to the mountain air unless they want to. They merely go upstairs to class. For visitors, the stunning use of structural concrete across the mountaintop is an exciting sight. The trip up the mountain to the university is now expedited, incidentally, by a four-lane highway.

No less striking, and the object of visits by many architects from the United States and Europe, is the university-in-one-building experiment at Scarborough College, a suburban branch of the University of Toronto. Ada Louise Huxtable, architectural critic of *The New York Times,* described it as combining "two of architecture's most progressive trends: Megastructure (huge buildings of multiple small units) and New Brutalism. This simple, stunning structure of rough concrete is a continuous circulatory system embracing classroom units and student spaces."

There are other interesting examples of dramatic architecture. Champlain College, for example, located on the fourteen-hundred-acre campus of Trent University, near Peterborough, Ontario, resembles an Inca temple, and the campus, which straddles the Otonabee River, is unified by an ingeniously constructed footbridge. Trent opened in 1964 with 102 students, by 1974 it expects 3,000.

The growth, or explosion, of construction for higher education in Canada since 1960 has been extraordinary. In 1954 the total current and capital expenditures for all universities came to $88 million. By 1964–65 these expenditures had risen to $563 million. They totaled more than $1 billion in 1968 and are expected to reach $2 billion by 1975.

Education at all levels in Canada is primarily the business of the provincial governments. But the federal government makes grants and other contributions to support the provinces' schools. From 1965 to 1968 the federal outlay jumped from $40 million to $500 million.

This expansion represents a belated effort to catch up with countries that are more educationally advanced. A study released in November, 1966, showed that proportionately twice as many Americans as Canadians have completed high school or university education. That is why Canada now spends more of its national income on education, according to United Nations figures, than does any other country —8.5 per cent, compared with 6.5 per cent in the United States and 7.5 in the Soviet Union.

The new universities catch the eye of visitors—and they should. But they do not eclipse the old institutions that have grown up with Canada and are an important part of its history. In the older, eastern provinces universities were often the initial order of business for the church establishments. The Roman Catholic and Anglican schools came first, but they were soon followed by those of dissenting faiths and secular groups. There was a time in the nineteenth and early twentieth centuries when sectarian rivalries founded more colleges than the small population could support or use. In Nova Scotia alone, for example, King's College opened in 1790, Dalhousie in 1838, Acadia in 1838, St. Mary's in 1841, St. Francis Xavier in 1853, and Collège Sainte Anne in 1890. In 1892 these six institutions had a total staff of 82 and a combined student body of no more than 533; they conferred just 124 degrees.

This mushrooming of colleges brought on an investigation by a royal commission. Its report in 1906 resulted in the reorganization of the sprawling University of Toronto and set a trend toward secular universities, which often contained sectarian and theological colleges on their campuses as affiliated or federated institutions. On the other hand, the University of Ottawa, established in 1848 by the Oblate Fathers, long remained a Roman Catholic institution, besides being one of Canada's few truly bilingual universities—some courses were taught in French, others in English. It became nondenominational in 1966 simply to qualify for a share of the Province of Ontario's educational funds.

In recent years facilities costing many millions of dollars have been built at the older schools: a fourteen-story, $6-million social science building at the University of Alberta, an $8.5-million medical building at Dalhousie University in Halifax, a $10.5-million library at McGill University in Montreal, a $4-million sports center and a $14-million nuclear physics laboratory at the University of Montreal, a $10-million research library in the humanities and social sciences at the University of Toronto, a $3.5-million arts building at the University of Manitoba, and a $6-million biological sciences, oceanography, and fisheries group at the University of British Columbia—to cite only a few examples.

This rapid expansion of Canadian higher education has not been without its growing pains. The most acute problem has stemmed from the absence of a reservoir of teachers, especially in the area of advanced studies. It had always been the practice of Canadian scholars to go to Europe, most frequently England, or to the United States for the advanced degrees they needed to join the faculties of Canadian universities. Many times they remained abroad, developing careers in foreign lands. There are probably very few American universities that don't have some Canadians on the faculty. All in all, the steady drain of academic reserves from Canada has been a cause of harsh complaints by college deans and administrators.

Ronald Baker, head of Simon Fraser's English department, told a reporter: "When I was staffing the university, I could have taken the whole Ph.D. population production in Canada and still not have had enough."

Scholars from Britain have helped fill the gap, and immigrant teachers still come from France, Germany, Scandinavia, South Africa, India, and Japan. But recently there has been a tremendous rise in the number of American instructors. This worries many professors and Canadian nationalists. They see their universities being overrun and warn that this new "invasion" may be more dangerous to Canada's identity than the huge United States investment in the nation's industry or the pervasive cultural hold of American movies, television programs, books, and periodicals.

Despite the great demand for college professors in the United States, many Americans come to Canada seeking among other things, better economic and academic opportunities and a more congenial atmosphere—political or social. As a result, Britain, formerly the principal source of instructors, has yielded first place to the United States. In 1967 a total of 1,876 Americans crossed the Canadian border to take teaching posts in various schools, 857 of them in colleges.

There is no record of how many Americans are on Canadian faculties today, but two English professors at Carleton University in Ottawa conducted a study in which they found that Americans occupy the majority of chairs in many departments. What alarmed them was their discovery that the number of Canadians on university staffs across the country in 1968 had fallen below 50 per cent. They found that ten members of York University's sociology department, including the department head, were Americans, while only three were Canadians. Of thirteen professors hired by the English department at Loyola College in Montreal over a three-year period in the late 1960's, eleven were Americans and one was a Canadian who had gotten his degree in the United States. At Simon Fraser University in 1969 Americans made up most of the 68 per cent of the faculty that was non-Canadian.

Canadian intellectuals deplore the fact that so many Americans are teaching sociology, economics, and political science. In Ontario, in 1970 one in four full-time instructors in the humanities is a United States citizen. Some Canadians feel that such teachers are habitually inclined to think along American lines and to believe in American political principles that may differ sharply from those of Canada. They have been called missionaries for the "American Way of Life." Many of them require that U.S. textbooks be used in their classes.

In a survey of some of these Americans, we found that a large number are beginning teachers who are getting their academic feet wet at a Canadian post and gaining the experience that will enable them to return to better jobs in the United States. But sometimes they are more radical than their Canadian associates, and in matters of civil rights and the war in Vietnam they show themselves to be emotionally involved in problems that Canada does not yet suffer.

Moreover, radical young American teachers have helped to direct the attention of Canadian students to American problems, and as the more militant Canadian students tend to follow patterns of American student action in demanding greater participation in university govern-ment, the British-oriented Establishment is fearful that this "Amer-ican" trend may expand under the influence of the younger instructors from the United States.

Having said this, one hastens to add that many of the American teachers who have come to Canada have accepted their place in Canadian society in all good faith and have donated years of service to the advancement of Canadian culture. One of these is Dr. Fred-erick Elkin, chairman of the sociology department at York University. A graduate of the University of Chicago, he crossed the border to teach at McGill. Now in his early fifties, he is looked upon as one of Canada's most eminent sociologists. After ten years at McGill, during which he mastered French, Dr. Elkin transferred to the University of Montreal. He has written articles and books on Canadian sociological subjects, including a book on the family in Canada.

In an interview he rejected the idea that "foreign orientation" has created a problem for Canadians. Sociologists, he said, "become in-terested in people and conditions where they are."

"Americans," he continued, "may come here because they are fed up with Vietnam, or are pacifist, or are neutral politically. They may be American-oriented, but after a breakthrough period they pick up Canadian material and use it. It just takes a little time.

"This inflow of American teachers is not the same thing as economic take-over. American teachers who come here are not American pa-triots—if they were, they wouldn't leave the U.S. They aren't reporting to American head offices, or sending corporate profits back home. I think they become 'good Canadians.' I'm still an American, not that I'm anti-Canadian, but because I hesitate to affirm nationality of any kind."

Dr. Elkin speaks for a hard core of scholars who resist the proposals made by young Canadian nationalists for quota safeguards. Some advo-cate requiring universities to employ enough Canadians to insure that Canadians remain, or become, a clear two-thirds majority of the full-time faculty in each department. This would, of course, upset the time-honored "academic competence" standard of faculty appointment. The proposal is, moreover, repugnant to those Canadian professors who think of themselves as members of an international fraternity that is above chauvinism.

As long as the demand for teachers remains high, salaries in some of the Canadian universities will be greater than they are in many of the smaller American institutions that attract young, inexperienced instructors. A large number of American teachers conceded in interviews that "good financial offers" had attracted them to Canada. Others said they liked the "relaxed climate" on Canadian campuses, where they could make more of an impact "as individuals" and where they found themselves under less pressure to become Ph.D.'s or to "publish or perish."

Canadian scholars differ on what the future holds. James Steele, an English professor at Carleton, has predicted that the influx of American instructors will be accelerated because increasing numbers of Americans in Canadian universities are now in a position to hire teachers. "If the trend continues, we Canadians will be a very small minority in a few years," he told a visitor.

Frank Milligan, assistant director of the Canada Council, takes the opposite view. It is a "disappearing problem," he contends, because Canada's graduate schools are growing and advancing. "Canada's supply of graduate scholars will be equal to the demand by 1972, certainly by 1974," he said. In his opinion, it would have been "impossible" to expand Canada's universities without importing teachers from the United States. "Trained, able Canadian teachers just didn't exist," he declared, "and we decided we wanted to grow fast anyhow."

In any event, it is becoming less and less necessary for Canadian students to go abroad for advanced study and research. The Canada Council, based in Ottawa, is the quasi-governmental agency responsible for awarding grants and fellowships to promote the arts and the humanities in Canada. Winners of doctoral fellowships from the council may use them anywhere. But, according to Mr. Milligan, two out of every five winners in 1968 chose to study in Canada, and, he added, "there is a fair chance that we will hit 50 per cent soon."

In 1969 the U.S. Defense Department made sixty research grants to individuals at thirteen Canadian universities. They were working on such diverse subjects as high-velocity launchers, missile aerodynamics, and the use of drugs to improve military performance. So far this aspect of the American invasion of Canada has raised no significant complaints.

Many American students, too, are being attracted to Canada's new and old campuses. There is no audible objection to them as yet, perhaps because they form too small and scattered a minority to be conspicuous. The Department of Immigration issues about five thousand student visas a year to young Americans for study in Canadian universities. The largest single group of students goes to the University of Toronto; in 1969–70 there were 1,126 Americans in a student body of 25,000. That same year McGill University had 987 Americans in a total enrollment of 14,000.

At least a few Americans will be found attending almost any university in the country, for a variety of reasons. For example, every summer about four hundred Americans attend a special six-week course in French at Laval University, Quebec, while one hundred enroll in regular winter terms in which all instruction is given in French. Most of them come there for degrees—graduate or undergraduate—in the Faculty of Letters, but one or more Americans are usually to be found in Laval's departments of agriculture, medicine, theology, science, education, and business administration.

Canadian universities offer American students, no less than teachers, certain opportunities worth thinking about. In some schools and departments the "rat race" for admission is not nearly as tough as it is in the United States. Moreover, tuition fees are generally much lower. At the University of Toronto, Canada's largest and most prestigious institution of higher learning, tuition averages $500 a year, a fraction of that charged by comparable universities in the United States. At McGill tuition fees in 1969–70 ranged from $636 in the Faculty of Arts and Sciences to $740 in Engineering and $800 in Medicine. The excellent reputation of both the medical and engineering schools at McGill has attracted American students to its campus for many years.

American students are admitted on the same scholastic basis, and at the same tuition rates, as Canadian students are. And there are no national enrollment quotas. The only requirements on crossing the border, other than a letter of acceptance from a Canadian university, are a student visa and evidence of adequate funds to carry one through a specified term of study. The visas are obtainable from Canadian consulates in the United States. Americans are never required to hold passports when entering Canada.

To some observers, it seems that too much is made of the Americanization of Canadian universities, when it is, in fact, the British influence that has long dominated campus life. Subtle efforts are made to offset the American academic "invasion" by recruiting English teachers. The efforts must be subtle because Britain resents the "brain drain," which has become so heavy that Britain regularly sends a man to Canada to lure her specialists home again.

In September, 1968, a leading authority from the Royal Postgraduate Medical School at Hammersmith, London, came out to open a new medical school at McMaster in Hamilton, Ontario. He was followed within a week by his right-hand man in the London establishment, and within the year four other specialists, three junior doctors, and several high-rating medical technologists were scheduled to join him. But no one has voiced alarm over the "danger" of British influence at McMaster Medical.

Britons fit easily into Canadian academic life because Canada's universities are structured along the lines of the Oxford-Cambridge plan, which clusters several colleges within each university. English customs are maintained, as well. When a fourth college was opened at York University, Colonel R. S. McLaughlin, for whom the new college is named, and Dr. George Tatham, its master, were led into the building by a bagpiper. At almost every public event in Canada the guests of honor are "piped" to their seats, though the man in kilts and sporran may never have seen Scotland. At York University the student piper was named Borya Nakonecznyj!

*Elizabeth II of Great Britain—the Queen of Canada—
visited her American domain in 1967 and again in 1970.*

7 The British Influence

"We still share the same Queen."

The British influence in Canada is apparent when the guard is changed at the national parliament.

Oɴᴇ ᴏꜰ ᴛʜᴇ distinguishing characteristics of Canada is the persisting influence of her two founding nations—the French and the English, or the Charter Peoples as they are sometimes called. But while French Canadians insist on the living influence of what is termed the French Fact, British Canadians west of the Ottawa River will deny as often as not that the British Fact still exists.

"British influence? That's past history."

Two men among many questioned agreed—one a deputy minister in the federal government, the other a distinguished newspaper columnist. Both laughed at the very idea that British influence was still a significant factor. "Not since the First World War," they said.

Their attitude reflects Canada's growing nationalism, which gained impetus during the centennial celebration in 1967. The growing pride of Canadians in themselves as Canadians makes some of them highly critical of American influence on Canadian life, as expressed in everything from cars to comic books, TV dinners to TV programs. As for British influence, though—"Hardly a trace of it left."

They can believe what they are saying because the British influence in Canada is so all-pervasive that they have grown as accustomed to it as to the air they breathe. Both men, the deputy minister and the columnist, are in themselves walking evidence.

They are both of British descent, as are the vast majority of Canada's elite, the men who dominate the country's economic, political, educational, and religious life outside Quebec. Even in that province the economic elite is still largely of British blood, a fact that has been a chief cause of separatist sentiment.

Both men are the sons of successful professional men, both attended private schools before going on to the "right" colleges. The deputy minister also spent some time at Cambridge. (A spell at Cambridge or Oxford carries great weight in Canada, though a graduate degree from Harvard is now almost as good.) Both men belong to a very good men's club, the Rideau Club in Ottawa, which is right across Wellington Street from Parliament, where so many of the club's members have served with distinction.

Today in Canada, much more than in Britain itself, the right background, schools, clubs, and even religion help a man to get ahead. Catholics, unless they are French Catholics, are in a distinct minority among the elite, and Jews, however wealthy, have little influence. And although there are millions of immigrants and sons of immigrants in the country, people of "foreign" descent—that is, of other than British origin—have but a limited chance of attaining high positions.

This is not a matter of opinion but a simplified summary of the findings in John Porter's well-documented six-hundred-page book *The Vertical Mosaic,* an "Analysis of Social Class and Power in Canada." Its publication in 1965 has been described as a "bombshell," for Canadians had long assumed that their mosaic-type social structure, in contrast to the American melting pot, produced an ideal classless society in which immigrant peoples could preserve their native cultures while enjoying all the benefits of democracy. Professor Porter's study, however, showed that the two Charter Peoples, the French and the British, had kept power in their own hands, with those of British origin dominant everywhere outside Quebec. There are forces for change at work, but as of now, men of British descent (English, Irish, or Scottish) largely constitute Canada's Establishment. And many members of that Establishment, such as the two men quoted earlier, continue to cling to their notion of Canada, despite Porter's findings.

The British influence pervades the whole structure of government. Like England, Canada has no constitution in the American sense. Her government was set up under the provisions of an English law, the British North America Act, adopted by the British Parliament in London in 1867 and amended by it several times since, as recently, in fact, as 1964. Step by step under additional statutes emanating from London, Canada attained her independence. The British North America Act and these other laws are popularly considered to be Canada's "constitution."

Until 1949 the British North America Act was interpreted by the Judicial Committee of England's Privy Council, but since that time the Supreme Court of Canada has been its final arbiter. The British Parliament passed a statute in 1949 that implied "domiciling" the amending power in Canada, but by 1970 the federal government in Ottawa and the regimes of the ten provinces had not yet been able to agree on a formula for amending the BNA Act at home. So that power still rests with the British Parliament.

As the official *Canada Year Book* states, "Also characteristically British is the lack of specific 'bill of rights' clauses in the Act and of any legal definition of the principles of responsible government." It was felt that these rights were already established in Canada wherever English common law and the customs, usages, and conventions of the British parliamentary system were entrenched in 1867—in other words, everywhere outside Quebec. Within Quebec the Act confirmed some aspects of the existing French system and guaranteed certain religious and linguistic rights.

Under the BNA Act the "One Parliament for Canada" includes the Queen (the nominal executive head with the Governor General as her representative), an appointed Senate (with no more power than Brit-

128

ain's House of Lords), and an elected and all-powerful House of Commons. There is no division of powers as in the American system, although the appointed judiciary is independent of parliamentary control. Instead, as in England, both executive and legislative powers are exercised by the Commons.

While the Governor General has the formal authority to summon or dissolve Parliament and to assent to bills, all in the Queen's name, he receives no guidance from Westminster. Instead he acts on advice given by Canada's Prime Minister or Privy Council (a committee of cabinet ministers) or in accordance with Canadian parliamentary conventions. He makes no independent political decisions and is not, as some Americans assume, the head of the government. The Prime Minister is. Indeed, the Governor General is chosen by the Queen on advice from the Prime Minister. Since 1952 the governor-generalship has been held by Canadians rather than Britons. The term of office, by custom is usually five years.

Following an election, in accordance with parliamentary convention, the Governor General asks the leader of the party that has won the largest number of seats to form the government. The leader of that party automatically becomes the Prime Minister and usually chooses his cabinet from elected members of his party. Most cabinet ministers (called, incidentally, ministers of the Crown) head government departments as they do in the United States, but that is about the only point of resemblance to the American system.

In other words, Canadians do not vote directly for their chief of state. They vote, rather, for the representative of his party in their riding, which is similar to an American Congressional district. There can be no splitting of the ticket in Canada. Voters in the 1968 election who wanted Pierre Trudeau for Prime Minister had to vote for their local Liberal. A vote for the local Conservative was a vote for Robert L. Stanfield as Prime Minister, since Stanfield, the former premier of Nova Scotia, had been chosen leader of the Conservative party. Some ridings did elect members of the New Democratic or Creditiste parties, though neither party had any hope of forming the government.

In 1968 Trudeau's appeal was sufficiently strong for his party to win a majority in the Commons. But a Canadian government can be plagued, as Prime Minister Lester B. Pearson's was during his entire administration, by the lack of a majority. Pearson's Liberals held the greatest number of seats, but remained a minority in the Commons as a whole. They were able to stay in office only because one of the smaller parties—in their case, the Creditiste party—supported them in votes that could have dissolved Parliament.

Parliament is dissolved, and a new election called, whenever a key government measure is defeated in the Commons or a vote of "want of confidence" is passed. Canadian party discipline makes such a vote unlikely if the government has a majority. With a majority a party can hold office for five years.

A coalition of members of the two leading parties against the government, a frequent occurrence in the United States Congress, is not possible in Canada. A member of the government party may oppose a measure in caucus, but if the majority of the caucus supports it, he must vote for it on the floor of the Commons or lose his party standing. Such a rule in the United States Congress would mean that a southern Democrat, say, who voted against a bill recommended by a Democratic President not only could not thereafter sit as a Democrat but also could not again run for election as a Democrat—unless and until the party restored his good standing. No wonder that in Canada, as Philip Givens, former mayor of Toronto and now a Liberal M.P., has said, a government member must "vote like a wooden soldier," even for a measure he may know very little about or actually wish to defeat.

A prime minister who does not enjoy a majority need not suffer the situation for five long years. Any time he thinks his party has gained enough popularity to win more seats, he can ask the Governor General to dissolve Parliament and call an election.

While Canada has more frequent elections than the United States, she has, however, had fewer prime ministers in the past century than the United States has had Presidents. This stems from the fact that there is no limit to the number of terms a prime minister may serve—as long as he remains leader of the winning party. Mackenzie King, as has been mentioned, was in power for a total of twenty-two years, and John A. Macdonald, Canada's first Prime Minister, for nineteen.

If a prime minister wishes to resign, his party can continue in office without an election. Whoever is chosen by his party to succeed him as leader automatically becomes prime minister. Thus when Lester

Pearson wished to step down at age seventy, he first notified his party. In convention—and it was an exciting contest—the Liberals named Pierre Trudeau to be their leader after Pearson's resignation took effect. Trudeau therefore became Prime Minister without an election, though he immediately asked the Governor General to call one, since he wanted more support in the Commons than Pearson had had. He got it. In the United States, by contrast, a change in Presidents without an election has occurred only when the incumbent has died or been assassinated.

Voters in Canada elect not only the government but also its "Loyal Opposition." The party with the second largest number of members is so designated, and its leader occupies an official residence in Ottawa —though not quite so imposing a one as the Prime Minister's. A tourist can glimpse the latter through a screen of trees on a high bank of the Ottawa River at 24 Sussex Drive. The opposition residence, with the Scottish name "Stornaway," is at 541 Acacia Street.

Finer than either is the Governor General's establishment, Rideau Hall, which is actually the Queen's palace in Canada, in which she stays during visits to the capital. It is almost directly across from the Prime Minister's house, and in summer its façade and gardens can be viewed when the Governor General is installed at the Citadel in Quebec. A mock changing of the guard, performed by a piquet—so spelled in British army regulations and in Canada, although Americans would call it a picket—in scarlet coats and bearskins, takes place daily in summer under the eye of the actual guard, the Mounties.

The Canadian system is all very British, though many Canadians have almost forgotten the origin of their parliamentary government. The system also prevails in the provinces, although the Commons in each is called the Legislative Assembly, except for Quebec's National Assembly and Ontario's Provincial Parliament. The provinces, with the exception of Quebec, have no senates, but each has a lieutenant governor who is appointed by the Governor General "in Council," that is, with the advice of the federal powers. A lieutenant governor's authority in a province is as restricted as the Governor General's is on the national scene. The provincial party leader in office is usually called a premier, although one or two aggressive premiers have insisted on being addressed as "Prime Minister." By tradition, however, there is only one Prime Minister—the Prime Minister of Canada.

The system being British, so are its trappings, and so is the behavior of the Commons in session. A traveler might enjoy verifying this for himself if he happens to be in Ottawa when Parliament is sitting.

In summer the best show in town is the changing of the guard on Parliament Hill. This does not involve the actual relief of one force of guardsmen by another, as is the case at Buckingham Palace in London. It is a spectacle staged for the benefit of visitors every morning at 10 o'clock, except in case of rain. Then the game is called for fear of ruining the guardsmen's handsome bearskin shakos and crimson jackets. The last performance takes place on Labor Day. Thereafter the best show in Ottawa is staged inside Parliament.

Parliament, when its work allows, recesses for two months in summer. The date on which it reassembles is determined by the date on which it recessed. If a visitor finds Parliament in session, he will probably enjoy attending the Question Period that opens each day's business. It starts at 2:30 P.M. on Monday through Thursday and at 11 A.M. on Fridays, and runs from forty minutes to an hour.

It's nothing like the boring scene that often confronts a visitor to the U.S. Senate or House of Representatives: a dozen men at their scattered desks listening, or not listening, to a member droning through a speech for the benefit of the *Congressional Record*. The whole Parliament is expected to attend the Question Period—including the Prime Minister and, until Trudeau's time, his entire cabinet. (About the Trudeau variation, more later.) The opposition is out in force and ready for blood.

But the fun begins before the Commons assembles, so the visitor should arrive early at the door of the tall Peace Tower. A guard will direct him to the line of people waiting for seats in the visitors' gallery. That line is a handy point from which to view the opening act—the parliamentary parade.

With a handful of guards to clear the way, the procession is led by the Sergeant at Arms of the Commons, shouldering the mace. He is wearing a "civil uniform" patterned on the English mode—which suggests a simplified version of eighteenth-century dress—a crisply starched English barrister's bib, and a Wellington hat (that's a bicorn that is worn fore and aft as the Iron Duke wore his, not crosswise in

*The governor general, the queen's representative, opens each session
of parliament.*

Napoleon fashion).

A visitor should not let this uniform distract him from the mace itself,
all 59 inches and 17½ pounds of it, elaborately ornamented and finished
in silver gilt, the technical term for gilded silver. This is the symbol of
royal authority, and unless it rests on a table in the Commons, that
body is not officially in session.

The original mace, in use in the Assembly of Upper Canada since
1792, was taken to the United States when Toronto (then York) was
raided by the Americans during the War of 1812. So Allan MacNab,
Speaker of the Assembly from 1837 to 1841, suggested that five hundred pounds be spent in London to have the largely wooden original
replaced in silver. It was so done and became the mace of the new

Commons when Canada became a Confederation in 1867. Then in 1916 most of the Parliament building in Ottawa was destroyed by fire with a tragic loss of life. All but a portion of the mace was ruined. But that portion was incorporated in the one that the visitor sees today, which was presented to Canada by the sheriffs of London.

Every province and territory of Canada has its mace. That of the Northwest Territories is especially picturesque. The rod itself is the spiraled horn of a narwhal, very like the legendary unicorn's horn for which even the great Queen Elizabeth mistook the long ivory tusk of that member of the white whale family. The mace is ringed with walrus tusks and ornamented with bands in an Indian pattern and with Eskimo bone carvings, the whole native design topped by a crown lined with red velvet. Most maces are, however, wrought in silver, perhaps washed in gold.

There is a fine silversmith in Victoria, British Columbia, who is noted for the work he did on that province's mace and also for the chains of office he has made for many mayors across Canada. It's a poor town that can't afford this very English symbol for its top man. In Ottawa His Worship wears the chains spread over the breast of a business suit.

But in Parliament they do things with more ceremony, so let's get back to the procession. Following the Sergeant at Arms comes the Speaker, attended by two pages in Eton jackets; he is followed by the Clerk (pronounced "clark") of Commons, the Assistant Clerk, and the Second and Third Assistant Clerks. Each wears that barrister's bib, a tricorn hat, and a black robe reaching to midcalf. The robe is copied from the one worn by a Queen's Counsel in English courts and is made of silk. Underneath his robe the Speaker wears a business suit, but the clerks wear civil uniforms. All march with solemn step past the line of visitors.

In their wake come the Members of Parliament in casual clusters. There is the Prime Minister himself, chatting with a group of his ministers. A visitor with a sharp ear may eavesdrop. He probably won't hear anything of importance, but in few other circumstances will he stand so close to Canadian notables. As yet, however, no teen-age girl has broken out of line to kiss the P.M. English decorum prevails.

Not until the Commons is seated are visitors allowed into their gallery, which is, unfortunately, behind the Speaker's canopied chair. People in the side galleries, reserved for VIP's and families and friends of members, can watch that important official in action.

He must make firm and instant decisions on the parliamentary propriety of every question and answer. Since the members persistently try to get an oratorical thrust past his guard, his is no easy task. He must also be bilingual, since members may speak in either of the Charter languages—French or English—and he must rule in whichever language the member uses. The visitor, incidentally, can get a simultaneous translation (and hear better) by using the earphone hanging on the right-hand side of his seat.

If the Speaker loses control of his unruly flock, an unseemly scene may ensue. The man who lets that happen is forever disgraced, and in his humiliation he may resign—a far cry from the happy day when the Commons elected him to his high post, so high that he had to pretend to be reluctant to take the chair and the Prime Minister and the leader of the Loyal Opposition had to take his arms and in a mock scuffle force him out of his member's seat and into the chair. This scuffle is a British tradition, too, but Canadians are so used to it that they tend to believe it entirely "Canadian."

During the Question Period inquiries are directed to the minister in whose area of responsibility they fall, or in his absence, to the Prime Minister. The P.M. and his cabinet occupy the center seats on the right-hand side of the hall, with all the members of their party ranged around them. Members who do not hold an office in the government sit in the rear rows, hence the slightly derogatory and distinctly British classification of them as "backbenchers."

All opposition party members sit on the left-hand side, with the leader of the Loyal Opposition directly opposite the Prime Minister. In the front row with him sits his "shadow cabinet," a term familiar to visitors to the English Commons. In Ottawa the visitor is handed a chart showing where each member is seated and so can locate anyone in whom he has a particular interest.

An American is usually surprised to find cabinet ministers facing a daily barrage of questions from the opposition. Each of them is a department head carrying a load of work that he must interrupt to be present. What's more, he must have at his finger tips the information needed not only to answer expected queries but to reply to surprise attacks. Until Trudeau became Prime Minister, the entire cabinet was expected to attend, although the British have not required all ministers to be always at hand for some years.

Trudeau announced to Parliament early in his administration that certain ministers would be absent on fixed alternate days to allow them to do the expanded work he had imposed. He hoped the opposition would, in a minister's absence, hold the questions directed to him until the following day, since few questions were so pressing as to require immediate answers. But the opposition was indignant over this break with tradition and proceeded to harass the Prime Minister by directing to him questions that were intended for an absent minister. It seemed, indeed, as if they deliberately held questions until a minister was absent, directing few queries to those ministers present. So they kept the Prime Minister bobbing up and down in his seat, affording visitors more opportunity to see Trudeau in action than might otherwise have been the case. This tactic disturbed his equanimity not at all. Usually he responded with a dismissive gesture, saying that he would refer the question to the absent minister. Where he could answer with a barbed quip, he was quick to do so.

The pointed and even venomous question is an accepted opposition weapon, although the dart must be thrown with ostensible politeness in order to get it past the Speaker. The old "Chief" of the Conservative party, former Prime Minister John Diefenbaker, has always been a master of the question loaded with innuendo. This is all in the English tradition, as is the response of a side when they think their man has scored a point. Then, to the surprise of American visitors, they pound on their desks like schoolboys—but not too long, lest they bring down the wrath of the Speaker. And like dismissed schoolboys, the majority of members troop out when the Speaker says "orders of the day," which indicates that the Question Period is over. Only those interested in the next business on the agenda remain. The rest return to their offices or go to meet constituents or generally manage to escape the dull debates.

For the first session of a new Parliament an elaborate and very British ritual is performed. A "new" Parliament always follows an election, but an election is not always necessary to bring about a new Parliament. The Prime Minister, acting through the Governor General, may prorogue the old Parliament and call for a new one the very next day if he wishes. Then the Governor General, wearing a uniform heavily encrusted with gold and a befeathered tricorn, rides to the Parliament building in the state carriage escorted by Royal Canadian Mounted Police on horseback with pennons flying. (Most Mounties are no longer mounted, alas, but travel by squad car and wear their red coats only on ceremonial duty.)

Seeing the Governor General pass along his route is about all of this ceremony that a visitor will catch, for most of it takes place in the Senate and seats in the galleries there are at a premium. The wives and daughters (and "their sisters and their cousins and their aunts") of members of the Commons, senators, and leading government officials will be in attendance, elaborately gowned, hatted, and gloved, looking formal indeed in the morning light. The gowns may hint of Paris or New York but the hats are often distinctly English—befeathered toques or beflowered tulle turbans, ideal for weddings and the Governor General's annual garden party.

At the opening of a new Parliament, when it is time for the Commons to proceed to the Senate for a "joint session," the Gentleman Usher of the Black Rod, who corresponds in the Senate to the Sergeant at Arms in the Commons, marches up to the big doors of the Commons, closed for the occasion, and knocks three times with his rod. When the doors are opened, he stands at the bar of Commons until he is admitted to the floor, where he bows first to the members and second to the Speaker and then delivers a message to the Commons from the Governor General. Only then does that body parade to the Senate.

The Governor General wears his befeathered hat throughout the ceremony. As the representative of Canada's royal ruler he uncovers his head before no man. Hat firmly on, he is conducted to the throne that the Queen occupies on her visits. There he reads the "Speech from the Throne." Neither he nor the Queen has any part in writing it. As handed to him by the Prime Minister, it is simply a statement of the Government's legislative program for the new Parliament. It consists, therefore, of a rather dull listing of measures, which makes the Governor General's task, as one commentator put it, "like reading a menu aloud." There has been talk of scrapping this unexciting performance, but in the English tradition it goes on and on.

The same ceremony takes place at every new provincial assembly, with the Lieutenant Governor, hat on head, droning out the speech handed him by the Premier.

Members of Parliament may take a coffee break in the morning instead of tea in the afternoon, but otherwise countless English customs prevail. Any change can cause a fuss.

In Quebec, however, the French-Canadian provincial government has been quietly altering this picture. In the autumn of 1968, for instance, bills were introduced and quickly adopted that changed the name of Quebec's Queen's Printer to (in English) Quebec Official Publisher and (in French) *Editeur Officiel du Quebec* and allowed provincial statutes to be identified by session and calendar year. Previously, statutes passed in, say, 1945 were identified as having been adopted in the ninth year of the reign of King George VI (9 Geo. VI), as they still are in Ottawa, where the Queen's Printer occupies a building just down the hill from Parliament.

Up Ottawa's Wellington Street in the opposite direction is Canada's Supreme Court Building. The Court consists of a chief justice and "eight puisne judges," all in the black gowns and white bibs seen on the "Servants of Parliament." "Puisne" simply means "associate." There is also an Exchequer Court, consisting of a president and "four puisne judges," similarly attired. This court hears "claims made by or against the Crown in the right of Canada," the official *Canada Year Book* explains. We explain in our turn that this means cases against the Canadian Government. The Exchequer Court also serves as a Court of Admiralty in Canada. Canada's federal judges, incidentally, wear their distinctive garb everywhere in the country. In the high Arctic the roving judge may bed down in a sleeping bag, but before he tries an Eskimo case involving a murder on a seal hunt, he will don a black robe and white neckcloth.

It must be admitted that Parliament has made one notable break with British custom. On May 22, 1919, the Commons passed a resolution requesting His Majesty (George V at that time) to refrain from bestowing titles on Canadian citizens. This policy was reversed in 1933, when a Conservative Government under Prime Minister R. B. Bennett recommended a number of such awards, which were duly included in the King's Honours List on New Year's Day, 1934, and again in 1935. Prime Minister Mackenzie King came back into office later that year, and his government reverted to the 1919 policy. No titles have been granted since, though in 1942 a special parliamentary committee agreed that His Majesty's subjects in Canada should be eligible for "Honours and Decorations, including awards in the Orders of Chivalry, which do not involve titles." But Canadians who have titles from an earlier day or from 1934–35 are accorded them.

Provinces and territories all have their coats of arms, topped by a crown in every case, including that of Quebec. Canada's national coat of arms is an intricate affair with the lion and the unicorn where one might expect the beaver and the moose. Visitors are, of course, aware of the crown on highway markers, but most do not know that the motorcycle cop who gives the speeder a ticket is not, properly speaking, a policeman—he's a constable, unless he has risen to the rank of sergeant. Outside the Province of Quebec, when a constable joins the force, he (like all other peace officers) swears allegiance to the Queen. In Quebec they changed that oath in 1967. There allegiance is now sworn to "constituted authority," which is much less colorful.

Many Canadians are genuinely outraged by such changes. In 1968 the Maritime Loyalist Association adopted a constitution that required members to swear to protect the Queen and to disclose any plots against her and her family. When the Toronto *Daily Star* came out editorially for a Canadian republic, a columnist on another Toronto paper proposed the appointment of a Queen's Champion in each province to defend Her Majesty "from the fast-rising incidence of treason in Canada."

Most Canadians feel neither strongly for nor against the Queen. The London *Times* correspondent reported that their attitude was largely one of indifference, but "indifference" may not be quite the right word. They seem to take her for granted, but they turned out in great numbers to cheer heartily during her visit in 1967. Among those who showed up were Ontario hippies and teen-age Québecois shouting *"Vive la reine."*

As part of its 1967 celebration of the Confederation centennial, the National Gallery in Ottawa staged a magnificent "Pageant of Canada," which told the country's story from its beginnings to 1867 through a display of portraits, busts, sketches, medals, silver pieces, Champlain's astrolabe, and other memorabilia. In the main pavilion, draped in royal purple trimmed with elaborate Victorian fringes and tassels, were several portraits of the young Victoria—alone or posed with her husband and small children. But nowhere in the entire display was there a single portrait of a Canadian. Not one of the Canadian Fathers of Confederation, not even Canada's George Washington, her first Prime Minister, John A. Macdonald, was there. The notables were all French or British, largely the latter, as hardly a Canadian noticed. The display had been assembled by Dr. Roy Strong—who is now the director of Britain's National Portrait Gallery.

A brilliant show during the Queen's visit in 1967 occurred on Parliament Hill when she presented new regimental flags to several units. There were men from the Canadian Black Watch swinging by in their dress kilts to the music of their pipe band. There were guardsmen in their red coats and bearskins. Even the military engineers were decorative in elaborate epaulets of chain mail. While Canada has taken the almost revolutionary step of unifying her forces, with soldiers, sailors, and airmen all eventually scheduled to be clothed in the same dark green, the government has allowed the men to keep their traditional dress uniforms and, in most cases, their historic regimental names.

Names and uniforms have on occasion given rise to confusion. Robert Nielson, an editorial writer for the Toronto *Daily Star*, reported one such incident in a recent article: "Could we wonder that President Nasser of Egypt, in 1956, with British invasion troops still in his country, boggled at the idea of admitting a Canadian regiment named the Queen's Own Rifles? That little case of suspicious identity almost denied Canada a place in the United Nations mission which for eleven years policed a precarious peace in the Middle East."

An English reporter for the London *Observer*, Barrie Stuart-Penrose, writing about Quebec in October, 1968, was surprised by still another aspect of Canada's military tradition: "One curious historical paradox strikes any visitor to the Citadel. The French-speaking soldiers all wear uniforms of the British Grenadier Guards and although they drill in British military fashion, the orders are given in French."

Tradition prevails even when the boys are having fun. When the Royal Canadian Hussars give their annual ball, their armory in Montreal is decorated with regimental colors, and a guard of honor in the Hussars' full-dress uniform greets the guests. Following dinner the traditional Cavalry Canter takes place, to music played by the regimental band.

The military don't have a monopoly on this sort of glamour. Not only do the Royal Canadian Mounted Police stage a Musical Ride—patterned on the one performed in British tattoos by the royal household cavalry—but so does the Metropolitan Toronto Police Force! It has become a major tourist attraction. When not performing the ride, members of the troop, in their dress uniforms with helmets and

English football—rugger—is played at the University of Toronto.

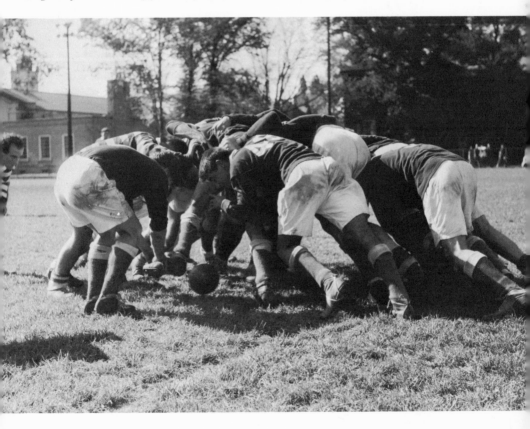

bamboo lances imported from Pakistan, stand mounted guard at Toronto's new city hall.

Another sort of English ride takes place in London, Ontario, during that city's annual Old English Fortnight, usually the first two weeks in July. Then Lady Godiva, wearing apparently only a long blond wig, rides through the town on her white horse. It's all part of a swinging British scene, with bobbies and beefeaters, double-decker buses and a London pub, on hand for the tourists. There are also cricket matches, and on this London's own Thames River, regattas.

While this festival is an obviously contrived affair, the traveler in Canada can see dozens of genuine manifestations of the English influence. Outside Quebec the majority of place names, not just of towns but of counties, streets, and even country roads, are British in origin. Rivers, lakes, and provinces may have Indian names, but the places where men settled were named by Britons pressing west, many of them Hudson's Bay Company factors setting up posts.

Occasionally, to be more distinctly Canadian, some English place names have been changed to Indian ones. So Bytown, named originally for Colonel John By of the Royal Engineers, became Ottawa, and York, named for the Duke of York, became Toronto. But more often the reverse has happened. The capital of Saskatchewan was originally called Wascana, an Indian name meaning "Pile of Bones"—buffalo bones, that is. It was changed to Regina in honor of Queen Victoria. A neighboring province honored royalty on an even larger scale by calling itself, in all its vastness, Alberta after Prince Albert, the Queen's consort.

A few immigrant groups of other nationalities have had their way in naming settlements, but the two largest towns in southwest-central Ontario, where the German Mennonites settled in great numbers, are named Waterloo and Kitchener.

More important than primacy in place names is a major advantage that Britons enjoy over other immigrants, including Americans. Under the existing franchise act, they can not only vote but also hold public office after only a year's residence and without becoming Canadian citizens. They are not considered "foreigners." "Foreigners," including immigrants from that other founding nation, France, must reside in the country for five years before they can become citizens, and only

142

then can they vote.

In much legislation of the past the term "British subjects" has been used in referring to Canadians generally. A proposal made to the Ontario Assembly in 1968 to substitute the words "Canadian citizens" caused considerable alarm. The Minister of Municipal Affairs explained that the change would disfranchise 184,000 British subjects now living in the province who had never become citizens. Several municipalities would also be deprived of able council members.

But this special privilege is in danger. In Ottawa in late 1968 Secretary of State Gérard Pelletier indicated that he would recommend it be eliminated by an amendment then being drafted to the Citizenship Act. There were immediate reactions in letters to the editors of various newspapers. One writer declared that "Britain is not a country like any other . . . we still share the same Queen. Above all, we owe the Canadian fact in the New World to the British soldiers who kept our southern neighbors at bay." The United States, that is. Such an amendment would certainly face a fight in the Commons, if not a prior one in the Government's own party caucus.

Nevertheless, when the British Broadcasting Corporation filmed an unprecedented and extended visit with Queen Elizabeth II at Buckingham Palace in 1969, the complete B.B.C. film was not shown in Canada. Instead, the government-subsidized Canadian Broadcasting Corporation presented the Queen of Canada to her subjects in the American version, in which twenty minutes had been cut from the original running time to make the film fit into the one-hour limit imposed by an American network—less, of course, time out for station identification and commercials. *Lèse majesté* indeed.

8

The Canadian Mosaic

"Canada is a land of no one ideology, no single vision;

it is a cultural free port . . . ."

Left, an Ojibwa Indian. Above, a Ukrainian festival takes place in Edmonton, Alberta.

The Mennonites were among the first non-British groups to settle in western Canada.

Having lived abroad for several years, the last five of them in Canada, we found that listening to the 1968 American election returns was a novel experience in one respect. The names of Congressional candidates showed a striking variety. The countries of origin of some of those names we could guess; others left us baffled. But the roll of winners and losers testified anew to the many ores that have gone into America's melting pot.

Canada's elections are quite different. In our four years north of the border we have listened in on two of them, and the vast majority of Parliamentary candidates have borne names of either British or French origin. Only occasionally did an "ethnic" name appear on the tote board. Yet Canada is a vast mosaic of peoples.

It is said that nearly a hundred languages are spoken in the land. More than a quarter of the citizens are labeled "ethnic"—the polite Canadianism that denotes "foreign" or foreign origin one or more generations back. Also distinct ethnically, although hardly foreign, are Canada's two hundred thousand Indians and thirty thousand Eskimos. The 1961 census listed thirty-two thousand Negroes, but there are thousands more now. From two hundred thousand to four hundred thousand or more Canadians are métis, people of mixed white and Indian blood. But one would hardly know any of this from the election returns or from the news stories about men appointed to prominent posts in business or government.

Not until 1957, in fact, did Canada choose as her prime minister a man with neither a French nor a British name—John Diefenbaker, who obviously had some German background. And remember that Germans settled in Canada as early as the English. The Diefenbaker surge also brought to Ottawa an ethnic Ukrainian Minister of Labor, an ethnic Italian Parliamentary Secretary, a Chinese M.P., and an Indian Senator.

The election of Prime Minister Trudeau eleven years later, representing another surge toward a united Canada, carried thirty-three "ethnics" to Parliament—"more," according to Stanley Haidasz, Parliamentary Secretary of Polish origin, "than there has ever been." Several bore names that did not sound foreign, but David Lewis, for example, is of Polish-Jewish descent, while Herbert Gray is of Russian-Jewish extraction. So, in a country that is 27 per cent "ethnic," non-French, non-British membership in Parliament as Trudeau took office stood at roughly 12 per cent. His enlarged cabinet of twenty-nine men (no women, but then only one was elected an M.P.) included at first just two ministers of non-French, non-British blood: Otto Lang, Rhodes scholar and Dean of Law at the University of Saskatchewan, and Bud Olson, businessman and farmer from Medicine Hat, Alberta. Then, in 1969, Herbert Gray was appointed minister without portfolio and became the first Jew ever named to the cabinet in Ottawa. In 1970 a Trudeau appointment proved another first for Canadian Jews when Mr. Justice Bora Laskin was named to the Supreme Court.

The "ethnics" seem to do better on the local level. They are readily elected to the provincial assemblies. A few have become premiers of provinces. Toronto has had two Jewish mayors, and the long-time mayor of Winnipeg, Stephen Juba, is a Ukrainian.

In the United States we are attuned to names like Roosevelt, Eisenhower, La Guardia, Lehman, or Ribicoff. A second-generation American of Greek descent is currently Vice President. But America is a melting pot, and Canada a mosaic whose dominant pieces remain the two Charter Peoples, the British and the French. From its very first step toward nationhood—the Crown-enforced union of Quebec and Ontario in 1840—those two peoples have kept their distance from each other. That beginning set the pattern the country would follow in the future.

The 1840 union was the result of a report made by John George Lambton, the Earl of Durham, after he had been sent over to investigate the 1837–38 revolts in Quebec and Ontario. Significantly, those rebellions were separate uprisings whose leaders did not coordinate their assault. Why not? Two quotations tell a good part of the story.

One of Durham's young investigators noted that the Québecois, being French, "have all the national conceit of that people. They consider themselves superior to all the other peoples, and too good to mix with any other race." They still feel much the same way. With some basis in fact, they believe their culture to be superior to any other in Canada, and many of their intellectuals are obsessed with trying to purify it of American and British-Canadian influences.

As for the British colonists, in his official report Lord Durham said, "accustomed to form a high estimate of their own superiority, they take no pains to conceal from others their contempt and intolerance of their usages." In time this attitude toward the French Canadians, though not toward others of different cultures, was modified in Ontario. It persists, however, in the western provinces. For decades condescension was the best a Québecois could expect from a British Canadian.

So culturally the two peoples went their respective ways, the French Canadians fighting hard and well to keep their language and religion intact. Britons living in Quebec maintained their separate communities, so that even today, Westmount, the very heart of Montreal, is a very British, very prosperous English-speaking enclave. French-Canadian settlements in eastern Ontario have likewise maintained their own

148

character.

Other historical factors helped piece together the modern mosaic. That first union consisted of only two provinces, unhappy pulling in harness, while other settled areas of what is now Canada remained apart. Nova Scotia, New Brunswick, and Prince Edward Island continued as separate colonies. Far-off Newfoundland did not even consider itself a part of the mainland. Though Confederation finally came in 1867, Prince Edward Island, as we have said, did not join Canada until 1873—and Newfoundland kept its distance until 1949!

Not only did these small provinces maintain their own particularisms, but within their small boundaries people of different national origins tended to "keep themselves to themselves." In New Brunswick and Nova Scotia, Acadians who had hidden in the woods to escape expulsion by the British stayed there, building up struggling little communities away from the areas that the English had taken over. Exiled Acadians who later trekked back to their homeland found the English well settled on the farms that had once been French. The returnees were allowed to establish fishing villages along the less desirable stretches of the Nova Scotia coast. There they are still, as the summer visitor poking along the rocky shore can discover for himself, tiny settlements in which not English but Acadian French is spoken.

If the tourist looks sharp, he'll find other villages in which a different people settled by themselves. These are the all-black communities inhabited by the descendants of slaves who reached Nova Scotia by various routes. Some were brought in by early eighteenth-century settlers, others by Tory slaveowners during the American Revolution. But many refugee owners found themselves too impoverished to keep slaves and so freed them. In the rock-bound, still-wild colony, how were the blacks to live? Their condition became so pitiful that the British Government shipped more than a thousand of them back to Africa in 1791. Thousands more refused to go, and squatter settlements of Negroes slowly grew up on unclaimed land. During the War of 1812 some five hundred more blacks arrived aboard British warships. They had fled from Chesapeake Bay plantations to beg the British forces raiding the area to carry them to freedom. These slaves were probably taken to Halifax as spoils of war, but they were eventually freed there. After 1833, the year slavery was abolished in the

Italian boccie *players in a Toronto park*

West Indies, it was gradually eliminated everywhere in the Empire, and British North America became the goal of runaway slaves from the Southern states. Few came to Nova Scotia overland. Most runaways arriving there were Negro crewmen who had managed to jump ship in some port of the colony. (Slaveowners found it profitable to hire out to ship's captains the best carpenters and coppersmiths among their slaves.) Such crewmen were welcomed in the black settlements and readily found work in nearby white towns.

Today the roads leading to Nova Scotia's Negro villages are admittedly poor, the schools that serve them distinctly inferior, but the inhabitants run their own communities, however poverty-stricken, and enjoy a separatism that young black militants in the United States are demanding for their people. Some Canadians tend to see this separatism as a better answer to the Negro problem than the integration that has been America's goal.

The summer visitor to Digby, a popular tourist area, will find on its fringes just such a village. It's called Jordantown; it's unpainted, generally unserviced, but all black. Digby people admit they have done little to help the Negroes, but they also say they have done nothing to harm them. There's no overt discrimination, and the doings of the blacks are written up in the local paper "just like news from any other town."

Outside Nova Scotia, Negroes generally do not live in isolated communities but cluster in the eastern cities, particularly Montreal and Toronto. Their number is difficult to estimate. Reference books offer totals for Canadian Negroes that range from thirty-five thousand to eighty thousand, without giving data sources. The Department of Immigration does not release statistics on the race or color of immigrants, only on their country of origin. Most of those arriving from the West Indies can be presumed to be black, but there is no way to determine the number of Negroes who enter from the United States or Great Britain. To enter officially, unsponsored immigrants must possess occupational skills needed in Canada. But many blacks undoubtedly come from the United States as tourists and simply stay, never registering as "landed immigrants." There has also been extensive Negro migration to Toronto from other parts of Canada. Though Nova Scotia authorities claim that half the blacks in Canada live in that province, numbers of them are known to have left for the better job markets of Ontario. Others have come from Montreal after finding their lack of French an increasing handicap. Then, too, Ontario has an anti-discrimination law, as Quebec does not. So in Canada heads can easily be counted twice. A safe estimate of the total number would probably be fifty thousand, but only the 1970 census will tell.

West of Ontario the number of Negroes is negligible. The black comedian Dick Gregory, performing in Vancouver, quipped: "There is absolutely no bias in Vancouver. I know because I just had dinner with your Negro."

In Canada, in the areas the white man conquered, most Indians live apart on reservations as they do in the United States. But the Indian in the eastern United States was nearly exterminated, and at best he was driven away from the centers of population. In Canada he was treated less ruthlessly. There are reservations near almost every large Canadian city as well as others off in the desolate bush. These bits and pieces—color them red—dot the whole Canadian mosaic.

One of the most historic is right at hand for the average visitor. This is Caughnawaga, the Mohawk Indian reservation near the south end of the Mercier Bridge to Montreal. Catholic Iroquois, called French

A German folk dancer at a folklore pageant in Montreal

Mohawks, were settled here in the early days of the Quebec colony (1667). At the Sunday Mass, which is well worth attending, the liturgy is sung in Mohawk, one of Canada's one hundred languages.

Akin to the Indians were the métis, the mixed bloods on the prairies, descendants of the early French-Canadian voyageurs and their Indian brides. Their tragic story will be told later in this book, but suffice it to say here that they twice revolted in defense of their "nation"—in 1869–70 and again in 1885—twice were put down, and in the end their

152

leader, Louis Riel, was hanged. Had their rights been recognized, or had their revolts succeeded, there might now be a large métis enclave in the heart of Canada.

Instead, while there are a few substantial communities in Manitoba, such as St. Boniface, where French is still the first language, most of the métis settlements are pathetic fragments in the Canadian mosaic, clusters of shacks in the bush or on the fringes of new boom towns, inhabited by people without the rights the treaty Indians enjoy and living in worse poverty than the descendants of slaves. Many of them have learned neither French nor English but speak Cree, an Indian language.

Indians who have left the reservation fare as badly as the métis. In northern Ottawa their shacks cluster on what is literally the wrong side of the tracks, the north side to which the electric power lines do not reach. Even the squad cars of the Ontario Provincial Police turn south at the tracks, not bothering to patrol the Indian villages.

Most of the population of Quebec was hotly on the side of the métis during the rebellions, most of the population of Ontario bitterly against them. So the episode deepened the differences between the Charter Nations. Thereafter the mosaic pattern was no longer a matter of historical accident. By the time Canada finally experienced a massive onrush of immigrants from Europe, it was one of the established principles.

Immigration to Canada had a slow growth. On her great new prairie-land, besides the disaffected métis, was a group of Scottish settlers who had been encouraged to immigrate by Thomas Douglas, the Earl of Selkirk. A few of the more venturesome from Ontario had also taken up land there. Late in the nineteenth century Canada still needed thousands more, but wanted those of her own choosing. Since Britain and Germany, needing workers for their expanding industries, discouraged emigration to the "new Siberia," Canadian agents concentrated on German population pockets in Austria-Hungary and Russia.

These people were Mennonites and Hutterites who had been pushed steadily eastward by religious persecution. By 1870 the countries that had once accepted them were exhibiting a new intolerance. So they organized a mass flight to new lands. Most of them settled in the Dakota Territory of the United States, but several hundred of the "Russian" Mennonites of Germanic origin reached Canada in 1874. Assured of exemption from military service and the right to educate their children in their own schools, they settled in eight townships of southern Manitoba that had been provided for them and built up a flourishing farm community around a town they named Steinbach. (In 1965 we heard the Parliamentary candidate for that riding address his audience in German.) Many other Mennonites joined them, and by 1880 there were six thousand in the new province.

Most people traveled to Manitoba by way of the United States, going first to Fargo in the Dakota Territory and from there taking a boat up the Red River. (Since the river flows north, they actually sailed "down" it to Manitoba, but it's up on the map, and we'll leave it at that.) Other immigrants took the "trail" the government had blazed from Port Arthur, Ontario, to what is now Winnipeg, 433 miles away, covering 137 miles on land and the rest by navigable water. Six hundred settlers used the trail the first year it was open. More would not come until the going was easier.

Canada's West, in other words, was not colonized by men in covered wagons, who blazed their own way, settling on whatever pieces of land they fancied and setting up in time a primitive system of law. Most Canadian pioneers traveled in homogeneous groups to areas that the government had chosen for them and to which the "law" had preceded them. There was none of the frontier independence—and little of the violence—that characterized American settlement.

Few came until a railroad had been built to carry them, a railroad that was Canada's very lifeline, the almost legendary Canadian Pacific. The very building of the line brought in more foreigners than already lived in the territory across which the navvies pushed an average of two and one-half miles of track a day. On the eastern stretch most of the crew members were Italians, transients from the States who went back there if they survived. Thirty men died along one fifty-mile stretch that wasn't exceptionally difficult, most of them killed by the dynamite that they had to use frequently and often mishandled. The work was even more brutal in the mountainous West, where contractors brought in seventeen thousand coolies to carve out the roadbed over the passes.

Many of the Chinese went home with their hard-won money. Thousands stayed, however, huddling in shacks along False Creek in what is now Vancouver. But completion of the railroad brought depression, and the rowdy whites thereabouts resented the cheap competition for the few jobs. A mob burned down the shacks of the Chinese, but couldn't drive the Chinese out of town. They fled to two back alleys that are the present-day center of Vancouver's Chinatown. To placate the enemy in a largely womanless settlement, the Chinese did woman's work as houseboys, laundrymen, and cooks. Some eighty thousand more had arrived by 1914.

Chinese immigration to Canada was restricted for only one period—from 1923 to 1947. Since 1947 Chinese have entered in a steady flow, more than six thousand in 1967 alone. These latter-day arrivals are fugitives from an antipathetic regime; they are skilled workers, professionals, wealthy businessmen. Thanks to them, Vancouver has its first all-Chinese bank.

Thousands stayed put in Vancouver's Chinatown and in Toronto's, but thousands more have broken the mosaic pattern. Sons and grandsons of the first cooks and houseboys have scattered all across Canada, setting up restaurants in towns so small that the owner and waiters are often the only Chinese for a hundred miles. Even if they were ever really trained in Chinese cuisine, they probably couldn't get the right ingredients in Moose Jaw. Besides, they cook to suit their customers. So not only will the sweet and sour pork be too sweet, but there may also be a surprising sign in the window: "Homemade pizza our specialty."

The immigrants who came on "the cars" after the railroad tracks had been laid were usually directed on their way. Their destination was, in most cases, arranged with government agents before they left their homelands. One such group was composed of Hungarians organized by Count Paul d'Esterhazy. They were settled in 1888 in what became known as the Esterhazy District of Saskatchewan when that part of the Northwest Territory became a province. Another group was established at Hun's Valley in Manitoba's Riding Mountains.

Such arrangements didn't always work out entirely as expected. In 1899 an extraordinary party of Russians settled on land set aside for them, again in Saskatchewan. They were Dukhobors, 7,500 members of a sect whose doctrines, Canada was told, were very like those of the Society of Friends. The Dukhobors were sponsored by Count Leo

Tolstoy himself, and happy with Count Esterhazy's Hungarians and Lord Selkirk's splendid Scots of an earlier time, Canada welcomed them.

Whatever understanding there was between the sect and the government rapidly became a misunderstanding on such questions as land tenure and the education of Dukhobor children. In 1903 the Dukhobors organized a protest. Extremists gathered at one village and stripped themselves in preparation for a nude march on the little town of Yorkton. The nudes that the police finally corralled were no young sylphs but hefty middle-aged men and women, many of them wearing only their heavy shoes—the better to march and kick with.

Before an extremist group of Dukhobors would pay taxes, it would burn down its communal buildings. A schoolhouse to which it objected might go the same way. If any of the men or boys were taken in on suspicion of arson, wives and mothers would appear at headquarters and begin stripping. Since they wore numerous peasant skirts and petticoats over long baggy underpants, the process usually took long enough to allow the authorities to bundle the partly clothed women into the nearest cells.

Several mass nude strikes took place before the Dukhobors' leader advised his people, in a deathbed message in 1939, to give up communal life and obey the laws of Canada. Most did so, but a schismatic sect called the Sons of Freedom remained occasionally troublesome.

In their need for settlers the federal and provincial authorities were sometimes too generous in the promises they made to religious sects. These promises were not always kept, and some were never even tested. In the 1880's Mormons south of the border were disputing the question of polygamy with the United States Government. In 1887, in consequence, a group of forty-one Mormons migrated to a corner of southwestern Alberta (not yet a province). Where the town of Cardston now stands, they soon erected a sawmill, flour mill, and cheese factory. They introduced irrigation into western Canada, but not, as it turned out, polygamy. Three years after they arrived, the Mormon Church discontinued multiple marriages.

By 1896, despite all Canada's efforts to entice various immigrant groups, only fifty-six thousand homesteads had been taken up, and sixteen thousand of these had been abandoned. So the government and

A Canadian of Chinese ancestry farms in British Columbia

156

the Canadian Pacific Railroad together mounted a noisy campaign. Pamphlets selling the soil of the Canadian prairies to prospective farmers were printed in twenty languages. A world boom in wheat underlined the message. Besides, the new minister in charge of immigration, Sir Clifford Sifton, had decided that "a stalwart peasant in a sheepskin coat . . . is good quality."

So the hearty peasants came in swarms: Russians, Ukrainians, Estonians, Poles, and from a corner of the old Austro-Hungarian empire, Galicians. The North Atlantic Trading Company was paid a bonus of two dollars a head for every Galician "colonist" landed in Canada, five dollars for each head of a family. In the next fifteen years more than two million new Canadians arrived, a third of them from Continental Europe.

The peasants were often shunted toward less desirable land and into the roughest, hardest jobs. They traveled on "colonist cars," with stoves for cooking and plank bunks for sleeping. Those from northeastern Europe generally ended up in the bleaker, colder northern sections of the western provinces. Perhaps they were sent there on the theory that anyone brought up on the climate of the steppes was better adapted to Canada's worst areas than an effete American or Briton would be.

During their first winter the Ukrainians in their sod huts endured incredible hardships, but they did endure. Today they flourish as farmers, businessmen, professionals, and virtually everything else. Most of them live in Manitoba, where an annual National Ukrainian Festival is held with a splendid choir, all manner of dancers in authentic costumes, demonstrations of their traditional artwork, and hearty servings of Ukrainian food. In 1968 the festival was staged early in August at Dauphin, two hundred miles north of Winnipeg. For the visitor who can't get to the festival, there is a Ukrainian Culture Museum in Winnipeg itself. The Ukrainians are strongly represented in Saskatchewan, too, where one out of every eight voters is of Ukrainian origin.

Of the great surge of immigrants to Canada before 1914, one third came from the United Kingdom, but thousands of these men went home to fight in World War I, never to return. Another third were Americans who came in response to advertisements placed in seven thousand U.S. newspapers, offering free land to any man who would work it. The Americans usually arrived with more money in their pockets than the Slavic farmers did. They could afford to buy farm equipment and set their families up in some comfort. And as their countrymen had done ever since the eighteenth century, they fitted right into the English-Canadian scene, never forming a separate piece of the mosaic.

World War I dammed the stream of immigrants, which would never again reach the flood proportions of 1913, when more than four hundred thousand arrived. In two later years, however, 1957 and 1967, the total number entering did exceed half the 1913 figure. In 1957 the Hungarian Revolt and the Suez crisis stimulated the flow. In 1967 the chief stimulus was economic discontent in Britain and Italy. The refugee Hungarians in 1957, and the ten thousand Czechs fleeing the Russian military occupation of their country eleven years later, have been about the only arrivals from eastern Europe since the Iron Curtain clanged shut.

Before it could close, however, thousands of Estonians, Latvians, Lithuanians, and Poles escaped, but these were not peasants in sheepskin coats to be herded on their way. Among them were business leaders and industrialists, educators and scientists, professional men and artists. They came as individuals, and their gifted individuality has strained the structure of the Canadian mosaic. Of like character were the Jewish refugees from Germany and Austria, Russia and Poland. Almost to a man they settled in the cities.

Since World War II a half million newcomers have wrought enormous changes in Toronto, once the bastion of stuffy "Empire" conservatism. Today one hears a babble of tongues in that metropolis. There are restaurants featuring the cuisines of a dozen countries. Textile, garment, and furniture design has been transformed by gifted "ethnics." One of the most successful designers, who also manufactures intimate apparel of her own contriving, is an attractive young woman of Lebanese origin, Claire Haddad. The design for Toronto's superb new $30-million Science Centre, the Ontario government's centennial project, was the work of a young Japanese-Canadian, Raymond Moriyama. At one time the assignment would have gone automatically to a resident architect of English origin. Recently Moriyama has enjoyed another triumph with his far-out plan for Toronto's

159

mammoth future zoo.

Despite the strain put on the mosaic by the individuality of latter-day immigrants, urban growth has tended to follow a mosaic pattern. This is neatly illustrated in Oakville, near Toronto, a former resort town where the Ford Company has built a Canadian factory. In six years Oakville's population has grown from ten thousand to twenty-seven thousand. Sixteen-Mile Creek, in the center of town, arbitrarily divides the Wasps, who live to the east, from the Portuguese and Italians, who live to the west. The latter seldom cross the bridge.

Most of the relatively late comers have been too busy adjusting to a new land, establishing themselves economically, or striving for professional or artistic recognition to concern themselves with politics. Happy to enjoy the cultural independence allowed them, they have not yet seriously threatened English-French dominance. But will their children stay content?

The sons and grandsons of some of the earlier immigrants have begun to organize a third force in Canadian life. In 1968 a Thinkers' Conference on Cultural Rights brought to Toronto delegates of ethnic organizations from across Canada. Speaker after speaker warned the delegates of the dangers in the trend "toward a monolithic society in Canada." They were told to support official biculturalism, to maintain the French presence in Canada, lest the British element be attracted to the concept of the American melting pot, "hardly a desirable prospect."

Peter Swan, director of the Royal Ontario Museum, said he found Canadians to be lacking in pride of ethnic cultures. "I do not mean," he explained, "the pride, say, of the Japanese in . . . being Japanese. I mean the pride of the rest of us in their 'Japanese-ness.' Pride that we have, for instance, so many Italians who could contribute without limit to the multicolored fabric of our society, pride in our Indians, our Greeks, our Poles, our French and even in our British."

Yet for the "ethnics" to dream of themselves as a unified third force is oversimplification, according to Royce Frith, a member of the Royal Commission on Bilingualism and Biculturalism. In doing so, he said, "they would identify less with their own groups and would thereby hinder their contribution to Canada."

While the French and British contributions to the mosaic are given

Canadian Ukrainians have preserved their culture while helping to develop the prairie provinces.

official support in Ottawa, those of other nationalities must be financed by the "ethnics" themselves. The Ukrainian Canadian Committee is very discontented with this situation. Ukrainians are the second largest, and most vocal, of Manitoba's racial groups, and in 1968 the committee asked the provincial government to allow any minority language to be taught in the public schools of areas predominantly populated by that minority. (Under a proposed federal law the French in Manitoba would enjoy bilingual instruction.)

But Manitoba knows from experience the trials of a multilingual school system. In 1897 the Manitoba School Act, designed to please everyone, provided that "where ten of the pupils speak the French language (or any language other than English) as their native language, the teaching of such pupils shall be conducted in French (or other such language) and English upon the bilingual system."

By 1916 the Minister of Education was complaining at length about his difficulties. In one school there were twenty-seven Poles, ten Germans, and seven Ukrainians. Polish-English and German-English teachers handled the lot, with the Ukrainian youngsters being taught only in English, although they overheard a lot of Polish and German. Teachers who spoke English and Hungarian or English and Ukrainian were in great demand, however inadequate they might be as pedagogues. Finally the minister had a request for a teacher who spoke Gaelic as well as English (there were plenty of Scots in Manitoba, too), and he gave up. The province promptly abolished all bilingual schools —to the outrage of the French-speaking inhabitants, who contended that their constitutional rights under the British North America Act had been violated.

Generally the home and the church have been expected to provide language instruction. In Toronto, for example, in addition to their regular schooling, twelve hundred young Orthodox Greeks attend "ethnic" school two or three times a week. There, little girls, with dark hair pulled into tight braids and gold earrings in their pierced ears, pour over Greek textbooks. Ukrainian Catholic nuns run four day-schools, while Ukrainian Catholic Basilian Fathers staff a high school with two hundred students. At Christ the Saviour Church Hall the Grand Duchess Olga School holds sessions every Saturday in Russian literature, history, music, and folk dancing.

162

Dancing is one of the major expressions of ethnicity. At the Toronto Buddhist Church 150 young people, mostly Japanese, have been taught ceremonial dances. At the right season a visitor may see them perform, as we did, in the big square in front of Toronto's soaring new city hall. That mid-July day the kimonoed Bon Odori dancers were celebrating the feast of O-Bon, which marks "the oneness of life." They were also demonstrating the multiplicity of cultures in Canada.

Linguistic differences, native dances and foods, fancy dress on certain occasions—all are encouraged in the mosaic. But in Canada, as in the United States, there's a limit to tolerance. The Hutterites have discovered that.

In 1874, when the Russian Mennonites emigrated to Canada, some of the Hutterian Brethren decided to stay on in the Dakota Territory. Other groups joined them in 1875 and 1877, and for more than forty years they prospered in isolation. By 1915 there were 1,700 of them, living in seventeen "colonies." These were large farms where the quaintly dressed, German-speaking Hutterites, usually in groups of a hundred, lived self-sufficient, disciplined communal lives. Their system was based on their interpretation of the ways of the early Christians, who, according to the Bible (Acts 2:44–45), "had all things common" and "parted them to all men as every man had need." They were also pacifist, to such a degree that they would not defend themselves against even the most flagrant aggression.

When the United States entered World War I, they were obvious targets for local "patriots." True to their principles, they stood by meekly when a mob attacked one colony, driving off two hundred steers and a thousand sheep. There was no provision in the draft laws then for conscientious objectors. Hutterite boys had to either submit to the draft and ask for noncombatant duty when they reached boot camp, usually without success, or go to prison.

Four boys, sent to Alcatraz and Fort Leavenworth, were refused clothes and blankets, were forced to stand for hours out in the cold, or were manacled to bars so they had to stand on their toes. Two died as a result of these abuses, and the other two were later discharged, completely broken. Consequently, in 1918, all but one colony emigrated to Manitoba and Alberta.

The Canadian Government, as it had to other pacifist sects, assured them military exemption. Furthermore, they would not be required to take an oath in court; they could live as a "commonwealth"; they could establish independent schools for their children. So many of Canada's stalwart young farmers had gone to war and been killed that the country needed men to work the land, and the Hutterites were welcomed.

They settled on prime farm country, shrewdly chosen by these expert farmers, and not only did they make the earth yield bumper crops but they themselves followed the Biblical injunction to "be fruitful and multiply." There are now ten thousand Hutterites in Canada, since their number has been doubling every sixteen years.

As each colony outgrew its land, the brethren bought more of the best available; they had the funds to outbid any independent farmer. They now own approximately a half million acres, in fifty-eight colonies scattered across southern Alberta. Their steady acquisition of land led the Alberta legislature to put restrictions on future purchases. Under a provincial law the Hutterites cannot buy additional acreage within forty miles of an existing colony, a new colony cannot possess more than 6,400 acres, and land must be offered for public sale for ninety days before the Hutterites can buy it.

In 1964 a Hutterite colony defied the act by purchasing 6,240 acres from four farmers. The Premier of Alberta brought charges against the colony in 1965, and early in 1969 the Supreme Court of Canada ruled that the province had the right to regulate and control in the public interest "the use of large areas of land in Alberta for the purposes of communal living."

By 1954 there were twenty-two colonies in Manitoba, farming a total of eighty-five thousand acres. In the next ten years seventeen more were established. In Saskatchewan the Hutterites have only seven colonies. But everywhere there has been agitation against them, although not legislative action as in Alberta. In the heart of Canada's Bible Belt what is the objection to these people who live so strictly by the Good Book?

As might be expected, it's basically economic. The Hutterites have been spreading out on the land at a time when much of Canada's rural population has been drawn to the cities. The shopkeepers in the small farming towns have been losing customers, and they deeply resent the

Hutterites, who grow most of their own food, bake their own bread, make their own clothes, including shoes, and build their own simple functional furniture. They buy the best farm machinery and trucks (wholesale where they can), but no automobiles, television sets, radios, musical instruments, cigarettes, indoor toilets, or toilet articles. Salt, sugar, and coffee are often purchased wholesale, too. They do not vote or take any part in community affairs; but they pay their taxes and cost the provinces nothing, for there is no crime among them, and they educate their own children and take care of their own sick and aged.

Yet men in the prairies have been known to get into a red-faced fury at the very mention of the word "Hutterite." There has been talk of mob violence, but in Canada that possibility is very unlikely. Any further action taken against the brethren will most probably be legal, encouraged by the 1969 Supreme Court ruling.

The mosaic system seems to work—up to a point. The distinguished Canadian historian William Kilbourn in his *Making of the Nation*, written for a centennial series published in 1967, describes it best: "Canada is a land of no one ideology, no single vision; it is a cultural freeport . . . this Austro-Hungary of the new world, with its two official peoples and its multitudes of permitted ones, its ethnic islands and cultural archipelagos."

What, besides geography, holds it together?

9

The French Fact

"Vive le Québec Libre" or "O Canada, Notre Patrie!"

Left, an oddly named Quebec village.
Above, one of Quebec's many farmers.

Quebec's fleur-de-lis flag is more prominently displayed there than the Canadian Maple Leaf.

Crossing into Quebec from the United States is always a pulse-quickening experience. When an American sees the word *douane* (customhouse) at the border stop, he is immediately aware of *la diffé-rence*. Even though the customs official, after a quick glance at the American's license plate, courteously does his questioning in English, the visitor starts his journey into Quebec knowing that he is in a foreign country. Perhaps the customs man's accent, or the trim of his moustache, or his non-English, non-American style of shoes play a part in this awareness.

The names on the land change. The St. Lawrence River is suddenly Fleuve St. Laurent. Quebec, itself, is pronounced "Kay-bec." And then begins that tremendous and often mystifying procession of saints. From St. Adalbert, near the northern border of Maine, to St. Zotique, in the southwest corner of the province, there are no fewer than 760 Quebec towns named for saints. They constitute nearly half the municipalities in the province. A lack of enough saints to go around results in duplication that may confuse travelers. There are twenty-three St. Jeans, eighteen Ste. Annes, and fifteen St. Françoises.

To avert chaos and madness in the post office, many of the more popular saints have acquired compound names that intrigue visitors, who may find them hard to pronounce. There is, for example, Sainte Euphémie sur Rivière du Sud and St. Étienne de Beauharnois. Some names, such as St. Calixte de Kilkenny, hint at Quebec's biculturalism; here a colony that was originally Irish was swamped by a later wave of French Canadians.

The Quebec Geographic Board keeps asking town councils to change to non-saint names, and recently St. Agricole de Terrebone became Val des Lacs. Gradually more changes may occur, to the relief of tourists and Quebec map makers. But the names are rooted in history and tradition. The saints took over geographically in 1855 when the United Parliament of Lower and Upper Canada (Quebec and Ontario) gave municipal status to all Roman Catholic parishes.

Quebec's peculiar French-English, Catholic-Protestant mixes are apparent in other names, too. In Montreal one may have a bite at the Grey Nun Snack Bar or the Holy Family Restaurant. There is the Christ-Roi Valet Service, the St. Pierre Drive-Yourself, and the Notre Dame des Victoires Cleaners. As for historical figures of old New France, they also live on, thanks to Champlain Carpets, Montcalm Auto Body, and Maisonneuve (the founder of Montreal) Bowling Lanes.

French purists in Quebec deplore this Anglicized sign language in "the second largest French-speaking city in the world"—the first being Paris, of course. Their struggle to keep Montreal, and Quebec, French goes doggedly on. St. James Street, the center of Montreal's financial quarter, has recently become rue St. Jacques. (Imagine Wall Street suddenly called rue de la Muraille.) Cathedral Street is strictly rue de la Cathédrale, and the sign on the bridge over the Ottawa River, which the tourist crosses as he drives west out of Montreal, was recently changed to read "Lac des Deux Montagnes," the name given by early Quebeckers to the historic Ottawa's estuary, which is dominated by two Laurentian hills.

So Quebec *is* different. Why? How did it become what it is? Knowing the answers isn't required to enjoy the fine scenery and the "*hospitalité* spoken here" charm emphasized in the travel advertisements. But a trip to the province will mean more, and be a lot more fun, too, if one is cognizant of what lies behind the *hospitalité*. Command of a few words of French would also be a convenience.

First, though, a brief geography lesson.

Quebec covers 594,860 square miles, about 15 per cent of the total area of Canada. It is the largest Canadian province and has been called "Canada's Texas." Climatically it is Texas blended with Alaska. In the south it has orchards and farms (some growing tobacco), while around Ungava Bay, 1,200 miles north, it is barren rock with tundra or muskeg in summer and snow and ice in winter.

Quebec's sheer size and geographic situation reinforce the notion of some Québecois that their province is a nation, especially when they ignore (as does the official map of Quebec) the boundary with Labrador, the mainland portion of Newfoundland. Quebec and Newfoundland quarrel about this. Quebec, in any event, is all but surrounded by salt water—Hudson Bay on the west, Hudson Strait on the north, and the Gulf of St. Lawrence on the east, with the St. Lawrence estuary dipping into its southern region.

Tourist maps of Quebec often do not bother to show the northern half of the province lying above the 52nd parallel. There are simply no roads or railroads there. Few Québecois have availed themselves of the limited air and boat services to the area, but mining operations in the Ungava region have now created a few settlements. Mostly the land and water are left to the Eskimos and to American sportsmen who fly in by charter plane for a few days of expensive hunting and fishing.

The five and a half million Québecois still find plenty of room in the comparatively narrow St. Lawrence-Ottawa river valley. It is, after all, fifteen hundred miles long and up to four hundred miles wide. It extends from the mining and timber settlements north and east of Ontario, to the Gaspé Peninsula, where tradition and occupation are maritime.

Nearly half the population lives in the heartland of Quebec, which

170

extends 175 miles from Quebec City southward up the St. Lawrence to Montreal. Here are the oldest towns, the oldest roads, the oldest families. Jacques Cartier explored the Gulf of St. Lawrence in the 1530's. Samuel Champlain founded what was to become Quebec City in 1608, and the Jesuit missionaries, including Père Marquette, and the fur traders followed. For 150 years settlements—Quebec City itself, Trois Rivières (Three Rivers), and Montreal—grew up.

Under the French colonialist system the king deeded large areas of land to his chosen seigneurs. These feudal lords assumed responsibility for bringing in settlers, habitants, who cleared off trees, worked the farms, and answered the seigneurs' call for road building and military service. Habitants serving their seigneurs pushed back the woods to clear the long, narrow strips of farmland that one can see, even today, reaching up from the shore. Every farm needed some frontage on the great river; besides, the low shoreland was always richer, and no one wanted to be cut off in the less fertile backlands. As generations passed, the land became divided into ever narrowing strips.

Driving northeast from Montreal on Route 2 through Repentigny, Saint Sulpice, and Berthierville, and then through Trois Rivières to Cap de la Madeleine and Donnacona and finally Quebec City, one encounters history on nearly every mailbox. The descendants of the Normans and Bretons and others who settled here in the seventeenth century are still on the land. There are, for example, the Le Royers, the Cherriers, the Benoits, the Bourgeaus, the Lévesques, and many others. Their farms, after 250 years, are still arduously tilled for fruit, vegetables, and small crops. Dairying is an important part of the farm industry. The houses and barns are seldom pretentious, but they stand solid against the winter snows and in summer gleam with fresh paint—bold blue, green, chartreuse, or shrimp pink. Some display all these colors.

This was old New France, and in many stretches of the provincial hinterland it's still there. One may find it in the Richelieu River valley. It may be seen running north from Lake Champlain and the St. Lawrence, or on a side trip north from Cap de la Madeleine, near Trois Rivières, 103 miles up the St. Maurice to the lumber town of La Tuque.

But France's dream of exploiting Canada while the English were settling the American colonies was dashed in 1759, when General James Wolfe stealthily maneuvered his British regulars up the cliffside at dawn to defeat a surprised French garrison on the Plains of Abraham, now a handsome park site just beyond the old walled city of Quebec. French military forces abandoned Canada, and the British redcoats took command.

With the departing French troops went most French civilians of wealth and learning. For them the future in a British-held Canada looked bleak indeed. Left were sixty thousand hardy commoners—farmers, trappers, and voyageurs—to fend for themselves.

These habitants established what is known in Canada today as "the French Fact." The story of how they survived and multiplied (one hundred times in two hundred years) is one of hardship and struggle that still continues. Mason Wade, an American historian, has written a comprehensive account in his book *The French Canadians, 1760–1967,* recently updated and reissued in two thick but interest-packed paperback volumes.

The abandoned habitants clung together, working in French, teaching in French, and praying in French. Unlike migrants of many nationalities, including the French in the United States, the French Canadians preserved their Frenchness. This, in essence the French Fact, at once plagues modern Canada and gives it the heritage of two great cultures—French as well as English.

But the habitants' steadfast solidarity also isolated them. While English Canada was reaching out to the United States and through the British Empire, now the Commonwealth, to the world and keeping up with it, the Québecois drew inward. While English Canada and the United States were advancing economically, politically, and socially into the twentieth century, Quebec, preserving its seventeenth- and eighteenth-century ways, grew backward and poor. The French Fact became a costly heritage.

The quaintness that is publicized to attract visitors and that visitors undoubtedly enjoy proved a mixed blessing. It is abhorrent to present-day Quebeckers pressing for evolution—or revolution.

"We can't be an inner colony any longer," says René Lévesque, who leads a movement to break Quebec away from the rest of Canada. "You know, quaint old Quebec—a sort of nice reservation inside the

172

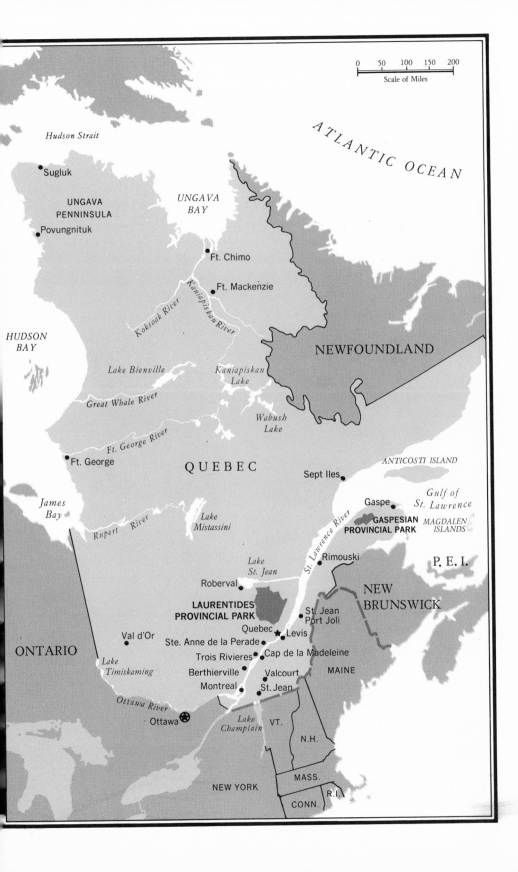

Scale of Miles
0   50   100   150   200

ATLANTIC OCEAN

Hudson Strait

• Sugluk

UNGAVA
PENNINSULA

*UNGAVA
BAY*

• Povungnituk

• Ft. Chimo

• Ft. Mackenzie

Koksoak River

Kaniapiskau River

*HUDSON
BAY*

Lake Bienville

*Kaniapiskau
Lake*

NEWFOUNDLAND

Great Whale River

*Wabush
Lake*

Ft. George River

• Ft. George

QUEBEC

ANTICOSTI ISLAND

• Sept Iles

*James
Bay*

Rupert   River

*Lake
Mistassini*

Gaspe •

*Gulf of
St. Lawrence*

GASPESIAN
PROVINCIAL PARK

*MAGDALEN
ISLANDS*

St. Lawrence River

• Rimouski

P. E. I.

*Lake
St. Jean*

Roberval •

LAURENTIDES
PROVINCIAL PARK

NEW
BRUNSWICK

ONTARIO

• Val d'Or

Ste. Anne de la Perade •

Quebec ★ • Levis

St. Jean
Port Joli

*Lake
Timiskaming*

Trois Rivieres •

• Cap de la Madeleine

Berthierville •

Valcourt •

MAINE

Montreal •

• St. Jean

Ottawa River

⊗ Ottawa

*Lake
Champlain*

VT.

N.H.

NEW YORK

MASS.

R.I.

CONN.

country."

A restlessness began to stir the old order in the early 1900's. There was resentment over the backwardness of the average French Canadian and over the domination of what economic development there was by English-Canadian and American management and capital. Quebec was attracting industries because of its reservoir of ores, timber, and pulp, its cheap hydroelectric power, and its cheap French-Canadian labor.

Ambitious young Québecois fretted over the fact that the classical colleges run by ultraconservative Roman Catholic priests prepared French Canadians for careers in the priesthood, law, and education— never for engineering, finance, or business management.

They fumed even more when Maurice Duplessis, provincial premier for all but five years from 1936 until his death in 1959, ran Quebec as though it were a fiefdom. He made all the arrangements with industrialists, and in exchange for their political support, he promised them cheap and trouble-free labor.

Duplessis and the Roman Catholic hierarchy maintained a similarly cozy arrangement. The safe, old-fashioned schools were bound to a rigid status quo. Training in technology or science was never countenanced, and the so-called manual-training courses for boys were confined to the level of handicrafts. In the late 1950's boys were still being taught how to make birch bark canoes.

Among those who protested the state of affairs in Quebec was Pierre Elliott Trudeau, a French-Canadian law student fresh from studies at Harvard, the Sorbonne, and the London School of Economics. He became Prime Minister of Canada in 1968. But in 1950 he helped found the Montreal magazine *Cité Libre* and wrote essays in it attacking Duplessis.

Dissident forces rallied around Jean Lesage, the province's Liberal party leader, and when he won the election of June, 1960, the Quiet Revolution was on. This "revolution" has often been confused in outsiders' minds with the 1963 Montreal mailbox bombings that maimed and killed. It has been misidentified with the hostile demonstrations against Queen Elizabeth II and with other overt acts by extremists.

The Quiet Revolution was, in fact, a reform program pushed over a six-year period by Lesage and his long-repressed supporters. Its aim was to haul Quebec quickly into the twentieth century. The first orders of business were transferring the school system from church control to secular administration and modernizing education. High schools were centralized and equipped with laboratories and up-to-date machines. In these projects Lesage had the full cooperation of new, enlightened church leaders, headed by Paul-Emile Cardinal Léger, then the Archbishop of Montreal.

The provincial legislative assembly passed laws giving women full rights, strengthening labor unions, providing social services, and encouraging investment in industry.

The Lesage government eventually ran into trouble in the conservative rural regions, where the big new schools were sometimes so centralized as to require pupils to take long interurban bus trips. More importantly, the villagers lost the feeling that their schools were actually theirs. The political and social reforms made less of an impact than did the inevitably higher taxes. Many henchmen of the late Premier Duplessis complained of the loss of patronage. To farmers in the hinterlands all the road building seemed to involve high-speed multilane highways and fancy cloverleaves around Montreal, while rural needs were neglected.

Lesage's Liberals lost the 1966 election to the inheritors of Duplessis' National Union party. Daniel Johnson, the new Premier, could not repeal the Quiet Revolution, although he tried to slow it down while he coped with the rising discontent in a prospering electorate over Quebec's subordinate place in the Canadian Confederation.

Québecois argue today over whether the Lesage government tried to do too much too fast. Some believe its program was the beginning of a renaissance that will enrich life, culturally and economically, for all Canada in generations to come. Others protest that it raised Quebec to that state of a little learning that is proverbially so dangerous. It expanded the universities, but it also set the campuses aflame with extremism, with students asserting that all of Quebec's ties to English Canada should be burned.

These extremists came to dominate Quebec's New Left in the 1960's. Although factious and splinter-prone, they rallied around René Lévesque, one-time Lesage reform minister, to form a consolidated political organization that brought them into the Quebec body politic in the election of April, 1970.

Mr. Lévesque founded this organization, *Le Parti Québecois*, on a platform calling for complete political independence from Canada without severing the economic umbilical. In short, the party demanded that Quebec become a sovereign state with a Common Market relationship with Canada. Feasible or not, this solution to Quebec's problem was made to sound reasonable, if not inevitable, by the persuasive and disarming Mr. Lévesque. The former Montreal journalist and television personality excited a large following of young radicals while winning over several thousands of traditional conservatives who had reluctantly lost faith in the faltering National Union government. Jean-Jacques Bertrand, a well-meaning party wheel horse who had succeeded to the premiership on the death of Mr. Johnson, lost his grip trying to hold both the traditionalists and the separatists. In the end, Premier Bertrand's uncertain control over Quebec affairs allowed old businesses to fail, new business ventures to lapse, and unemployment to rise severely.

Alarmed both by Mr. Bertrand's waverings and by the upsurgence of Lévesque separatists, the voters in decisive numbers deemed it wiser and safer to return the government to the Liberals who had promised federalism and prosperity. Robert Bourassa, a Harvard- and Oxford-trained economist, became, at thirty-six, the youngest premier in Quebec history. He won the election by arguing that Quebeckers wanted employment ("good jobs" in French), not separatism. He agreed with his fellow Quebecker Prime Minister Trudeau that Quebec, liberated from ignorance, political corruption, and church conservatism, could best preserve its French culture and attain its aspirations by taking part wholeheartedly in the federal state that is Canada. All Quebec needs, in the Trudeau-Bourassa view, is a little elbowroom through changes in Canada's constitution.

Routing the National Union party, Bourassa Liberals won an extraordinary majority of legislative assembly seats—73 out of 108. But the separatists won at least a moral victory. The Parti Québecois captured 23 per cent of the popular vote and put separatists (seven) in the assembly for the first time. But while the party became a fact of political life in Quebec, its leader, Mr. Lévesque, lost his seat to a

Liberal, and his role as separatist leader was thrown in doubt.

However, if the separatists are relatively few in the total electorate, their voice is loud and boisterous in the cities. In Montreal they have demonstrated at every opportunity against federalism and have now abandoned the cause of bilingualism in Quebec for that of French-speech-only in schools, in the street, and in places of work. In one 1969 instance a separatist-nationalist demonstration protesting the use of the English language at McGill University ended in riotous window-smashing in downtown Montreal. As usual, the so-called English Establishment places—Eaton's Department Store, Birk's Jewelry store, and Morgan's (now owned by Hudson's Bay Company)—were hardest hit.

Prime Minister Trudeau, though a French Canadian, is anathema to the separatists, simply because he entered federal politics and has become the champion of the "one Canada, one nation" concept.

In June, 1968, separatist demonstrators tried to break up the annual St. Jean Baptiste Day parade with homemade bombs because Mr. Trudeau sat in the reviewing stand with Quebec dignitaries. The Prime Minister dodged the Molotov cocktails, refusing to leave the platform while Montreal police in riot regalia beat off the demonstrators and arrested about a hundred.

The St. Jean Baptiste Society, named after Quebec's patron saint, had always been a nonpolitical, patriotic organization. Its annual parades were gala displays featuring pretty girls, marching bands, and colorful floats—a June 24 attraction that tourists often compared with the New Orleans Mardi gras. But after 1968 the society took a turn toward separatist militancy, and in 1969 it openly declared itself on the side of the separatists.

Hopefully, with elected representatives in the provincial assembly in a position to give the separatists an official outlet for their views, they would feel less impelled to demonstrate on the streets. They had always disavowed any responsibility for the bomb-throwing and window-smashing tactics. However, at the outset of the 1970's it was clear that conservative Quebeckers of whatever party made up the vast majority and looked to Mr. Bourassa's new government to restore economic stability and confidence in Quebec's future as a province of Canada.

The idea that Canada might really be "two nations"—English

Canada and French Canada—has been rejected for the time being. It probably will remain so as long as Trudeau is Prime Minister and Mr. Bourassa the Premier. But separatism or no, change is in the air in Quebec. Scientists, engineers, and business managers—as well as classical scholars, lawyers, and teachers—are streaming from the universities. In large measure they built Expo 67, they are designing Montreal's skyscrapers and high-rise apartment houses, and they built the city's remarkable new subway called Le Métro. They constructed the great new hydroelectric dams on the Manicouagan River to supply power for the growing French-Canadian industry.

What the traveler to Quebec may look forward to, therefore, is a view of the oldest continuously inhabited area of North America in a state of turbulent modernization. It will offer many faces—quiet villages dominated by those tall-spired gray stone churches, the new Montreal, and to the north, land so forlorn and remote it can be seen only from a boat or a plane.

Montreal itself presents many faces. There are the new man-made islands of Expo 67, with many of the far-out pavilions intact. How soon will they become dated, as did many of the wonders of the world exhibitions of yesteryear? Now the city is happily planning for 1976, when the summer Olympic games will be held there.

Montreal, whose population today passes two million, is a city of industry, commerce, and finance. It is, in fact, as Chicagoesque as it is Parisian. Although a thousand miles from the Atlantic, it is a great transoceanic port. It is the major transshipping point in North America for wheat from the prairies. Those tall grain elevators along the harbor hold twenty-two million bushels of grain. In the constantly growing cluster of high buildings downtown are the head offices of the two major transcontinental railway systems, of Air Canada, of the International Civil Aviation Organization, and of the International Air Transport Association.

Modern Montreal is also an ancient town. Mayor Jean Drapeau, the man chiefly responsible for Expo 67 and for bringing in the summer Olympics, has preserved the town's impressive Old Quarter. Its narrow streets are not hospitable to automobiles, but those undertaking walking tours will encounter friendly bilingual hosts in the antique shops, the museums, and the little French restaurants. The bronze tablets along the way summarize the story of a landing place for inland voyageurs that became a trading post that became the fur-trading capital of the world. One becomes acquainted with historic names, such as Adam Dollard des Ormeaux, heroic defender of the early city against the Indians, Lambert Closse, first commandant of the Montreal garrison, and Pierre le Moyne, sieur d'Iberville, who went on to found Biloxi, Mississippi.

From atop Mount Royal, the backdrop "mountain" that gave Montreal its name, there is a spectacular panorama of the city, the harbor, the site of Expo 67, and the entrance to the St. Lawrence Seaway. One discovers, too, why Montreal has been called *La Ville des Clochers en la Verdure* ("The City of Belfries in the Greenery"). Some five hundred churches and chapels are sheltered by the trees.

Perhaps the most original work in the field of Canadian culture is being done in Montreal. It is certainly the center of contemporary painting and sculpture, although the English Establishment's Montreal Museum of Fine Arts on Sherbrooke Street is not the place to discover this. One does better browsing among the innumerable shops of art dealers in the neighborhood. Often one may find representative canvases by Jean-Paul Lemieux and Jean-Paul Riopelle, to mention two of the most prominent Quebec painters. Lemieux often paints solitary figures on vast, lonely landscapes, against empty skies. Riopelle's canvases are brilliant abstractions.

If one wants to sample the difference between the English and French Canadas, he must ride Le Métro, Montreal's subway. It was built in the mid-1960's, shortly after Toronto constructed a subway that is comfortable, clean, and austere. But Montreal's sleek aquamarine trains glide along on rubber tires. The city spent one million dollars just to decorate the stations with brilliant tiling and abstract murals created by Montreal artists. There are more than a score of stations, each one different.

The hub of the performing arts in Montreal is the Place des Arts, French Canada's version of Lincoln Center. It contains a 3,000-seat opera house named for Wilfrid Pelletier, a former conductor of the Montreal Symphony who also conducted at the Metropolitan Opera House in New York. It is also the home of the Montreal Symphony. The 1,300-seat Maisonneuve Theatre presents outstanding visiting

Visitors to Expo 67 view a dramatic exhibition in the British pavilion.

troupes, and an 800-seat Port Royal Theatre offers recitals and chamber music concerts.

The French-language theatre in the Place des Arts and elsewhere in the city is lively; it is worthwhile to consult the newspapers for English as well as French presentations.

Montreal has as many good restaurants as it has churches, and no matter how long the visitor stays, he need not eat twice in the same place, although he may often want to. The enticements range from coffeehouses on Mountain Street to the Café de Paris at the Ritz Carlton.

Chez LouLou, with its French bistro atmosphere, is a rendezvous for artists, writers, and the intelligentsia in general, both genuine and pseudo. Le Drug Discothèque, an avant-garde meeting place created by artist François Dallegret, has become a landmark easily recognized by its façade of heavy chain drapery.

There is, of course, The Coffee Mill, a straight English-style coffeehouse noted for its cold sherry soup. The Pam Pam specializes in a mixed grill, and The Rose Marie has a Hungarian chef who prepares a tasty chicken paprika with nocki. Ben's Delicatessen is particularly busy after the theatre, and at the already mentioned Grey Nun Snack Bar one may buy a good hamburger.

Montreal's cuisine is really international, but visitors sooner or later seek out the French places. There is no more delightful or rewarding pursuit in North America than researching Montreal's French restaurants. The way to start is with a reliable guidebook, obtainable at hotels and bookstores.

Here are a few Montreal restaurants recommended by the authors:

Excellent French cuisine and service: Chez Bardet, 591 Henri-Bourassa Boulevard East; Chez La Mère Michel, 1209 Guy Street.

Excellent Provençal menu with appropriate décor: Chez Fanny, 1279 St. Hubert Street.

Seafood: Chez Pauze, 1657 St. Catherine Street West.

Steaks: Moishe's, 3961 St. Laurent Boulevard.

Crepes: Crêpe Bretonne, 808 St. Catherine Street East.

French-Canadian cooking in the Old Quarter (Le Vieux Montreal): Les Filles du Roy, 415 St. Paul Street East; Auberge le Vieux St. Gabriel, 442 St. Gabriel Street.

French cuisine in a bistro setting: Chez Son Père, 907 St. Laurent

Boulevard.

Hotel dining rooms: Café de Paris, Ritz Carlton Hotel; roof dining room, Château Champlain; Beaver Club, Queen Elizabeth Hotel. Le Vaisseau d'Or (The Golden Ship) in the Hotel Windsor is a concert dining salon where good food and wines are served to the accompaniment of baroque music played by a twenty-piece orchestra. When Bach or Vivaldi is on, dinner conversation is off. Montreal's Mayor Jean Drapeau is often there to greet guests; he is the proprietor.

Like the hockey stars of the Montreal Canadiens, the city's medal-winning chefs are well known and numerous. The Swiss-born Rodolphe Doseger, of the Hotel Bonaventure, was a captain of the Canadian team at the 1968 culinary Olympics in Frankfurt, Germany. His co-captain was Pierre Demers, the French Canadian who presides over the kitchens of the Ritz Carlton.

Quebec Province, unlike Ontario, has few cities. In essence, there is Montreal and there is Quebec City. Tourists leaving the former usually head for the latter. They exchange the excitement of a cosmopolis for the charm and quaintness of French Canada's oldest town. It is all French except for the 10 per cent English minority. Its business is, and always has been, government administration. But with the Quiet Revolution it has acquired a skyline and sprawling suburbs.

Most interesting for visitors, however, is the old gray stone city sheltered by the great Gibraltar-type rock. The walls are still there, and thanks to persistent campaigning by the mayor, the seventeenth- and eighteenth-century atmosphere is coming back to life. Only two high structures—the Canadian Pacific's Château Frontenac and the office building of the Price pulp and lumber enterprises—violate the low historic horizon. One may hope and expect that there will be no others. High-rise, according to present planning, is for outside the walls.

Walking down the narrow and winding rue St. Louis, one may have to step off the sidewalk now and then to avoid the fallout from sand-blasters removing layers of latter-day stucco and paint from old stores and dwellings. Re-exposed, the original stone blocks reveal once more the good taste of the architects and the skill of the ancient stonecutters and masons.

Taxis and buses penetrate the walled town, but as in old Montreal, it is best to map out walking tours. The shops are clustered conveniently around the Place d'Armes in the shadow of the commanding Château Frontenac. While the shops are mostly of the souvenir variety, requiring little time to explore, the Musée du Fort in their midst is well worth twenty-five minutes for its electronically animated diorama of the six battles of Quebec. Included is a vivid summary of the drama on the Plains of Abraham on the morning of September 13, 1759.

In approaching this decisive episode in Quebec's history, an American had better forget that James Wolfe, the British general, actually won. The fact that the mortally wounded Wolfe was victor over the mortally wounded Montcalm is never mentioned and is gradually being erased from the record. In 1964 a primitive wooden statue of Wolfe that had stood for decades in a high niche over a street in old Quebec was removed. A separatist leader had warned the owner that if the general wasn't taken down, the building would be bombed. Taking heed, the owner called in the authorities, who arranged for a corps of regimentals to transport the general to asylum in a museum inside the Citadel. There he now stands in state, protected by the Government of Canada.

The Citadel remains a "British" stronghold in French Canada. It is maintained by the federal government, and the Governor General of Canada, the British monarch's personal representative, usually spends a month or two in summer residence there. It was in the Citadel, three hundred feet above the St. Lawrence, that President Roosevelt, Prime Minister Churchill, and Mackenzie King, the Prime Minister of Canada, conferred during World War II.

The Citadel is guarded ceremonially by Canada's famed French-speaking regiment, the Vingt-Deuxieme, popularly known as the "Van Doos." This regiment, which played dramatic roles in both world wars, is stationed at Val Cartier, outside Quebec, but mounts a changing of the guard ceremony in town for summer visitors.

Aside from the private quarters of the Governor General, the Citadel is a restored fort open to the public.

On the Plains of Abraham, beyond the Citadel, is the beautifully kept Battlefields Park, with flower gardens, ancient trees, lawns, and monuments. Statues of both Montcalm and Wolfe are there, but the old notation identifying the British general as the "victor" in 1759 was recently removed. He is memorialized simply for having been mortally wounded on the battlefield.

And never look for Wolfe's Cove, the English name for the inlet where the general's troops began their daring nighttime ascent to the Plains. Maps and guides to Quebec call it *Anse au Foulon* (Fuller's Cove), as it was named before Wolfe came on the scene. About the only manufactured export of New France in old times was the flax grown in the fields around Quebec and treated at the cove of the fullers.

In the park is the Quebec historical and arts museum. It deserves priority in any visitor's itinerary. The provincial Ministry of Cultural Affairs has rearranged the displays according to modern techniques. On view first are the usual memorabilia, but the visitor soon moves on to highly interesting exhibits of eighteenth-century silversmithing, early Quebec wood carving (which in the area of church art was gently moving if never dramatic), and highly enjoyable portraiture and landscapes. Here one may view canvases by Cornelius Krieghoff and see how charmed he was with the country of the habitants, especially in winter. There is also Joseph Legaré, a French Canadian who did remarkable genre scenes of his own time (the mid-nineteenth century) and historical re-creations.

Most visitors see Quebec City in summer, although skiers and Winter Carnival visitors are breaking down the seasonal limits of touring. On starlit, perhaps moonlit, nights tourists from Ohio stroll the Dufferin Terrace—the Château Frontenac's boardwalk—to think their own thoughts and watch freighters bucking the tide to Montreal. Probably they do not pay much attention to the young girls promenading by, until those girls are intercepted by young men. After animated introductions the encounters are resolved by two-by-two retreats into the darkness.

Too many discussions, too many books, treat Quebec as though it were only a problem. Binding two cultures together is as difficult in Canada as it has been elsewhere. But it is not an insoluble problem, as Switzerland, with three languages and cultures, has proven.

Too little has been written about the contribution French culture can make, and has made, to Canada—and to North America, too. When the Quiet Revolution tries to build up and expand French education and the use of the French language, it not only preserves French

A young Quebecker offers homemade model boats for sale.

Canada but performs a service for which we should all be grateful. It enriches Canada as a whole and the environment in which all North Americans live.

Surely Americans, as well as English Canadians, should be happy to have first-class French universities in neighboring Quebec. While a year at the Sorbonne in Paris is as rightly coveted by students as a year at Cambridge or Oxford, Quebec universities may soon offer excellent opportunities for French education—without the cost of transatlantic travel. And the universities *are* excellent on the classical level, although the French spoken elsewhere may not be of the purest variety.

There are many jokes among the Québecois about the French spoken in the province. Prime Minister Trudeau, who grew up with it, once called it "lousy." Professor Emile Bessette, who teaches French literature at the University of Montreal, says that of the three thousand words making up the basic French-Canadian vocabulary nearly half are Anglicisms. While most Quebeckers are sensitive to criticism, they are nevertheless making sincere and strenuous efforts today to improve their speech. This is why the government made an arrangement with France a few years ago to exchange students, teachers, books, and radio and television programs. Surely the caliber of Quebec's French will not improve if its people mix only with their English-speaking neighbors. There are more French Canadians, as it is, who speak acceptable English than there are English Canadians who speak even passable French. This is one reason for the patois often heard in Quebec. Another factor, of course, is the archaic forms preserved by the habitants' long isolation.

Yet out of Canada's problems with language has emerged a vital and exploding culture. In 1965 Edmund Wilson, in his *O Canada—An American's Notes on Canadian Culture,* praised much of the literary output to that date. And the output is continuing.

Among the established Quebec writers, two must be mentioned, one a novelist, the other an actor-playwright.

Gabrielle Roy, a leading author in both French and English, is not a Québecoise. She was born in 1909 in St. Boniface, a French-speaking community just south of Winnipeg, Manitoba. She taught school, became interested in the theatre, and went to Paris to study drama. On her return to Canada in 1939 she began writing for magazines in Montreal, and in 1945 she was widely praised for *Bonheur d'Occasion,* a novel of life in an industrial district of that city. It was published in English as *The Tin Flute.* Other novels followed, and with them came France's prestigious *Prix Fémina* and the medal of the French Academy. Miss Roy, as a novelist, was one of the first to discuss the two Canadas, a theme also pursued in the novels of Quebec's leading English-speaking author, Hugh MacLennan of McGill University.

Gratien Gélinas, born near Trois Rivières (also in 1909) of a French-Canadian father and a Scotch-Irish mother, is one of Quebec's outstanding personages of the theatre. He is known across Canada as a playwright, director, producer, and actor. He was still an insurance salesman in 1939 when he became an "attraction," doing sketches in Montreal cabarets. He went into radio, then television. He did a play, *Tit-coq;* entitled *Little Rooster* in English, it toured cities from coast to coast and reached Broadway. He has earned critical acclaim and has been hailed as "the Charlie Chaplin of Canada."

These are veteran artists, but the new wave is winning French awards, too. Marie-Claire Blais, a very young Montrealer, took the coveted *Prix Medicis* for one of her novels. To improve the quality of Quebec's French and promote its French culture, the Ministry of Cultural Affairs grants $100,000 a year in subsidies to writers and publishers. And $30,000 more is distributed to prize winners for works offered in literary competition.

Expo 67, therefore, is not the only evidence of the lively state of the arts and sciences in Quebec. Many young Québecois exuberantly feel themselves breaking out of the ancient cocoon. They find the air electrically charged with excitement. It is natural for them to lash out against the British and charge that the English Canadians wove the cocoon. It is natural, too, for them to reach out to France, not only for culture but also for guidance, especially when de Gaulle himself shouted *"Vive le Québec Libre."*

But visitors to Quebec must note that a great majority of Quebeckers —certainly a majority of the voters—are alarmed that the old protective covering is breaking open so rapidly. For all the confinement, the cocoon was comfortable and snug for 250 years. As recent elections have shown, most Québecois would like the Quiet Revolution to be cooled to a gradual evolution.

An American in Quebec will soon sense vibrations, however, and he may be startled the first time he hears a hotheaded separatist say "I am a Québecois, not a Canadian."

Or should an American on a vacation or a short visit be concerned about Quebec's future? Why not pay for the charming quaintness, the French atmosphere and delectable food, the enchanting scenery, and, perhaps, fine fishing, and let it go at that when coming back across the border?

What, in fact, would happen if a majority of the people of the province he has just visited were Québecois through and through and wanted no part of the rest of Canada? Not one of the twenty million Canadians today foresees a civil war like the horror that the United States experienced from 1860 to 1865. Yet it is hard to believe that the Prime Minister of the hour would not rise to declare: "A house divided cannot stand."

The defection or secession of Quebec would lead to the fall of Canada as our northern neighbor. Alone, Quebec would have to lean for economic and political support either on France or the United States. Any idea that France, for all of General de Gaulle's words of affection, would take a fledgling Quebec under her wing runs counter to 250 years of history. If France could afford such a move, would the United States, under the Monroe Doctrine, tolerate such interference on this continent? An Americanized Quebec however, would be self-defeating, with the French Fact disappearing into the melting pot.

It would be a sad time for all. English Canada could easily disintegrate, with the Boston-oriented Maritime Provinces reaching as quickly as possible for New England, and British Columbia becoming British California.

Quebec is, then, the keystone of Canada in a very real sense. With it Canada is a difficult marriage, but without it Canada would not be Canada.

As the late Premier Daniel Johnson once said: "It might be better to amend the marriage contract [that is, revise the Canadian constitution] than to go through all the hardships and explosive damages of divorce."

La Belle Province, alone and isolated, would not be a gay divorcée.

10

The Mics, the Macs, and the Micmacs

"We may be needy, but we can still afford the luxury of self-government."

*ft, François, one of Newfoundland's fishing out-
rts. Above, artisans in a Nova Scotia shipyard.*

A nineteenth-century primitive painting of Maritime Micmacs

Aɴʏ Aᴍᴇʀɪᴄᴀɴ ᴡʜᴏ is tired of neon-lit tourist strips, of shoulder-to-shoulder summer cottages shutting out his view of the sea, and of garish billboards blocking off the distant mountains will find that Canada generally provides the most convenient escape. For haunting loneliness within easy reach, for the strangely foreign in the midst of the familiar, he might well take a long look at Canada's Atlantic Provinces.

The seagirt cluster, comprising Newfoundland, New Brunswick, Nova Scotia, and Prince Edward Island, is in some ways the very essence of the Big Land, though much smaller and poorer than the

192

rest of the country. The impoverished four would probably do better economically under a single provincial government, and for more than a century a Maritime Union (without Newfoundland, the other three have always been called the Maritimes) has periodically been discussed. In fact, Canada's larger Confederation grew out of one such proposal in the 1860's. While the big Confederation eventually came about, a Maritime Union never has, although the idea is again in the air. Each of the little provinces has been too independent in the past for union, forever pulling and hauling against any central authority. As a Prince Edward Islander said, "We may be needy, but we can still afford the luxury of self-government." With the bigger, richer provinces tending to take the same attitude, Canadian unity has always been precarious.

Quebec nationalists are in fact Johnny-come-latelies on the secession scene. Nova Scotia threatened to secede a century ago. Prince Edward Island refused for years to become part of the Confederation. And Newfoundland would not join Canada until 1949, after a bare majority of the islanders had approved the union. Perhaps this individuality is due to the fact that so many of these people *are* islanders, cut off for a good part of every year from easy access by the rest of mankind. Even today, the Atlantic Provinces remain, as Canadians say, "a place where you can't get from here to there," especially during the winter.

Newfoundland is the tenth-largest island in the world—with a population of less than half a million. Prince Edward Island, with a population of 100,000, must be one of the world's smallest islands having its own legislature. Parts of Nova Scotia are recognized islands: minute Madame Island and big and beautiful Cape Breton Island, itself almost cut into two segments by Bras d'Or Lake. Indeed the whole of Nova Scotia is surrounded by open water except for the sixteen-mile boundary, itself a river, that it shares with New Brunswick, and no point in the province is more than thirty-five miles from the sea.

This mosaic of land and water is also, like the rest of Canada, a mosaic of peoples. In Nova Scotia Scots, Irish, English, Germans, French Acadians, and a few Negroes go their cultural ways, with the Micmac Indians in the background, as they have been ever since Champlain's day. The Scots easily dominate the whole. They are strong on Prince Edward Island, too, while on Newfoundland the people are largely of Irish and Devon English descent. In New Brunswick the majority are English—many descended from refugee Tories —but 40 per cent are Acadian French.

The ever-present sea has created this complexity of peoples and has influenced the whole course of the provinces' history. When European countries began expanding westward, this stretch of the North American coast was closest to Europe, and it was here that many of the earliest explorers landed first.

There is mounting evidence that Leif Ericson's Vinland was at L'Anse aux Meadows in northern Newfoundland. For decades archaeologists sought Vinland much farther south, because of the wild grapes that Leif had reported to be flourishing at his settlement. They were unaware of the marked change in climate that took place in that area after Leif's day. But Viking sites on Greenland have revealed that the southern coast of that country was richly productive farmland centuries ago, and similar weather conditions probably prevailed on Newfoundland.

The archaeologist who has insisted most stubbornly that Leif was on Newfoundland is an Oslo man, Helge Ingstad, who had been digging at L'Anse aux Meadows on the north coast for seven seasons before he made a significant find in 1968. He had previously discovered traces of thirty buildings, but no artifacts. Articles of everyday use are always easier to pinpoint in time than stone walls. So, although the foundations he had uncovered followed characteristically Norse plans, opponents could still argue that they had been laid by fifteenth-century Basques, for instance, who are thought by some authorities to have fished the Newfoundland Banks.

But Ingstad persisted, and in 1968 he finally found a belt buckle that has been identified as a type used in Norway from the ninth to the eleventh centuries. Somehow it had escaped the Eskimos, who are thorough scavengers, picking a site clean of any useful metal, bone, or wood. Although he found no additional artifacts in the summer of 1969, Ingstad will doubtless persist in his excavations.

It is hard to determine the number of times Newfoundland was discovered. Officially, John Cabot did so, entering the harbor at what is now St. John's on the evening of St. John's Day, 1497. He promptly claimed this "New Founde Isle" in the name of his sovereign, Henry

VII. The place became such a base for fishermen of all nations that England had to keep reaffirming her right of possession. In 1528, on King Henry's orders, a merchant named Bute founded a colony there. In 1583 Sir Humphrey Gilbert claimed Newfoundland for England again, this time in the name of Queen Elizabeth I. Captain Hayes, who commanded that expedition's *Golden Hind,* described St. John's as a populous place much frequented by ships.

A brief drive from St. John's brings the tourist to Conception Bay, where the Portuguese discoverer, Gaspar Corte-Real, claimed the island for *his* king in 1500. Had he explored the place thoroughly, he would have learned that he was three years too late. At the extreme north side of the bay, on a rock standing at the base of a cliff one hundred feet from the sea, Cabot and his crew had inscribed their names. Even today, the words "IO CABOTO" can plainly be seen, and there are traces of the other names.

The Basques used as their harbor a point on Newfoundland's south shore, which they named Placentia, described in 1611 as a place of considerable trade. Then, in 1662, the French moved in, determined to control the island that commanded the entrance to the Gulf of St. Lawrence. The French built impressive fortifications, a monastery, and a church, of which nothing remains now but a few old cannons besides a handful of moldering Basque gravestones near the Anglican church. The Basques left a bigger monument to their presence in the Newfoundland dog, said to be a cross between Basque ships' dogs of the powerful Great Pyrenees breed and Canadian wolves.

There's little other trace of its ancient past left on Newfoundland today. St. John's was fought over, looted, and burned too many times for early structures to have survived. The town was attacked by a Dutch squadron under the famous Admiral Michel de Ruyter in 1665, by the French from Placentia in 1696 and again in 1708, and finally by the French from Quebec in 1762. The old port took additional punishment when English troops from Halifax recaptured it. Other early settlements had similar histories.

There weren't many. Colonies were encouraged only during Newfoundland's early years. A few settlers came in under the aegis of Lord Baltimore, who was finally driven to Maryland by the climate. Others arrived from the Isle of Jersey and from Ireland. By 1633, however,

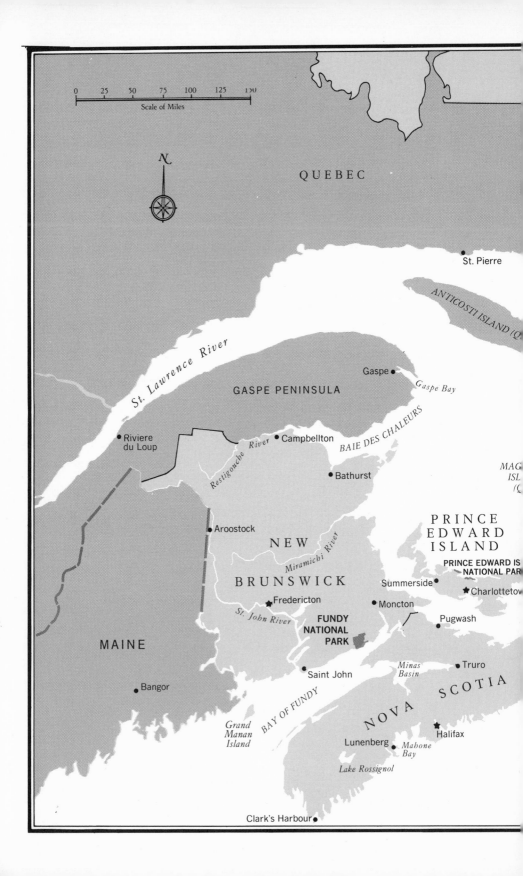

0   25   50   75   100   125   1ᴉ0
Scale of Miles

N

QUEBEC

St. Pierre

ANTICOSTI ISLAND (Q

St. Lawrence River

GASPE PENINSULA

Gaspe

Gaspe Bay

Riviere
du Loup

Restigouche River

Campbellton

BAIE DES CHALEURS

Bathurst

MAG
ISL
(Q

Aroostock

NEW

Miramichi River

PRINCE
EDWARD
ISLAND

PRINCE EDWARD IS
NATIONAL PAR

BRUNSWICK

Summerside

Charlottetow

Fredericton

St. John River

FUNDY
NATIONAL
PARK

Moncton

Pugwash

MAINE

Minas
Basin

Truro

SCOTIA

Saint John

Bangor

BAY OF FUNDY

NOVA

Grand
Manan
Island

Halifax

Lunenberg

Mahone
Bay

Lake Rossignol

Clark's Harbour

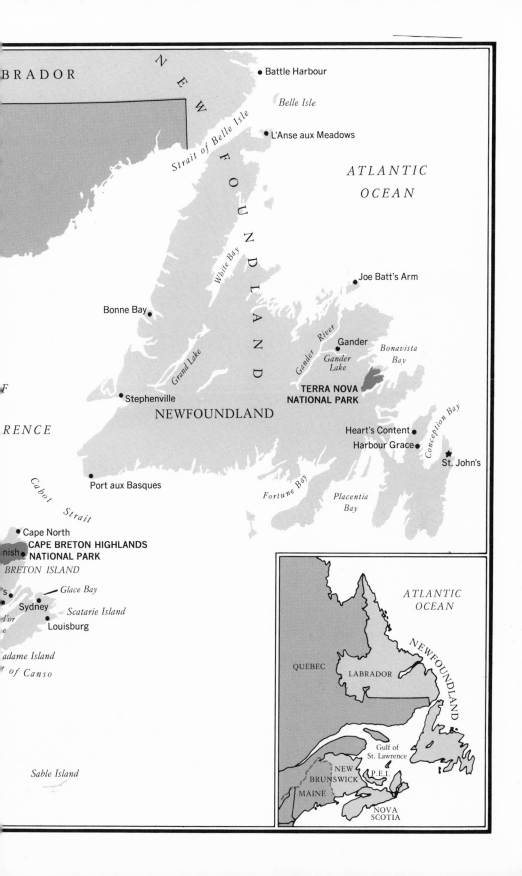

powerful merchants from the west of England had a monopoly on the fishing trade. Wanting no competition from colonists, they persuaded the English government to pass laws calculated to make settled life on Newfoundland impossible. One law forbade chimneys on houses so that no one could live through the Newfoundland winter. Another forbidding the cultivation of land was designed to starve out those who had endured the cold. Then there was the custom whereby the first fishing captain to reach Newfoundland each spring became the island's "admiral" for the season. This potentate was regularly so brutal to the settlers that it's a wonder they didn't abandon the place and leave it as the merchants wanted it, "a great ship moored near the Banks for the convenience of English fishermen."

But the settlers refused to leave. Instead, they scattered to the remote coves that fringe Newfoundland's six thousand miles of coastline. There they built and cultivated and fished as they pleased in tiny hamlets clinging to the rocks above many a wild shore. Using for fertilizer small smeltlike fish, the capelins, which swarm into the coves at certain times of the year, they grew vegetables. On the hillsides they picked various wild berries. They kept cows and goats for milk and meat and hides, and sheep for wool. Almost to the day in 1949 that Newfoundland entered the Canadian Confederation, the Newfies— say it with a smile—were as self-sufficient as early pioneers.

Fishing was their life, and in those days there was a steady demand, particularly from Europe, for the cod that they caught from small boats and then salted and dried in the sun and the wind on platforms thrust high on thin stiltlike legs. There were by then 1,900 outports with their fantastic names: Tickle Cove and Blow Me Down and Joe Batt's Arm, Ireland's Eye and Heart's Delight and Heart's Content. With a total of forty miles of road on the island, the outports could be reached only by boat. The inhabitants had their own patois and songs and foods.

As late as 1949 they still lacked electricity, telephones, roads, schools (to any extent), doctors, and nurses. Not knowing what they were missing, they were illiterate but content, until the time came when a one-man cod-drying operation could no longer provide even the barest of livings.

Big European trawlers operating offshore were scooping up the fish for modern processing plants back home. Indeed, the Russians had a seagoing plant right out there with their fishing fleet. Perforce, the provincial government had to resort to "centralization," encouraging fishing families, by substantial money grants, to move to central locations, which could then provide enough men to operate diesel-powered craft and to run a modern packing plant. At these enlarged ports there would also be enough people to support schools, power lines, telephones, and medical services. At last report, people from three hundred outports had accepted the government's offer. Not a few migrants took their houses along, floating them to new locations on rafts made buoyant by a base of empty oil drums.

The rest of the outports keep going with the help of welfare checks. Change is slow. For years to come travelers will still be able to photograph those fantastic tiny settlements that are like nothing else in North America.

For all its quaintness, Newfoundland was twice the scene of important breakthroughs in modern communications. One outport already mentioned, Heart's Content, was a center of world attention on July 27, 1866, when the *Great Eastern,* the "iron" ship that was almost a myth, laid in its deep cove the western end of the second transatlantic cable. The first had been a three weeks' wonder, until it expired. But from 1866 until today the connection at Heart's Content has never been broken. On the top of St. John's Signal Hill thirty-five years later, in December, 1901, a dapper little Italian, Marchese Guglielmo Marconi, received the first transatlantic wireless signal sent from his station at Poldhu, Cornwall, in England. He had chosen Newfoundland because it was the North American point nearest Europe.

For the same reason the backward little island, where most of the natives traveled in rowboats, was the take-off point for four of the earliest transatlantic flights. The first was piloted by Albert C. Read in a U.S. Navy flying boat in May, 1919. He came down in the Azores before going on to Lisbon, so it wasn't nonstop. The first nonstop flight, made by Alcock and Brown, left St. John's on June 14 of the same year and reached Clifden, Ireland, in sixteen hours and twelve minutes. Wiley Post and Harold Gatty took five minutes more in their flight from Harbour Grace, Newfoundland, to Ireland in June, 1932, while Amelia Earhart, the first woman to fly the course alone, leaving in May of that year from the same old town, reached Ireland in under fifteen hours.

All of the bleak mountainous section of Canada's most easterly peninsula lies within Newfoundland's official boundaries. With its dark rocky terrain and freezing weather for eight months of every year, Labrador has been called "the land which God gave Cain," but its wealth of minerals and hydroelectric power may eventually make "haves" instead of "have-nots" of Canada's Newfies.

It is 565 miles by the rambling new Trans-Canada Highway from St. John's to Port aux Basques, where the Canadian National's car-and-passenger ferry debarks for North Sydney, Nova Scotia. That ferry trip takes nine hours. But in summer anyone who prefers less driving and more time at sea can turn off the highway some thirty miles out of St. John's and take a short stretch of gravel road to the Argentia ferry, which takes seventeen hours, from 8 P.M. to 1 P.M. the next day, to cross.

Air service between Newfoundland and the rest of Canada, particularly the Maritimes, is constantly expanding, although fog may close down the airport at either end of a flight. A real Newfoundland fog, which the summer traveler probably won't encounter, is so horrendous that Newfies are rather proud of it. The thick brown stuff doesn't just hang there like the pea soup of London; "it flows steady as a river."

Since fog has long been the bane of the Maritimes, the foghorn was appropriately invented there by another of those artistic souls who have provided answers to so many of Canada's problems. Robert Foulis, engineer, artist, inventor, and musician, was teaching music at Saint John, New Brunswick, when he got the idea for a foghorn. Telling his daughter to play the scale over and over while he walked a hundred paces down the street, he discovered that at that distance he could hear only the low notes on the piano. It was a deep bass horn that was needed. In 1854 he built one, powered by steam but manually operated. Money was collected to install the first of these gadgets on Partridge Island to warn ships of danger. Though foghorns were soon in wide use, Foulis did not benefit by his invention and died penniless.

While Newfoundland has been described as a great ship, Nova Scotia has been called a huge wharf serving anything that floats. Though the province is less than 400 miles long and only 100 miles at its widest point, it has 4,600 miles of saltwater coastline. To tuck all that into limited space, that coastline is intricately convoluted, with innumerable little coves, several big deep bays, and an arm of the Bay of Fundy so long that it almost cuts the province in two. Around every bend on any coast road there's a magical and usually solitary cove, so it's a poor traveler who can't find one bit of seashore to himself. Dotting the waters off Nova Scotia's tattered south shore are innumerable small islands, many of them sites for lighthouses. The province has 365 lights, the most picturesque, as the Tourist Department warns camera fans, "accessible only by boat."

The most famous of its islets is probably Oak Island in Mahone Bay, where Captain Kidd is reputed to have buried his treasure. Oak Island lies off the village of Western Shore, and in 1795 three young men from the village who were hunting on the island stumbled on an old ship's block hanging from a limb of a huge oak. Beneath this rig, which had obviously been used as a derrick, there was a significant depression in the ground, thirty feet in circumference. The young men hurried to the mainland for shovels, tales of pirates heard since childhood spurring them on. Back they came to dig and dig and dig. Ten feet down they encountered a layer of oak planks, twenty feet down a second layer of planks, this one covered by charcoal. Hauling up the dirt became more and more of a problem as the plank layers continued to a depth of ninety feet, the last one being covered with putty. At ninety-six feet water rushed in, flooding the young men out of the pit. In some fashion an underground channel had been used to protect whatever was buried down there. Every attempt to get past that barrier has failed, no matter how ingenious the scheme.

The digging, however, still goes on, although men have died in cave-ins, and so many shafts have been sunk in nearly two hundred years that no one is certain now where the digs started, since the old oak is gone. But there's something there. Borings made in the 1890's established the presence of three oak chests at 160 feet. Some say that the bit came up once with three gold chain links caught on its tip.

Three young Nova Scotians out hunting in 1968 had better luck, but they knew before they started just what they were looking for. One of the three, Alex Storm of Louisburg, Nova Scotia, had done enough research in Sydney and in Ottawa to be certain that at least one impor-

Burgeo, an outport community on Newfoundland's southwest coast

tant British warship, the *Feversham*, had gone down in 1733 near Scatarie Island off Cape Breton's east coast.

So the three skin divers did their hunting on the boulder-strewn sea bottom. They eventually came on cannons, twenty of them, which led straight to several pieces of eight in perfect condition. In their jubilance the young divers performed an underwater jig.

"I'm sure," Storm told reporters, "the fish thought we had gone mad."

What they brought up in the end was one of the finest collections of early North American coins yet discovered, as well as many from South American mints. Most important were the Dutch silver daalders, used as currency in New York when it was New Amsterdam. Many are so rare that their value has yet to be determined.

For Storm and another of the young men, Harvy MacLeod, this was their second find. In September, 1965, with a third man, they had brought up a haul of gold and silver from the wreck of the eighteenth-century French ship *Le Chameau*. The French vessel was found off Louisburg, roughly ten miles west of the later discovery. Ownership of that booty, whose value has been estimated from $10,000 to $100,000, was tied up for some time in litigation, but in 1969 the Nova Scotia Supreme Court gave possession to Storm. He and his partners will soon be off on other searches, first through archives and then in deep waters. There's more than fish to be found in the seas of Nova Scotia.

Under those same seas off Cape Breton Island during the last two centuries men have risked their lives digging for the stuff that used to be called black gold—coal. Veins of coal found on the island led not only deep into the earth but down under the Atlantic itself. At Sydney Mines, which the traveler on the ferry from Newfoundland will pass going into Sydney Harbor, one such mine runs under the sea for four miles. Most of these mines are being phased out, not because they make killing work for men, but because their production is uneconomical.

But anyone curious to know what it's like down there can drive to the Miner's Museum at Glace Bay for a trip down into a miner's life. The place is not so much a museum as a "happening." The visitor dons a heavy rubber coat, boots, and a helmet for the descent into damp, dark coal seams, where ex-miners acting as guides show how they used to work, crouching down hour after hour, in sharp danger every time they blased out a new face of coal. But the life seems to have its fascination. Many miners from Cape Breton are emigrating to Alberta and British Columbia to work in new mines out there.

The shabby industrial area around Sydney, once a source of wealth to absentee owners, now a problem area for both provincial and federal governments, is the only spot of blight on one of the world's most beautiful islands. But Cape Breton Island is more than a delight to the eye. Within its small compass, a hundred miles as the crow flies from Canso Causeway to Cape North, a surprising variety of attractions can be found. Tourist traffic, however, has not yet been heavy enough to prompt the building of many inns and motels. So visitors should make reservations.

A major attraction is the fortress of Louisbourg twenty miles south of Sydney on a windswept corner of the island. In the center of a three-hundred-acre park, the government of Canada is busy with the biggest restoration it has yet attempted—the reconstruction of the greatest fortress built in America. Its construction took the French more than twenty years—from 1713 to 1740. Its reconstruction began as a make-work project for the unemployed miners of the area, but it has developed into a source of national pride. Archaeologists, historians, and engineers, working side by side with ex-miners retrained in stonecutting, masonry, wrought-iron work, and timber hewing, have made striking progress on a historical display that may come to rival Virginia's Williamsburg.

Already the tower and massive chimneys of the Château St. Louis have erupted on the park's skyline. When completed, the château will have 120 rooms and will house one of the finest collections of eighteenth-century French furniture on the continent. The beautifully furnished Governor's Wing was opened in September, 1969. But the château is only a part of the complex being built around the King's Bastion, the fortress's main focal point. The whole restoration is so extensive that visitors are bused around it. They are not only shown through completed buildings but taken to view continuing excavations.

Anyone whose interest is modern science, not ancient history, can swing through the island to the Alexander Graham Bell Memorial

Museum at Baddeck. For thirty-six years Bell came to Cape Breton every summer; he died there and was buried, as he had planned, on the side of a mountain near Baddeck. To him, Cape Breton was reminiscent of his native Scottish highlands, though the weather there was probably better. But he was never idle, summer or winter, and in his laboratory he and a group of young men he had gathered around him made notable scientific discoveries. Their contribution to modern life is clearly set forth in the displays at the handsome museum.

Not only does the scenery on this side of the island remind one of The Highlands, but so do the people. On this east coast a visitor may catch a phrase spoken in Gaelic as he wanders through the villages. At St. Anns, just up the road from Baddeck, is the only Gaelic college in North America, where summer visitors can observe outdoor classes in Gaelic singing, bagpipe music, and Highland dancing. During the second week of August the Gaelic Mod, an annual festival of Celtic culture, takes place. We've been told, though we never found the place, that near St. Anns there is a black settlement whose people speak Gaelic, having learned it decades ago from their Scottish neighbors.

The west coast of the island is largely inhabited by Acadian French, and among its many charms for the eye is the artistry of the women who make the famous Cheticamp needlepoint rugs. With smiling faces they actually welcome tourists who come to watch them at work.

Three miles north of Cheticamp is the western entrance to the Cape Breton Highlands National Park and to the park section of the drive that encircles the northern half of the island, the Cabot Trail—one of the glories of Cape Breton, with magnificent views on every hand. Unavoidably sharp curves and steep grades force a leisurely pace. There is a spectacular gorge in the park and surprisingly, as the trail winds down to the east coast, a wide sandy beach at Ingonish.

At Indian Brook an interested driver can turn off the trail toward the Englishtown ferry and Big Bras d'Or, where he can take a boat trip to Bird Islands. From early June to late July seafowl in immense numbers—cormorants, razor-billed auks, puffins, Mother Carey's chickens, and terns—nest on these two little islands.

While there is a concentration of the Scottish influence on Cape Breton, the skirl of the pipes can be heard in many other areas of Nova Scotia, which sports a tartan cover on its official road map. At Pug-

206

A festival at St. Ann's Gaelic College on Cape Breton, Nova Scotia

wash, where the street signs are in both Gaelic and English, the "Gathering of the Clans" takes place on July 1. From then until the middle of August a series of Scottish Concerts and Highland Games flourish at points around the province. On driving out of a small town, it seems very natural to read on a road sign, "Will Ye No' Come Back Again?"

Many do return year after year to their bit of Nova Scotia: a Sunday painter to try again to capture on canvas the rocks and water at Peggy's Cove, an angler not just to fish for trout but to enjoy his nightly dinner at the restaurant a village woman runs in her own home, a rock hound to search the Bay of Fundy's shores for amethyst and agate, chalcedony and malachite, and expert on tides to get his daily view of Fundy's great bore of water, twenty-five to thirty feet high.

One American goes to Lunenburg just to sit and whittle while he watches men shape beautiful boats in the old way. Now and then it's a schooner that comes off the ways, one of the ships for which Nova Scotia was once famous. They're coming back now as big sporting craft, with schooner races held off Lunenburg early in July. The shipyard at Lunenberg that specializes in schooners also built the replica of the *Bounty* that was used in the movie, and in 1969–70, a replica of the twenty-gun Revolutionary War frigate H.M.S. *Rose,* which will eventually dock at Newport, Rhode Island, where it will serve as a waterfront pub and marine museum.

At one time Nova Scotia rated fourth in the world in registered tonnage, all of it wooden sailing vessels. Nova Scotians built, as well as sailed, many a famous three-master. The coming of steam put an end to the province's era of greatness. Paradoxically, it was a Halifax man who pioneered regular transatlantic steam navigation—Samuel Cunard, founder of what later became the Cunard Line. In 1840 the company he organized had four ships in operation that crossed on schedule, the first in the world to do so. They sounded the knell for ships that depended on wind and weather.

The history of Nova Scotia's capital, Halifax, is rich in paradoxes from its beginnings until today. The sedate, middle-sized city, described recently by a western Canadian as "contemplating the moss in its navel," has in its more than two centuries of existence periodically been the scene of wild excitement, wide-open vice, pageantry, and violence.

Built on the wooded ridges that surround one of the finest landlocked harbors anywhere, Halifax was founded in 1749 as a British military base. Thirty-six years earlier in 1713, England had taken possession of the Nova Scotia mainland under the Treaty of Utrecht, while France kept Cape Breton Island, separated from the mainland by only the

208

narrowest of straits. In 1713 France had also begun building its great fortress of Louisbourg, which was completed in 1740, and from this base French privateers raided Massachusetts vessels fishing the Grand Banks off Newfoundland. In 1745 the outraged New England colony had assembled an unsoldierly army led by the militarily inexperienced William Pepperell, and to the world's astonishment, that force of farmers, woodsmen, and townspeople had captured the great French stronghold. In the war with France, however, Britain had come out second best, and in 1748 she had calmly agreed to return Louisbourg to the French, to the further outrage of the American colonists. (Their grievance on that score was one of the causes of the American Revolution.) To sooth their fears of more trouble with the French, a fortress was built at Halifax, and in 1758, after a siege in which young General Wolfe distinguished himself, Louisbourg was retaken and razed to the ground.

The siege took longer than had been planned, and by the time Louisbourg fell, it was too late in the season for the visitors to return to Quebec City, icebound in winter then as now. Several regiments and warships therefore wintered in Halifax, and the advantages enjoyed by this protected but warm-water harbor were at last realized. His Majesty's Navy began to build there the largest dockyard in the American colonies, and Halifax became, almost accidentally, a naval base, growing in importance until it occupied one corner of the "marine quadrilateral" (the bases at Malta, Gibraltar, Bermuda, and Halifax) on which the British Navy relied during its greatest decades. The Citadel that crowns the town was manned by British troops until 1906, but it was the navy yard that set the seagoing tone of Halifax, the navy yard that was still bustling when the crumbling Citadel was used only to house prisoners of war. Prince George, later King George V, commanded the gunboat *Thrush* on station at Halifax in 1890, while his son Albert, later King George VI, came there as a midshipman on H.M.S. *Cumberland*. Today the Citadel is a colorful museum, its very lack of military importance having preserved it, while the old dockyard was torn down in 1939 to make way for a modern naval base no more colorful than a big industrial plant.

Since its founding Halifax has been overrun during every war, as it was, remember, in 1776, when Howe arrived from Boston with his army and eleven hundred Tory refugees. A train of civilians always follows an army. The soldiers' and sailors' wives and children create problems enough during the food and housing shortages war inevitably creates, but worse problems arise as the prostitutes, confidence men, gamblers, and thieves flock in to prey on the uniformed men. A red-light district grows up overnight, and in Halifax it has always centered around Water Street near the docks and Brunswick Street, which leads down from the Citadel. A small-town police force is not equipped to cope with an invading army of crooks, so the Halifax police have generally left that problem to the military, who can't always cope either. Water Street has been the scene of wild roistering ever since the days when sailors wore brightly striped jerseys and shiny black leather "sailor" hats above tarred pigtails. When a drunken lot of them came roaring down a street, nice ladies hurriedly retreated indoors. A soldier or sailor angered by high local prices, by the high rents charged his dependents living in the town, by the consequences of his own indulgence—the fleecing in a brothel or the misery caused by rotgut—blamed not himself but Halifax. So in 1918, and again in 1945, servicemen rioted, and in their attacks on the Halifax police and the Halifax shops they were eagerly joined by the waterfront toughs and the transient criminals.

In 1918 the sailors' riot was an additional blow to the town's battered head that Haligonians found hard to forgive. From the day the Citadel was built in 1749, townspeople had been uneasy about the munitions stored there. With every new war the tonnage of explosives on hand at Halifax showed a fearful increase. On December 6, 1917, a single French steamship, the *Mont Blanc,* had a devilish brew aboard, consisting of 2,300 tons of picric acid, 200 tons of TNT to set it off, 61 tons of explosive acid, and a deck cargo of benzene in tins. Nevertheless, naval authorities allowed the ship to enter Halifax harbor to take her place in a convoy being assembled there. While passing the city at eight in the morning, she collided with the Norwegian Belgian Relief steamer *Imo,* without much damage to either ship. But the benzene tins were punctured, and fire broke out on the *Mont Blanc.* Men from the dockyard and a British cruiser hurried to fight the blaze.

A few minutes after 9 A.M. the *Mont Blanc* exploded and vanished, except for one cannon found bent like wax and her one-half-ton anchor, which came down in a woods two miles away. One square mile of Halifax, its north end with all its houses, churches, schools, warehouses, wharves, factories, a rail terminal, and one dockyard, was blown to bits. Citadel Hill protected the south end of town from complete destruction, but everywhere window glass was shattered, doors blown off their hinges, and plaster knocked down. In Halifax and the largely naval town of Dartmouth, which had grown up across the harbor, fourteen hundred men, women, and children were killed instantly or buried under debris and burned to death. Six hundred more died later of their injuries, two thousand were mutilated or blinded by flying glass, and other thousands bound up their wounds as best they could. More than six thousand people were left homeless, and other thousands were ordered out of their shattered houses at noon on that dreadful day because the raging fires had set an army munitions magazine alight. While these refugees trudged toward safety, Canadian sailors managed to get into the flaming magazine, turn on the water cocks, and flood it. Those who had homes still standing were told they could return to them, and once there, they worked frantically, nailing old boards, blankets, carpets, anything with some thickness, over gaping doors and windows to shut out the cold and the advancing snow. All that night a blizzard raged over Halifax, burying under a pall of snow the ruins in which living people were still trapped; some were found alive days later.

The Haligonians left to recover from this disaster were mostly women, children, and older or physically unfit men; of Halifax's prewar population of fifty thousand, an estimated six thousand men had enlisted in the armed forces. For these suffering people, the first and most efficient help came from Massachusetts, which sent a completely outfitted relief expedition by sea. Long after the disaster the Massachusetts Relief Commission, financed entirely by American money, continued its clinics, housing and welfare work, in Halifax. Relief funds from all over totaled $30 million, but the material damage done, not to mention the physical injury, amounted to at least $35 million. So the riot started by sailors the following May deeply angered civilians who had suffered grievously from a Navy error.

In 1945, however, the Navy redeemed itself in the eyes of the Haligonians. By 1939 a new magazine, designed to serve the Canadian Army, Navy, and Air Force in the area of Halifax, had been completed on Bedford Basin across the harbor from the north end of Halifax. Munitions were stored in small brick structures, each surrounded by a rampart of earth and concrete that would confine any blast that could be set off by the limited quantity of munitions held by each structure. After V-E Day, 1945, however, Canadian naval craft from the Atlantic theatre unloaded such vast quantities of torpedoes, depth charges, mines, and bombs that there was not enough room inside the magazine buildings to store the lot. Much of the lethal stuff was piled in outdoor dumps. Somewhere the authorities also stored enough of a new explosive called RDX to blow Halifax off the map. Then, on the evening of July 18, an ammunition barge exploded at the new magazine's jetty, without causing a major blast. But a series of concussions began as the exposed dumps caught fire. If the flames had reached the store of RDX, a catastrophe equaling, or worse than, that of 1917 would have resulted. So the north end of Halifax was evacuated according to plan; a ten-mile-long mass of vehicles crawled over the one protected road. For more than twenty-four hours the menacing fireworks continued, several of the worst blasts coming in rapid succession at 4 A.M. Buildings rocked, but did not fall. By evening the refugees from Canada's powder keg were told they could safely return home.

North End Haligonians who had refused to leave had seen Navy volunteers desperately battling the inferno all through the night. Later all Halifax was able to observe squads of Navy men moving to safety live shells and other explosives that had been flung around by the blasts. Such unwavering heroism dispelled all the old resentment against the Navy—once British, now Canadian. When, in 1968, Canada's armed forces were unified and Canada's sailors were told they, too, would eventually be uniformed in the same deep green as the Army and the Air Force, Haligonians generally were as angry as the most anti-unification admiral. Navy blue proved to be their favorite color. And today Jack Tar, a giant effigy of the same roistering sailor who once drove nice ladies indoors, is the official symbol of Halifax's pleasant summer festivities for tourists.

The province's story abounds in such paradoxes. Most of its Irish

A herring seiner in Newfoundland

"Mics," for instance, are Protestants, while many of its Scottish "Macs" are Catholics, descendants of men who fought for Bonnie Prince Charlie and the Catholic Stuart kings. And while the Indian on Nova Scotia's coat of arms may be, in heraldic terms, "a Savage or a Wild Man Proper," he isn't a proper Micmac.

Today the Micmacs dress and act like any other Canadians. Whatever the current "civilization," Micmacs seem to adapt to it all too readily. Thus, when the British took over Nova Scotia in the eighteenth century, the area's Indians, after more than a hundred years of French rule, had little of the savage about them. They were, as they still are, Catholics, devoted especially to Saint Ann. Many of the men, certainly the chiefs, wore trousers and full-skirted dark blue coats, ornamented with braid and beading and porcupine quillwork in sophisticated patterns. The women's attire had something of the French peasant about it, with long full skirts and chic peaked bonnets, also ornamented with quillwork. Their household effects, too, had style; many a papoose slept in a handsomely decorated cradle.

In several of the museums around the Maritimes, specimens of Micmac work can be seen, notably at the New Brunswick Provincial Museum at Saint John. In the National Gallery at Ottawa a charming primitive painting of Micmac men and women canoeing shows how these museum pieces of attire looked on living models. As for Micmac behavior, when the English savagely drove the Acadian French out of their settlements, it was the savages who took in many of the refugees and sheltered them through the bitter winter.

A large number of Acadians fled to New Brunswick, which has been described as a "very British, faintly military province ringed by the Acadians." They settled in the north and the east where today New Brunswick shows its best and its worst. The Baie des Chaleurs is a noted beauty spot. The Miramichi and the Restigouche rivers are celebrated salmon streams and are fished by wealthy sportsmen. But some of the worst poverty in Canada can be seen on the fringes of this magnificent wilderness.

When, in July, 1960, Louis J, Robichaud became the first Acadian premier of New Brunswick, he launched an "Equal Opportunity" program that has benefited many of the province's desperately poor inhabitants. The provincial government has taken over a hodgepodge

214

of local governments, including once powerful county councils, the administration and full cost of education, health, welfare, justice, and tax collection. Some really appalling rural schools and their semiliterate teachers have been replaced by modern consolidated establishments under trained instructors. Volunteer welfare services that Dickens might have found wanting in his day have been replaced by state aid. Taxes on rural shacks have been cut by 75 per cent, while those on urban real estate and large holdings of unimproved land have been stiffly increased. Traditional taxes (personal property, head, and occupancy taxes) have been abolished, and a sales tax substituted. As Toronto's conservative *Globe and Mail* said, Robichaud "took a backward political province and with great political courage shook it into modern shape."

But industrial growth, on which Robichaud had counted for help in paying for his reforms, fell far below provincial hopes. Any considerable help from Ottawa has been deferred. Of necessity, the New Brunswick government in 1969 raised the sales tax to 8 per cent, imposed a 10 per cent income tax, and increased taxes on tobacco, liquor, and gasoline, always fiscal scapegoats. The poor being below the level of taxation, the burden fell on the middle- and upper-income groups. They are largely English, and the city of Saint John is their bastion.

Reform and its cost did not endear the Robichaud government to the province's richest man, K. C. Irving, who owns oil refineries and service stations, pulp mills and bus lines. More importantly, he owns one of the province's two TV stations, one of Saint John's private radio stations, and all five of the province's English daily newspapers, which are uniformly critical of the provincial government.

New Brunswick is small enough for one rich man to have great impact upon its life. Irving's predecessor in that respect was Lord Beaverbrook, financier, English newspaper publisher, and political figure, who was born in New Brunswick. He remembered his native province generously. There's hardly room to list his benefactions—theatres, university buildings, church bells, steeples, and scholarships—but in the provincial capital, Fredericton, the most conspicuous are the Beaverbrook Playhouse, home of the New Brunswick Symphony Orchestra, and the Beaverbrook Art Gallery, for which he not only provided the building but also the contents, his own personal but wide-ranging choices, including four paintings by his long-time friend, Winston Churchill. Down the street in Officer's Square there is a statue of "the Beaver," unveiled during his lifetime.

But no one man has ever dominated Canada's smallest province, stubbornly independent Prince Edward Island, which took her time, as we have said, in joining the rest of Canada, though one of the nineteenth-century Fathers of Confederation jokingly threatened to tow her into the St. Lawrence if she wouldn't come in on her own. But small as Prince Edward Island seems to Canadians, the province is twice the size of the smallest American state, Rhode Island. Unlike Rhode Island, Canada's Prince Edward Island really is an island, ringed round with sandy beaches and connected with the mainland only by ferries, whose car-borne passengers may wait seven to eight hours to cross during the peak midsummer season.

There has been talk for decades of a causeway, and the federal government was recently so near to building it that some approaches were under construction. But costs kept mounting. When the final figure threatened to reach $300 million, federal officials decided the project was "beyond the bounds of economic sense." Prince Edward Island's population, after all, is only 100,000. Ottawa promised to help improve the ferry service, but that was all.

Still the visitors come, addicted to the island's leisurely pace and to the islanders' politeness and soft, somehow Irish brogue. Irish refugees from the potato famine arrived here in large numbers, and inevitably the island's major crop is potatoes, but the Scots are here, too, and in force. Island politics can be confusing to outsiders because of all those MacDonalds and Campbells, though the natives sort them out with ease.

P.E.I.'s geography is simple enough. Its only "city," Charlottetown, the provincial capital, is really a neighborly small town of twenty thousand people with one movie house and one public bar. Summerside, with eight thousand people, is its biggest "town." Sulky racing is its principal sport, and its major tourist attraction is a small clapboard farmhouse that was the original for the fictional Green Gables in *Anne of Green Gables*. Readers of that girlhood classic turn up at the rate of a thousand a day in summer to tour the place. At the handsome theatre in Charlottetown's Confederation Centre, which also includes a library and art gallery, the steady hit of the annual summer festival is a musical version of *Anne of Green Gables*. The visitor without a teen-age daughter might entertain himself instead over a sparkling fresh P.E.I. lobster. The Island's second largest crop is still lobsters, and its second most popular sport is said to be lobster poaching, dropping a trap into another fellow's lobster bed.

Modernization may yet overtake the province, Canada's "million-acre farm," which has been discovering that farming on small holdings is uneconomical and that fishing in small boats no longer pays either. So there is a program under way to consolidate the many little farms into a few bigger ones that can be worked with machinery that a small farmer can't afford. And fishermen, too, are being encouraged, as they are in Newfoundland, to move to larger centers and to work with modern trawlers. But change on P.E.I. will come with the easy gait of a sulky race.

Of the young, impatient, and ambitious, 10 per cent leave the island for greener fields elsewhere, in Canada or in the United States. The brain drain from the Maritimes has, however, been going on for generations. These small provinces have contributed valuable men to other areas of the Big Land. Today many of the brightest lights in Canadian education, government, and communications are native Maritimers.

Ontario's fabulous Niagara Falls

11 The Queen Province

"Ontario seems the most Canadian province of Canada."

The Welland Canal, part of the St. Lawrence Seaway, permits ships to sail from Lake Erie to Lake Ontario.

To an outsider, Ontario seems the most Canadian province of Canada. If Quebec on the east seceded and British Columbia on the west went its own independent way, Ontario would remain the core of Canada, supported, for all their distrust of eastern industrialists, by the Prairie Provinces, and struggling to maintain some connection with the Maritimes. Such a tragic development would make Canada look as strange on a map as Pakistan, with her big western area out of all proportion to the tiny distant eastern bit. But there would be nothing strange about the character of the country: it would be staunchly Canadian. Every aspect of Canada that has been discussed so far—its difficult size, hard winters, never-ending struggle against American power, English heritage, and mosaic culture—is markedly evident in Ontario.

Just as evident is the provincial resistance to the federal authority. Ontario's attitude toward the government at Ottawa is displayed on any highway map. In Canada highways are the responsibility of the provinces. So the provincial government at Queen's Park in Toronto plots and maintains all the highways into Ottawa, the capital of the country and a major tourist attraction, which stands inside Ontario. The result of this division of authority will be a shock to the visiting motorist traveling from Montreal to Ottawa. He moves out of Montreal over the Metropolitan Thruway, a broad divided freeway that allows high-speed driving all the way to the Quebec border. An informed man, he knows that he is leaving a poor province for the richest province in Canada. At the Ontario border, however, he must pull up fast. The Quebec freeway immediately narrows to a two-lane road that stays two-lane the entire seventy miles to Ottawa. *Every* other Ontario highway into Ottawa is also two-lane, whereas a vast freeway complex girdles Toronto in acres of cement. The situation would be comic if the route between Montreal and Ottawa were not so dangerous. That twisting two-lane road carries a yearly average of fifty-five thousand cars a week. During summer weekends the figure must double. When the number of accidents on the "Killer Strip," as Ottawans label the Montreal road, became a public scandal, Queen's Park finally agreed to replace it with a four-lane highway within four years. The new highway should be open in 1973.

Toronto, conscious of its power and privilege as the economic and financial center of Canada, tries to treat Ottawa as just another small town, disregarding its status as Canada's capital and its metropolitan population, which has now passed the half-million mark. Although one young Toronto reporter, before he left for Paris, described Ottawa in print as "the dullest capital in the world," an official guidebook declares that visitors find "its calm graceful demeanor typically Canadian." There is some justification for both statements.

In the areas over which the National Capital Commission has authority—the Parliamentary complex, parks, and parkways—Ottawa still has charm. The parkways along the river and beside the carefully preserved Rideau Canal were praised by another departing reporter for their "shimmering greenery in August." They are, of course, brilliant with millions of tulips during the annual Tulip Festival in May, and the Parliament grounds are bright with the red coats of the changing guard any summer morning. Sussex Drive, where the Governor General and the Prime Minister have their official residences, leads to another attractive area, Rockcliffe, the close-in suburb where most diplomats live.

With its mushrooming growth since 1965 the center of Ottawa has lost much of its calm and grace. The Dutch elm blight and the high-rise blight have, between them, destroyed the character of many a dignified block. Big handsome houses have been torn down to make way for apartment buildings resembling vertical ice trays, giving added chill to the winter landscape. Many vanished houses are still listed in the only guide to historic Ottawa. With a very few exceptions, high-rise office and apartment buildings are done in "Contractors' Modern." In their wake, streets are perpetually torn up for the installation of new facilities, sidewalks are in disarray, and the skyline is gap-toothed where it is broken by large, bleak parking lots. This is all the more unfortunate because Ottawa's remaining big buildings of an earlier day have a grace of their own. Purists may carp at Parliament's Victorian Gothic style, but for the average man, it has a satisfyingly "Canadian" feel. So does the French château aspect of a neighboring big hotel, which on winter nights looks like an illustration for a fairy tale.

As Expo 67 demonstrated to millions, Canada also builds outstanding modern structures. An exciting example, on Ottawa's central Confederation Square, can be toured daily. This is the new National Arts Centre for the performing arts—designed by Fred Lebensold—which opened on June 2, 1969. In its cluster of concrete hexagons massed to form a modern castle on the banks of the Rideau Canal, there are three unusual auditoriums, the smallest a highly experimental theatre, the largest a magnificent "opera house" with a stage nearly as large as that of the Metropolitan Opera in New York's Lincoln Center. There the comparison ends. Ottawa's "Met" is much more original in style, a tremendous bubble or cage with a velvet-black steel framework outlining walls of glass from which tiers of boxes seem to hang suspended in space. Its great curtain is a huge tapestry in glowing colors. Even

Toronto's impressive city hall at nig

those who "don't like modern architecture" find the effect magical.

The visitor who manages to see Parliament in session in the afternoon and to enjoy a performance at the Centre—opera, ballet, concert, or theatre—in the evening will gain some insight into Canada's heritage from the past and her promise for the future. He might well also visit the National Gallery, just across Elgin Street from the Centre. The Gallery has a balanced collection of moderate size, strong, as it should be, on Canadian art, which unfortunately is often displaced to make room for visiting exhibitions of far-out modern art, most of it American. The Mall, nearby, is an attractively laid-out pedestrian shopping plaza. Except for two native arts shops, notable for the Eskimo, Indian, and French-Canadian work they keep in stock, Ottawa stores still seem geared to the city's small-town past.

On a sunny summer day one of the real pleasures of Ottawa is the regular Ottawa River excursion. The boat leaves from a dock at the foot of the remarkable series of Rideau Canal locks alongside Parliament Hill. The trip gives the tourist a sense of the sweep and majesty of the Ottawa, the watery path of the voyageurs. Today's traffic, interesting in itself, consists largely of huge rafts of logs heading for the pulp mills on the Quebec side.

When Queen Victoria chose as the capital of Canada the community that was then called Bytown—named for Colonel John By, who built the Rideau Canal—her choice shocked the Ontario Establishment. They looked down on it as a roistering lumber town, its streets muddy paths from one tavern to the next. Some historical resentment of the upstart may lie behind Toronto's current attitude.

From Ottawa the roads lead west with topographic tidiness into the three broad strata that make up Ontario. The southeastern, or lowest, layer occupies the gentle lowlands of the St. Lawrence-Great Lakes region, an area of fairly moderate climate, productive farmland (particularly in the Niagara Peninsula), expanding population, and intensive industrial growth. Ontario is as big as France, West Germany, and the United Kingdom put together, but its population includes less than seven million people, most of whom are crowded into this one-hundred to two-hundred-mile wide lower strip, which represents less than one fourth of the province's total area. This attractive region was naturally the first to be settled and was for decades thereafter the point of greatest conflict with the United States. Most of Ontario's historic sites dot this ribbon of land, and it is here that the present American industrial and cultural invasion is most evident.

North of the lowlands the vast Precambrian Canadian Shield rears up, a great rocky plateau stretching across Canada from Labrador to the Manitoba border. It is strewn with lakes, 250,000 of them in its Ontario sector alone, much of it is beautiful and, to the north, rich in ores. As farmland the thinly covered ancient stone broke the hearts of most of the pioneers who ventured this far. In central Ontario descendants of those who hung on live in hard poverty where they try to farm rocky soil. Others have given up; and abandoned farms, their barns and sheds fallen in, mark the roadside for many a mile. Around the next bend, however, the motorist may be surprised to see prosperous rolling farmland, usually lying in a wide river valley.

But around the lakes, large and small, that lie within 150 miles of Toronto and other populated points to the south, who needs to farm when there's good money to be had from the summer people? This second and central strata of Ontario is Getaway Country, holiday land for the province's city dwellers and for thousands of Americans, too. There are now two hundred thousand cottages clustered around Lake Simcoe, the Muskoka Lake Region, Georgian Bay, along the Trent Canal system, and as far as the Haliburton Highlands. Their waters are abuzz with three hundred thousand pleasure craft. Ontario people generally are so determined to acquire their piece of not-too-distant lake front that salesmen have been taking them out in snowmobiles to view sites in winter. In their hurry to have country places they're not overparticular about the designs of the prefabs they put up. As one manufacturer said, "They buy any old model so long as if flushes and makes ice cubes."

Thousands of other vacationers live aboard their boats, to the mounting concern of the provincial government. Having fled the pollution of Lake Ontario, these summer sailors are now beginning to pollute smaller and more vulnerable waters. The Ontario authorities still manage to protect magnificent stretches of unspoiled wilderness and its wild life, but they have their difficulties. Most of the province's great Algonquin Park, three thousand square miles of it, can't be reached by automobile. To penetrate its beauties for any distance, a

A summer cottage in the Muskoka region, about one hundred miles north of Toronto

man must go either on foot or by canoe. The campsites that can be reached easily are, however, so overrun in summer that one of the park's finest lakes has already been polluted.

Many small towns in the Getaway Country just shut up shop in winter. Others have a vigorous and distinctly Canadian life the year round. Such is Orillia, on the northern side of Lake Simcoe, which Stephen Leacock, the Canadian humorist, gently satirized as Mariposa in his *Sunshine Sketches of a Little Town,* delightful background reading for a tourist. At first Orillians were indignant at the fun Leacock had poked at them, but today the town proudly boasts that it is the "original Mariposa," and Leacock's summer home there is a museum.

North of this seasonally lively strata Ontario is wilderness and bush all the way up to and a little beyond 56° north, halfway up the western shore of Hudson Bay. The bush is broken here and there by several

mining towns, some of them booming, like Sudbury, "the nickel capital of the world," others, particularly the gold-mining towns, with their glory gone. Some of these look very like the false-fronted towns of America's early West. Hunting is a big sport, but up there, man is still outnumbered by the moose, deer, beaver, and bear. This is the near north, part of what Richard Rohmer, a Toronto lawyer with a big dream, calls "Mid-Canada"—on his map, a tremendous arc of land reaching from Labrador on the east to the Mackenzie River on the west and up the Mackenzie to the Arctic. In Ontario it takes in this third strata and then dips slightly south to include the muskeg region north of Lake Superior. Rohmer sees the Mid-Canada Development Corridor, which he and others are researching, as the next stage in Canada's development, a second tier that will one day be as populous and busy as the tier along the American border. Such a corridor, if it ever develops, will take time, imagination, planning, and billions of dollars. It will also force improvement of existing forms of transportation or the invention of new ones. This isn't the Arctic, but it is cold country where for months of every year harbors are iced over and roads lie buried under deep snow. Cargo submarines, hovercraft, and pipelines for carrying such solids as grain and ore could provide transport for the corridor. Subterranean shopping malls are no novelty in Canada, but the dreamers also speak of bubble-top cities, heady talk for a part of Canada in which much of the present housing consists of an occasional trapper's cabin or a tiny trailer village for loggers. This strata of Ontario couldn't even be crossed by a car in summer until that stretch of the Trans-Canada Highway was opened in the early 1960's.

The traveler who would like to tour that northern frontier before the high-rises spring out of the bush can head north on Route 17 out of Ottawa, drive two hundred miles to North Bay, and from there make a five-hundred-mile loop around the mining country on what one Tourist Department handbook calls a "Circle Tour from the Trans-Canada Highway." The tour takes the adventurous traveler north on Route 11, good road all the way, to Porquis Junction and then south and west back to the Trans-Canada on routes 101 and 129. These two routes, broken by long stretches of graveled road, go through very lonely country. On the return half of the loop, it might be better to stay on Route 101, called "The Golden Route" because of the gold mines that line it. At Timmins, a gold-mining center, the tourist can cut back across to Route 11.

Much of even this shorter route is bleak, but all of it has romantic associations. From Ottawa to North Bay the motorist drives alongside the water route of Champlain and many other early explorers. At Mattawa, where a river of that name enters the Ottawa, the road turns west as the voyageurs did. With the help of the Mattawa River and a couple of small lakes, the voyageurs were only a short portage away from North Bay on Lake Nipissing, which they crossed to reach the mouth of the French River leading into Georgian Bay and Lake Huron, part of the Great Lakes system. This was the path that took Père Marquette to the American Midwest and La Salle down the Mississippi. A companion of Champlain's, Jean Nicolet, who himself explored Lake Michigan, Green Bay, and the Fox River in what is now

Wisconsin, set up a fur-trading post at North Bay, the first commercial establishment in Ontario, long before there was any settlement on the southern tier. In fact, this northern waterway was more traveled in the seventeenth century than the Mississippi-Missouri system would be for another hundred years. Yet, even today, people living on the edge of North Bay are not surprised to see a moose amble across the lawn.

Though explorers, soldiers, traders, and trappers passed through this region in surprising numbers, it wasn't really settled until the turn of this century, when ore strikes brought in prospectors, miners, and managers. Most of the big strikes were almost accidental. When the builders of the Canadian Pacific, the railroad that shaped so much of Canada's history, were cutting through the Canadian Shield up there, at a point three miles west of the new station at Sudbury, a blacksmith named Tom Flanagan noticed metallic glitter along the face of the cutting. His find was stuff called "Old Nick's Copper," later shortened to "nickel," and consigned to Old Nick because miners considered it a nuisance—until a use for it was finally found. Today Sudbury is the nickel capital of the world, not just to its own chamber of commerce, but in sober fact.

Another accidental find, also attributed to a blacksmith, was made in 1903 at Cobalt, the first stop in that Circle Tour. Some say the blacksmith threw his heavy hammer at what he took for a fox's eyes gleaming in the dark, a gleam that proved to be the world's richest silver vein. In its heyday Cobalt had a floating population of twenty thousand. The lucky ones who struck it rich overnight became "silver kings." The unlucky could at least walk Cobalt's Silver Sidewalk, still to be seen. Enough young Canadians went through there before 1914 to make "The Cobalt Song" familiar to most of the Canadians who were in the trenches in France during the first World War. Someone had only to start singing "The Cobalt Song," and the ditty would be quickly taken up all along the line:

> *Where all the silver comes from*
> *And you live a life, and then some!*

The rest of the words are a guide to several of the towns on the Circle Tour:

Porcupine's a muskeg, Elk Lake's a firetrap,
New Liskeard's just a farming town
And Haileybury's off the map.
But it's hobnailed boots and a flannel shirt
And it's Cobalt town for mine.

Today Cobalt looks like a deserted set for a Hollywood western, with some of its houses built of railroad ties and dynamite boxes. It does have a colorful mining museum. Haileybury, where many of the silver kings built their big houses, boasts a "Millionaire's Row" among its tourist sights. New Liskeard is still a farming center, lying in a rich agricultural belt of one million acres. As for Porcupine, Cobalt people were just jealous of that collection of brawling camps where the miners really struck it rich, digging out $15 billion worth of gold in fifty years. In 1909–10 the equipment for Porcupine's mines had to be transported thirty-two miles from the railroad by trail and canoe. Today, its heroic past a memory, Porcupine is simply a solid trade center for northeastern Ontario. The best-known town in the area is probably Timmins, which has the second-largest gold mine in the world (the Rand in South Africa is the only one larger). There are conducted tours of the mine to show visitors how gold ore is handled, although the guide may not explain that the stuff is hardly worth mining these days. At Kirkland Lake big mines standing in a row make up its "Golden Mile," and some of these can also be toured.

It was to Kirkland Lake that a Maine man, Harry Oakes, came with a packsack and $2.56 in his pocket to stake a claim that in time made him the rich Sir Harry Oakes. He survived the dangerous wilderness days, only to be mysteriously murdered years later in his luxurious establishment in the Bahamas. Ontario's moneyed men have a weakness for the Caribbean. Edward Plunket Taylor, the province's most potent financier today, lives down there. Through the years of bitter winters, Canadians seem to dream of being rewarded in the end with life on a tropical island.

"All that glitters" may not be gold but stuff of greater value in today's technology. Just off the Trans-Canada a hundred miles west of Sudbury, with its riches in nickel, is the modern bonanza town Elliot Lake, Canada's uranium center. Elliot Lake went through one boom that

sputtered out, but now a second boom is building up. In mid-February, 1968, Elliot Lake was the scene of an old-style claim-staking race with modern trimmings. In a one-hundred-thousand-acre area known to be rich in uranium, men raced in zero weather and blowing snow—by airplane or snowmobile if they could afford them, on snowshoes more often than not—to spots they had picked in advance. Until noon on Monday, February 19, however, not a stake could be driven legally. Patrolling inspectors, harassed by the weather, tried to enforce that rule, but there were rumors of a few men who got the jump on the rest in the hard work of claim staking. If so, none were caught.

Under the regulations of a claim-staking race, a prospector places his No. 1 post—a tree he has squared or a post he has brought with him—inscribed with his name, mining license number (a license costs five dollars), and the date and hour. From that post he marches 1,320 feet due south, using a compass and blazing his claim as he goes by scoring trees or setting small stakes. There he places his No. 2 post, inscribed as No. 1 was, and from that point he turns west and, following the same procedure as before, installs No. 3 at a distance of 1,320 feet. From No. 3 he marches north to install No. 4, and then east, setting markers between the posts all the way, until he is back at No. 1, with his claim of approximately forty acres exactly fenced by his four inscribed posts and his markers. Only then is he ready to mail or take his application to the nearest mine recording office, where, after payment of ten dollars, it is put on record.

Normally a prospector will stake about twenty claims—an experienced man can plot out three or four a day—before recording the whole lot at one time. (The license allows the holder up to ninety claims.) In the Elliot Lake race, however, men had to rush, staking only one or two claims before racing off to Sudbury or Sault Ste. Marie, each about a hundred miles away, to record them. Forty light planes were waiting at Elliot Lake to take men who could afford the fare to a recording office. The rest turned that stretch of the Trans-Canada into a speedway.

The big operators hired whole camps of stakers, paying a man twenty-five to fifty dollars a day to stake and register claims in his own name before turning them over to his employer. Working smoothly in areas their employers' experts had indicated, these crews probably

232

got the pick of the pay dirt. Undoubtedly American money was involved, since the economic invasion of Ontario has pushed well north of the border region where military invaders were always halted. In 1970, the economic invasion was also checked when the Canadian government decided to restrict American control of uranium mines.

Today American military men have reached northern Ontario, helping to man the NORAD base at North Bay. NORAD stands for North American Air Defense, the joint American-Canadian program with overall headquarters at Colorado Springs, Colorado. The base at North Bay is responsible for the Northern Region, which covers all the air approaches to the great industrial centers of the eastern United States and Canada. To meet that responsibility, a Canadian Bomarc Squadron at North Bay maintains a state of constant readiness, and fifty-six Bomarc surface-to-air atomic missiles are poised to streak off in sixty seconds to strike enemy bombers four hundred miles away, the enemy bombers that would follow up an atomic attack. These missiles are controlled from the fantastic underground headquarters, called The Hole, around North Bay and the base itself.

To reach headquarters, a man with a pass to get him through the first gate must drive down a mile-long, 12 foot by 12 foot tunnel blasted out of the rock, and at the tunnel's end, through the nineteen-ton blast doors painted bright blue. Beyond, a three-story windowless office building with a heavy steel framework stands free, its walls and roof clear of the rock, in a deep man-made cavern gouged out of the ancient stone. Inside that "office," and watched by intent young Canadians and Americans, are banks of radar scopes, part of the intricate northern radar network, and two three-hundred-ton computers, which gather and correlate all intelligence flashed into the base from far-off DEW (Distant Early Warning) line sites and from the interceptor squadrons and another Bomarc squadron that are attached to this command but stationed elsewhere. There are also bevies of secretaries and clerks who march out of The Hole at 5 P.M. to catch their buses as casually as if they were leaving an ordinary office.

If the men at the scopes spotted enemy ICBM's, however, warning would be flashed to Colorado Springs, the blast doors at North Bay would clang to, and the four hundred people working that shift in The

Hole would stay there, whatever happened elsewhere. They would be furnished with all the normal amenities, beds, baths, and meals, while waiting for manned bombers to follow up the missile assault. When the bombers came on the screens, the Bomarcs would be launched, but only after a Canadian officer had turned his key in his lock on the controls and an American officer had turned his, having been authorized to do so by the Prime Minister of Canada and the President of the United States respectively. At least that's the theoretical plan. All sensitive jobs in The Hole are done by two men working together, one a Canadian and one an American. "On the theory," a reporter was told, "that a nut is possible on any job, but two nuts at the same time are unlikely."

From North Bay only the most determined tourist will go the whole way west—more than one thousand miles by Route 17 of the Trans-Canada—to the Manitoba border. The stretch beyond The Lakehead, as the Thunder Bay area is commonly called, is the real Mid-Canada Corridor, wild and largely undeveloped, with few roads and even fewer railroads. Even the main transportation channels through this part of the province can be severed in strange ways. At one point at the head of Lake Superior, where the Trans-Canada Highway and the Canadian Pacific rails run side by side, heavy rains in 1968 broke a beaver dam. Does that sound harmless? The resulting flash flood smashed the highway's paving into chunks, gouging holes thirty-five feet deep in some places, and tore up the tracks. Two years before, a flood caused by beavers derailed the CPR's crack *Canadian* near there, killing two people. Canada's national symbol, the beaver, builds dams high enough to pile up a mighty wall of water.

In northwestern Ontario and in Manitoba east of Winnipeg freight is hauled to isolated communities in winter over an extraordinary network of temporary roads, two thousand miles of them. They're man-made snow roads that simply melt away every spring and must be rebuilt every winter. The company that does this job and runs "trains" over its network is operated by three stalwart brothers of Icelandic descent. The oldest brother, Svien Sigfusson, spent twenty-seven years finding the right routes for the trains—through bush and across muskeg—and throughout the winter he checks the network constantly from a little, ski-equipped Cessna plane. The trains that travel these snow tracks are "cat trains," each consisting of a powerful five-ton Caterpillar tractor hauling five wooden freight sleighs and a caboose where the crew sleep and eat while the train pushes steadily on. Right behind it is a second train—for safety's sake, the trains travel in pairs. Each pair is called a "swing," with the "cat skinner" on the lead train acting as the swing boss. The company had twenty-two swings in operation during the winter of 1968–69, operated by crews that worked six hours on and six hours off around the clock, remaining on their trains out in the bush for as long as ninety days—and liking it.

The weather may range from 30° below to 55° below for days on end, and there is no roof on the cab of a cat—so the driver can jump clear if his heavy tractor breaks through the ice. It happens often enough for the crews to call the resulting delay "downtime." Over the years more than one hundred cats have gone through the ice, all retrieved by means of a block-and-tackle technique that Sigfusson perfected. Ice that will bear the weight of the big tractor will take the freight sleighs easily enough. So through the dark winter they carry everything—drums of oil, packets of tea, building materials, schoolbooks—to isolated Indian settlements, church missions, hydroelectric stations, and Hudson's Bay posts. As the trains crawl along at five miles an hour, their crews see little life in the snowbound woods around them, perhaps only wolves running in a pack behind the caboose, waiting for the cook to throw out scraps.

The wilderness has its addicts, men who come to northern Ontario year after year to hunt and fish off in the bush. The non-addict had better turn south at Sudbury, where another branch of the Trans-Canada comes up to join Route 17. In a matter of miles he will be in one of the loveliest areas of the Getaway Country, the Georgian Bay region, its waters dotted not with a thousand islands but with thirty thousand. For all its ebullient holiday life, this is historic country, and for a look at the remarkable work Canadians have been doing lately in reconstructing their past, the visitor should swing off the Trans-Canada at Waubaushene and proceed to Midland, the peninsula's chief town.

Just outside Midland stands a remarkable palisaded village, the carefully researched re-creation of the fortified mission headquarters that the Jesuits built here in 1639, at a time when most settlers in the New World—the few there were at Jamestown, New Amsterdam, Plymouth, and Quebec—clung to the Atlantic shores. In that year sixty-six Europeans built a village among the Huron at Ste. Marie, deep in the heart of the continent. Most of the colonists were French, but there were two Italian Jesuits among them and a tailor named Dominie Scot. Inside the palisades they built two churches and a hospital, living quarters and a cookhouse, stables and a blacksmith shop, a dispensary and a carpenter's shop. To bring in supplies sent from Quebec by water, they set up a miniature system of locks and canals.

Five of their priests were martyred, and on a hill overlooking the site, the Jesuit Martyrs' Shrine towers up. Goya, surprisingly, did a lurid painting of the deaths of two of the priests. Unfortunately, by 1649 the once powerful Hurons, who had responded to the fathers' preaching and teaching, had been decimated by famine, epidemics, and worse, by the Iroquois. Ste. Marie, the fathers decided, must be abandoned, but not to the Iroquois. They themselves put it to the torch. Three centuries later, Ste. Marie began to rise from its ashes. Now it is complete in every detail. Nearby, a Huron village of the same period has also been reconstructed. In it there is, incidentally, a sweat bath, not unlike a sauna.

For contrast, some English aspects of the peninsula's history can be seen at Midland's twin town, Penetanguishene (the French- or English-speaking citizens of this truly bilingual community call it Penetang). Here, on a neck of land beside a large bay, the British built a naval base in 1814 "for His Majesty's Vessels on the Upper Great Lakes." Penetang, they believed, could rival Detroit as a center for the northwest trade. It never did, and the base itself eventually fell into disuse. Today "The Establishments at Penetanguishene," not yet entirely restored, can be visited, as can the delightful little Anglican church of St. James-on-the-Lines, built in 1836, with its center aisle made unusually wide so that the troops could march into church four abreast. On the right wall a memorial tablet reproves posthumously a trooper who perished in the snow after drinking too well at a tavern in the town. A matching tablet was put up in expectation of the death of his drinking companion, who managed, however, to survive. That tablet is still blank.

Such restorations and reconstructions—"rebuilts" they're sometimes called in Canada—are scattered across Ontario's southern layer.

A reconstruction near Midland, Ontario, of the palisaded village that Jesuit fathers built on the spot in 1639

For such a peaceable people, a surprising number of these are forts, twelve in Ontario alone. In the United States one's guide around a historic site is often a middle-aged woman in curls and billowing skirt, while in Canada the guide is equally often a college boy in bright jacket and brass buttons. This relish for period uniforms is, of course, in the British tradition, though Quebec forts, too, deck their resident "soldiers" in elaborate uniforms. If the local historical attraction isn't a fort, it's probably a "Pioneer Village." The most elaborate collection of period buildings moved to a chosen location, Upper Canada Village near Cornwall, has been discussed. In 1969 there were four other pioneer villages in Ontario, and there may be more now. During the school year they are aswarm with children happily absorbing Canadian history.

Near Ontario's southern border, on the outskirts of the small town of Dresden in Kent County, there is a modest historical complex that is visited by thirty thousand people a year. Its center is the weathered two-story frame house that was once the home of the Rev. Josiah Henson, although few of the tourists who wander through it know him by that name. They have come to see "Uncle Tom's Cabin" (Canadian cabin, that is), since Henson is reputed to have inspired Harriet Beecher Stowe's story. He certainly inspired the development of a black community in Kent County, and his grave stands in a cemetery for escaped slaves just across the road. One generation's hero can become a despised symbol to the next, so few black militants visit Uncle Tom's grave. They might if they knew more about him. In 1852 he advocated separate schools for Negroes—"we would thus gradually become independent of the white man for our intellectual progress, as we might also for our physical prosperity."

In 1969 the descendants of some of his black neighbors, busy farmers, had never heard of the Black Panthers. These men all had stories about their grandfathers' escape routes north and the life they lived after reaching Canada. (The grandfather of one of them spent his first eighteen months housed in a hollow tree.) Kent County's older men might not feel at home, however, in Toronto's "soul food" restaurant, the Underground Railroad, decorated to look like a hideway for slaves bound for Canada. It does a thriving business in chitterlings, pig's tails, and corn bread, collard greens, black-eyed peas, and fish gumbo. A

Black and white Canadians watch a parade at Windsor, Ontario.

chain of like-named restaurants is planned for the United States.

The Underground Railroad is more elaborate than many of Toronto's dozens of "ethnic" restaurants. Most are simple places that serve their national dishes to newcomers longing to eat in the old familiar way, be it French, Hungarian, German, Italian, Portuguese, Mexican, West Indian, or Turkish. That doesn't exhaust the list. Even Canadian migrants are catered to, so a Newfoundlander or a French Canadian can also find his native food (there are more people of French descent in

Among Toronto's many ethnic restaurants is this one, established by black immigrants from the United States.

Ontario than there are in Louisiana). Many of these cafes are simple establishments simply named. The Famous Dairy Restaurant, for example, specializes in what its proprietor, Moshe Nachum, calls "Israeli" food, really Middle Eastern dishes any Egyptian or Jordanian would recognize.

The Toronto mosaic is intricate indeed, with a half million immigrants having entered the city since the end of World War II and more arriving every year. They have transformed staid old "Hogtown" to such a degree that a Torontonian declared in 1968, "with a few more sidewalk cafés, it would be a Continental city." When he said it, really Continental cafés could not be operated, for under Ontario's liquor laws open-air drinking was illegal. Cocktail lounges were largely confined to hotels, where any drinking was done behind heavy curtains.

At open-air cafés, the customers could not order anything stronger than coffee, and even in hotels a visitor could not be served a drink in his room! In 1969, however, changes were made in the liquor regulations that promise to make a sidewalk *apéritif* or a beer possible in summer.

Great numbers of Toronto's immigrants, some just beginning to make a place for themselves, others having found their place an insecure one, live in the poorer areas of town. There, people of one nationality may be in a majority on one side of the street, while across the way or a block over, people of another origin cluster together. The mosaic winds in, out, and around in a dizzy fashion, and inevitably there are clashes, chiefly among the youths, restless in Toronto as elsewhere.

A few of these clashes have been racial, a new sort of trouble for Toronto. Since 1966 blacks have been coming into the city in greater numbers, chiefly from the West Indies and Nova Scotia, though there are probably not more than ten thousand of them. Whatever their place of origin, they seem to stick together, as white immigrant boys do not, and most of the blacks are militant. A social researcher, himself a Negro, in a report made for the Ontario Human Rights Commission, said that the blacks had driven the whites away from two youth centers, either by their aggressiveness toward whites "irrespective of racial or ethnic backgrounds" or by their "open vandalism" when exclusive black programs were not set up.

The retreating whites, according to the report, indulged in sporadic conflicts of their own. The Italians raided Portuguese territory, and vice versa. Since both Italian and Portuguese parents keep their young girls in at night, their boys, hunting for "chicks," raided dances given by white Maritimers. There was frequent fighting and "very little other social interaction." Mentioned also were troubles between Italians and Jews, between Anglo-Saxons and Poles. The report did not pretend to be definitive. There are undoubtedly many other patterns of conflict. The mosaic society seems to function no more ideally than the melting pot.

And it is in Toronto that the mosaic is most evidently breaking up, with newcomers of talent and training refusing to be shunted into ethnic groups and gifted descendants of earlier immigrants making major contributions to the city's life. A symbol of the change in the very character of Toronto is its graceful, imaginative new city hall. The plan for this very original structure, which has given a heart to the modern city, was chosen in an international competition. It was won by the late Viljo Revell, a Finnish genius who died in his prime. Revell, however, was not a Canadian. The design chosen for the really splendid new Science Centre, opened late in 1969 but intended as Ontario's centennial project, probably represents a more significant development. As we have said, the design was the work of a young Japanese-Canadian, Raymond Moriyama, whose unusual plan for the city of Toronto's 1,200-acre future zoo has also been accepted. In music, too, there have been changes. The distinguished Czech refugee, Karl Ancerl, succeeded Seiji Ozawa, a Japanese, as conductor of the Toronto Symphony, which was led for twenty-five years by Sir Ernest Mac-Millan. The Czech opera star Jan Rubes and his wife Susan founded the Children's Museum Theatre and the Young People's Theatre. In a thousand other ways, in Canadian television programs originating in Toronto, in the arts and crafts displayed in commercial galleries, in the clothes and other wares displayed in the many distinctive small shops, a tourist can discover for himself the influence on Toronto's life that lively newcomers have already exercised.

But the old Torontonian custom of spending one's weekends in the country still prevails. Although the city has many parks and wooded ravines and maintains a certain spaciousness, the newcomers have joined the lemming-like rush to the Getaway Country every summer weekend. Of course, most of the people working in the city came originally from small towns across Ontario and the Prairie Provinces or from villages in Italy or Portugal or Germany, for which they may continue to feel some nostalgia. With open country so close at hand, away they go.

If Toronto has changed beyond recognition, London, Ontario, has not basically altered since 1900. It has grown, but its industries are of the neat, unobtrusive sort. There, on a fork of the Thames River, a visitor can examine one of Canada's last Anglican strongholds. Of its population of two hundred thousand, 73 per cent are of British stock. There is probably a millionaire for every one thousand people, and a good majority of the top two hundred will be related to each other, will

242

attend an old Anglican church, will belong to the London Hunt and Country Club, and *may* belong to the London Club, a highly selective masculine inner sanctum, whose members by an unwritten rule do not discuss women or politics. The changing temper of the University of Western Ontario in London, these people feel, has made that actually moderate educational institution "a hotbed of radicalism." It was a young Anglican priest from the university who denounced the members of the interlocking elite in London for their complacency and prejudice, among other sins. They really have no prejudice against Jews and Catholics, but at the club, "one naturally wants to see one's friends." London also has a small military establishment, and more brigadiers retire there than to any other base in Canada. The only newspaper, the London *Free Press,* is run by a fourth-generation publisher, and generally the old families have things their way. The fox-hunting season opens in late September. There are two hunts a week; the biggest is on Thanksgiving, which in Canada comes on the second Monday in October. An American's only opportunity for a look at London's elite would be at a Sunday service in St. Paul's Cathedral, or at Cronyn Memorial Church, or at St. John's in Arva (a wealthy suburb). Hume Cronyn, the actor, is a member of one of London's oldest families, but he fled the town.

Anyone who travels from Porcupine to London (where some of Porcupine's gold may have wound up) will get the whole range of Ontario. Canada, and all its complexities, take on dimension here.

12

The Company
of Adventurers

"It is an institution operating at a profit."

Above, a replica of the Nonsuch. *Left, an Eskimo takes white fox skins to the Hudson's Bay store in Spence Bay.*

The Hudson's Bay store at Coral Harbour, Northwest Territories

DISTINCTIVELY CANADIAN is the famous Hudson's Bay blanket of heavy white wool with a bold striped border of red, green, and yellow. Indian chiefs wore it as a regal cape. Many Americans prize it for its fine quality and weight, even today when steam-heated apartments and feather-weight electric blankets have made it somewhat unnecessary, not to mention old-fashioned. In being so, however, it is all the more symbolic of its remarkable manufacturer, a firm that went into business

in Canada in 1670—three hundred years ago—as "The Governor and Company of Adventurers of England trading into Hudson's Bay."

A visitor entering Canada west of Toronto will encounter Hudson's Bay stores soon after he crosses the border, and he would keep on encountering them should he travel by dog sled, mechanized toboggan, bush plane, or canoe all the way to Cape Parry in the Arctic.

Old forts across the prairies remind today's traveler that Hudson's

Bay men were often the first settlers in the Canadian west. Coming down by canoe and portage trail from York Factory, the company's initial export point on Hudson Bay, the fur traders staked out their first fortified post near the fork of the Red and Assiniboine rivers, now downtown Winnipeg.

A stone fort that the Hudson's Bay Company built in the 1830's, Lower Fort Garry, twenty miles north of the fork, stands today, scrupulously restored. Buildings, including a fur loft, a bakery, a jail, and residences, are in good repair, and visitors are welcome to inspect the stone-walled enclosure and bastions of the thirteen-acre area of fortifications, now a National Historical Park.

Upper Fort Garry, erected in the fork of Winnipeg's two rivers, has largely disappeared. The preserved original stone gate is called by Winnipeggers the "Gateway to the Golden West." Appropriately, this remnant of fur-trading days is just across Main Street from the block-square Hudson's Bay House, the present North American headquarters of this remarkable New World business enterprise.

The company built Lower and Upper Fort Garry, Fort Edmonton, Fort Victoria, and many other forts to protect its domain, which covered all of Canada's great northwest. Around the forts Canada's western cities grew up. Fort Edmonton is now Edmonton, Fort Victoria today is Victoria. These cities, like Winnipeg, are provincial capitals.

Right on top of Lake Superior, two hundred miles north of Duluth, Minnesota, lies an Ontario town newly called Thunder Bay. It was, until 1969, two rival ports that owed their being and growth to the fur trade that Hudson's Bay men started and fought for. One town, Port Arthur, was a Hudson's Bay post established in 1804 to protect the firm's territorial claims against a challenger, the North West Company, which had recently erected an outpost at nearby Fort William.

Canadians refer to these neighboring towns collectively as The Lakehead. For it is in their fine harbor that much of the grain from the prairies is taken from railroad cars to be put aboard bulk vessels. In spite of the grain glut, it is still one of the sights of Canada to see the long, low-slung freighters take on their golden cargoes, then, sitting low in the water, steam out into the Great Lakes to begin the long voyage to feed the world. The freighters fly the flags of Europe, Asia, and

Africa, not to mention the Americas.

Since there is no distance between the present-day towns, the residents of Port Arthur and Fort William finally agreed to a merger in the interests of economy and efficient administration. But whether all the people of Thunder Bay will soon come together spiritually remains to be seen.

"From the start, they didn't get along," commented a journalist recently. "Gang fights over the drop of a whisky glass gave way to battles over harbor dockage, and these gave way to fights over railway facilities." In the old days it was fur that flew.

Fighting in those old days broke out wherever Hudson's Bay men were challenged. Hudson's Bay factors—a company name for trading-post managers—were already old-timers in most places when the early homesteaders began to arrive in the nineteenth century. There are northern outposts today where the key men are still the Royal Canadian Mounted Policeman, the Oblate missionary, and the Hudson's Bay factor, who may sometimes double as postmaster and justice of the peace.

The 245 stores flying the H.B.C. ensign today range from $10-million department stores to one-room trading posts so remote that they can be stocked only once a year—in summer when the ice melts, permitting the supply ship to make its annual rounds.

But as visitors soon discover, "The Bay" is no ordinary business in Canada. As one of its managers put it, "it is an institution operating at a profit." In a recent year the "institution" netted an after-tax profit of $14 million on gross sales of more than $400 million. The sales involved the extensive fur trade that persists, mineral rights to some 4.5 million acres of oil-rich western Canada, and the continent-wide wholesaling of Hudson's Bay products—tobacco, bonded liquors, and, of course, the blankets. It is a lively, picturesque institution whose sales counters or trading posts, wherever they are, attract thousands of tourists every year. Nevertheless, it was not retailing or mineral prospects that made Canada a land of great promise for the first adventurers who came to Hudson Bay. It was the tremendous wealth of fur-bearing animals to be harvested from a wilderness inhabited only by scattered Indians and Eskimos.

The adventurers arrived, incidentally, aboard the sturdy forty-three-ton ketch *Nonsuch*. A replica of the vessel was constructed as part of the company's three-hundredth anniversary celebration in 1970. That replica was built in Devon, England, and brought to Canada.

The story of the company starts with King Charles II making his favorite cousin, Prince Rupert, who had distinguished himself as a great cavalry general in the Civil War, head of a group of eighteen English noblemen and merchants who were to be "true and absolute Lordes and Proprietors" with rights to "sole Trade and Commerce" in all the territory draining into Hudson Bay. (The charter called it Hudson's Bay, and the company retains that spelling in its name.)

With no maps to study, the king was unaware of the extent of his bounty. But in his eagerness to (1) encourage English discovery of the Northwest Passage, (2) involve English capital in the profitable fur trade, and (3) head off the French in Canada, Charles transferred to private ownership an area of 1.5 million square miles. Rupert's Land, as the region was named, was about the size of European Russia.

Later Parliament leased further territories to the company, extending the Hudson's Bay realm to the Pacific, the Arctic, and Alaska. The proprietors then owned all of Canada except the settlements around the St. Lawrence River and the Great Lakes. When the United States strode out for its Manifest Destiny and "Fifty-four Forty or Fight" in the 1840's, it took on not England or an English colony directly but the Hudson's Bay Company.

The adventurers and proprietors lived up to their names. The company's history could well be told in profiles of bold, colorful, and often courageous men. Reaching Hudson Bay in the early 1670's, they raised the H.B.C. ensign first over a few trading posts along the shoreline— Charles Fort, Moose Factory, and Fort Nelson, now York Factory. The red ensign incorporated the British Union Jack, with the bold white initials H.B.C. emblazoned in the lower right corner. Some Canadians will tell you irreverently that the letters stand for "Here Before Christ." The company is the only private establishment ever allowed to adapt the Union Jack for its own purposes.

In 1690 Henry Kelsey, at the age of twenty, paddled westward up the Hayes and Saskatchewan rivers. The first white man on the Canadian prairies, he discovered the buffaloes on the plains of Manitoba.

Samuel Hearne, pushing northward, became the first white man to reach the Arctic Ocean overland. Hudson's Bay fur traders were soon battling French entrepreneurs out of Montreal, and the story of the company's first century is one of building stockades and trading posts, defending these establishments, and often losing them to French and Indian attacks.

The British defeat of the French at Quebec in 1759 ended the European power struggle in Canada, but H.B.C.'s wars were far from over. Its adventurers were soon vying as fiercely as ever with another Montreal rival, the North West Company, formed by Scottish Canadians eager for fur fortunes in the great Canadian woods. These hardy wilderness men respected no boundaries and pushed canoe routes up the rivers and over lakes and portages to the Rocky Mountains and the Pacific. They even ventured into the territories that became Washington and Oregon in the United States.

Bloody conflict lasted, including the Port Arthur-Fort William confrontation, until the North West Company sold out to Hudson's Bay in 1821, making it the undisputed master all the way to the West Coast. H.B.C. even set up trading posts in San Franscisco and Hawaii and tangled with the East India Company over rights to exchange pelts for tea in China.

Dr. John Rae of the H.B.C., a five-time Arctic explorer, earned a reputation as a fast man on snowshoes. For example, starting out from Moose Factory in what is now northern Manitoba, he once traveled one hundred miles in twenty-four hours. Rae, a handsome Scotsman who came to Rupert's Land as a surgeon in the early 1800's, worked his way around by canoe and sled until he had delineated the Arctic coastline of Boothia Peninsula. Later he won an award of 10,000 pounds sterling for finding authentic traces of Sir John Franklin's ill-fated voyage of 1845 in quest of the Northwest Passage.

George Simpson, a stubby Scotsman, acquired the sobriquet "Little Emperor" because, as the company's first governor-in-chief in Canada, he organized its fur-trading operations on a grand scale. "Simpson," says a company historian, "made decisions on the spot. It took 18 months for the proprietors in London to receive a report on what he had done. By that time they could only approve an accomplished fact."

A popular portrait of George Simpson shows him in his canoe on a wilderness waterway. He sits tall in a black frock coat and top hat. Red-shirted Iroquois paddlers propel the craft swiftly forward, and a Highlander with bagpipes is poised to pipe the "Little Emperor" ashore at the next stop.

Samuel Black, John Bell, Robert Campbell, and others explored the interior of British Columbia. The company built Fort Yukon and traded in Alaska when that territory was Russian.

All this enterprise was founded firmly on profits. The European appetite for furs seemed to be insatiable for at least a century and a half. And the supply of beaver, white and silver fox, lynx (used for the busbies of British hussars), marten (Canadian sable), ermine, and other pelts was inexhaustible—thanks in part, say Hudson's Bay historians, to the company's conservative practices.

The only problems were trading efficiently with the Indians and Eskimos and encouraging them to bring their pelts in quantity to the trading posts, often hundreds of wooded miles from the trapping grounds. Since there were no other places to spend money but at the posts, trade became a matter of barter and bargain. Hudson's Bay detractors say that the native trappers "bartered" and the Bay men did the "bargaining." And profits, enabling the company many times to pay dividends of 50 per cent of the value of a shareholders' stock, are said to have been made at the expense of the poor Indians and Eskimos in want of trinkets, rifles, or a bottle of whisky.

The company motto, "Pro pelle cutem," inscribed on its elk-and-beaver coat of arms, is variously translated. A company historian has said that the literal "the skin for the fur" was intended to mean "a skin of goods for a skin of fur, in a word, a fair deal." But jokers say the words stand for "a skin for a skin."

The profit situation began to change in the 1840's when silk replaced beaver in top hats. The bottom fell out of the fur market. By 1860 Parliament had allowed Hudson's Bay rights in territories beyond Rupert's Land to lapse. In 1867 Ontario, Quebec, New Brunswick, and Nova Scotia formed the Confederation of Canada, and this led to the end of the great trading company's monopoly in the Canadian northwest. Two years later the company surrendered or "traded" its rights in Rupert's Land to the new Canadian government for 300,000 pounds sterling, seven million acres of land in the country's "Fertile

Belt," and small areas around all the trading posts.

Now came a dramatic turn of events that changed the face of western Canada and transformed the company of the fur-trading adventurers. They had been in the land for two hundred years, but the Canadian west remained pretty much as they had found it. The beaver was busy at his centuries' old tasks, and the buffalo still roamed. From Toronto to the Pacific Coast there were only about thirty thousand white people who had braved the inhospitable prairies and mountains. Farming techniques that produced prosperity in the humid soil of the eastern regions did not work in the arid west. Crop failures, locust invasions, and dust storms required more adjustments than ordinary immigrants could bear. The Indians and half-breed métis, a few missionaries, and the Hudson's Bay employees were the hardy exceptions.

But in Ottawa the government of the fledgling Canadian Confederation needed control of the west to head off the Americans. South of the border the Civil War had only temporarily diverted thoughts of Manifest Destiny. President Grant now hinted that the British might be willing to give up some Canadian land in order to settle what became known as the *Alabama* claims, which were claims for damages inflicted on the North during the Civil War by the *Alabama* and other British-built Southern raiders. Grant made it apparent, in any event, that he felt Canada would sooner or later be absorbed by the United States.

Knowing well that if the Canadians didn't populate and develop the west soon, the Americans would, Prime Minister John A. Macdonald began to prepare for settlers by setting up a government in advance. He named one of his cabinet ministers "Lieutenant Governor of Rupert's Land and the Northwest Territories" and sent him on his roundabout way (of necessity through the United States) to Fort Garry. A survey was initiated on the rectangular township plan used in Ontario. The "most desirable immigrants" were expected to come from that province, where the plan was familiar to farmers. No cognizance was taken of the people already living there.

But the métis, largely French and Indian mixed-breeds, had settled long before on the Red River around Fort Garry. They were nearly six thousand strong, descendants of those intrepid canoeists, the early voyageurs, and themselves hunters and trappers, traders, storekeepers, and boatmen. They were directly or indirectly dependent on the Hudson's Bay Company and took pride in the freedom they enjoyed under it's paternalism. In contrast, the "new government men" from Ottawa were suspect, and the fears of the métis were aroused as soon as these eastern agents moved in to take control of the new Confederation's prairie territories. Before Queen Victoria had officially approved the sale of Hudson's Bay land to Canada, agents began surveying every bit of ground, including the strips along the river banks on which the Hudson's Bay Company had long ago settled hundreds of "its" people.

Under the leadership of Louis Riel, the métis revolted in 1869. They forcibly stopped the new lieutenant governor at the American border and then took Fort Garry, where they set up their own government with Riel as president. With Donald A. "Labrador" Smith, the Hudson's Bay man, acting as go-between, Riel held the Ottawa authorities at bay for a year, until, after ninety-six days of cross-country travel, troops arrived from Ontario. Riel fled to the Dakotas, from which he returned fifteen years later to lead another revolt, this time in Saskatchewan. It was during this second revolt that Van Horne of the Canadian Pacific Railway got soldiers out there in a hurry—eleven days.

"Labrador" Smith didn't succeed in mediating for the métis during the first revolt, but he retained their confidence when he later ran for a seat in the federal Parliament. He coolly transported métis traders from one polling place to another at the Hudson's Bay Company's expense to insure his majority. "And the fur traders," reported Douglas MacKay in his history *The Honourable Company,* "with the implicit obedience of their training . . . accept[ed] it all with amusement as part of new duties under a new régime." Eventually one of Smith's elections was upset on charges of corrupt practice.

Smith was knighted by Queen Victoria and later raised to the peerage as Lòrd Strathcona. In London he is remembered for equipping and maintaining at his own expense a cavalry regiment (Lord Strathcona's Horse) for service in the Boer War. But where did the money come from? Winnipeggers recall him as the slick land salesman who invested the savings of his fellow company officers and paid them 3 per cent interest while he acquired for himself enough shares of Hud-

The Bay outpost at Broughton Island, Baffin Island, is shown at the onset of the brief warm-water season.

son's Bay Company stock to insure his appointment to the company governorship in 1889.

Various homesteading measures were adopted to promote settlement in the west. More important than any of them was MacDonald's promise of a transcontinental railroad, a promise that brought Manitoba (Riel's name for that part of Rupert's Land) into the Confederation in 1870 and British Columbia in 1871. The territory between eventually became the provinces of Alberta and Saskatchewan. He also promised law and order by establishing the Northwest Mounted Police, that romantic constabulary now known as the Royal Canadian

Mounted Police. Sir John dressed the Mounties in red tunics to make them resemble British soldiers, whom everyone then respected and admired.

With the railroad and the Mounties went people, first as construction workers, then as tradesmen, and finally as homesteaders. Emigrants from other hard lands, among them Ukrainians and Icelanders, stayed to overcome the grasshoppers, the dust storms, and the cruel winters and to grow the grain whose shipment made railroading profitable. The process revived the Hudson's Bay Company, for while the settlers drove out most of the fur-bearing animals, they needed goods of all kinds. They needed stores to supply them.

The railroad obligingly (but basically for geographic reasons) ran from one Hudson's Bay post to another, forming a chain of communications, a defense line, and gradually an artery of trade fed by the growing agriculture. Towns and cities grew up in the wake of the railroad and its branch lines—Fort Garry (Winnipeg), Calgary, Regina, and Vancouver, the mainland terminal of the Canadian Pacific. As cities, Saskatoon and Edmonton awaited the coming of the Canadian National.

Wherever the railroad brought in the business, Hudson's Bay converted its old trading-post facilities into department stores, and the phenomenon of "Harrod's on the Prairies" developed. Fine new establishments modeled after London's famous department store sprang up. Unfortunately some of them became white elephants because pioneer housewives looking for dishpans and heavy woolens found emporiums loaded with English merchandise, like fine china and Sheffield plate, for which they had little use or taste.

Looking back, the Hudson's Bay deal with the new Ottawa government seems a fabulous one for the company. The seven million acres in Alberta, Saskatchewan, and Manitoba, which showed nothing but buffaloes and prairie grass, actually covered oil, gas, ore, and potash deposits of untold value. But all that the proprietors in London knew at the time was that they owned limitless horizons of unpromising plains. It was theirs to dispose of, and they felt that they had better get started. Donald A. Smith went west as the Hudson's Bay Company's chief liquidator. It was on the way to this assignment that he fell into his role of mediator in one of Canada's most celebrated re-

The skidoo is quickly replacing the dog team in the North.

volts. For, regardless of ups and downs, the company was the institution that people in the west looked to for guidance and protection long after the new federal government in Ottawa came into being.

Smith's liquidation was followed by a period of thorough reorganization that lasted fifty years. But Hudson's Bay remained a delightfully Old English establishment until 1970, when on the adventurers' three-hundredth anniversary it was finally decided to move headquarters from the paneled walls of Hudson's Bay House, Bishopsgate, London, to Winnipeg. The directors announced their decision after an annual meeting that had received a report showing that 97 per cent of all Bay business was transacted in Canada.

Viscount Amory, the governor, announced that upon his retirement within a year, he would be succeeded by the Bay's first Canadian governor.

The managing director, whose headquarters are in Winnipeg, is James R. Murray, a Winnipegger who was a career officer in the Canadian foreign service before coming into the business in 1951. Murray is responsible for giving "The Bay" its new look—shortening the name for the benefit of the copywriters, replacing dark, "dignified" colors with eye-catching yellows in window displays, and giving managers free reign to pep up salesrooms with mod shops and discothèques.

Besides new colors, there are new accounting systems and new buildings. And there is a new approach to trade.

Cape Parry and Sugluk, both in the Arctic, now stock "ski-doos," the mechanized toboggans that have replaced dog sleds. The stores at Yellowknife, in the Northwest Territories, and at other remote points offer a Hudson's Bay U-Paddle Canoe rental service. For twenty-five dollars a week a venturesome voyager can pick up a canoe "here," cruise the abundant rivers and lakes, and leave it "there"— the next post.

And all the remote posts now stock refrigerators. "Of course, we sell them to the Eskimos," said Clem Pigeon, the manager in Aklavik. "Few Eskimos today live in igloos. Food will spoil in their oil-heated houses, same as in yours, without an icebox."

But Clem Pigeon still takes furs in payment when his customers offer them. The Eskimos, said an H.B.C. northern executive, "have seen governments, and other companies, come and go. Only The Bay has stayed."

In recent years the Canadian government, through its Department of Northern Development, has moved into the former Rupert's Land with multimillion-dollar school and welfare programs. Government checks are part of the economy. Latter-day adventurers and proprietors are waiting to move in, not so much for fur as for oil, gas, iron ore, potash, and a dozen other minerals with which Canada is blessed. But the Hudson's Bay Company plans to carry on up there, too. It has built a new store at Deception Bay, in northern Quebec, where the Asbestos Corporation, Ltd. recently opened a mine.

Hudson's Bay celebrated its tercentenary in the Year of Our Lord 1970. But for the "Company of Adventurers" it was the year Outfit 300. "Outfit" is the term for the annual supplying, or outfitting, of the posts. And Hudson's Bay still counts the years that way—right back to the landing of the ketch *Nonsuch.*

Recently at a ceremony at Lower Fort Garry, Hudson's Bay officials turned over to the government of Canada the deeds to grounds around old York Factory up on Hudson Bay.

In accepting title to the historic property, Jean Chretien, Minister of Northern Development, noted that this once thriving port for shipping western Canada's principal exports, furs, was now "inaccessible." There are no roads there today, and the place is so remote that it isn't feasible yet to develop it for tourists.

But, added the minister, "the isolation of today is not permanent." The day will come, he said, when York Factory "is once again on the paths of the traveler."

For three hundred years, Hudson's Bay fulfilled the provision of its 1670 charter that the British monarch collect as an annual tribute from Rupert's Land the skins of two elks and two beavers. This obligation was omitted from the 1970 charter, which authorized moving the home office to Canada. However, the Bay's officials decided not to change custom precipitously. When Queen Elizabeth II visited Winnipeg for a centennial celebration in July, 1970, she was invited to a ceremony at the rebuilt Lower Fort Garry. Perhaps for the last time, Hudson's Bay factors approached the monarch with the traditional tribute. They presented the Queen with the skins of two elks and two beavers.

The Big Lonely and the Big Sky in Saskatchewan

13 Big Lonely

"Here is a different breed of Canadian, the true 'New Canadian.'"

Banff, Alberta, lies at the foot of the Cascade Mountains.

From Lake Superior to the Rockies lies the tremendous expanse of the Canadian prairies, which hoboes riding the rails call the "Big Lonely." Manitoba, Saskatchewan, and Alberta are among the areas of the civilized world least worried about the population explosion. There is one square mile for every 5 of the 3,350,000 people in those provinces. And the gradual movement of half of them into the half-dozen largest cities leaves the prairie country lonelier than it was a hundred years ago when the Indians and métis pursued the great herds of roaming buffaloes. The Montreal artist Jean-Paul Lemieux has movingly caught the loneliness in his canvas *Midnight Train,* now hanging in the National Gallery in Ottawa. It shows flat, endless land, snow-covered and without sign of native life—but in the distance a night train, diminishing in perspective, is making its solitary way to a destination beyond the horizon.

With the coming of modern transportation and instant communications, the prairies may not be as lonely as they look, but they are still big. The horizons are straight and long, the skies are high, the fields are as oceans, and the people stand tall against the harsh weather. It is difficult to tell a Calgary man from a Texan—and he frequently is a Texan. There is a joke that says Dallas men and their women go to Calgary to escape that closed-in feeling. The twenty-five thousand or so Americans in Calgary include farmers, cattlemen, oil prospectors, business tycoons, bankers, and speculators. Many of the destitute Okies who somehow reached Alberta during the depressed 1930's are now living there on their capital gains.

An American on the Canadian prairies sees much to remind him of home on the range, American style—rugged individualism, conservative thinking, Bible Belt religion. Ernest C. Manning held the premiership of Alberta for twenty-five years, urging the wheat farmers to greater production, carefully parceling out oil-field concessions, and teaching a Sunday afternoon Bible class on the radio. When he retired in 1968, he left behind him a provincial government that stood as a monument to a quarter century of prairie prudence and disciplined husbandry.

But the sooner an American visitor realizes that he is not at home —that Winnipeg is not Minneapolis, or Saskatchewan, Kansas—the better. Nowhere in Canada do Canadians admire Americans more than they do on the prairies, but at the same time, there is no place where they cherish their Canadianism as much. The mosaic pattern of living—the unity of the diverse many—has worked better in the open prairies than in the urban east. In the time and space of the "Big Lonely," settlers from Europe and Asia, clinging to Old World cultures, became Canadians without first becoming English or French.

Here is a different breed of Canadian, the true "New Canadian." Cut off socially and physically from the east, he has survived the hardships of pioneering, the bitter cold, the dust and the droughts, the hordes of insects, and above all, the loneliness. He feels that he did it on his own and is today ready to stand up to any Establishment man from Toronto or Ottawa. On the slightest provocation he will tell an American to go back where he came from.

The first non-English, non-French, non-Establishment Prime Minister of Canada came from the prairies. John George Diefenbaker, of German parentage, grew up in humble pioneer surroundings in the Saskatchewan wheat country. As an ambitious young "progressive" lawyer, he came out of the west with the impetuosity of Lochinvar and the oratorical strength of William Jennings Bryan. He first captured the Conservative party, then swept the entrenched Liberals out of office to become Prime Minister in 1957.

Perhaps it was prairie individualism that made Mr. Diefenbaker a champion dissenter and a poor political organizer and administrator. He lost to the resurgent Liberals in 1963, but has carried on as an irascible voice in the Parliamentary Opposition. Mr. Diefenbaker represents a characteristically western Canadian free-swinging conservatism that resembles the old radical republicanism of the American West. In Canada the prairie conservative is the product of no establishment. He is a rebel. Affluence growing out of trade in wheat, livestock, oil, and potash may have subdued the radical in him and perhaps diluted the spirit of rebellion. But he is still no conformist, and the Riel Rebellion was by no means the last civil upheaval on the prairies.

A strike of building and metal trade unionists broke out in Winnipeg in May, 1918, and before it was over, forty-one days later, thirty-five thousand workers, both organized and unorganized, had walked out in sympathy. The immediate objectives, collective bargaining and industrial unionism, would be taken for granted today. But fifty years ago these goals were a generation ahead of their time. The only unionism then accepted by government and business was that of crafts and trades, which divided labor's strength. In the east leaders of such unions usually worked with the governments, and for that reason they had lost their hold on radical labor unionists in the west.

As the Winnipeg strike gathered momentum and won popular support, it became not only the instrument of the unionists but also the voice of the poor and the downtrodden. They demanded the downfall of big business and the end of governments that catered to "the interests." While Prime Minister Arthur Meighen, an eastern Conservative, inevitably denounced the strikers for seeking "the perfection of bolshevism," thousands more workers walked off their jobs in Winnipeg. They closed down the stores, the telephone and telegraph services, public transportation, and the mails. Milk and bread deliveries were maintained only at the insistence of the strike committee.

The workers' drive for One Big Union collapsed on a bloody Saturday in June, when fifty Mounties on galloping horses charged surging crowds on Main Street, firing their revolvers and whaling away with baseball bats. Two died in the gunfire, thirty demonstrators fell under the blows, and six Mounties were carried to the hospital.

The charge of the Mounties broke the strike. Gradually the men went back to work. But most of the militant leaders who were arrested, jailed, and prosecuted became martyrs and heroes. Some of them lived to change the politics of the prairies. One, J. S. Woodsworth, who was jailed on charges of seditious libel as editor of the strike bulletin, organized the Cooperative Commonwealth Federation, a party of socialist reform. He was its national leader during the depression of the 1930's.

The C.C.F. won the Saskatchewan elections in 1944 and gave the province an out-and-out socialist government for twenty years, before yielding finally to the Liberals under Premier Ross Thatcher, the champion of "100 per cent free enterprise." Saskatchewan socialists established the first free public medical care plan in North America. Meanwhile, Alberta's Mr. Manning, though an archconservative by present-day standards, rose to power in the 1930's as a Social Crediter advocating wholesale distribution of wealth through government certificates of credit.

The C.C.F. eventually became the left-wing New Democratic Party, which has continued to hold the support of most labor unions. The new party's efforts to build a strong national structure on the old C.C.F. foundations have as yet failed. Nevertheless, in 1969 the New Democrats upset the reigning Conservatives in Manitoba to form a socialist-minded provincial government for the second time in Canada. Again it was on the prairies.

The visitor to the Canadian prairies today traverses the geographic, and in a sense the historical, heartland of North America. Anyone putting his finger on the center of the map of this continent would find it very close to Winnipeg. Sixty miles directly south of Winnipeg is the border village of Pembina, North Dakota, the oldest community on the northern plains. Its name, originally Pembian, comes from the French rendition of a Cree-Chippewa term for the prairie cranberry used in pemmican, a concentrated food made by the Indians.

Pembina was inhabited by 1780, and local historians say that the first white children in the Canadian-American plains were born there. Two babies were delivered in the same week—one to English parents down from Hudson Bay, the other to a Quebec mother who had accompanied her voyageur husband into the Wild West. Pointing out Pembina's mixture of races, which became typical of the Canadian prairies, Joseph Kinsey Howard, the late Montana historian, wrote in *Strange Empire:* "Americans may find it odd that this American town was the first prairie headquarters of the thoroughly British Hudson's Bay Company, that it once was owned by a Scottish earl, and that it once was peopled almost entirely by German and Swiss mercenaries, veterans of some dog-eared European war."

But more than this. Pembina, a town of eight hundred, which one sees as he enters Canada by the Red River route, was the "capital" of the métis, the mixed white and Indian people whose attempt to form a nation for themselves in the "Big Lonely" was one of the most dramatic episodes in Canadian history.

Legend says that this prairie heartland was a crossroads much earlier than is commonly believed. In 1898 a farmer near Kensington, Minnesota, dug up an inscribed stone. Scholars say the inscription appears to date from the fourteenth century and to give an account of a massacre of a group of Norse explorers by Indians at this site in the Red River basin in 1362. Were Norsemen in the mid-continent of North America more than a hundred years before Columbus reached the West Indies?

Why, in any event, did these immense lonely prairies become a "crossroads"—for the Indians coming in from Asia, for English adventurers moving down from Hudson Bay, for French voyageurs traveling west from Quebec, and later for Americans from the south and Pacific mountain men from the west?

The answer is that the prairies, after the antediluvian ocean had receded, became a vast sea of grass drained by great rivers. Three mighty waterways begin in the prairie basin—the Nelson River flowing north to Hudson Bay, the St. Lawrence-Great Lakes system draining into the Atlantic Ocean, and the Missouri-Mississippi, which carries some Canadian prairie water to the Gulf of Mexico.

The soil deposit on the prairies is a dark loam, often twelve inches deep. The thousands of square miles of grass once fed millions of buffaloes. The rivers supported populations of fur-bearing animals. The animals drew first the Indians, then the white men. Despite all the the empty space, the two races never found room enough to live together on equal terms.

A conflict involving a people who were part Indian occurred just a century ago and was touched upon in the preceding chapter. Whether Louis Riel, who brought it on, was a martyr or a traitor is still being debated. He was hanged for leading two rebellions of the métis against the new Confederation of Canada. But his memory lives. He has the folk-hero stature of, say, John Brown in the United States. A stream of books, a play, and an opera have been written about him. Trudeau, shortly after becoming Prime Minister, went to Regina, Saskatchewan, to unveil a statue of Riel. A leading Canadian folk singer has made popular a haunting song entitled "Riel! Riel!"

The Riel legend has so embedded itself in Canadian life that many Canadians are convinced that had the rebel won, the prairie heartland would today be a huge French-speaking province, if not an independent republic.

The métis were a by-product of the fur trade. The men who canoed westward for furs, especially the French-speaking voyageurs, took up with Indian women. While there was intermarriage in many tribes, the Cree were especially favored, according to Joseph Kinsey Howard. "The white men found their women more attractive, more dependable morally—they eagerly embraced Christianity—and more intelligent than those of other tribes. Half-breed girls were especially desirable; early travelers reported they were often 'of classic beauty.'"

The proportion of Indian blood gradually diminished, and the term "half-breed" became inaccurate. The name métis, French for mixed blood, was favored and is still being used by the people themselves.

Métis were relatively few in number until the victory of the British

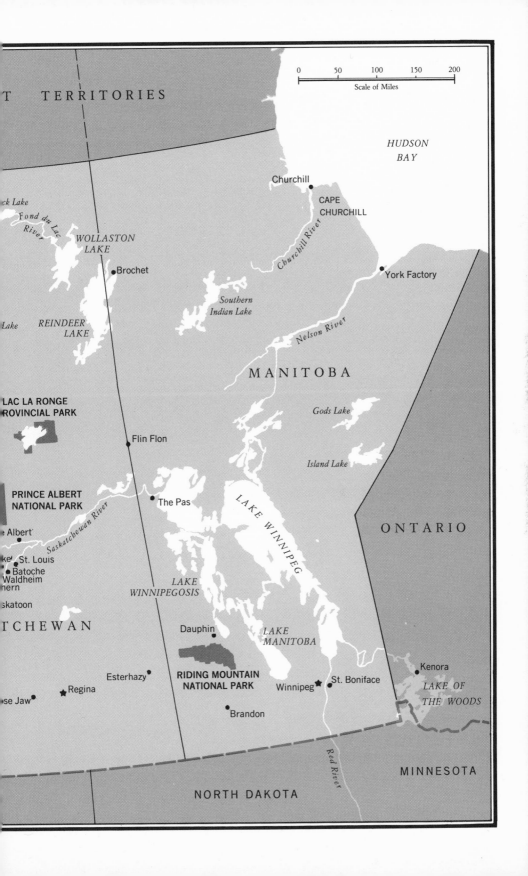

T E R R I T O R I E S

0   50   100   150   200
Scale of Miles

HUDSON
BAY

ck Lake

Fond du Lac River

WOLLASTON
LAKE

Churchill

CAPE
CHURCHILL

Churchill River

●Brochet

York Factory

Lake

*Southern
Indian Lake*

REINDEER
LAKE

Nelson River

M A N I T O B A

Gods Lake

LAC LA RONGE
PROVINCIAL PARK

●Flin Flon

Island Lake

PRINCE ALBERT
NATIONAL PARK

Saskatchewan River

●The Pas

O N T A R I O

Albert

ke St. Louis
●Batoche
Waldheim
hern

L
A
K
E

W
I
N
N
I
P
E
G

ke

skatoon

LAKE
WINNIPEGOSIS

T C H E W A N

Dauphin

LAKE
MANITOBA

Esterhazy●

RIDING MOUNTAIN
NATIONAL PARK

Winnipeg ★ St. Boniface

Kenora

LAKE OF
THE WOODS

★Regina

se Jaw●

●Brandon

Red River

MINNESOTA

NORTH DAKOTA

over the French at Quebec in 1759 started a new migration of French Canadians to the plains. By 1850 there were at least thirteen thousand métis in western Canada, while other thousands had crossed into the western United States. In Canada they remained a minority among the Indian tribes, but outnumbered the whites in the settlements.

Although they roamed, seeking furs and following buffalo herds, they developed a culture and economy. They were, says Howard, "the best boatmen, the best guides, the best hunters, trappers and traders." Some white men out to exploit the west made the mistake of thinking the useful métis obsequious.

After 1867 the British Government, as we have already noted, persuaded the Hudson's Bay Company to cede its northwest territories to the new Canada. While negotiations for the transfer went along smoothly, no one bothered to tell the Indians or the métis. The Indians continued their tribal ways without immediate protest. But the métis were alarmed when they learned, after the deal was made, that their "nation" had been sold to a "foreign power." When the first Canadian government survey team arrived to lay out roads and three-hundred-acre farm plots, the leader who directed the métis to step on the surveyors' chains to halt the intrusion was Louis Riel.

Riel, a black-haired, dark-skinned, stocky man, who was, in fact, no more than one-eighth Indian, had gone to school in a Montreal seminary. He had lived for a time in the United States. But he considered himself a métis prairie man, and as such he resented both the intrusion of the Canadian advance agents and their arrogance. They made no secret of their belief that the métis men were shiftless and their women loose.

The métis had been much happier and freer under Hudson's Bay Company rule, and Riel hastened to Fort Garry to raise the British Union Jack in defiance of the advancing Canadian authorities. As has been told, Ottawa sent out Donald "Labrador" Smith to pacify Riel. But Riel, proving himself an able leader, held his métis firmly together and staved Smith off until the spring of 1870, when the government of Canada offered acceptable terms. It promised to make Manitoba the fifth province—the first since Confederation—and to guarantee French schools for the métis and full protection in the use of the French language.

270

Unhappily, Riel's own amnesty was not guaranteed. When Canadian troops arrived to establish law and order, Riel found it expedient to slip across the border into American exile. But in one sense the refugee, rather than Prime Minister Macdonald, was the real Father of Manitoba.

The métis, being in the majority in the new province, elected Riel *in absentia* to be their first representative in the House of Commons at Ottawa. He was smuggled into Ottawa to sign his name in the register of the Commons, but he never took his seat. During the next fifteen years he spent several months in a Quebec asylum, then returned to the United States and acquired American citizenship. Riel suffered from a mania that made him feel, as did Joan of Arc, that he had a divine mission to free his people.

In 1884 he came back to Canada at the call of métis, who were rebelling again, this time in Saskatchewan. The drama of his life was now swiftly approaching its climax. The man who was a mystic revolutionary, who had been a member of the federal Parliament, stood up against the troops of the Crown. But he would not truly fight. Military strategists argue to this day that had Louis Riel given his military commander, Gabriel Dumont, his head, the métis would have won their nation.

Dumont, called "Prince of the Prairie," was a brilliant guerrilla fighter who applied the same techniques to attacking redcoats that he had used to hunt buffaloes. He drove them into "pounds," then let his sharpshooters pick them off at will. He scored at Fish Creek on April 24, 1885; and at Cut Knife Hill the métis and allied Indians under their leader, Chief Poundmaker, fired scrap iron and any other missiles available to drive back troops armed with cannon, long-range rifles, and the new Gatling gun, the first machine gun.

Dumont won battles, but Riel would not permit him to follow up his ambushing tactics and wipe out the enemy. Riel, the religious visionary, always prevailed. Some thought him still insane, others called him the "prophet of the prairies," but all followed him, including Dumont.

Meanwhile, as previously related, William C. Van Horne, the American-born builder of the Canadian Pacific, realized that the Riel Rebellion afforded him an opportunity to prove his unfinished railroad's worth to the government. Although long stretches of track were still unlaid, Van Horne fulfilled his promise to transport militia units from eastern Ontario to Saskatchewan in eleven days. Where there was no trackage—a total distance of a hundred miles—Van Horne used carts, wagons, and sleighs instead of trains. In later life he said that had it not been for Riel, the transcontinental railroad would not have been completed for many years. The rebellion dramatized the need for it, and a hitherto balky Parliament provided the necessary financing.

Some historians are certain that Dumont, if left to his own devices, would have harrassed the troop movements and perhaps prevented the federal forces from reaching the decisive battleground. At Batoche, in central Saskatchewan, the métis and Indians were crushed. Riel was captured and put on trial in Regina as a traitor. Standing in the dock, a squat figure with a full black beard, Riel, then only forty-one, rejected his lawyer's plea of insanity—the only plea that might have saved his life.

"Though it would be easier for me today to plead insanity . . . I have this satisfaction," he told the court, "that if I die I will not be reputed by all men as insane, as a lunatic."

He was convicted, and a board appointed by the government found him sane enough to be hanged. In Ottawa Prime Minister Macdonald, despite the implications for French-English disunity, refused to reprieve the condemned man. Riel was executed. Was he a martyr? Or a traitor? Was Canada defeated no less than Riel? His death stirred up English and French antipathies anew. There were riots in Montreal.

Meanwhile, Dumont, the métis' brilliant guerrilla fighter, escaped to the United States, and in later years he appeared in Buffalo Bill's Wild West Show.

Canada eventually won the west. Unhappily the métis, who were the best plainsmen on the land, never overcame their defeat. They can be found today on the fringes of society around booming towns. They are as underprivileged and as unacceptable as the Indians—and even more dispossessed. There are no métis reservations in Canada.

In striking contrast to the métis are the New Canadians, who pushed in after the building of the transcontinental railroad, and especially after 1900. The Canadian ideal of "unity and diversity" is nowhere better realized than in, say, Winnipeg.

The capital of Manitoba, which a century ago was a remote trading post, is now a metropolis of 500,000 people. It sprawls, but its prosperity is also pushing it skyward. A thirty-two-story office building marks the intersection of Main Street and Portage Avenue, reputed to be the windiest, and in winter the coldest, street crossing in North America. Two rival department stores, The Bay (Hudson's) and Eaton's, are described as "neighbors on the sunny side of Portage." One merchant explained that shoppers refuse to cross to the shady side "for fear of freezing to death—even when there's a bargain over there." All winter long, whenever the thermometer rises above 20 degrees below zero, Winnipeggers take it as a sign of spring.

Founded by Englishmen and Frenchmen, the city is now largely in the hands of people of other ethnic extractions. At least fifty-five thousand Winnipeggers are of Ukrainian background, fifty thousand are Germans, and there are large numbers of Poles, Icelanders, and Scandinavians, a few Italians, Chinese, and Japanese, and "even some Americans."

An estimated total of 150,000 Winnipeggers read newspapers printed neither in English nor French. The *Mennonite Review,* a German-language paper, is more than a hundred years old. The Icelandic *Logberg Heimskringla* has been published for seventy years. The *Canadian Farmer,* with a circulation of seventy thousand, contends that it is the oldest and largest Ukrainian-language journal outside of the Soviet Union.

Winnipeg's North End, where most of the New Canadians live, supplies a liberal share of the dancers in the world-traveling Royal Winnipeg Ballet. Its musicians fill many chairs in the Winnipeg Symphony Orchestra. It sends actors to the distinguished Manitoba Theatre Centre, whose one-time director, John Hirsch, emigrated to the Shakespeare Festival in Stratford, Ontario, and has since worked on Broadway. From the North End, too, come some of Canada's famous names in hockey—Bill Juzda, Terry Sawchuk, Wally Stanowski, and Bill Mosienko.

Another product of the North End is Stephen Juba, the first non-English Canadian to become mayor of Winnipeg. Of Ukrainian extraction, he is now in his fourth term, having won repeatedly over Establishment—i.e., English—challengers.

The grain elevators at Estlin, Saskatchewan, tower over the fields and barley harvesters.

Mayor Juba is fond of conducting tours through the new, glistening white city hall, built "right where Skid Row used to be." The town's slum has become a municipal complex, accommodating not only the city hall and the police and fire departments but also a fine new Arts Center. Other city landmarks include the pseudoclassic legislative building, notable both for the "Golden Boy" statue atop its 225-foot dome and for two immense bronze bison that guard the grand staircase inside.

The Winnipeg Art Gallery offers visitors a growing collection of Canadian paintings and an impressive display of fine Eskimo art and sculpture, much of it from settlements on Hudson Bay. There is also a provincial museum, with Indian and pioneer relics arranged to dramatize Manitoban history.

Tourism has only recently come to the prairie provinces, but each of them—Manitoba, Saskatchewan, and Alberta—now has an active travel department staffed by energetic, helpful, informed men and women who are full of ideas for sightseeing, camping, dining, and lodging.

Visitors in prairie cities used to be at the mercy of the old railroad (Canadian National or Canadian Pacific) hotels, whose main business today is housing conventions and government conferences. But new hotels and motels, with modern accommodations at every price range, are now in operation. Accordingly the "châteaus," as the old railroad hotels are commonly called in Canada, have improved their plumbing, brightened their décor, and enlivened their cuisine.

Good restaurants, in and out of hotels, abound in Winnipeg. Their specialties are steaks, sometimes offered by the pound, and freshwater fish. We find nothing more delectable than the Winnipeg gold-eye, a smoked fish introduced sixty years ago by the first chef of the Royal Alexandra (Canadian Pacific) Hotel.

But a traveler through the prairies, unless he uses the airlines or railroads, must expect many hours of driving—hot in summer, cold and perhaps hazardous in winter—through wheat fields and open spaces that, while monumental and momentarily exhilarating, may become monotonous. In winter, in fact, the prairies are too bleak, cold, and uncertain for cross-country pleasure.

One engrossing pastime for motorists leaving Winnipeg in any direction is collecting absurd names of towns. The towns themselves are seldom notable, but one delights in passing through Flin Flon or The Pas, both in Manitoba, just to tell the folks back home of having been there. Both are somewhat out of the way, but if one cares for such things, Flin Flon, 450 miles northwest of Winnipeg, offers guided tours through its Hudson Bay Mining and Smelting Company plant. Recently, too, visitors have been pausing at the main highway entrance to photograph a statue designed by Al Capp, the American cartoonist. The Pas, south of Flin Flon, has an old Anglican church whose pews, altar, and religious carvings are the work of ship's carpenters—members of an expedition to find the missing Arctic explorer Sir John Franklin. The expedition spent a winter there, and the carpenters didn't waste their time.

Saskatchewan, on and off the Trans-Canada Highway, is more and more wheat. Some visitors come away convinced that there are more grain elevators than people. Human beings aren't evident in the daytime, but one of the haunting sights in the world of travel must be passing through Saskatchewan on a night of the harvest moon. Then the tractor-drawn reapers may be seen moving through the fields, their headlights poking through the frosty air like fireflies in a New England glade.

And who would not be charmed to discover, on the Trans-Canada just west of Moosomin (pop. 1,088), a road marker pointing to Esterhazy (pop. 423), which is just a wheat field or two from Stockholm (pop. 229). Mozart (pop. 50) is a grain-elevator town south of Quill Lakes. Awaiting one farther west are Moose Jaw (pop. 20,496), whose principal businesses are railroading, flour milling, and meat packing, and Swift Current (pop. 5,074), which has Canada's only helium plant. Prince Albert (pop. 17,067), just south of the geographic center of the province, is the jump-off point for most of northern Saskatchewan. It has sawmills and flour mills, sells farm machinery, and still trades in furs.

However, Regina (pop. 131,127), the capital, and Saskatoon (pop. 115,892) are the principal cities to visit. Rivalry between them is so keen that the University of Saskatchewan, seated in Saskatoon, now has a fast-growing division in Regina.

Regina was established in 1882 as a cluster of tents at the crossing of the new Canadian Pacific Railroad and Wascana River. The river, it was said at one time, "could not make up its mind which way to flow over the flat plain." But now, transformed into a lake, it is the heart of the Wascana Development Project, a multimillion-dollar center designed by the Japanese architect Minoru Yamasaki. It is the setting for government and university buildings, public parks, picnic grounds —and the new statue commemorating Riel. The recently relocated early pioneer home of former Prime Minister Diefenbaker also stands here.

Reginans judge the age of various sections of town by the height of the trees. In the beginning "there wasn't a sprig anywhere around," reported one old-timer. Over the last fifty years thousands of trees have been imported, painstakingly watered in summer and protected from the prairie blizzards in winter. Beyond the downtown areas, where the firs and maples may rise above the gabled houses, trees are no more than roof high, and in the suburbs, where the streets run straight into the open prairie, homes stand out in their fresh pastel paint because the trees are still only striplings.

It is in Regina that the Royal Canadian Mounted Police, which began as the Northwest Mounted Police, has its principal training grounds. Its headquarters were once there, too, but they are now in Ottawa. On the barracks grounds on the outskirts of Regina, visitors can see the recruits learning how to get their man. The parade grounds and museum are open daily from 8:30 A.M. to noon and from 1:30 P.M. to 5 P.M. Constables conduct guided tours, during which the future Mounties can be seen working out at karate, jujitsu, and markmanship. Ironically, there isn't much horsemanship anymore, as previously noted, because the only Mounties who are mounted today are the very few who participate in ceremonial functions. All the others perform their duties on foot or in automobiles.

Nevertheless, visitors are now and then lucky enough to catch one of the wonderful mounted musical rides being rehearsed for a special occasion. And every day at 1 P.M. they may observe the regular military drill.

The barracks museum contains fascinating relics of cases solved by the Mounties. One display recounts the Riel affair. It was at these barracks that Riel was executed.

278

Downtown again, one should visit the Saskatchewan Museum of Natural History, with its flora and fauna of the Canadian prairies. Dr. Fred Bard, the director, has created dramatic dioramas showing the mighty moose guarding his herd, birds in flight, coyotes fighting over a buffalo carcass, and Indians hunting or working the buffalo hides.

Saskatoon, 160 miles to the north, is topographically more interesting than Regina. It straddles the twisting South Saskatchewan River at the juncture of the treeless plains and the park country of the north. Within the river's many loops are sloping enclaves of trees, flowers, and shrubs. Saskatoon, in fact, got its name from the Indian word for a wild berry that grows there in profusion.

Most visitors head for the Western Development Museum to see a collection of the farm equipment that won the west for the pioneers. The old steam tractors and combines are shown in action in summer at the "Pion-Era" performances staged at the museum.

A favorite cultural attraction is the new Mendel Art Gallery and Civic Conservatory, beautifully situated on the riverbank. It is named for Fred Mendel, the town's wealthy meat packer and philanthropist, who built the gallery and placed in it part of his collection of Canadian paintings. Hundreds of other canvases by leading contemporary European artists hang in Mr. Mendel's private quarters in the main building of Intercontinental Packers Limited, from which he directs a $10-million-a-year business.

The University of Saskatchewan arranges tours of its campus and gray stone buildings, among which are the new $15-million Medical College and Hospital, the University Picture Gallery, and several museums of special interest, notably the W. P. Fraser Herbarium in the department of biology.

Sensing that many tourists might not know what to do with the province's great open spaces except speed through them as fast as the law allows, the Saskatchewan Centennial Corporation worked out a series of Vacation Trails in 1965. These are routes for motor trips of two hundred miles or so out from the cities. Folders and maps outlining the trails may be had for the asking at tourist information offices throughout the province or by writing the Saskatchewan Travel Bureau, Department of Industry and Information, Regina.

As an example of the trails, there is one, dedicated to Louis Riel, that starts at Saskatoon, follows Route 11 north to Waldheim, continues to Rosthern, Duck Lake, and St. Louis, and then returns to Saskatoon by a different way. One passes the site of Fort Carlton, an old Hudson's Bay post that later became a Northwest Mounted Police station. But the historical highlight of the trip will be the Batoche Rectory site, where the métis under Riel's General Dumont met final defeat at the hands of the government forces. The trenches dug by the victors are still visible, and Dumont's grave is situated on a bluff overlooking the South Saskatchewan River, within sight of the church and rectory, which date from 1884.

Alberta, geographically, is the Colorado of Canada. Its eastern half is in the prairies. Its western half rises ever so gently, and at Calgary, as at Denver, one gets one's first thrilling glimpse of the Rockies in the distance.

Alberta's culture and economics, however, belong to the prairies. Calgary's population of 330,575 includes wheat and cattle men, oil drillers, and above all, stampeders. The Calgary Stampede, which overtakes the city for a week every July, is the annual call of the Wild West. But when it is over, Calgary settles back to its conservative prairie ways.

Yet times are changing. Sunday sports were legalized a few years ago, and it became lawful recently for grocery stores to open on Sunday. But Sunday cocktails remain taboo unless ordered with meals in licensed restaurants. Indeed, not so long ago cocktails on any day were forbidden anywhere outside one's home—a result of Premier Manning's Baptist fundamentalism.

Mr. Manning didn't drink alcoholic beverages, and he preached abstinence on his Bible hour, which led to suggestions that the Premier was allowing his personal preference to stand in the way of freedom to drink liquor. Mr. Manning put the question to a referendum. When the imbibers won in 1964, he acquiesced. Alberta didn't get saloons, but places where one could order whisky or a martini opened for business.

"I think you will agree," one of Mr. Manning's aides told a visitor, "that here in Alberta we have some of the nicest, cleanest cocktail rooms to be found anywhere in Canada or the U.S.A."

But never, as yet, on Sunday.

Bighorn sheep at Rocky Mountain National Park, on the Alberta British Columbia border

280

Chuck-wagon races at the rodeo at Swift Current, Saskatchewan

Calgary sits dramatically on the bluffs and plateaus where the Bow and Elbow rivers join. This was a Canadian Pacific town, and the railroad's hotel was named for Captain John Palliser, discoverer of Kicking Horse Pass in the Rockies, through which the tracks now run. A Canadian Pacific subsidiary is developing the two-block Palliser Square downtown. It includes a revolving restaurant with a hundred-mile view atop the six-hundred-foot Huxley Tower.

The promoters of the annual Stampede have done so much to identify Calgary with their super-rodeo that tourists may wonder why they should bother to visit the city at other times of the year. The Stampede, attracting as it does the star stunt men of the world of cow-

282

boys and Indians, is in Calgary to stay. It is big, noisy, and exciting.
Thousands of visitors adjust their vacation schedules to take it in.

But the Stampede is not all there is to see in Calgary, thanks to the
work of two historical foundations acting in cooperation with city
and provincial officials. The Glenbow Foundation, incorporated by
the Eric L. Harvie family in 1955, devotes its energies and funds to
preserving the heritage of western Canada. Its staff includes archaeologists, librarians, and artisans capable of restoring any relic from an
old clock to a broken-down steam locomotive.

The foundation lends its pictures, art objects, books (fifteen thousand
volumes), and archaeological artifacts (thirty-five thousand items) to

schools and museums. But it maintains its own museum, too, in co-operation with the provincial government. The museum is at Seventh Avenue and Fifth Street in southwest Calgary and is open Tuesday through Friday from 10 A.M. to 9 P.M., Saturday from 10 A.M. to 5 P.M., and Sunday from 11:30 A.M. to 6 P.M. There is no telling what one might see, since the collection grows steadily and displays change constantly. There is, for example, a remarkable exhibit of western firearms that includes a flintlock rifle like the weapon Louis Riel carried and the 1876 Winchester rifle used by the Mounties against Riel's rebels. Calgarians say that two kinds of guns opened the Canadian west—the kind that was given to the Indians and the kind that was used by the white law-and-order men when they fought the Indians. Both kinds may be seen at the Glenbow Foundation's museum.

Calgary's second historical foundation, the Woods, is responsible for the recently developed and still growing Heritage Park—sixty acres in a crook of the Elbow River in a southwestern section of the city. The Heritage Park Society now has the backing of the city and the Glenbow Foundation in this delightful, if modest, version of Disneyland. For twenty-five cents children and grownups can ride an old-fashioned three-coach train, pulled by a 1905 steam locomotive driven by a retired C.P.R. engineer. They can cruise the park's Glenmore Lake aboard a two-hundred-passenger stern-wheeler. They can climb the palisades of a restored Hudson's Bay fort, pet the park animals, watch the blacksmith shoe horses, and buy a newspaper printed on a pioneer press. There's nothing in the park that isn't in western Canada's past, boasts an official brochure, "except the modern washrooms."

The provincial capital, Edmonton, not to be outdone by Calgary, has its answer to the Calgary Stampede. It is the Klondike Days, a two-week festival in midsummer that puts less emphasis on cowboys than it does on gold-rush gaiety and girls. During Klondike Days the mayor of Edmonton rides to work in a horse-drawn carriage and is greeted on his arrival at city hall by girls in Klondike tights and tassels.

Edmonton, with a population of 376,925, is the seat of new-found oil operations, and Edmontonians no longer compare their boom town with Calgary but rather with Montreal. In the last decade it has acquired forty-one buildings that are from six to thirty-five stories tall. The highest is the new Canadian Pacific hotel, the Château La-combe, a significant addition to the skyline because Edmonton is on Canadian National's main line, not the C.P.R.'s.

Calgarians charge that Edmonton has no right to a Klondike fair, since the Klondike, a river that struck it rich, was, and still is, in the Yukon. No matter, retort Edmontonians. One of them said: "Edmonton's annual exhibition was just another fuddy-duddy fair until we took over the Klondike. This is war."

Driving west out of either Calgary or Edmonton, one is, within an hour's time, in the passes of the Rockies leading abruptly and spec-tacularly to the Continental Divide. There the prairies end. Behind lie Canada's heartland and breadbasket, the plains. Ahead is the land of mountains and the Pacific Coast. Crossing the Continental Divide at Banff and Jasper has awed travelers for two hundred years. Today a splendid stretch of highway engineering enables a driver to negotiate Rogers Pass with ease, but it is still awesome.

14

British California

"We like being Canadians, but we're just hardheaded

when it comes to economics."

*ft, a Kwakiutl totem at Alert Bay. Above, the
ovincial capital at Victoria illuminated at night.*

Snowy peaks tower over Vancouver in this view to the west. The planetarium and centennial museum are in the foreground.

BRITISH COLUMBIA, to the reporter of the London journal *Truth* in 1881, was "a barren, cold mountain country, that is not worth keeping."

No one would make that statement today, although a consensus about the province is far from formed. Quite unbarren, British Columbia shares with the world its gamut of products, from salmon to silver. While up north there are trappers and lumberjacks who feel the bite of the Arctic winter, there are Vancouverites playing golf in February, and in Victoria, gardeners in the suburbs show off their tulips in March.

Not for a long while has any Canadian questioned British Columbia's "worth." Rather, some British Columbians today voice doubts about "keeping Canada" with all its problems of identity, bilingualism,

Quebec, and the always precarious relationship with the United States. From Vancouver, all of Canada east of the Rockies is as remote as if it were seen through the reverse end of a telescope. Toronto is a speck on the horizon. Ottawa is weak and insignificant. And Quebec is barely visible.

The average British Columbia businessman thinks his taxes support the poorer provinces—meaning most of the rest of Canada. He thinks British Columbia would be better off going it alone or joining the United States, never doubting that the province would be welcome.

While the separatist spirit is strong in British Columbia, it is as yet neither as well organized nor as articulate as it is in Quebec.

"We are not emotional about it, as they are in Quebec," said a Vancouver politician. "We like being Canadians, but we're just hard-headed when it comes to economics. There is a lot of the Yankee in us."

To such men, the United States border means less than any inter-provincial boundary. They go to Seattle or San Francisco to make a deal with greater ease then they would go to Winnipeg or Toronto. Their wives go along to shop. And families that spend their vacations camping within British Columbia think about going to Las Vegas or Hawaii.

The hundreds of eastern Canadians who cross the mountains every year to retire or get rich, or both, breathe the fresh, salty air and begin thinking expansively, too. They start calling Canada's Pacific Coast province the state of "British California."

Its 366,000 square miles of land and fresh water cover an area larger, in fact, than the combined area of California, Oregon, and Washington. Its mountains, rising sharply from the Pacific coast, give the landscape a rugged, dramatic third dimension, climbing from sea level to the eleven-thousand-foot-high peaks of the Rockies. Its eastern boundary includes a five-hundred-mile sector of the Continental Divide at its highest.

Today's jet-plane passenger flying west over the Divide, about a hundred miles west of Calgary, views, on a clear day, a spectacular corrugation of snow-streaked mountains—range after range—black canyons, and rivers. The mountain system is more complicated than it is farther south.

The dramatic effects continue after the traveler lands. On the limousine ride away from Vancouver International Airport, Vancouver is seen as a jigsaw puzzle of bays, inlets, and picture-post-card peaks.

The warm Japan Current of the Pacific Ocean gives the British Columbia coast, especially Vancouver and Victoria, the provincial capital, an English winter, including the rains and fogs. The warm damp air pushes up the seven thousand miles of fjords to the rain forests. There, standing in luxuriant growth, are pines, cedars, and the great Douglas firs, some of which sprouted about the time of the fall of Rome.

The rainfall from the humid sea air gives rise to three great rivers—

the Columbia, which British Columbia shares with the United States; the Fraser, which empties into the Pacific just below Vancouver; and the Peace, which runs east from the Divide across the northern country to Alberta, eventually joining the Mackenzie River system to the Arctic Ocean.

The middle river, the Fraser, drains a high plateau in the interior. This is Cariboo country, settled a hundred years ago by cattlemen who introduced the Texas longhorn stock that is still thriving there. Some of the cowpokes are Indians, riding as often as not these days a motor runabout or a helicopter. At newly restored Barkerville the high-living fortune hunters who arrived in the area during the gold rush of the 1860's are memorialized.

Gigantic hydroelectric power developments on the Columbia and Peace rivers operate large modern pulp and paper mills. But British Columbia—despite the cosmopolitan population and the urban culture of Vancouver—is predominantly rawhide country, the rowdiest frontier in North America today.

In the booming mining and lumber town of Prince George at the confluence of the Fraser and Nechako rivers, five hundred miles north and inland from Vancouver, traditional frontier society blossoms every Saturday night. George Street, the main thoroughfare, is aglow with neon lights and free-spirited loggers and construction men. Indians mingle in the crowds that include immigrant workmen from all parts of Europe and the United States.

"I wouldn't venture down there with a necktie on," advised an up-town innkeeper. "They'll know you don't belong here, and you might get jostled around."

Hard liquor flows with frontier freedom, and visitors are told that the Royal Canadian Mounted Police has more constables per capita stationed here than in any town in Canada. But in a recent interview the mayor stated that all was well in Prince George, that the law was in control. "You will find more churches here than beer halls," he said.

Indeed, there are churches of at least twenty denominations. Some are old, some strikingly modern; all are well attended. Prince George also has a large vocational school and a junior college with three hundred students and two thousand acres of campus. In addition, there are an excellent golf course, a fine new curling rink, two little theatre

Cattle graze by the Fraser River in the Cariboo region.

groups, and Fort George Park, on the site of the old Hudson's Bay Company fort. So much for the new frontier in British Columbia.

The Gang Ranch in the Cariboo Mountains is larger than the King Ranch in Texas. The Douglas Lake Cattle Company ranch around Kamloops is as big as the state of Rhode Island; Queen Elizabeth II and Prince Philip were lodged there during a visit in 1959. The respect given British Columbia beef on the tables of Canada is as deserved, if not as widespread, as the praise heaped on British Columbia salmon. Cattle and fish both contribute importantly to the economy.

However, British Columbia is above all a land of forests. Timbering, lumbering, pulp and paper manufacturing, are billion-dollar-a-year industries. The province's forest products make up 11 per cent of all Canadian exports to the United States.

The demand for the raw materials in the United States, and increasingly in Latin America and Japan, is causing an explosion in the economy. The lowly minerals—iron, coal, lead, copper, oil, unknown, or valueless, in the days of the rush for the glamorous furs and gold—are the fuels of modern industry. British Columbia is richly endowed in these and strategically located to supply the needs of that part of the world touched by the Pacific.

By 1972 an American mining company expects to be taking four million tons of coal annually from a mountain at Natal in southern B.C. Computer-operated trains, one hundred cars long, will carry the coal to a new deepwater harbor at Roberts Bank, south of Vancouver. There it will be loaded on super-freighters for export. Japan, alone, will take forty-five million tons, worth $650 million at present prices, over a fifteen-year period. But the company's deposits contain at least six billion tons of good industrial coal, enough to keep the mine operating at its initial rate for a thousand years!

This is only one known reserve. There are many others for various minerals, and the search continues in a frenzied race of geologists and their technicians by jeep, helicopter, and on the offshore seas, by boat. Mining companies are breeding like rabbits, and their penny stocks fill the Vancouver Stock Exchange with excited, sometimes frantic speculators looking for a "quick windfall" and hoping for some new bonanza.

Despite the sprawl and enormous size of the province, the tourists' British Columbia is not too difficult to reach. One's introduction to it is most likely to be Vancouver, whose downtown is just fifteen miles north of the U.S. border crossing at Blaine, Washington. Ever since Captain George Vancouver's explorations in these parts in 1792–94, the site at the mouth of the Fraser River has been considered the Pacific outpost of the British Empire. Captain Vancouver circumnavigated the island that bears his name and at whose southern tip is Victoria, the provincial capital.

As might be expected, vestiges of Empire persist to this day. The doorman at the new and expensive Bayshore Inn in Vancouver goes about his duties in the full rig of a Tower of London beefeater. Vancouver clubs and eating places offer sherries and British brands of beer. British Navy Rum, not seen much anywhere else, is in demand here. The casual attire is tweedy, and the accent of speech not just English but British. An engineer from the Maritimes, an Acadian fluent in French and English, not only found his French useless in Vancouver but also found that his Atlantic-oriented English was considered an oddity.

"People didn't know what I meant when I used the expression 'au courant,' " he told a visitor. "My secretary didn't know how to spell 'résumé.' " That "au courant" (well informed) and "résumé" (review or outline) are French words now widely used in conversational English elsewhere carried no weight in Vancouver.

Princess Anne certainly found it all familiar when she and her mother stopped over in Vancouver on their way to Australia in 1970. "Mother, this is just like home," she was overheard to say to Queen Elizabeth as they entered the Hotel Vancouver through a welcoming crush of two thousand people.

Once ensconced in one's hotel room, however, overlooking the Capilano peaks, the sea, or the harbor, one thinks not of London but of San Francisco. And it is to California that Vancouver is really oriented. It no longer seems ironic that Queen Victoria selected the name British Columbia for her westernmost province, Columbia being the poet's name for the United States. Metropolitan Vancouver is, in flavor, Pacific West Coast. If it isn't, truly, "the San Francisco of the North," it compares readily with Seattle or Portland.

Vancouver has its detractors, usually Canadians, who call it "Regina with mountains." To be sure, commerce in Vancouver is centered around the same stores found across the prairies and through Ontario—Hudson's "The Bay," Eaton's, Simpson-Sears—and the cavernous château-type hostelry run by one of the transcontinental railroads. The Canadian National's Hotel Vancouver, however, is now under Hilton management.

Yet, the salubrious weather and the salt air lift Vancouver enough above the humdrum to attract more newcomers today than any other Canadian city except industrial Toronto.

Like the booming California cities, Vancouver draws all kinds of people—workers, pensioners, the idle rich, religious eccentrics, and a fair share of "kooks." Vancouver may be the only city in the world with a subsidized Town Jester. In 1968 Polish-born Joachim Foikis, thirty-six, received $3,500 from the Canada Council, which noted that many people think Foikis made "a serious contribution to the self-awareness of the entire community." He bobs up at meetings of the

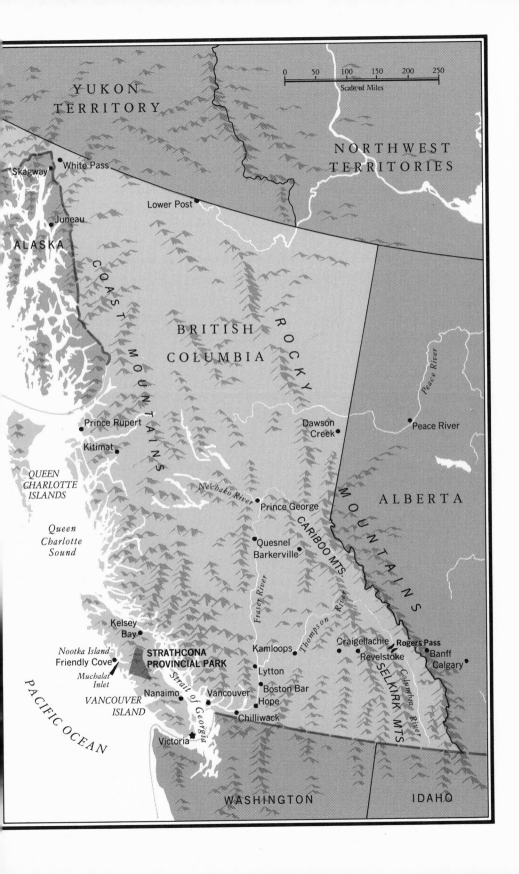

city council to needle, in a genial way, politicians with inflated egos. He comes to other public forums primed with embarrassing questions.

"Dressed in traditional fool's motley, he has nursery rhymes for children and metaphysical riddles for adults," said the Canada Council of Mr. Foikis's frequent appearances in Vancouver's downtown courthouse square.

But it is often hard to pick out the official jester, for Vancouver has become a mecca of hippies, whose dress, behavior, and outcries are more outlandish, and frequently funnier, than any offerings of the jester. On Georgia Street severe steel-rimmed eyeglasses are worn both by elderly pensioners out shopping and by long-haired youths walking with their short-skirted girls. And in the same block the passer-by may be asked to buy both the latest issue of the Salvation Army's *War Cry* and the latest avant-garde publication, whose militant young publisher might get into trouble for printing four-letter Anglo-Saxonisms.

Vancouver's divorce rate is the highest in Canada, and Lions Gate Bridge across Burrard Inlet rivals San Francisco's Golden Gate span in both elegance and number of suicide leaps.

The visitor, however, need not be eccentric to have fun. Vancouver has the largest Chinatown in Canada, within walking distance of downtown hotels. Even without diplomatic relations with Communist China, Canada carries on a trade that supplies Vancouver's Chinatown with objects and goods actually made on Red China's mainland. Chinese imports from Formosa, Hong Kong, and even Japan are also on the shelves of lively stores, some of which operate more on the scale of supermarkets than of Oriental shops.

Chinese immigrants enjoy a respected status in British Columbia. One of them became mayor of Kamloops, the cattle town previously mentioned. In Vancouver the twenty thousand Chinese-Canadians are by no means confined to Chinatown. Many of the businessmen live in the well-to-do north shore suburbs and belong to the parent-teacher associations of English schools attended by their children. Most of the wealthy suburbanites go to Chinatown to shop or have dinner at any of several good Chinese restaurants, including the Chinese Smorgasbord. Prices are pleasantly reasonable.

Vancouver has a new opera house and concert hall, the Queen Eliza-

A church for Chinese-Canadians

beth, whose calendar of coming events is always worth watching. It has museums of many descriptions. But before embarking on a tour of them, a visitor should be told about what most critics, we believe, would agree is the outstanding manifestation of indigenous art in Canada. This is the wood and argillite carving of the Haida, the Salishes, the Chimmesyans, the Kwakiutls, and the Nootkas, all tribes of Pacific Northwest Indians.

Where these Indians came from in prehistoric time is a mystery. But when the white man arrived—the fur traders and explorers seeking the elusive Northwest Passage—the Indians could show them many evidences of sophisticated living. They inhabited the rain forest country of the jagged shore of the mainland and the offshore islands from Vancouver Island north to Alaska. They dwelled in large cedar-plank houses. They fished industriously for salmon and hunted sea mammals. They accumulated wealth, and remarkably, developed customs centered around the conspicuous display of that wealth.

Their great winter ceremony, the potlatch, consisted of feasting, dancing, and taletelling, but it reached its climax in an extravagant exchange of gifts. A donor won the immediate respect of his neighbors, and also rich material reward, for a recipient kept his self-respect by returning the favor with a gift more impressive and more expensive than the one he had received. It is said the potlatches sometimes ended in the impoverishment of a disliked person.

The wealth took the form of highly developed art—copper plates, goat-hair blankets, and more notably, carvings in wood and stone so stylized that they seem modern today. The Indians' cedar sculptures are of such grandeur that to call them totem poles, which technically many of them are, seems almost sacrilegious. On cedar trunks four and five stories high, West Coast Indian artists sculptured features of men and animals related to legends of the Raven and Eagle clans. The sculptures appear to rise to the sky, and at one time the coastal country was literally forested by them. The Indians also carved wooden ceremonial masks that are as lean and stark as some of the best art of Africa. They are decidedly more colorful.

The Haidas also developed a technique for exquisite relief-carving on argillite. This is a velvety fine black stone that allows the shaping of cameolike figures. The substance found in the Pacific Northwest coastal country might be said to resemble the finest antique Wedgwood basalt. The stone is related to shale and slate, but during eons of time it has metamorphosed until it no longer has a slaty cleavage.

In Vancouver's new centennial museum, part of the McMillan Planetarium, there are not only exhibits of fine argillite pieces but also a graphic step-by-step explanation of the carving technique. Not to be

298

missed is the display of works done in the early years of this century by Edenshaw, considered the master of Haida argillite artists.

Because of the brittle fragility of the stone, fine argillite work is harder and harder to find outside museums. However, Vancouver and Victoria shops offer interesting contemporary specimens of the art. But with the better examples finding their way into permanent museum collections, quality argillite carvings may soon become as expensive as old Chinese jades.

The totemic art is also going to museums. Sculptures fifty and sixty feet tall are hardly suitable for private collecting. Cedar is perishable, and the Indian "forests" have almost lost their treasures. Some, alas, have fallen only to rot. They are photographed, vine-covered and split, like the ruined monuments of Angkor Wat.

A dance mask worth seventy-five dollars in 1955 would bring ten times that amount today. Production simply isn't keeping up with demand. Therefore, one should keep an eye cocked for Indian displays, the most rewarding of which are found in the Vancouver historical museum (in the planetarium building) and at the new Victoria provincial centennial archives and museum, across the street from the Empress Hotel.

The totem sculptures are everywhere, inside and outside. That is why one should know about them before venturing out. There is a fine example on the grounds of the Vancouver Marine Museum, which also displays the *St. Roch,* the R.C.M.P. schooner that in 1940–42 made the first Canadian voyage through the Northwest Passage. Stanley Park has a fine grove of impressive poles (as well as a popular aquarium complete with a living whale). Each pole tells in symbolic heads and figures the triumphs and tragedies of a tribe, or perhaps, the story of the artist's life. The University of British Columbia has an outdoor display of totem poles as part of its reproduction of a Haida Indian village.

With so much of their art on display in Vancouver and Victoria, it is hardly necessary to track down the West Coast Indians in their home settlements, although they are a perfectly amiable people. They inhabit the rain forest country of the mainland and the thousands of islands extending north to Alaska.

Before cruising north, however, there are a number of short sea trips around Vancouver to be considered, thanks in great part to the up-to-date and economical ferry services provided by the government of British Columbia.

The first trip should be to Vancouver Island to visit Victoria. The route, via Nanaimo, is, in fact, an extension of the Trans-Canada Highway, which after a one-hour-and-fifty-minute ferry leap from downtown Vancouver, or from Horseshoe Bay in West Vancouver, completes its cross-country run in a sixty-mile stretch southward to the provincial capital. A new hovercraft service now makes the run across the Strait of Georgia in fifty minutes, but it takes no cars.

There is also a shorter highway-ferry route to Victoria by way of Tsawwassen in south Vancouver. On a fine day or a moonlit night when the frequently scheduled boats ride through the islands, it is an enchanting respite from hours at the steering wheel. All ferries take passenger cars, and the Vancouver-Victoria buses use them, too.

Victoria is slow-paced, genteel, and very British. The sixty-five-year-old Empress Hotel, the Canadian Pacific's monument to Edwardian living, serves tea and crumpets at 4 P.M. in the main lounge. There is a glass-enclosed botanical garden off the lobby, and on a summer's day, there is, or was until recently at least, bowling on the green.

A few years ago the Canadian Pacific's efficiency men despaired of the old Empress's ability to cope with a new trade that craved cocktails more than tea. On Saturday nights all was peace and calm in the Empress, while the tourists went elsewhere for their weekend partying. In the old days when public power was unreliable, the Empress had built its own electricity plant; unfortunately, the direct current it produced would operate neither television sets nor electric razors.

While none of this bothered the Canadian pensioners and the English trippers very much, American tourists deserted the old English Empress in droves for the new motels offering all the modern amenities, and swimming pools to boot. Word spread that the Empress was dying and that the fortress castle would have to be demolished.

Never did alarm inspire a more heroic rescue. Bury the Empress? It would kill Victoria. The demolition men were sent away, and in rushed Leslie Parkinson, a Canadian Pacific hotel veteran with an old-timer's true appreciation of tradition and plans for a proper renovation. His job was to sweep away the cobwebs while preserving the old way of life. Quite naturally, Mr. Parkinson called the $4-million renewal project "Operation Teacup."

The result is a remarkable compromise between the Claridge and the Hilton. There is a television set, as well as a bath, in every room, and usually a fireplace, too. There is a parking lot beside the bowling green. The old library has become a cocktail lounge. But the tea salon is preserved intact.

"One can renovate the Empress," commented Mr. Parkinson to a guest. "One can never really modernize it."

The teatime patrons, usually elegant dowagers and their straight-backed gentlemen escorts, have their moments of doubt about this. The swingers have their foot in the door, and as the days roll on the tea circle grows smaller and quieter. The day will yet come, they know, when the television sets, the radios, the electric razors, the automatic elevators, and that noisy damnation of a cocktail bar will overwhelm the old nostalgia.

Victoria must be one of the few capitals in which a photographer can frame in one shot an Edwardian-type hotel, an ocean liner, and an ornate, domed parliament house. Out of his window at night the Empress guest sees the inner harbor with its ships at call and the sprawling government building lit up, in Edwardian style, by chains of electric bulbs.

And at the same window next morning he may very probably find a sea gull on the sill pecking at the pane for a breakfast handout. The Victoria gulls' uncanny sense tells them when room-service tables roll in. The sea gull is an irresistible panhandler, but it is wise to offer him his snippet through the narrowest slit under the window. Otherwise he may boldly step inside to attack the breakfast spread voraciously, or in his outburst of appreciation, gobble up the handout and with it a piece of one's finger.

Also within camera range of the Empress is the new centennial museum with its remarkable Indian exhibits. And just around the corner is Thunderbird Park, full of those impressive totem poles mentioned earlier. In the opposite direction is Victoria's downtown district, with the English bone-china shops one would expect in British towns. And out of town a way are the famed Butchart Gardens, with their array of flower beds that only English green thumbs seem able to produce.

Even Victoria, however, is close to the frontier and wilderness. The best way to sample it may be a trip to Strathcona Provincial Park, which covers a half million acres of wilderness almost in the center of Vancouver Island. The route to the park is through Campbell River, a Georgia Strait town 165 miles north of Victoria. There, one can take an all-day, bus-boat excursion to Gold River and Friendly Cove.

For a twelve-dollar round-trip fare, the bus leaving Campbell River at 8 A.M. takes its passengers across the island through the northern neck of Strathcona Provincial Park to Gold River on Muchalat Inlet. After lunch, excursionists board the converted mine sweeper *Uchuck* for a thirty-mile voyage down a thickly forested fjord. The destination is Friendly Cove on the Pacific side of the Island. While history associates this settlement of sixty inhabitants with Captain Cook, Canadian archaeologists recently found relics reminding today's visitors that the Spanish were there, too.

When Cook ventured into the bay in 1778, he renamed the Nootka village of Yuquot Friendly Cove because of the warm reception given him by the natives. The new name was retained by John Meares, the Englishman who came ten years later to build the shipyard from which he launched the schooner *North West America*. Meares' stay was cut short by the arrival of a Spaniard, Estevan José Martinez, who seized the *North West America* and built the military quarters recently excavated.

Friendly Cove is still a friendly place. The Indians offer visitors woven baskets and the remarkable Maquinna hats, conically shaped headgear made from the inner bark of cedar. Friendly Cove has only three totem poles, but there are three very fine carvings guarding the approach to an oceanside graveyard.

Visitors traveling across the British Columbia mainland can head in many directions. But three possibilities should be considered first. One is the "inside passage" up the coast by boat, car, or bus to Prince Rupert and the return by highway through the interior. A second suggestion is to follow, for a stretch at least, the Alaska (Alcan) Highway. The third is to travel the Trans-Canada Highway from Vancouver up to and over glorious Rogers Pass.

Both the Canadian National and the Canadian Pacific have scheduled Inside Passage (Vancouver to Alaska) cruises. And there are air-rail-sea-bus combination tours providing all the services and conveniences of modern "package" tourism.

A recommended do-it-yourself way, ideal for motorists with families who have not booked package tours well in advance, is the ferry-highway route. At present no vessel of the B.C. Ferry Line goes the whole distance up the coast to Prince Rupert. But one can negotiate the 550-mile trip by boarding the ferries where they exist and driving the rest of the way. For example, take the ferry in Vancouver and cross over to Nanaimo on Vancouver Island. Then drive up Route 19 for 219 miles to Kelsey Bay. There *The Queen of Prince Rupert* sails at 1:30 P.M. every other day in summer for the enchanting 330-mile, overnight voyage to Prince Rupert. The *Queen* makes no stops, but her wake often brushes island shores, making passengers feel they are as close to the sights and sounds and the people as they would be if they were driving their car up a highway.

While few voyagers would think to count them, there are said to be about eleven thousand islands between Vancouver and Prince Rupert. Some of them are tips of mountains rising steeply from the sea. Others have lumber camps clinging desperately to their cliffs. Here and there are isolated villages, including a few Indian settlements.

At Prince Rupert passengers can transfer to other ships for Alaska points, and one reason for doing so would be to embark at Skagway on one of the world's most remarkable railroad trips. The railroad is the White Pass and Yukon Narrow Gauge Railroad. While cars and buses are put aboard flatcars, passengers take to the observation coach for the 110-mile ride over the "Trail of '98," the path of the gold rush. The narrow tracks laid down in 1900 head almost at once into the twists and turns of the Alaskan coastal range. The roadbed is an engineering marvel, and the train moves slowly enough for picture taking. Since dining cars were never built for the W.P.&Y.N.G.R., there is a lunch stop along the way. The train eventually reaches Whitehorse in the Canadian Yukon.

But back to British Columbia. From Prince Rupert, Highway 16 leads across to Prince George, cited earlier, and from there one may take the road south following the Fraser River to Quesnel and eventually reach Vancouver. Turn east at Quesnel for a sixty-mile side trip to Barkerville, the historic gold-rush town recently restored and brought to life in summer festival events. It was named for Billy Barker, a naval deserter who first found gold there in the 1860's. At one time it boasted the largest population on the coast north of San Francisco. When the gold petered out, it became a ghost town, until the British Columbia government restored it for tourists.

There is a stretch of the Alaska Highway cutting up from Dawson Creek to Lower Post, B.C. From there it continues to Whitehorse and Fairbanks, Alaska. This World War II vintage road is still gravel, and it calls for careful planning of provisions, fuel, and overnight stops —which may, of course, include camping.

It would be too bad to visit British Columbia without traversing the excellent Trans-Canada Highway that leads from Vancouver up the Fraser River valley to the Thompson River, then branches east, passing through Kamloops and Revelstoke, to negotiate glorious Rogers Pass over the Continental Divide to Banff and Calgary.

The trip east starts unsensationally enough, out of Vancouver's endless suburbs. (One learns that "up the Fraser" is the only way "the mountains let the city grow.") But the fun begins at Chilliwack and at Hope, where the foothills of the Rockies swing the river from its southern course west toward the ocean.

The canyon country begins very soon, and one is suddenly in the treacherous region that challenged Simon Fraser 150 years ago. That explorer, canoeing downstream, bartered with the Indian navigators at what is now Lytton. According to his journal, "Here I obtained, for an awl, passage to the next village, a distance of three miles through strong rapids." Today one stops at Spuzzum for a tankful of gas to take him through Hell's Gate and Boston Bar.

One scales the canyon, a towering mountain on one side, an abyss on the other. Hundreds of feet below, a transcontinental train crawls like a caterpillar over a slope and around a curve.

The Thompson River at Kamloops courses through cowboy country, and having passed through that area, one starts the climb to the Rockies. The Rogers Pass stretch of the Trans-Canada Highway cuts one hundred miles off the old route. (The latter follows the meandering Columbia River, which fooled early explorers by flowing north before bending west and south.) The summit of the pass is 4,300 feet high.

The problem of engineering a highway there, however, was not so much the rough landscape as the snow. Every winter 340 inches of snow falls on the Selkirk Mountains, and avalanches are a threat every minute of the day and night. To make the road reasonably safe, engineers devised the snowsheds that we have mentioned before. In summer, driving in and out of snowsheds seems ridiculous. But in winter they make this part of the Trans-Canada possible.

Just east of Rogers Pass one is on the Continental Divide and in the lap of the landmarks, Jasper, Lake Louise, and Banff. If he doesn't apply his brakes, the motorist is in Calgary and out on the prairies before he knows it.

He is in a different country. When it is reached, some Canadians will say, "We are back in Canada." But a British Columbia Canadian will look back with a sigh.

A word to campers and outdoorsmen: the official British Columbia Tourist Directory—obtainable from the Department of Travel Industry, Victoria—catalogues hundreds of provincial and national parks and wilderness areas (9.5 million acres in all) with their camp sites, lodges, motels, and picnic areas. It gives detailed information about where, when, and what to hunt and fish and a complete list of licensed guides available.

Unless he is a resident of British Columbia, the law says that he must have a licensed guide when he hunts big game and on bagging an animal must go at once to the nearest government agent or conservation officer to pay a trophy fee. The fee for a mountain sheep is seventy-five dollars; for a mountain goat, forty dollars; for a grizzly bear, sixty dollars; for a black bear, five dollars.

It is illegal to "shoot from a vehicle"; to "hunt any game from a sailboat"; to "allow the guide to kill game for the hunter"; to use any "electrically operated calling device" in hunting game; or to "shoot hawks, eagles or owls."

An Eskimo youth practices using his whip.

15 North to the Pole

"Oh, people of the north don't bother to sleep much in summer."

Eskimos in Cape Dorset, Northwest Territories, apply designs to fabrics.

Most travelers to the Canadian north come back stricken with Arctic fever, a euphoric affliction that can strike suddenly and is virtually incurable. It may attack one on spying a tiny yellow flower pushing through the tundra, on first seeing the midnight sun, on first actually touching an iceberg, or on witnessing a lemming rush madly over the encrusted snow as though he were being chased by a whirlwind. Or one may be smitten on receiving the soft smile of a young Eskimo mother when the papoose on her back is praised.

For the Arctic is not always cold and dark. From April to October the sun shines for twenty to twenty-four hours a day. We have seen Eskimo boys in Inuvik playing in full light at midnight.

"When do you sleep?"

"Oh, people of the north don't bother to sleep much in summer."

Arctic fishermen go forth at "night," when tales seem to grow even taller than they do at more conventional hours. In the north, a good teller of tales can say that the trout that got away was three feet long and weighed sixty-two pounds—and make it sound convincing.

In winter the driven snow becomes so hard that the caribou and musk oxen must paw it vigorously for nibbles of moss and tundra underneath. But when the spring sun melts the snow, fields of exquisite flowers burst over the ground. The colors range from delicate pastels to poppy reds and daffodil yellows. While trees do not penetrate the Arctic tree line, there are myriad little flowers wherever there is land. At Mary River on northern Baffin Island we saw flowers carpeting the side of a mountain of solid iron ore, a vein so rich it could feed the steel furnaces of Pittsburgh for a generation or two.

On a return flight from Alert in late April our Canadian Forces pilot made a short swing over Greenland to show us the mighty Humboldt Glacier. The frozen river, at least five miles across at its mouth, sheered off at the edge of the Kane Basin. Then, in the icebound sea, we saw a startling procession of icebergs. Hundreds of them were held waiting for the thaw that would let them proceed on their oceanic odyssey.

Viewing icebergs from twenty thousand feet is no preparation for experiencing one close up. Our plane circled around one caught for its second winter at Pond Inlet, Baffin Island. It rode with the aloofness of a Cunard *Queen* at anchor. In silhouette in front of the low-lying sun it was not black; it was translucent in greens and blues, and its edges threw off sparks like a monstrous diamond.

Our pilot said that the iceberg was probably two miles offshore, although it seemed no more than a stone's throw away. Next morning a group of us followed the Governor General of Canada on a hike out over the harbor ice to inspect the iceberg. We proved the pilot right. Scrambling over the rough shore ice, we thought he may have underestimated a bit.

In the early morning the iceberg was so veiled in mist that our cameras couldn't pick out the barest outline. Gradually it loomed forbiddingly over us, and we advanced cautiously over some loose ice to touch it. A few agile members of the party started to climb it, but found its sides too craggy and steep. An hour later, when we were boarding our plane, the mist had burned off, and our iceberg stood out clearly in living color, jagged as an Alp.

On Melville Island we saw a new Canadian oil derrick operating six hundred miles north of the Arctic Circle. It seemed to stand alone on an acre or two of snow-cleared land. The empty plain stretched to the horizon on all sides. But it wasn't empty, for immediately outside the clearance were the fresh tracks of caribou, musk oxen, white foxes, and Arctic hares, and inevitably, the faint tracings of some scurrying lemmings.

Some travelers to the north never leave. In Yellowknife we met Peter Baker, who calls himself the "Arab of the Arctic." He was born a baker's son in Lebanon. He migrated to the United States about sixty years ago, only to hear the call of the Canadian north. In Yellowknife, Northwest Territories, he became a trader supplying merchandise to the Indians in exchange for furs, in competition with the Hudson's Bay Company. He lived close to the Indians and learned the language of the Dogrib tribe. He prospered and stayed. As time went on, he returned to Lebanon for visits, but he became a staunch northerner. A few years ago he won a seat on the Territorial Council. The Indians around Yellowknife helped him defeat the rival candidate, the local Hudson's Bay manager.

The north has several breeds of inveterate professionals—the Hudson's Bay factor, the Mountie, the mission priest—who come for a short tour and wind up staying. Recently two newcomers have joined the hardy lot. They are the bush pilot and the crusading editor.

In a sprawling country without roads, where sparse populations do not warrant scheduled airline operations, the bush pilot in his light plane that can take off on short notice on wheels, skis, or pontoons is the man to take you where you want, or have, to go. These most daring of Canadians are becoming true folk heroes. They fly tens of thousands of miles every year over uninhabited, monotonous landscape, finding their tiny and uncertain destinations without radar. The bush pilot's country is often unmapped. Temperatures may drop to 50 degrees below zero. There is no radio link with civilization. Often their compasses are useless because the magnetic pole is so close.

Their passengers may be prospectors, surveyors, industrialists, priests on "parish" rounds, an urgently expectant mother, or perhaps, a sportsman from New York, Chicago, or Kansas City.

One April day Bob Engle, flying our party out of Frobisher Bay, brought his venerable DC-3 over Cape Dorset just as snow began to fall. He circled once or twice, saw his way clear between the open water and the shore hills, and landed on the ice.

It hadn't occurred to him to turn back to Frobisher, which maintains an improved airport. But once on the ground, Bob saw the snow turn to sleet, the clouds settle around those hills, and the wind point out to sea. While his passengers enjoyed lunch and a visit to the handicraft shop, Bob's copilot wielded a broomstick against the ice on the DC-3's wings, and Bob concentrated on his takeoff.

The tops of the hills disappeared in the lowering clouds, and the runway over rough shore ice toward the sea became definitely downwind. (Planes normally take off against the wind.) An ordinary pilot would have waited for the weather to change. But Bob had the Mounties' radio report that the weather at Cape Dorset might be closing in for days. ("One couple who flew into Dorset for lunch," Bob recalled, "stayed for three weeks, waiting for the weather to clear.")

The copilot once more knocked the ice from the wings. Bob put his passengers aboard, tried the downwind, out-to-sea run, and failed. The plane could not pick up the speed needed to be air-borne. He tried three, four, five times. Then, after he had decided to give up, the wind shifted a few degrees, and instead of having it at his back, it became a slightly more favorable cross wind. Gunning his engines, he put the plane through a run and a jump, and the wings, to applause in the cabin, carried us into the air.

"When you want to fly," said Bob, "all you have to do is get the cockpit over the fence and the rest will follow."

Bush pilots like Bob Engle seem a reckless bunch. But really they never are. They take meticulous care of their planes, nursing them like pets. They know the planes' performance and limitations exactly, and in an emergency will never take less from them than the limit. They know every trick of the trade and will remorselessly try one after the other to find the one that works.

Clennell H. "Punch" Dickins, who has been bush piloting in the

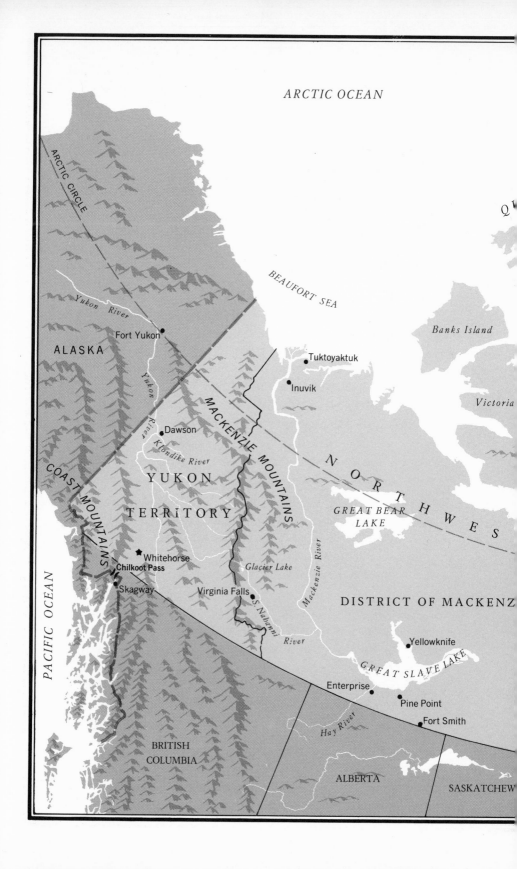

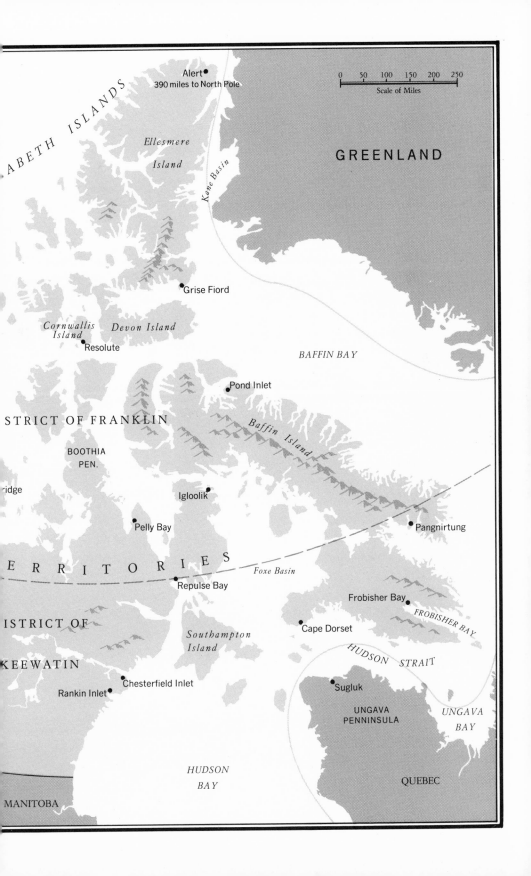

north since the 1920's, created what is generally regarded as the ideal bush plane, the Beaver, out of his experience. It is an all-metal craft with big loading doors, a high-power radio, and a short takeoff capacity. The United States Air Force has bought a thousand of these Canadian-made craft. Later Dickins helped develop the Otter, the Caribou, and the Buffalo for use in the Canadian environment. In fact, these aircraft names are familiar to fliers around the world, and the United States has bought many of the planes for the war in Vietnam.

Flying out of Resolute, bush pilot Weldon Phipps delivers and picks up explorers or scientists near the Pole. He delivers supplies and drilling equipment to oil-surveying teams on Arctic islands. "The polar pack is absolute garbage," Mr. Phipps told a reporter in Resolute. "The ice is just piled up and tossed around there. It's all rubble." Yet, as a bush pilot, Phipps manages to land there.

No less remarkable is the school of frontier journalism that gives the Canadian north a freedom of the press seldom attained anywhere else in the world. An official party headed by the federal Minister of Northern Development landed in Whitehorse, the Yukon, to find at its hotel copies of the Yukon *Daily News* with a banner headline reading, "Another Junket Stays for Dinner." The fact that on the junket were a Cabinet minister, the governor of the Bank of Canada, the chairman of the Economic Council of Canada, and a dozen nationally prominent businessmen and labor leaders did not faze Ken Shortt, the *Daily News* editor.

This newspaper's brashness might be partly explained by the bumptious journalism of its older competitor, the Whitehorse *Star*. Such headlines as "Booze Boosted," reporting a rise in liquor prices, endear the *Star* to visitors.

In Yellowknife Ted Horton, editor of the *News of the North* and former mayor, reported in strictly northern terms a national railway strike that had gripped southern Canada. He lamented in three short paragraphs that during the strike no telegrams could be sent out of Yellowknife because the Canadian National Railways operated the telegraph service.

In Fort Smith Jim Whelly, editor of the *Norther,* renounced news items about ladies' teas and men's fishing conquests to devote his columns to "important developments in the North." "What they do in Norway or in Siberia to solve problems of cold climate and remoteness should be of interest to us," he told us.

In Inuvik, the new government town inside the Arctic Circle, Tom Butters, editor of the *Drum,* tries to serve the cause of the fifteen hundred Eskimos and Indians in his town. One article explained the Eskimo's fear of dying away from home if he accepted government offers to send him "outside," meaning Edmonton, for special treatment.

Editor Butters prints his weekly multilingually—in English, Western Arctic Eskimo, and two Indian dialects. "This is crudely produced and readers are warned to expect that the *Drum* will be a primitive instrument of communication for some time to come," he warned in his first issue. He added that his motto would be "Today's newspaper is tomorrow's toilet paper." The subscription, he said, would be four dollars a year "in cash or kind." "Fish is O.K.," he added.

The Canadian north is divided into two political regions, neither of which has, as yet, the status of a province. They are territories: the Yukon, which covers 215,346 square miles, and the Northwest Territories, of 1.3 million square miles. The Yukon, the smaller and relatively more compact, has the largest city—Whitehorse, whose population is about five thousand. Less romantic than it once was, it is nevertheless prosperous. Guests in its half-dozen hotels and new motels may very easily include Japanese or Americans in town to discuss with Canadian government men some deal in asbestos, silver, lead, zinc, coal, oil, or any of a score of other deposits now known to lie underground in the region.

The north initially attracted fur traders and missionaries, but its first rush followed the discovery of gold on August 17, 1896, at Bonanza Creek, a tributary of the Klondike River near present-day Dawson, Yukon Territory. George W. Carmack and two Indian companions, "Skookum" Jim and "Dawson" Charlie, made the discovery with the aid of some data that had come to them from Robert Henderson, who had spent two years prospecting thereabouts. A rush rivaling the one California experienced in 1849 ensued, and men from far places came to find their fortune in the Canadian north.

Dawson was 500 miles north of Whitehorse, and Whitehorse was 110 miles by hazardous mountain trail from Skagway, and Skagway was 2,000 miles from San Francisco. But in the next eight years uncounted thousands of gold seekers tumbled in and out. Some left broke, but altogether more than $100 million worth of gold was taken from Klondike creek beds. Whitehorse, Dawson, Hunker Creek, Cariboo, and Gold Bottom were founded as settlements. Indeed, Dawson, with a population of twenty-five thousand, was the largest city north of Winnipeg. A town where so many people were digging all day and spending their gold all night inevitably became the "Paris of the North."

Visitors now have a good opportunity to see what this Yukon "Paris" was like. The federal government spent $400,000 to rebuild the ruins of Arizona Charlie's palace grand saloon and opera house to its former splendor. Arizona Charlie, really Joe Ladue, arrived in Dawson shortly after the strike, not to pan for gold, but to give it a center of recreation and culture. His entertainers included such favorites of the day as Diamond Tooth Lil, Golden Gut Gertie, and Klondike Kate.

A recent Conservative government justified the expense of restoring Arizona Charlie's palace on the grounds that it was a historic place where, in addition to operatic performances, there were prayer services and Sunday-school classes for grateful or hopeful gold miners. We, however, got a somewhat different history from the vivacious hostess-guide, in 1890 gown and ostrich-plumed hat, who introduced herself as a "sporting girl." She explained that the nightly performances of *Gaslight Follies* now offered tourists in summer are patterned after the musical programs that Arizona Charlie's patrons used to see. But other entertainment is, she seemed to regret, no longer available. The saloon, while authentically refurbished and stocked with vintage bottles, sells no liquor. The champagne that the guide says went for twenty-five or fifty dollars a bottle no longer flows.

"The champagne," she explained, "was all the same, but the price varied with the selection of the dancing-girl drinking companion and the degree of privacy desired." A twenty-five-dollar bottle entitled the purchaser and his girl to enjoy the musical performance from a first balcony stall. For fifty dollars a lonely miner in from Bonanza or El Dorado for his Saturday night fling could sip his champagne on the third floor, where the stalls led, through a door with a key, to private rooms. Our guide said that the most celebrated of Arizona Charlie's hostesses "often attended these accommodations." As for the prayer meetings and Sunday-school classes, she had never heard of them.

The present Liberal government has earmarked $2 million for acquiring and restoring other historic sites in the Yukon during the 1970's. Scheduled to come to new life in time at Dawson are the Bonanza Hotel, Ruby Scott's place, the post office, a Presbyterian church built by miners, and a gold dredge on Bonanza Creek.

One night in 1906 a young teller in Dawson's Canadian Bank of Commerce attended a banquet honoring a departing business executive. What he heard and saw so impressed the young clerk that he wrote in verse an exuberant prophecy of things to come in the Canadian north. The poem, entitled "Bob Smart's Dream," by Robert W. Service, appeared in the next day's newspaper. It began:

> *This is my dream of Whitehorse*
> *When fifty years have sped,*
> *As after the Rogers Banquet*
> *I lay asleep on my bed.*
> *I tottered along the sidewalk*
> *That was made of real cement;*
> *A skyscraper loomed above me,*
> *Where I once remembered a tent.*

Bob Smart in later verses went on to cross "a big steel bridge," to hear the roar of quartz mills, and to sniff "the fumes of the smelter, and the sulphur made me sneeze."

The Klondike's gold rush passed, as millions of readers of *The Spell of the Yukon* well know. But Robert W. Service, the Klondike's balladeer, might find today's Canadian north no less inspiring. Gold has given way, but only to the new-found wealth of lesser metals.

Dawson's last gold dredge closed down a few years ago because operations were no longer profitable. The "Paris of the North" was given over to the tourists visiting Arizona Charlie's or the cabin where Service in later years rocked in his reed chair, philosophized, and pounded out ballad rhymes by the dozen. One may cash a check in the bank where Service clerked, and, of course, there are restaurants and bars where the weary traveler may get a drink or a snack, if not Arizona Charlie's entertainment, at today's going rate.

The White Pass and Yukon Railroad—that narrow-gauge, cliff-hanger, gold-rush train we've already mentioned—may strike tourists riding it to Whitehorse as a Toonerville Trolley. But it is expanding and modernizing all the time, preparing for the new rush of metals and coal from the Yukon highlands to the sea. Lead and zinc concentrates, trucked into Whitehorse from the Anvil Mine 230 miles to the northeast, are loaded today on container cars for transhipment by W.P.&Y. to Skagway.

Whitehorse also prospers from its situation on the Alaska Highway, which now brings in many tourists. This 1,523-mile road also makes it easier for mining promoters to reach their properties and haul in the equipment needed to develop them. The road, except for about four hundred miles in Alaska and the eighty-four-mile stretch out of Dawson Creek, B.C., is gravel, dusty and grimy in summer and treacherous in winter because of snow, ice, and drifts. Those who have toured its length call it the "longest and most rugged Main Street in the world." Some find its "ruggedness," its far-apart though dependable and courteous fueling stations and lodges, and its attraction for grizzly bears, moose, and wayfaring caribou a wonderful escape from civilization's claustrophobic traffic jams and monotonous dual-lane freeways. A lodge or roadhouse and filling station turn up every thirty or forty miles. One returning traveler reported the cheery helpfulness of his roadside hosts. At one house late at night he had found a light burning beside a little note: "Take any room with the door open. Settle in the morning."

Except for the lower Yukon, one encounters a very different kind of Canadian north. It is spectacularly stark country. The landscapes in summer are, in fact, lakescapes. In winter they are deserted seas of ice and snow. The mountain ranges are heroic, and in the eastern Arctic the coastlines are processions of dramatic fjords. Here, in the endless expanse of forests and tundra, lies the world's largest reservoir of fresh water. There are no roads outside the settlements except the dusty lane that links Yellowknife to Edmonton.

Both the Northwest Territories and the Yukon are subject to federal authority. In 1967, however, the federal government partly relieved the sting of "colonialism" by giving the Northwest Territories, as it had already given the Yukon, a capital of its own, Yellowknife, to which the territorial bureaucracy was moved from Ottawa. By increasing the number of elected members on the Territorial Council, the government gave the people in the north more self-government. For a long time to come, however, the northern Canadians will depend on the federal government for schools and public welfare, jobs, law enforcement, and financial largesse.

Stuart H. Hodgson, the first commissioner of the Northwest Territories to live in Yellowknife instead of Ottawa, must travel thousands of miles every year to visit his people and find out about their problems. His responsibilities begin at the Yukon border and extend east through the Canadian archipelago.

Alert, Canada's most northern habitation, which has no Eskimos but supports a Canadian armed forces base and a weather station operated jointly by Canada and the United States, is just 450 miles from the North Pole. Admiral Robert Peary began his historic sled dash for the Pole at Alert in 1909, and a cairn marking his takeoff point still stands. Alert is 2,600 air miles from Ottawa and about the same distance across the polar wastes from Moscow.

While the country is big, the people are few. The Yukon has a population of 15,000, including 12,500 whites, nearly 2,500 Indians, and 50 Eskimos. The 30,000 inhabitants of the Northwest Territories include 12,000 whites, 7,000 Indians, and 11,000 Eskimos. One hundred years after Confederation, 99.75 per cent of the Canadians cling to the south, with only 45,000 living north of the 60th parallel, where the territories begin.

But the solitude of most of the north is even more severe than these figures make it seem, for at least two thirds of the people live in the relatively hospitable Mackenzie River valley, north of Alberta. Life there centers around a few towns: Fort Smith, the former headquarters of federal services; Pine Point, a new zinc- and lead-mining center; Hay River, the Great Slave Lake terminus of a new spur of the Canadian National Railway; Yellowknife, the new capital; Norman Wells, the site of World War II oil-drilling operations; and far within the Arctic Circle, Aklavik, the old Eskimo-Indian trapping settlement, Inuvik, the federal government's new $50-million city dedicated to northern development, and finally, Tuktoyaktuk, whose few hardy Eskimos survive the ice and slashing winds of the Beaufort Sea with the help of jobs and trade generated by a nearby station of the Distant Early Warning (DEW) defense system.

The whole eastern Arctic is inhabited by a few hundred whites and fewer than ten thousand Eskimos, who cling to the seaside coves and fjords in reach of good hunting and fishing. Such settlements as Cambridge Bay on Victoria Island, Chesterfield Inlet and Rankin Inlet and Igloolik on Hudson Bay, Grise Fiord on Ellesmere Island, and Cape Dorset and Pangnirtung on Baffin Island are picturesque but completely isolated outposts that survive with the aid of federal welfare, contributing nothing to the development of the interior. The federal government now has ambitious plans to expand the town of Frobisher Bay into a distribution center to serve the eastern Arctic as Yellowknife and Inuvik serve the west. That the new Frobisher Bay will attract increasing numbers of prospectors, investors, and industrial developers is, at present, an earnest hope.

However, Yellowknife, whose name is related to the discovery of gold there about the same time as the Klondike gold rush, seems now, as territorial capital, destined to be the most important city in the Northwest Territories. It is also the one most accessible to tourists and has, in fact, a tourist information center called Travel Arctic—address, Yellowknife, Northwest Territories, Canada. Yellowknife already has 3,200 inhabitants, and more, especially government employees, are moving in every week. The government has built a thirteen-story apartment building, the first high-rise dwelling in the north and the nearest approach there to Service's "skyscraper." Pacific Western Airlines brings in jet aircraft on a scheduled basis, and a number of chartered airplane services to points as yet on no one's timetable are available.

Raising buildings in the north requires special techniques, and Canadian engineers have made study trips to Russia to look into methods found successful in Siberia. Like Russia's north country, the Canadian north has an underlay of frozen ground. Permafrost, as it is called, often penetrates as deep as two thousand feet, freezing the ground as solid as rock. This is fine as long as the ground remains frozen, but a heated building resting directly on the ground, or built into the ground, melts the permafrost, and the foundations then become soft and unstable. Buildings throughout the north, therefore, are built on stilts, which permit a free circulation of cold air over the frozen ground. For the same reason, conventional water mains and sewers will not work in the north. To cope, Canadian engineers have developed the Utilidor overground pipelines. In Inuvik and Frobisher Bay visitors have to climb over the pipelines—boxed and insulated—that supply residents with steam heat, running water, and sewage disposal.

Because of some mysterious disturbance of the permafrost, the whole town of Aklavik in the Mackenzie delta began to sink a few years ago. Unable to find any solution, government authorities built the new town of Inuvik on higher ground and invited the Aklavikans to move in. But the nine hundred Eskimos and Indians who had lived there for generations, tending their muskrat traps and selling their furs to Hudson's Bay, refused to move. They preferred the old life in their old town, even though it might be disappearing from sight. Today, while Aklavik continues to sink, the population has grown to about twelve hundred, and the Hudson's Bay Company recently built a new $100,-000 store.

Communities from Aklavik to Grise Fiord are bleak by southern standards, but houses there look much like houses in any low-cost suburban development. In most settlements even the Eskimos are provided with prefabricated, two-and-three-bedroom houses heated with oil and lighted with electricity. Toilets are indoors, and most kitchens, contrary to popular belief, have some form of refrigeration. Eskimos *do* buy iceboxes. They are learning to freeze the meat from the hunt, storing it for the months when hunting is poor.

It is heartening to see the Eskimos, as at Grise Fiord, living in homes that provide all the amenities of modern life with the exception of television. However, it is surprising to see the Eskimo men come out of these houses, pull their parkas over their heads, hitch their dogs to a sled, and ride out over the ice to shoot a polar bear or harpoon a seal. It is out on the ice that the hunter builds his igloo to shelter him while he stalks game for several days, perhaps for two or three weeks. When he returns home, he spends days curing his skins by stretching them on frames in the sun. It is not uncommon to see the skin of a white fox or an Arctic hare swinging on the line along with the family wash.

The problem of harnessing the Eskimo's undoubted talents, including his quick, flexible mind, his good humor, his eagerness to take on a new job, and his patience in learning how to do it, is a perplexing one for Canada. Children learn lessons quickly at school, even when they have to learn in English, but they receive little help at home from parents who never went to school and speak only Eskimo. There is no industry, aside from the government, to employ the young people, who become frustrated and embittered. Yet the government cannot let them alone to go their old ways, nor can it afford to pass up the opportunity to employ in some constructive way the only people who have proved they can survive, if not prosper, in the inhospitable north. Eskimos have done it for centuries.

One project, however, is producing results. The program to develop Eskimo carving promises both an occupational release and a means of self-support. Eskimos, lacking metals and wood, have worked for centuries in stone, the bones of animals, and the tusks of walruses and narwhals. These are the hard materials from which they made their weapons (harpoons and arrows), utensils (whale-oil lamps), and ornaments (beads and clasps).

Not so familiar until recently were the sculptures that the Eskimos carve from the same soapstone and ivory, with the same files, chisels, and knives. This Eskimo art reflects the Eskimo's simple life, but subtly shows his intimate knowledge and understanding of the animals that are so much a part of his life. The polar bear, the seal, the walrus and narwhal, and the wild goose are favorite subjects. Eskimo artists depict these animals in all attitudes of action and repose. Often the Eskimo himself is portrayed—the hardened face of an old man, the hunter attacking his quarry, the mother toting her papoose.

The best Eskimo pieces seemingly take the least work. One is told that an artist believes he does not create a beast or a human being, but merely releases whatever was in the raw rock or ivory. He studies his stone carefully until he thinks he sees something, or someone, inside, then puts his file and chisel to work as economically as possible. A polar bear in noble stride may "come out," a seal may have rolled on his side with one flipper waving in the air, or a goose may be sleeping with its head tucked under a wing.

The Eskimos' elaborate mythology has lent itself to the graphic arts. Government instructors have taught them the technique of print making. They have taken to this with characteristically effective results.

322

Polar bears in Norwegian Bay, Northwest Territories

Eskimo women are especially good print makers. The best artists, so far, have come from the eastern Arctic—Cape Dorset, Pelly Bay, Igloolik, Chesterfield Inlet, and Rankin Inlet. But ever since their work first caught the eye of travelers to the north, carving has become a growing craft industry. The Department of Northern Development sponsors classes and shops where the carvers and print makers may have their work appraised by councils of their peers. Government handlers then ship the chosen works, which eventually make their way, after moderate markups, to retail stores in the south.

Government buyers periodically tour Eskimo villages and bring out "Eskimo art" by the planeload. It is to be hoped that the resulting prosperity does not corrupt the artists or encourage them to sacrifice, particularly in their carvings, the inherent simplicity that is often moving and majestic. Eskimo art has become fashionable across southern Canada. Like all folk art, it has personal appeal that cannot be subjected to usual standards of art criticism. Some of it is in the high classic vein often attained in primitive art. Much of it is charming. A lot of it is simply crude.

When looking it over in shops, one might examine, particularly, any pieces from Cape Dorset. All pieces offered for sale are tagged with the name of the artist and his settlement. Dorset not only has interesting artists; the locale also supplies them with a good quality of greenstone that in the right hands produces carvings with the look and feel of jade. Pelly Bay is the center for small ivory pieces, such as exquisitely carved beasts and birds. A good Dorset polar bear, nine to ten inches long, can command a hundred dollars in a Toronto or Montreal shop. One of the Pelly Bay ivories may sell in the south for thirty-five or fifty dollars. There is, however, a wide range of prices.

The Northwest Territories government is promoting tourism and reports that about ten thousand visitors a year come up. There is no travel in the world like it, but because of the vast distances, the absence of roads and railroads, it is expensive, and out of the question during the long, dark winter that begins in October. But in summer one can drive to Yellowknife, if he doesn't mind a hot, dusty ride, or fly there and on to Inuvik by commercial planes that make daily flights from Edmonton. In the east there are flights from Montreal to Frobisher Bay several times a week, and connecting planes take one as far as

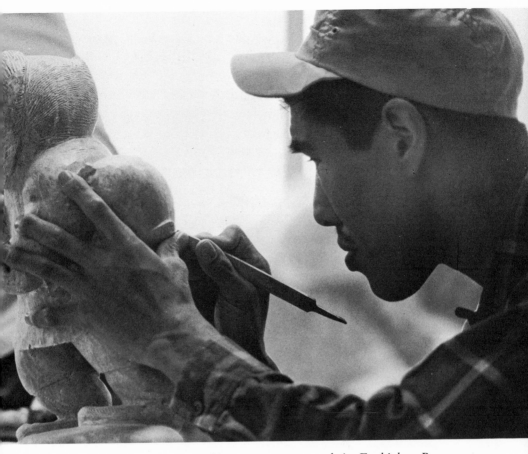

Meekeeseetee, an Eskimo carver, at work in Frobisher Bay

Resolute on Cornwallis Island. Until more sightseeing services and accommodations open up, hunting and fishing are the principal attractions outside Whitehorse, Dawson, and Yellowknife. There is also unlimited canoeing for the experienced and hardened water sportsman.

Hunting and fishing lodges are going into business in many remote places noted for their grizzly bears, moose, Dall sheep, or trout, grayling, and Arctic char. Great Bear Lake, 250 miles north of Yellowknife, has several fly-in fishing lodges, but because of their remoteness they cost each person $700 to $800 a week, transportation free from Edmonton or Winnipeg. If one wants Arctic fishing badly enough and has $1,000 to spend, he can have it for a week at Albert Edward Bay on Victoria Island, 225 miles inside the Arctic Circle. But one must remember that in summer, when the days are long, the fish bite around the clock.

Some eastern Arctic settlements, including Pelly Bay, have camps run by local Eskimo cooperatives that offer lodging and food for about fifty dollars a day, and sometimes hostels, with beds, indoor toilets, and cooking facilities, are available for less money. But travel agents and booking services hardly exist in this part of the world, and the adventurous traveler must go as far as he can commercially and then place himself in the hands of charter airlines whose bush pilots know where to go and how to get there.

As reporters we have traveled the north usually with government parties, once with the Minister of Northern Development and once with the Governor General of Canada, Roland Michener, on his first trip to the Arctic. The Governor General went there to impress upon the Eskimos the fact that they were Canadian subjects of Queen Elizabeth II, just as all other Canadians were. Whether the Eskimos were impressed they did not say, although their children waved homemade Maple Leaf flags and sometimes sang "O Canada" in Eskimo, English, and French. But there can be no question that the Governor General and his wife were impressed by what they saw of the north. Mr. Michener said that the distances and the incredible vistas of land, sea, and ice exhilarated him. He found the loneliness awesome.

Queen Elizabeth II made an unprecedented tour of the North in mid-summer of 1970. She, her husband, and their two older children traveled for five days across the Arctic from Frobisher to Yellowknife on a "people tour." Leaving traditional British pomp and circumstance behind, the royal family took informal walks through settlements, shaking hands and exchanging greetings. At Tuktoyaktuk the queen, tramping a dirt road, greeted her subjects wrapped in a hooded fur coat that the villagers had just presented to her. At Fort Providence to unveil a plaque to Alexander Mackenzie, she wore a pant suit for protection from insects.

The Eskimos and the Indians were charmed by the informality of these regal visitors. But did the queen inspire in these remote subjects a sense of true loyalty beyond the friendliness of a new acquaintance? Did she help extend the Arctic horizon to make these long-isolated people feel they belong to the great nation "outside"?

One may doubt this. And yet the loneliness, awful to southerners but cherished by Eskimos, will not last much longer. The trial voyages of the United States tanker *Manhattan* in 1969 and 1970 showed that the long-sought Northwest Passage may be realized. In the next decade or two new ways to force open the ice-choked channel may at last make it the practical water road to riches.

Thus, the sight of the *Manhattan,* a foreign vessel, in their Arctic excited all Canadians. It also aroused their deep concern. For while brightening the prospect of opening the earth's last great frontier, the *Manhattan*'s cruise raised vexing problems of sovereignty and control. Despite the voyage twenty-five years ago of the Canadian coast guard vessel *St. Roch* and the annual outport visits of Hudson's Bay supply ships, Canadians can hardly say they patrol the Arctic. They must do so, however, if they want to maintain Canadian control once foreign commercial vessels begin plying those waters.

The Arctic is easier to pollute than are tropical zones, because frozen waste simply does not decay and disappear. Sewage cannot be treated septically, and oil spilled on the Arctic ice and shores would lie there in a virtually solid state for decades. Extensive pollution of the land and sea would critically endanger the North's ecology.

Prime Minister Trudeau has said Canada must, at least, protect what he calls "the world's last big natural reserve." Not only the oil and ore but also the extensive wildlife must be conserved. The government is mindful that exploitation, trade, and commerce move a country forward, but almost inevitably leave pollution in their wake. It would be "irresponsible," Trudeau has argued, for Canada to allow her natural heritage to be destroyed, "either in the name of freedom of the seas or in the interests of economic development."

The government's first step was to declare Canada's dominion over navigation in Arctic waters one hundred miles out to sea. This means that all ships in the Northwest Passage must obey Canadian regulations designed to prevent pollution.

If, in the last third of the twentieth century, Canada can develop her north, open its resources to the world, and yet keep its natural and uncontaminated beauty, she will have performed a service for which all nations should be grateful in the years beyond 2000.

Prime Minister Trudeau, surrounded by his ministers, speaks to the House of Commons in Ottawa.

16 Will It Last?

"The direction of Canada's steps forward in the 1970's should be fascinating to watch."

Eskimo girl scouts wave crepe-paper Maple Leaf flags they have made to welcome the governor general.

THE CANADA WE have surveyed has a richer past than most foreigners and many Canadians appreciate. The country's vastness and rugged terrain have for centuries challenged exceptional men, from the early French explorers to modern Arctic adventurers. To lay hands on Canada's natural riches—whether furs, minerals, or oil—men have endured hardship and privation. The great American historian Francis Parkman found this history so engrossing that even blindness could not discourage his long pursuit of just one aspect of it—the French experience in the north country.

Though hardy men had reached its western mountains and even its Arctic north before American colonists had crossed the Alleghenies,

Canada remains a fresh country, underpopulated and largely undeveloped, a place where birds and beasts outnumber humans and sweeping solitudes lure men weary of cities. More than one third of its people are "new Canadians" in the real sense that their roots are not in the country's past. If one wants to experience the beauties and comforts of tradition—to see people behave pretty much as their ancestors did—one must go to the old countries of Europe and Asia.

The excitement of Canada is seeing its patterns change as its people seek new relationships among themselves and between themselves and foreigners, especially Americans. The election of Pierre Elliott Trudeau to the Liberal party leadership in April, 1968, and his accession to the prime ministry marked, many observers felt, a turning point in Canadian history. If so, what were the nation's new goals? The direction of Canada's steps forward in the 1970's should be fascinating to watch. Whither Canada?

After passing its one-hundredth birthday in 1967, Canada is much more untested as a nation than the United States was in 1876, its centenary. George Washington, as first President of the United States, and the early Chief Justices, notably John Marshall, had asserted vital powers for the federal government. A separatist movement in the South had tested the nation's unity. Rebellion had been put down in the terrible Civil War. By 1876 the concept of Manifest Destiny had prevailed from ocean to ocean. There was no longer any doubt that the United States would become one big nation, although the extent of its power and influence would not be known for another fifty years.

Canada still faces many of these great challenges, plus the formidable one of living in the shadow of the American Goliath. The Supreme Court of Canada, without constitutional foundations (it is a creature of Parliament), is respected but not necessarily obeyed. Ottawa treats the restiveness in French Canada with the caution displayed by antebellum Washington when it met turmoil in the South with compromises. No prime minister of Canada would, as yet, think of moving on Quebec with force, and some Quebec separatists are boldly confident that federal troops would never go into action to stop secession. History, of course, reports that virtually no one thought an American President would order United States troops to subdue the South, either. But irritations led to challenges, and challenges led to Fort Sumter, leaving a hesitant Lincoln no choice but to fight.

The present hope is that Prime Minister Trudeau, with his flair for the unusual, the different, the resourceful approach, will find a way to meet and overcome the challenges to Canada's life without a national breakup or civil war.

To do this, Newfoundland must grow closer to British Columbia than the people of those provinces can now imagine. Torontonians must come to think of their north in terms of the Arctic, not of the pleasant Muskoka summer-cottage country an hour's trip up Route 400. Prosperity, in the Canada of the future, must not mean booms in four or five cities while poverty grinds down great undeveloped regions, including all the north. Jet plane transportation and satellite radio and television communications can help remove the barriers of mountains, wilderness, water, and time zones. But what must, more importantly, come about in the 1970's is a positive Canadianism to replace the negative "non-Americanism" that too often marks Canadians today.

"What is a Canadian?" runs an old joke.

"Well, he's not an American."

Unless action is taken, such empty Canadianism will collapse before the pressures of north-south trade and cultural exchange, making Americans out of Canadians whether they like it or not.

Trudeau has prescribed a preventive course not radical in ideology or revolution but fundamentally rooted in rights and responsibilities for all Canadians. The French Canadian in Ste. Anne de la Pérade, the poor fisherman in the Newfoundland outport of Come-by-Chance, and the Eskimo hunter of Grise Fiord need not only the social welfare insurance that previous governments have provided but also a surge of pride in being Canadian. In many older countries, certainly in the United States, patriotism often becomes unpleasant and undesirable chauvinism. Canadians, wanting none of this, go to the other extreme. They must be the least patriotic people on earth, and certainly they are never guilty of chauvinism. A Vancouver journalist, in a conversation with the authors, spoke of national pride in country as though it were, indeed, one of the deadly sins. "That's the trouble with you Americans," he said. "You are proud. We Canadians are not like that."

If patriotic fervor will not induce the Canadian spirit to soar, as Walt Whitman used hortatory verse to arouse Americanism, perhaps

Trudeau can lift his countrymen upward and onward through the Just Society.

In simple terms, the Just Society would give Canadians a central government that is assertive and aggressive enough to command the respect of the provinces and sensitive enough to hear and heed the will of people scattered through five time zones. The government should speak French and English and inspire the many Canadian cultures to flower. It should become the final arbiter of resources development, so that well-to-do Ontario, British Columbia, and Alberta share more of their wealth than they now do with the poor regions of the east and the north. Also, sometime, somehow, Canada must replace her one-hundred-year-old London-based British North America Act with a strictly Canadian constitution. Since 1867 Canada has grown in so many ways that she needs a broad, basic, homemade charter in which Canadians can design their own pattern of life and the relationship they want to establish with each other and with the world. All this is essential if Canada is to develop as a nation.

The sweeping victory of the profederalist Liberals in the Quebec provincial election in April, 1970, was an encouraging development. In choosing Robert Bourassa to be their premier, the voters demonstrated their preference for a prosperous, stable society within the Confederation to an uncertain future as an independent state. While in the end 23 per cent of the voters supported separatist candidates, the deciding issue was federalism and economics. Many Quebeckers, old and young, voted for the separatist *Parti Québecois* not because they wanted to live in an independent French-speaking republic, but because they had lost faith in old parties and old leaders to improve their lot.

Mr. Bourassa, while leading one of the two old-line parties, proved that at thirty-six he was anything but an old leader. He persuaded a decisive number of voters that what they really wanted wasn't separation from Canada but confidence and jobs—the "opportunity to work" in the French language. He promised to develop Quebec's sense of security and pride as part of the Canadian family. He has a term of at least four years to fulfill his promise. If he fails, new pressures for separation are certain to return in full force.

The United States' need for raw materials, including water, is certain to be a constant strain not only on U.S.-Canada relations but also on the relationships between the Canadian provinces with materials to sell and those with nothing to sell. A civil war might unite Canada, as some historians believe it did the United States, but it would more probably destroy it. Another foreign war, as accounts of both world wars show, could rip asunder a country that has never wholly accepted the military draft and has been sympathetic on that account to American draft dodgers.

Americans who visit Canada may experience many surprises because too many of them know less about the divisions within this neighbor of theirs than they do about the conflict between the Arab countries and Israel. They will learn, surely, that it is a mistake to take Canada's friendliness for granted. David is still very wary of Goliath. The time when Americans automatically thought of Canada as a part of their Manifest Destiny is past. Thomas Jefferson, if living today, would never express the "hope" that Canada "join us in Congress and complete the American union." Most Canadians know that Americans aren't really plotting to absorb them bodily. But Canadians are uncomfortable when they hear Americans talk so much about being "close neighbors." Canadians would rather regard Americans as good foreign friends, or neighbors once removed.

James Eayrs, the University of Toronto political economist who has studied U.S.-Canada relations for a long time, wrote a few years back: "What is really required (if the American-Canadian relationship is to flourish) is a certain reserve, a sense of live and let live, even of aloofness on occasion, in the treatment of the smaller country by the larger. 'Good fences,' American leaders are fond of quoting on their Canadian visits, 'make good neighbors.' They could usefully remember that good neighbors make good fences."

The late Blair Fraser, another prominent Canadian writer who was deeply attached to the northland, once lamented the "development" that made "ugly little towns prosper (across southern Canada), all calling themselves cities and all looking like faithful copies of Omaha, Nebraska."

"This is not a Canada to call forth any man's love," Fraser wrote in his book *The Search for Identity*. "But just north of it still lies a different kind of land—too barren ever to be thickly settled, too bleak to be

334

popular like Blackpool or Miami. There is no reason to doubt that it will always be there, and so long as it is there Canada will not die."

Such an evocation of national feeling by a Canadian is as refreshing as it is moving. But it is already too late for Canadians to rely on their barren, bleak northland to safeguard their Canadianism. It is rather for Canadians, by joining finally and determinedly behind a common purpose, to develop earth's last great frontier into a country that will endure and could become one of man's finest achievements. There is still time for that.

Special Interest Guide

THIS SECTION OF OUR BOOK is designed to help travelers who always take abroad with them their personal enthusiasms— for modern art or old houses, for power dams or bird sanctuaries, for the particular aspects of the world they most enjoy examining. Astride one's hobby is a great way to see any country, as those who haven't yet tried it can discover for themselves. Pursuing a special interest takes a traveler down byways never glimpsed on the ordinary tourist route and may bring about chance encounters with the nicest people around —fellow enthusiasts, of course. Sportsmen know the truth of this. The trip to a remote fishing camp, the beautiful isolation of the place when they reach it, the talk around the fire at night, make it worthwhile even when their fishing luck is poor. Travel agents use the idea in special tours for playgoers or for balletomanes or for Bible students. We feel it is even more rewarding as a do-it-yourself project. The experts one meets along the way—an archaeologist on a dig, an engineer at a nuclear power plant, the curator of a historic house —will often really talk to one or two deeply interested individuals, whereas he will lecture a larger group. And nowhere will one be rushed, as happens on even the best of arranged tours.

So in this section, tourists used to having their avocations shape their vacations (and those who would like to try the plan next time) will find under the proper subheads brief descriptions of points of special interest to them. These listings are by no means exhaustive. We have chosen to recommend outstanding or unusual examples or those that seem to us characteristically Canadian. Some relate specifically to our text. Two other criteria affected our choices: a point of interest had to be reasonably accessible and open with some degree of regularity. This is not to say that we guarantee the road to a remote but interesting mine won't be gravel, or that the curator at a western museum won't be out harvesting if you arrive in autumn. Enthusiasts, we feel, are willing to take the rough with the smooth. They are also used to asking questions of local people before they start off.

We have not listed every local museum, summer theatre, dam, or historical attraction worth visiting if the tourist happens to be in the area with an hour or two to spare. We have listed the points of interest we think he should drive out of his way to see. Neither have we chosen to sponsor attractions that are simply commercial operations, unless they have been done with taste and/or authenticity. Of course, most boat and rail tours are commercial, but in Canada these are handled with a notable absence of honky-tonk. They are often crowded, however, particularly the special trains to unusual points. For that matter, during the summer it may be hard to get the right accommodations on the great cross-country trains, so reservations should be made well in advance.

The happy man or woman whose business or profession is *his* greatest interest used to be advised to forget it during his holiday, and therefore spent his time in a state of boredom, whatever the name of the actual state around him. Now, more and more tourists are finding that they understand and enjoy any country more if they look into the workings of their own business or profession in that country. For them the Canadian situation is ideal. Wherever they may be, the local tourist bureau or the chamber of commerce will be happy to tell them what factories or mines or colleges can be toured at what hours—or to arrange a special guided tour if the visitor so desires. Our suggestions along these lines have been more general; we have listed the really big operations and unusual small factories that anyone might enjoy visiting and that say something about Canada. Few American branch plants are listed. Here again, we don't guarantee that you'll get in everywhere; at that great copper and gold complex, or at that little organ factory, the workers may be out on strike when you arrive.

Because Canada is a developing country, its funds barely

cover its constant expansion. Its most pressing needs naturally come first. So any institution that requires a subsidy—federal, provincial, or local—can find itself forced to delay announced plans, cut back visiting hours, or even close down altogether. Only a few have done so, but consider, for example, the future of Montreal's Man and His World, as the continuation of Expo 67 is called. It is a large and lively point of interest any summer that it is open, but finding the money to keep it in operation in subsequent summers proved a major enterprise for the city's mayor Jean Drapeau, who dreamed up Expo 67 originally. Another mayor might not choose to spend so much time and money on it. So how long will the continuation continue? We have listed it, but the reader's guess is as informed as ours. As one attraction fades, however, two or three new ones open up. A new historical museum in Halifax was scheduled to open in mid 1970. In September, 1969, Winnipeg asked for bids on a new art museum to round out the complex of public buildings that help make it one of Canada's most surprising cities. When it is finally ready, Winnipeggers will let visitors know. Toronto is planning to build what the city says will be the largest zoo in the world, one that follows a highly original plan. It is scheduled to open July 1, 1973, but should be worth waiting for. Change is in the Canadian air, and without apology, we admit it is bound to affect this Special Interest Guide here and there. But its use will, we promise, enlarge your concept of Canada—even if you are a Canadian.

Archaeology

ESTABLISHED SITES

VIKING SETTLEMENT

L'Anse aux Meadows,
Newfoundland

*For more than seven years a determined
Norse scholar has been working at this
dig, slowly proving his point that the
Vikings reached this northernmost tip
of Newfoundland. Seven red-roofed
structures protect his extensive finds.
Trips to visit the site can be arranged
in summer at the Loon Motel, fourteen
miles from St. Anthony. St. Anthony
can be reached by a rugged but interesting drive, by Canadian National
Steamship, or by East Provincial Air-
ways from Gander.*

PICTOGRAPHS

Kedge Lake, Nova Scotia

*Pictures and symbols etched on slate
rock.*

INDIAN ROCK PAINTINGS

Bon Echo Provincial Park, Route 41,
Eastern Ontario

*Paintings on the scenic cliffs of Mazi-
naw Lake.*

THE SERPENT MOUNDS

Keene, Ontario

*Near Rice Lake, earth construction in
the form of a gigantic serpent, dating
from the second century A.D.*

PETERBOROUGH PETROGLYPHS

Lakefield, Ontario

*This extraordinary array of prehistoric
Indian figures etched in rock can be
reached from South Stoney Lake Road.*

INDIAN ROCK PAINTINGS

Near Agawa Bay,
Lake Superior Provincial Park,
Route 17, Central Ontario

*Paintings on the sheer cliffs of Lake
Superior are accessible via a short road
and a scenic trail, from the first Friday
in June to the second Sunday in September.*

STONE MOSAICS

Betula Lake, Near Seven Sisters Falls,
Manitoba

*Boulders laid out to represent huge
birds and animals on a spot sacred to
the Indians. Best viewed in summer.*

WRITING-ON-STONE PROVINCIAL PARK

Seventy-five miles southeast of
Lethbridge, Alberta

*Groups of simple incised portrayals of
a hunt, a fight, or a raid. Latter-day
Indians believed that they were made
by spirits. Some are reproduced on a
wall of the Provincial Museum at
Edmonton.*

NATIONAL MUSEUM DIG

Digby Island, Near Prince Rupert,
British Columbia

*A shell midden containing cemetery
areas, house remains, and artifacts
spanning a four-thousand-year period.
Write the National Museum at Ottawa
for permission to visit.*

PETROGLYPH PARK

One mile south of Nanaimo,
Vancouver Island, British Columbia

*Canada's rock formations lent them-
selves to this early type of Indian art.*

A summer dig at a Huron village
near Orillia, Ontario

Several Canadian universities and the National Museum of Man at Ottawa excavate prehistoric Indian sites during the summer months. The dig locations vary from year to year. Some are too remote to interest most visitors. Others are easily reached, and some allow the interested public not only to visit but also to participate. For information on the current plans and the status of visitors, archaeological buffs should write in spring to the chairman of the archaeology department at the university nearest the area they will be visiting:

THE UNIVERSITY OF TORONTO
Toronto, Ontario

MCMASTER UNIVERSITY
Hamilton, Ontario

TRENT UNIVERSITY
Peterborough, Ontario

LAKEHEAD UNIVERSITY
Lakehead, Ontario

THE UNIVERSITY OF MANITOBA
Winnipeg, Manitoba

THE UNIVERSITY OF CALGARY
Calgary, Alberta

THE UNIVERSITY OF BRITISH COLUMBIA
Vancouver, British Columbia

Archaeological buffs vacationing in Saskatchewan in the summer might enjoy lending a hand to the farmers, teachers, and businessmen from all over the province who work at licensed digs, Indian mounds, and other sites. Information may be obtained from:

SASKATCHEWAN ARCHAEOLOGICAL
    SOCIETY
c/o William Long,
857 Elphinstone Street,
Regina, Saskatchewan

Architecture

DISTINGUISHED PERIOD BUILDINGS STILL IN USE

PROVINCE HOUSE

Charlottetown, Prince Edward Island

Guided tours of the capitol are offered daily. Modern Canada had its beginnings in the Confederation Chamber here.

PROVINCE HOUSE

Hollis Street, Halifax, Nova Scotia

Canada's oldest (1811) and smallest seat of government is a fine example of the Adam style, with a library of particular charm. Dickens found the proceedings in this legislature "like looking at Westminister through the wrong end of the telescope." Tours daily.

GOVERNMENT HOUSE

Barrington Street, Halifax, Nova Scotia

Begun in 1800, the residence of the lieutenant governor has been called "Government House" since the days when the queen's representative really was the government. Not open.

THE HENRY HOUSE

Barrington Street, Halifax, Nova Scotia

A merchant's house built in 1818, this was once the home of one of Canada's Fathers of Confederation, William Alexander Henry. Today it is an attractive bar and restaurant, and can therefore be toured easily.

L'ATRE

La Famille (Ile d'Orleans),
near Quebec City, Quebec

Two ancient houses classified as historic monuments. One contains an excellent restaurant.

CHÂTEAU FRONTENAC

Quebec City, Quebec

In itself and in its location, the most impressive of the Canadian Pacific's château-style hotels.

HÔPITAL GÉNÉRAL DE QUEBEC

Boulevard Langelier, Quebec City, Quebec

In 1692 this general hospital was established by letters patent from Louis XIV. It is presently a hospital for the chronically ill, but it has been modernized so discreetly that it is the best preserved group of old French buildings in the province. The paintings forming the dadoes on the lateral walls of the chapel were done by a nun in the 1690's.

OLD MARKET

St. Paul Street East, Montreal, Quebec

The handsomely domed old central market has been restored by the city so that it is in period outside with efficient modern offices inside.

PARLIAMENT OF CANADA

Parliament Hill, Wellington Street, Ottawa, Ontario

Daily tours of this Victorian-Gothic complex, including the Library of Parliament—the earliest part. Public admitted to the House of Commons for Question Period and debates, Monday through Friday when Parliament is in session.

GOVERNMENT HOUSE

Sussex Drive, Ottawa, Ontario

The official residence of the governor general is not open to the public, but in summer, when the governor general is away, the grounds can be visited. The changing of the piquet guard can be viewed daily then.

VICTORIA HALL

Cobourg, Ontario

This town hall and courthouse has kept its 1860 furnishings. The courtroom is a replica of Old Bailey in London.

CITY HALL

Kingston, Ontario

When its cornerstone was laid in 1843, Kingston was the capital of the United Province of Canada, and the building was designed to house the legislature, which instead moved the capital to Montreal in 1844, leaving Kingston with a handsome city hall.

COUNTY COURTHOUSE

London, Ontario

Completed in 1831, it is patterned after Malahide Castle in Ireland.

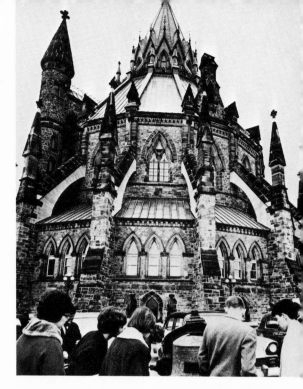

The Library of Parliament at Ottawa

OSGOODE HALL

130 Queen Street West, Toronto, Ontario

Built for the Law Society, circa 1829–32, this is a splendid example of Ontario's early public architecture. Expanded later, it now also houses the Appellate Division of Ontario's Supreme Court. Note the two cow gates in its handsome iron fence.

ST. LAWRENCE HALL

King Street East, Toronto, Ontario

Beautifully restored, this 1850 building is once again the city's community center.

VICTORIA CITY HALL

Victoria, British Columbia

The charm of this Victorian building has been pointed up with bright paints. For contrast, a modern shopping center was built around it.

CANADA'S "GRAND HOTELS"

These vast old establishments, either in a very British or in

341

"château" style, were built by railways or steamship lines for the grandiose comfort of well-heeled travelers. They still manage with a degree of modernization not only to keep running but to maintain much of their Edwardian style, with stained glass, armor, and afternoon teas in the lounge.

MANOIR RICHELIEU
Murray Bay, Quebec

BANFF SPRINGS HOTEL
Banff, Alberta

CHÂTEAU LAKE LOUISE
Lake Louise, Alberta

EMPRESS HOTEL
Victoria, British Columbia

OUTSTANDING MODERN STRUCTURES

CONFEDERATION CENTRE
Charlottetown, Prince Edward Island

Built to commemorate the first meeting of the Fathers of Confederation in Charlottetown in 1864, the Centre houses a theatre, art gallery, and library. The design, selected in a national competition, is by Dimitri Dimakopoulos of Montreal.

LE MÉTRO
Montreal, Quebec

Montreal's Métro demonstrates that a subway can be charming.

BIOSPHERE
Ile Ste. Helene, Montreal, Quebec

Buckminster Fuller's great shimmering globe was the United States pavilion at Expo 67. Now it is a permanent fixture on the Montreal landscape, to be used each season as the city authorities choose.

HABITAT APARTMENTS
Cité du Havre, Montreal, Quebec

Moshe Safdie's experimental housing development overlooking the St. Lawrence River was a sensational attraction at Expo 67. But as a permanent dwelling in the Canadian climate, it presents problems.

L'AUDITORIUM DES JEUNESSES MUSICALES DU CANADA
Mont Orford Park, Magog, Quebec

A curved, flowing, modern structure in a woodland setting.

MANIC V
135 miles by road north of Baie Comeau, Quebec

Part of Hydro-Quebec's chain of great power stations on the Manicouagan River, this giant dam is not only an impressive engineering achievement but a thing of beauty. Built on the multiple

Montreal's clean, attractive subway, Le Métro

vault system, it is 705 feet high, and its towering arches in a great curve make it more elegant than a Roman aqueduct.

CITY HALL–COURT COMPLEX

Brantford, Ontario

Designed in brutalist style by architect Michael Kopsa.

NATIONAL ARTS CENTRE

Confederation Square, Ottawa, Ontario

Fred Lebensold designed this opera house-theatre complex on the banks of the Rideau Canal, where it stands like a modern castle. Opened in June, 1969, it enlivens the whole Ottawa scene.

CITY HALL

Nathan Phillips Square, Toronto, Ontario

Frequent tours of Toronto's superb city hall are offered daily. Viljo Revell was the architect. Its influence has transformed Toronto, "given the city a heart."

ONTARIO SCIENCE CENTRE

770 Don Mills Road, Toronto, Ontario

Three different buildings interconnected on a twenty-acre wooded ravine make a strikingly successful modern museum. Designed by Raymond Moriyama.

PROVINCIAL MUSEUM AND ARCHIVES

12845 102nd Avenue, Edmonton, Alberta

A simple, functional design, given interest by the use of stone from several provinces of Canada. Note also the use of Indian petroglyphs for a mural effect on the outside wall of the auditorium.

POLICE STATION

Edmonton, Alberta

A striking structure where design is hardly expected.

CHÂTEAU LACOMBE

Edmonton, Alberta

An eighteen-sided tower hotel.

THE "NEW TOWN"

Gold River, British Columbia

One of six "instant" municipalities established in British Columbia since 1964, this one, almost in the center of Vancouver Island, is a handsome example. Note particularly the apartment complex. There are other "instant"

towns at Port McNeill and Rumble Beach on Vancouver Island.

OUR LADY OF VICTORY CHURCH

Inuvik, Northwest Territories

An Eskimo church in shape of an igloo. The pews and altar were carved by Eskimos.

See also NEW UNIVERSITIES under EDUCATION.

Art

INTERNATIONAL AND CANADIAN

Canada has no really great art museums, built up over the decades by extensive gifts or bequests from wealthy collectors. That pattern of philanthropy has yet to develop north of the border, due in part to Canadian inheritance and gift tax laws. Notable private collections have either been broken up and sold or remain inaccessible. However, Vincent Massey, first governor general of Canadian origin and heir to the Massey-Ferguson (farm machinery) wealth, did give his collection of modern English paintings to the National Gallery, and in his will he left the gallery his larger collection of Canadian art. Lord Beaverbrook not only built a small museum for the Province of New Brunswick but also stocked it with his own very personal art choices. But for the most part, Canadian museums have had to depend on federal or provincial grants for new acquisitions. These grants are never large enough to allow curators to bid for major art works in a competitive market. Northern galleries are, consequently, weak in European masterpieces, but they are fairly strong in Canadian art. Most of the artists represented will be new to Americans, who might well enjoy making their acquaintance. The McMichael Collection in Kleinburg, Ontario, is, in fact, entirely Canadian, and its gallery, built of massive logs, provides an ideal setting.

Museums

ARTS AND CULTURAL CENTRE

St. John's, Newfoundland

The multi-use Centre contains, besides a theatre, three art galleries and a teaching area for crafts. Near Memorial University.

CONFEDERATION CENTRE

Charlottetown, Prince Edward Island

This all-Canadian complex includes a theatre, art gallery, museum, library, and the Memorial Hall.

BEAVERBROOK ART GALLERY

The Row, Fredericton, New Brunswick

The Canadian-born British press lord's gift to his native province houses his collection, which includes four large paintings by Winston Churchill and a huge canvas by Dali, Santiago el Grande.

MUSEUM OF FINE ARTS

1379 Sherbrooke Street West, Montreal, Quebec

Those who saw the superb art exhibit at Expo 67 will be disappointed by the limited display here.

ART GALLERY OF HAMILTON

Hamilton, Ontario

Canadian and some European works are exhibited in this finely equipped building.

McMICHAEL CONSERVATION COLLECTION OF ART

North of Toronto, Route 400, Kleinburg, Ontario

The setting and the collection provide a sense of Canada at its most characteristic.

NATIONAL GALLERY OF CANADA

Elgin and Slater Streets, Ottawa, Ontario

Visitors will find a few pleasant surprises in the permanent collection. Outstanding loan exhibits on occasion.

ART GALLERY OF ONTARIO

317 Dundas Street West, Toronto, Ontario

More limited in its displays than it should be, given the city's size and wealth.

ROYAL ONTARIO MUSEUM

Avenue Road and Bloor Street, Toronto, Ontario

The Chinese collection is notable, particularly the funerary figures in pottery.

MENDEL ART GALLERY AND CIVIC CONSERVATORY

950 Spadina Crescent, Saskatoon, Saskatchewan

A "new" Canadian's gift to his adopted city is now the community's pride.

VANCOUVER ART GALLERY

1145 West Georgia, Vancouver, British Columbia

Its permanent collection is small, but under a vigorous director, major loan exhibits are featured from time to time.

Commercial Galleries

For a view of current trends in Canada, the commercial galleries are worth visiting. Naturally they are found by the streetful in Montreal and Toronto, but there are good shops in several other Canadian cities.

OPEN-AIR ART MARKET

Rue du Tresor, Quebec City, Quebec

In a narrow little street off the Place d'Armes, young Quebec artists put their wares up for sale every day in summer. Occasionally some really distinctive work can be found.

GALENE DENYSE DELRUE
451, St. Sulpice Street, Montreal, Quebec

DOMINION GALLERY
1438 Sherbrooke Street West,
Montreal, Quebec

WALTER KLINKHOFF GALLERY
1200 Sherbrooke Street West, Montreal,
Quebec

GALERIE GODARD LE FORT
1490 Sherbrooke Street West, Montreal,
Quebec

GALERIE LIBRE
2100 Crescent Street, Montreal, Quebec

GALERIE DE MONTREAL
2060 Mackay Street, Montreal, Quebec

GALERIE MOOS
1430 Sherbrooke Street West, Montreal,
Quebec

GALERIE SHERBROOKE
1196 Sherbrooke Street West, Montreal,
Quebec

WADDINGTON GALLERIES
1456 Sherbrooke Street West, also
Place Bonaventure, Montreal, Quebec

ROBERTSON GALLERIES
162 Laurier Avenue West, Ottawa,
Ontario

WELLS GALLERY
109 Metcalfe Street, Ottawa, Ontario

DUNKELMAN GALLERY
15 Bedford Road, Toronto, Ontario

THE ISAACS GALLERY
832 Yonge Street, Toronto, Ontario

CARMEN LAMANNA GALLERY
840 Yonge Street, Toronto, Ontario

MAZELOW GALLERY
3463 Yonge Street, Toronto, Ontario

THE DAVID MIRVISH GALLERY
596 Markham Street, Toronto, Ontario

GALLERY MOOS
138 Yorkville Street, Toronto, Ontario

JERROLD MORRIS GALLERY
15 Prince Arthur, Toronto, Ontario

THE POLLOCK GALLERY
599 Markham Street, Toronto, Ontario

ROBERTS GALLERY
641 Yonge Street, Toronto, Ontario

ALBERT WHITE GALLERY
25 Prince Arthur, Toronto, Ontario

Montreal's Museum of Fine Arts

JACOX GALLERIES
10518 99th Avenue, Edmonton, Alberta

ART EMPORIUM
2956 Granville Street, Vancouver,
British Columbia

BAU-XI
555 Hamilton Street, Vancouver,
British Columbia

DOUGLAS GALLERY
1724 Davie Street, Vancouver, British
Columbia

EXPOSITION GALLERY
151 Water Street, Vancouver, British
Columbia

GALLERY OF GOLDEN KEY
761 Dunsmuir Street, Vancouver,
British Columbia

OHLER'S GALLERY
2750 West Broadway, Vancouver,
British Columbia

ESKIMO AND INDIAN

In a special category are Canada's indigenous arts—those of the Eskimos and the Indians, particularly the west-coast Haida, Kwakiutls, and Chimmesyans—which have already caught the eye of international collectors. The response to Eskimo art has in fact been so enthusiastic that it has prompted natives of small talent to try their hands at carving, too. To buy wisely, the visitor might first inform his taste by studying museum collections. He should also look for the tags on Eskimo sculpture and the insignia in the margins of Eskimo prints, which show that the work has been evaluated and approved by the Eskimo Art Council of Canada. The Council also sets prices to make sure the native artist gets a fair return.

West-coast Indian art (casually labeled Haida) is not yet as popular with the general public. Most of the early pieces have been bought by astute museum curators or by such folk-art collectors as Nelson Rockefeller. In consequence, prices have risen astronomically. A very few coast Indians are still at work re-creating tribal myths in wood or stone or metal; they are dedicated artists who have not been commercialized. But in or out of museums and parks, Haida, Kwakiutl, and Chimmesyan work will prove a revelation to anyone who has a stereotyped conception of Indian art.

Museums

NEW BRUNSWICK MUSEUM

Saint John, New Brunswick

Micmac artifacts.

NATIONAL MUSEUM OF MAN

Metcalfe at McLeod, Ottawa, Ontario

This Victorian fortress of a museum has recently been completely reconstructed inside, the better to display its fine collections of notable early Eskimo carvings and some of the best west-coast Indian art to be seen in the east.

WINNIPEG ART GALLERY

Winnipeg, Manitoba

This provincial gallery has one of the best Eskimo collections in Canada and has greatly influenced proper appreciation of this art form across the country and abroad.

MUSEUM OF NORTHERN BRITISH COLUMBIA

Prince Rupert, British Columbia

TOTEM GROVE

University of British Columbia, Vancouver, British Columbia

A Haida house and other structures in a grove of totem poles. Also a fine museum of anthropology, where not all of its superb collection can be displayed.

TOTEM POLES

Stanley Park, Vancouver, British Columbia

The most photographed if not the most notable collection.

CENTENNIAL MUSEUM

Vanier Park, 1100 Chestnut Street, Vancouver, British Columbia

Among other interesting exhibits is a fine, small west-coast Indian collection notable for the carving in argillite by the Haida artist Edenshaw.

HERITAGE COURT MUSEUM

Victoria, British Columbia

A part of Heritage Court, the province's historial reference complex, the new Museum of Natural History and Anthropology's collection of west-coast Indian art should not be missed. Notice particularly the glass pavilion outside, which can be toured when the museum is closed (as it is on Mondays). Thunderbird Park is next door.

THUNDERBIRD PARK

Victoria, British Columbia

Totem poles in all their variety: heraldic, house frontal, memorial, mortuary, and welcome figures. Here, too, is the house of Mungo Martin, a Kwakiutl chief, one of the last great totem-pole carvers.

Native Art Shops

GRENFELL HANDICRAFT SHOP

Grenfell Mission, St. Anthony, Newfoundland

Eskimo arts and crafts.

SEA CAPTAIN'S LOFT

St. Andrews, New Brunswick

CANADIAN HANDICRAFTS GUILD

2025 Peel Street, Montreal, Quebec

Eskimo, Indian, and French-Canadian arts.

KEEWATINOOK

1455 Crescent Street, Montreal, Quebec

GALLERIE LIPPEL

2159 Mackay Street, Montreal, Quebec

COMPTOIR DU TOTEM

Place Laurier, Ste. Foy, Quebec

At Quebec City's shopping center, where an old village once stood.

GALLERIE ST. JEAN

1093 rue St. Jean, Quebec City, Quebec

Contemporary Canadian and Eskimo art.

GALLERIE ZANETTIN

Côte de la Montagne, Quebec City, Quebec

Contemporary Canadian and Eskimo art.

IROQRAFTS

Rural Route 2, Ohsweken, Ontario

Off Highway 6, two miles southwest of Caledonia, Ontario. A large wholesale-retail native Iroquois crafts outlet.

CANADA'S FOUR CORNERS

93 Sparks Street (on The Mall), Ottawa, Ontario

Eskimo, Indian, and other folk art.

LOFTHOUSE GALLERIES

223 McLeod, Ottawa, Ontario

Contemporary Canadian as well as Eskimo art.

THE SNOW GOOSE

40 Elgin Street, Ottawa, Ontario

One of the most discriminating Eskimo displays anywhere. Also more west-coast Indian art than is usually available in eastern Canada.

SIOUX HAND CRAFT CO-OPERATIVE

Standing Buffalo Reserve, Adjacent to Echo Valley Provincial Park, Saskatchewan

Wool tapestries and rugs in traditional Sioux designs. Open during the summer.

THE QUEST

Banff, Alberta

THE "BAY" DEPARTMENT STORES

Winnipeg, Manitoba; Calgary and Edmonton, Alberta; Vancouver, British Columbia

Because of the company's many posts in the Arctic, these and other Hudson's Bay stores generally have representative Eskimo art works on hand.

INDIAN CO-OP

First Avenue and Lorna Street, Whitehorse, Yukon

Indian handicrafts.

FOLK ART

Because of Canada's mosaic culture, more attention is paid to folk art than in the United States generally. In the province of Quebec, as might be expected, folk artists and craftsmen get official support and encouragement. The ebullient results—in ceramics, wood carving, and metalwork—can be found in dozens of small shops and occasionally at roadside stands. We list a few of the established shops there and elsewhere. (Some folk art is also on display at many of the native art shops already listed.)

In the Maritimes, too, folk art is encouraged, but success has been modest so far. Where Scots abound, hand-woven tartans are featured, and the weaving is superior. Fine needle points are made by French-Canadian women on Cape Breton.

Perhaps because their homeland is now absorbed into the U.S.S.R., the Ukrainians have been the most active group in the Canadian west in setting up folk museums. Ukrainian crafts are best found at church bazaars, especially those held at Easter, when elaborately painted eggs are featured. Other nationalities tend to show their talents at folk festivals where the music is played with zest, the dancers are expertly trained, and the costumes are often heirlooms. (See under Folk Festivals)

Folk Museums

MUSÉE DE LA PROVINCE DE QUÉBEC

Battlefields Park, Quebec City, Quebec

A splendid French-Canadian folk museum with a selective small display of Canadian and world art.

TARAS H. SHEVCHENKO MUSEUM

Route 5, two miles east of Palermo, Ontario

Ukrainian folk-art collection.

ARTS AND CRAFTS MUSEUM OF THE UKRAINIAN WOMEN'S ASSOCIATION

401 Main Street, Saskatoon, Saskatchewan

Open afternoons, Wednesday through Sunday.

MUSEUM OF UKRAINIAN ARTS & CRAFTS (MOHYLA INSTITUTE)

1240 Temperance Street, Saskatoon, Saskatchewan

Extensive displays in a variety of mediums.

DUKHOBOR PRAYER HOUSE

Veregin, Saskatchewan

A typical meetinghouse of the Russian sect has been restored and opened to visitors. It is still used for festivals.

GRAVELBOURG CATHEDRAL

Gravelbourg, Saskatchewan

Monsignor Charles Maillard spent fourteen years working on the frescoes of Saint Philomena in this church. She has been dropped from the Calendar of the Saints, but the frescoes remain.

UKRAINIAN PIONEER HOME

Elk Island National Park, Alberta

An authentic reconstruction of an early thatched cottage, complete with furnishings, tools, and ornaments.

UKRAINIAN MUSEUM AND ARCHIVES

Mundare (just off Route 16), Alberta

Folk Arts and Crafts Shops

MADAWASKA WEAVERS

St. Leonard, New Brunswick

Distinctive work is done by these well-established hand weavers.

ST. ANDREWS WOOLLENS

Douglas Street, St. Andrews, New Brunswick

The Merrill family has specialized in hand weaving for more than forty years. Grandfather is still the master craftsman, but the young men of the family give every promise of carrying on the family factory. Tweeds, wearing apparel, and blankets.

THE LOOMCROFTERS

Highway 102, Gagetown, New Brunswick

The Royal Canadian Air Force tartan was designed here. Replicas of historic weavings are displayed in the studio, one of the oldest buildings on the Saint John River.

BUTE ARRAN

Baddeck Bay Road 1½ miles from Baddeck, Cape Breton, Nova Scotia

LYNWOOD

Baddeck, Cape Breton, Nova Scotia

Antiques and Nova Scotia paintings, including some contemporary primitives.

348

CO-OPÉRATIVE ARTISANALE DE
  CHETICAMP LTEE

Cheticamp, Cape Breton, Nova Scotia

CRAFT CENTRE

1895 Granville Street, Halifax, Nova
Scotia

*Exhibition—but not sale—of work by
Nova Scotia craftsmen. The provincial
handicraft section annually publishes
an excellent booklet listing shops in the
province, "Handicrafts in Nova
Scotia."*

CULTURAL CENTRE

Jonquière, Quebec

Local craft displays.

LA CENTRALE D'ARTISANAT DU
  QUEBEC

1450 rue Saint-Denis, Montreal, Quebec

*Also at the Queen Elizabeth Hotel and
at 302 rue Craig Est and 403 rue Ste-
Catherine Est, all in Montreal.*

QUEBEC HANDICRAFTS CENTER

1450 Saint-Denis Street, Montreal,
Quebec

*A large display featuring items from all
over the province. Visits to handicraft
workshops can be arranged here.*

LA CO-OPÉRATIVE D'ARTS
  DOMESTIQUES

17 rue Desjardins, Quebec City, Quebec

All types of Quebec crafts.

STEFANOFF ART CENTER

Highway 11, Val David, Quebec

Bulgarian folk art for sale.

Boat Trips

Over Canada's complex of waterways, boat trips of all types and
durations are available to tourists.
Some are no more than short
sightseeing runs on inland canals;
others are voyages of several days
along coastal waters and across
open sea. But even the shortest
gives perspective on the country.

We have not listed ferries. They
are simply a fact of life in the
Maritimes. Two provinces can be
reached from the rest of Canada
only by ferry: Prince Edward
Island and Newfoundland. Below
Ottawa there are several little
ferries across the Ottawa River
that a car driver summons by
flashing his car lights day or night.
In contrast to these casual substi-
tutes for bridges, British Columbia has a provincially owned network of big modern ferries that
transform a transportation need
on that rugged coast into a real
pleasure. Many smaller ferries
are free there.

Since this is a guide to Canada
we have not listed west-coast
cruises that spend most of their
time in Alaskan waters.

NEWFOUNDLAND & LABRADOR COAST
  CRUISES

c/o Area Sales Manager, Canadian
National Railways, St. John's,
Newfoundland

*Cruises of various durations, sailing
from various Newfoundland ports, provide the best way to see the outports
and the beautiful Labrador coast.*

BLUE NOSE TOURS

6319 Allen Street, Halifax, Nova Scotia

*Two-hour sightseeing trip around Hali-
fax harbor and the northwest arm. Four
trips daily from July 1 to Labor Day.*

FUNDY ISLES TOURS

St. Andrews, New Brunswick

*Two-hour cruise in the Bay of Fundy.
Two o'clock daily in summer.*

SAGUENAY CRUISES

c/o S.S. Gala Navigation,
P.O. Box 546, Station N,
Montreal 129, Quebec

On the S.S. Varna, *out of Montreal, a week-long summertime cruise up the Saguenay River, down and over to St. Pierre, Miquelon, to Percé in the Gaspé, and then back to Montreal again. Bilingual.*

CRUISES TO THE ILES DE LA MADELEINE

Clarke Steamship Company, Montreal and Quebec City, Quebec

In the Gulf of St. Lawrence, 155 miles east of Gaspé, these sixteen wind-swept islands are dotted with small isolated fishing villages.

LOWER ST. LAWRENCE CRUISE

Lower St. Lawrence Transportation Company, Rimouski, Quebec

From April to November this six-day cruise takes the adventurous to fifteen tiny Quebec fishing ports on the north shore, all the way from Sept Îles to the Labrador border. Most of them can only be reached by water. One can also travel the Newfoundland coast to Labrador by Canadian National ship and return to the Canadian mainland by this line.

QUEBEC WATERWAYS TOURS

Quebec City, Quebec

The five-hour morning tour stops at Ste. Anne de Beaupré. The two-hour afternoon tour returning upstream gives a fine view of the Heights. In the evening a three-hour moonlight tour has charm if there is a moon.

KAWARTHA LAKES TOUR

Young's Point, Ontario

Tours of varying lengths through Stony Lake's 1,100 islands.

LAKEHEAD TOURS

Thunder Bay, Ontario

A water tour of developments at this Lake Superior port: the world's largest grain elevators, pulp and paper operations, shipbuilding, etc.

LIFT LOCK TOURS

George Street Wharf, Peterborough, Ontario

Daily tours available. The boat trip takes one up and over the world's

highest hydraulic-lift lock; boats are hoisted sixty-five feet.

MUSKOKA LAKES TOURS

Bracebridge, Ontario

Three-hour tours through the holiday lake country.

OTTAWA RIVER TOUR

Foot of the Rideau Canal Locks, Ottawa, Ontario

This one-and-a-half hour cruise on a splendid river offers some of the best views in the area.

RIDEAU CANAL BOAT TOUR

Below the Arts Centre, Ottawa, Ontario

A one-hour trip through Ottawa on the old and famed Rideau canal as far as Dow's Lake.

ST. LAWRENCE SEAWAY TOURS

Long Sault, Ontario

Daily tours of Lake St. Lawrence and the Seaway Power project.

SOO LOCK TOUR

Sault Ste. Marie, Ontario

One of the busiest waterways in the world. Daily two-hour cruises through the big locks from June 1 to September 30.

TORONTO HARBOR CRUISES

Foot of Yonge Street, Toronto, Ontario

Hour-long cruises of Toronto's harbor and island park lagoons in glass-topped excursion boats of the Amsterdam type. Every half hour from 10 A.M. to 10 P.M. in the summer.

30,000 ISLANDS CRUISE ON GEORGIAN BAY

Town Dock, Midland, Ontario

A five-hour cruise of the inside passage. Available from the last weekend in June through Labor Day.

30,000 ISLANDS TOUR

Parry Sound, Ontario

The tours from here last two and three hours.

THOUSAND ISLANDS TOURS

from Brockville, Rockport, Gananoque, and Kingston, Ontario

Most of these tours last about two hours. The most ambitious cruise is the five-hour trip from Kingston.

"NORTHLAND PRINCE" TOURS

Northland Navigation Company,
404 Hornby Street, Vancouver 1,
British Columbia

This company seems to make the longest trips in Canada's coastal waters, traveling from Vancouver on beyond Prince Rupert all the way to Alice Arm and Stewart on the Portland Canal, the border between Canada and Alaska.

MARGARET ROSE CRUISE

Out of Wrangell, Alaska

Though it leaves from Alaska on its 160-mile, four-day trip, this riverboat cruise is in British Columbia glacier country most of the time, pushing up and down the Stitkine River, fastest flowing in North America, with mountains overhead and seals in the water below. May through September.

NOOTKA SOUND CRUISE

P.O. Box 28, Port Alberni,
British Columbia

The cruise leaves from Gold River, to which passengers are bused from Campbell River. The M.V. Uchuck III winds through Nootka Sound on the rugged west coast of Vancouver Island to Zeballas, stopping on request at logging camps on the route. Not a luxurious trip, but distinctly different. Write for details.

OKANAGAN CRUISE

Penticton, British Columbia

Scenic day cruises on Lake Okanagan.

INSIDE PASSAGE CRUISE

British Columbia Ferry *Queen of Prince Rupert,* Kelsey Bay to Prince Rupert, British Columbia

This nonstop, 330-mile cruise affords a close-up view of the unforgettable landscape. It leaves for the north on alternate days. Reservations recommended well in advance. Box 1388, Victoria, British Columbia.

ALBERNI INLET TOURS

Port Alberni, British Columbia

Tours travel the inlet that runs deep into Vancouver Island from Port Alberni to the open Pacific. They go regularly to Bamfield, and on Mondays and Fridays they make the round trip to Ucluelet. Year-round.

NAHANNI RIVER SAFARIS

P.O. Box 33, Fort Nelson,
British Columbia

A rugged trip down one of the most beautiful and isolated rivers in North America. The actual starting point is accessible only by chartered plane.

YUKON QUEEN RIVER TOURS

Dawson City, Yukon Territory

Along the Yukon River with a stop at an Indian village and at the fish wheel where, during the month of July, king salmon are caught.

MILES CANYON CRUISE

Aboard M.V. *Schwatka,* Whitehorse, Yukon

A three-hour trip by motor vessel along the Yukon River route of the Klondike stampeders. Jack London was a river pilot here.

Books

The following stores are recommended for their stocks of old and new books, especially in the field of Canadiana:

BERNARD AMTMANN, INC.
750 Sheridan Street, Montreal, Quebec

WM. P. WOLFE
222 rue de L'Hôpital, Montreal, Quebec

OLD AUTHORS FARM
Morrisburg, Ontario

THE QUEEN'S PRINTER BOOKSHOP
Rideau Street at Mackenzie Avenue,
Ottawa, Ontario

New books, often colorful Canadiana, published by the government printer. Northern Cookbook, for instance, has

practical recipes for ptarmigan stew, standing rib of caribou, and seal flippers.

DORA HOOD'S BOOK ROOM
34 Ross Street, Toronto, Ontario

MARY SCORER BOOKS LTD.
214 Kennedy Street, Winnipeg, Manitoba

This firm also publishes under the name of Peguis Publishing Company at the same address.

M. G. HURTIG LTD.
10411 Jasper Avenue, Edmonton, Alberta

ADELPHI BOOKSHOP
822½ Fort Street, Victoria, British Columbia

Conservation and Natural History

Many of Canada's hundreds of national parks have been designed to suit the needs of a nation of sportsmen. Canadians are avid campers, fishermen, and hunters, and for them, more and more outdoor facilities are created every year. Provincial legislators who are niggardly with funds for art museums will allow money fairly generously to their park systems. Nevertheless the camping areas are often crowded. It hardly seems possible, since Ontario has 92 provincial parks, Saskatchewan 30, British Columbia 120, and the other provinces comparable numbers. In addition, there are the great national parks.

On the really big national and provincial spreads, however, comforts for visitors hardly make a dent. At Jasper National Park, tourists can dine in a sky-high restaurant after riding up Whistler Mountain in the Sky Tram. They can drive in comfort through the park on a splendid highway. But actually to see the whole of Jasper, they would have to spend days in a helicopter. Chibougamau Provincial Park to the far northwest in Quebec is one of the best-organized fishing and hunting centers in Canada. But planes are still the most practical means of transport into the park, and no matter how energetically it is exploited, it will probably remain in effect a conserved area for years to come.

All across Canada, enormous woodlands, thriving bird and animal life, high alpine meadows, and hidden lakes are protected chiefly by law but also by their very remoteness. The rough gravel roads into some of the choicest spots are not for the timid. Neither are the canoe routes that must be followed to penetrate beyond the fringes of other areas. The visitor to Mt. Robson Provincial Park in British Columbia can see fifteen glaciers in one fourteen-mile stretch, but he must hike the distance to do it. With effort, the truly interested can find in Canada some of the last primitive country left on this continent and enjoy it in well-earned solitude.

The provincial tourist departments, listed on page 381, will send sociable campers all the

352

data they need on parks with good golf courses, sunny beaches, organized play for the children, and summer art courses. They will also tell the sportsman in which park to hunt deer with bow and arrow or fish for speckled or lake trout. We list here only the parks that have extensive protected areas, and on these, too, the provincial tourist departments will provide full information. Parks with bird sanctuaries are listed separately below.

NATIONAL PARKS

WATERTON LAKES NATIONAL PARK
Waterton Lakes, Alberta

Adjoining the American Glacier National Park in Montana, this alpine park and wildlife sanctuary is made for walkers. Its animals allow people to come so close that park officials warn humans to use caution in photographing them.

ELK ISLAND NATIONAL PARK
Thirty miles east of Edmonton, Alberta

The big attraction here is not elk but freely roaming buffaloes, which sometimes cross park roads.

JASPER NATIONAL PARK
Reached by Routes 16 or 93, Alberta

One of Canada's most magnificent parks. Visitors can bathe in hot springs or scuba dive in the underwater labyrinths of Horseshoe Lake. The Columbia ice fields are a major point of interest. The highway has on occasion been closed by snow in August.

YOHO NATIONAL PARK
Eastern British Columbia

On the western slope of the Rockies. Among the many scenic splendors is Takakkaw Falls, one of the most spectacular in Canada. The waterfall is formed by "melt water" from the Daly Glacier in the hanging valley 1,200 feet above Yoho Valley.

Elk at Banff National Park

PROVINCIAL AND REGIONAL PARKS

CHIBOUGAMAU PARK
Northwest Quebec

Far to the north, this is one of Quebec's best-organized fishing and hunting centers. It can be approached from the new and growing town of the same name or from St. Felicien on its eastern side. But planes are still the most practical means of transport.

DE LA VERENDRYE PARK
Northwest Quebec

Five thousand square miles in area, this is one of Quebec's principal game and fish preserves. The limited game hunting is for Quebeckers, but for visitors the park is a fisherman's paradise. Three large establishments offer comfortable accommodations. The park is a long drive north, but it can be reached by plane. To fish some of its remote lakes, hydroplanes must be chartered.

Algonquin Provincial Park

Eastern Ontario

Nearly three thousand square miles of protected wilderness. The only road in is Route 60, which cuts across a southwest corner. There are, however, ten campgrounds and seven picnic grounds that lie within thirty driving miles of the west gate. Of the campgrounds, nine are on the shores of lakes, one is on the Madawaska River.

Killarney Provincial Park

North shore of Georgian Bay, Route 637, Central Ontario

One hundred and forty square miles of spectacular scenery, opened as a park in 1961. Some of Canada's best-known artists have painted this area, reaching it by canoe. For information on canoe tripping here, write the District Forester, Sudbury, Ontario.

Polar Bear Park

Hudson and James Bays, Near Moosonee, Ontario

A 7,000-square-mile preserve for, among other animals, Ontario's largest concentration of polar bears. Bearded seals, walrus, arctic foxes, and caribou are to be seen, but not hunted. There are also colonies of snow geese and blue geese. The park can as yet only be reached by chartered plane.

Quetico Provincial Park

Route 11, Western Ontario

One of the last great primitive areas—1,750 square miles—in North America. Access to historic canoe trails from several points along the park perimeter. Dawson Trail campground is the only developed area in the park. Booklets are available from the Ontario Department of Tourism.

Moose Jaw Wild Animal Park

One mile south of Moose Jaw, Saskatchewan

American bison at large in their natural habitat.

Dinosaur Provincial Park

Patricia, Alberta

Dinosaur skeletons that have been uncovered are displayed in their original positions. There is also an exhibit of other fossils found in the park. The prairie provinces have strict laws against removing fossils from protected sites.

Lakelse Lake Park

Kitimat Highway, 12 miles south of Terrace, British Columbia

One of the last homes of the trumpeter swan. Camping only.

Mt. Robson Provincial Park

Routes 5 and 16, British Columbia

Adjoining Jasper National Park, it is notable for its glaciers. On a fourteen-mile hike to Berg Lake, fifteen can be seen from the trail. Ice from Tumbling Glacier falls into Berg Lake. Mt. Robson is the highest in the Canadian Rockies, 12,972 feet. There are a variety of good accommodations nearby.

Strathcona Provincial Park

Vancouver Island, British Columbia

Almost a half-million acres of wilderness in the center of the island.

Tweedsmuir Provincial Park

British Columbia

British Columbia's largest and wildest park. Along the Atnarko River, in the park's south leg, is one of the largest concentrations of grizzly bears in the world. The park is named for the adventure-story writer, John Buchan, later Lord Tweedsmuir.

Wells Gray Provincial Park

Twenty-five miles from Clearwater, British Columbia

A vast park of waterfalls, varied and spectacular, the largest 450 feet high. Its million acres of protected woodland can be reached only after twenty miles of bad gravel road leading off the new Yellowhead Highway seventy-five miles north of Kamloops. Tourist facilities are limited, even on the highway.

BIRD SANCTUARIES

Witless Bay Islands

Nineteen miles south of St. John's, Newfoundland

Sea birds by the thousands cluster on these islands, easily viewed from regular sightseeing boats.

CIBOUX AND HERFORD (THE BIRD ISLANDS)

By motor launch off Big Bras d'Or, Nova Scotia

ILE BONAVENTURE

By fast ferry from Percé, Quebec

Now a federal sanctuary for millions of sea birds. Auberge Ile Bonaventure has rooms and cabins.

TIDAL FLAT FEEDING GROUND, CAP TOURMENTE AND ILE AUX GRUES

Thirty miles below Quebec, Quebec

As many as 80,000 to 100,000 greater snow geese rest here on their way south from the Arctic, from October to early November. At the end of the period, when the flock is at its peak, hunting is permitted.

JACK MINER'S BIRD SANCTUARY

Kingsville, Ontario

An estimated thirty thousand wild geese pause here on their way north (last ten days of March and first ten days of April) and south (last week of October, first three weeks of November). In either season, the best hour to visit is from 3:30 to 4:30 P.M.

JOHN E. PEARCE PROVINCIAL PARK

Two miles south of Route 3, Wallacetown, Ontario

Hawk migration point.

PRESQU'ILE PROVINCIAL PARK

Routes 401 and 2, Southeastern Ontario

A noted migration point on a peninsula connected to the mainland by a sand bar. The wilderness area provides nesting grounds for thousands of terns and gulls. In fall, pheasant shooting of stocked birds and waterfowl hunting are allowed by special permit. Open the second Friday in May to the third Sunday in September.

RONDEAU PROVINCIAL PARK

Route 3, near Morpeth, Ontario

One of the oldest Ontario parks, it is fully developed with five hundred camp and trailer sites. Its marshes and waters (Lake Erie) make it a remarkable point for watching migratory birds, especially ducks and shore birds. During the open season, waterfowl shooting is permitted under special permit. Opens the second Friday in May, closes the third Sunday in September.

UPPER CANADA MIGRATORY BIRD SANCTUARY

Off Route 2 near Upper Canada Village, Ontario

From the end of September until November 1, as many as five thousand Canada geese fly in to feed at 2:30 P.M. regularly. There are always more birds to be seen than people, even on weekends.

BIRD SANCTUARY

Last Mountain Lake, north of Regina, Saskatchewan

Established in 1887, it is the oldest in North America. Famous as a stopover for sand-hill cranes.

PELICAN ROOKERIES

Prince Albert National Park, Saskatchewan

Another common bird here is the double-crested cormorant.

DUCK LAKE WILDFOWL RESERVE

Creston, British Columbia

In the "Valley of the Swans" spring and fall migrations of white swans are to be seen.

FEATHERLAND BIRD RESEARCH FARM

1848 Burnside Road West, R.R. 3, Victoria, British Columbia

A private project of Mr. and Mrs. C. C. Hyndman, who have reared more than a hundred species of birds by hand and treated thousands of injured wild birds. The right letter from an earnest bird watcher might win an invitation to visit the farm.

ZOOS AND AQUARIUMS

BIOLOGICAL STATION MUSEUM

Bedford, Prince Edward Island

Local fish and shellfish in naturalistic settings.

AQUARIUM

Chemin Saint-Louis, Quebec City,
Quebec

*On the edge of a cliff overlooking the
St. Lawrence River, the Province of
Quebec opened an impressive modern
aquarium in 1959. Displays emphasize
the fish found in Quebec's infinity of
lakes and rivers and along its extensive coast.*

ORSAINVILLE ZOO

Quebec

*In a traditional French-Canadian vil-
lage setting, Canadian birds and
animals, including moose, beavers, and
caribou, are exhibited.*

ONTARIO ZOOLOGICAL PARK

Wasaga Beach, Ontario

*A one-hundred-acre zoo featuring a
beaver pond.*

VANCOUVER PUBLIC AQUARIUM

Stanley Park, Vancouver,
British Columbia

*A live whale and hydrophones for listen-
'ing to the dolphins.*

UNDERSEA GARDENS

Oak Bay Marina, Victoria,
British Columbia

*The world's largest natural marine
exhibit can be viewed from behind
glass. Among the many undersea
exhibits, a skin diver may occasionally
be seen getting a still closer view.
Illuminated at night.*

NATURAL PHENOMENA

ICEBERGS

Labrador Coast, Newfoundland

*Since bergs are common along this
coast in summer, passengers on any of
the pleasure cruises from St. John's that
swing around the island and then north
have a good chance to see them.
Mirages are also common in July and
August.*

A HIKE ON THE OCEAN FLOOR

White Head Island (near Grand
Manan Island), New Brunswick

*During a series of extreme low tides in
summer one can cross by the "Thor-*
*oughfare" to Ross Island; by "Cheney's
Passage" to Cheney Island; or by "Cow
Passage" to White Head, exploring the
actual ocean floor. A return in comfort
by modern ferry to Ingalls Head is
recommended.*

THE HOPEWELL ROCKS

Route 14
Hopewell Cape, New Brunswick

*Fundy's fantastically high tides have
carved giant columns and caves out of
the red sandstone of the area. All the
small rivers and creeks flowing into
Fundy Bay have a strange look at low
tide. High tide arrives in a bore at
Moncton.*

FISH ELEVATOR

Beechwood Dam, fifteen miles south of
Perth, New Brunswick

*A modern fish elevator lifts the Atlantic
salmon over a sixty-foot dam in the
Saint John River.*

FLOWERPOT ISLAND

Georgian Bay Islands National Park,
in Georgian Bay near Honey Harbour,
Ontario

*Of the thirty-nine islands or portions of
islands in the park, the most photographed is one hundred miles to the
northwest of most of the group. This
is Flowerpot Island, its two "flower-
pots," pedestal rocks topped with small
trees and shrubs.*

OWEN SOUND MILL DAM

Owen Sound, Ontario

*During the spring run, rainbow and
German brown trout climb Canada's
first fish ladder to their breeding pools
up the Sydenham River.*

PRAIRIE DOG TOWN

Near Val Marie, Manitoba

*One of the few remaining such "towns."
There are six colonies, including more
than a thousand prairie dogs. Also
believed living in this area is the rare
black-footed ferret.*

SOCKEYE SALMON RUN

Adams River near Salmon Arm,
British Columbia

*Mid-October. The Trans-Canada High-
way can be traveled to this brilliant*

natural spectacle in an equally brilliant autumn setting. For viewing only. The spawning fish must not be disturbed.

MISCELLANEOUS

SUNBURY SHORES ARTS AND NATURE CENTRE

St. Andrews, New Brunswick

At this old Passamaquoddy Bay resort, long popular with Americans, both children and adults enjoy not only art and handicraft classes but also intensive nature studies in an area rich in tidal flats and pools, lakes and marshes. All field classes, lectures, and films stress the preservation of natural surroundings. Associated with the University of New Brunswick.

PALISADES NATURE RETREAT

P.O. Box 1126, Whitehorse, Yukon

At the camp at the confluence of the Yukon and Pelly rivers, not only hunters and fishermen but also bird watchers and rock hounds are catered to. Some guides take out photographic parties, too.

Education

NEW UNIVERSITIES

SCARBOROUGH COLLEGE

Scarborough, Ontario

Canada's new universities have not had time to develop departments of interest to the specialist. But architecturally many of them are impressive. This one, just north of Toronto, is a striking example of the new "brutalism." Architect John Andrews had made even the smokestacks an element in his design.

TRENT UNIVERSITY

Peterborough, Ontario

An architectural surprise in a small-town setting, and on that account alone it is worth visiting. Ron Thom, architect, won four citations from the International College and University Conference for his design.

SIMON FRASER UNIVERSITY

Burnaby, British Columbia

This new university is a modern classic in a setting the ancient Greeks might have selected. Erickson, Massey was the architectural firm responsible for this and other outstanding modern designs in Canada.

MEDICAL SCHOOLS

DALHOUSIE FACULTY OF MEDICINE

Dalhousie University, Halifax, Nova Scotia

The only medical school in the Atlantic Provinces recently celebrated its centenary. Tours may be arranged through the University's information office.

MCINTYRE MEDICAL SCIENCES BUILDING

McGill University, Drummond Street at Mt. Royal Park, Montreal, Quebec

In this handsome new building several of McGill Medical School's distinctive units are to be found, including the Osler Library of the History of Medicine and the Institute of Aviation Medicine. Interested visitors are welcomed.

RESEARCH CENTERS

MARINE SCIENCES RESEARCH LABORATORY

Logy Bay, Newfoundland

Part of the province's Memorial University, this marine laboratory, shaped like a giant sea anemone, is one of the few using a continuous flow of water year round, and the only one so far north and working in unpolluted water.

INSTITUTE OF OCEANOGRAPHY

Bedford Basin, Route 7 near Bedford, Nova Scotia

A major east-coast research establishment and a very important one to the seagoing Maritime Provinces.

RESEARCH AND PRODUCTIVITY COUNCIL

College Hill Road, Fredericton, New Brunswick

The Council, set up by the provincial government, finds solutions to processing and business-management problems

for anyone who seeks and pays moderately for its advice.

THE GAULT ESTATE OF MCGILL UNIVERSITY

Off Highway 9 south of Montreal,
Mont St. Hilaire, Quebec

"The Mountain," rising 1,300 feet above the Richelieu River, was left to McGill in 1958. It has since provided a magnificent field laboratory in the natural sciences. The university also conducts some research into the mining industry there. Parts of the mountain are closed off to preserve the untouched natural environment. But on its 2,285 acres there are also miles of trails open to hikers, equestrians, skiers, and snowshoers.

THE MAGNET LABORATORY OF MCGILL UNIVERSITY

151 rue du Parc Industrial, Longueuil,
Quebec

This laboratory is devoted to the study of materials in high magnetic fields and to the development of magnet and cryogenic technology. Half its time is given to research requested by organizations or individuals who pay only for the cost of consumable materials. Visitors with this specialized interest should write the director, Dr. Richard Stevenson.

GREAT LAKES INSTITUTE RESEARCH STATION

University of Toronto, Kincardine,
Ontario

Laboratories conducting studies on Lake Huron's waters, shoreline, fish, and pollution are open to visitors, including groups, on application to the Director, Great Lakes Institute, University of Toronto, Toronto, Ontario. Arrangements can also be made, on application to the director, for visits aboard the Institute's research vessel, Porte Dauphine, *when it is in port.*

SPECIAL SEMINARS

DALHOUSIE INSTITUTE OF PUBLIC AFFAIRS

Dalhousie University, Halifax,
Nova Scotia

Under its director, Professor Guy Henson, the Institute holds four to six conferences a year on a variety of social problems. The Labor-Management Conferences have attracted particular notice. Some are held in summer. For information, write the director.

SEMINAR ON SHAW

Shaw Festival, Niagara-on-the-Lake,
Ontario

Under the co-sponsorship of Brock University, outstanding personalities lecture or lead discussions on George Bernard Shaw and his contemporaries. End of July.

SHAKESPEARE SEMINARS

Stratford Festival, Stratford, Ontario

Two seminars of a week's duration are held under the auspices of McMaster University. Limited to 150 persons. They take place during the last week in July and the first week in August. The closing date for registration is in mid-June. For information, write the Assistant Director of Extension, McMaster University, Hamilton, Ontario.

SUMMER COURSES

ORAL FRENCH SUMMER SCHOOL

University of Toronto, St.-Pierre Island,
St.-Pierre et Miquelon

Two four-week terms, one in July and one in August, are open to beginning, intermediate, and advanced students of French. Students are billeted in French homes on the island, off the coast of Newfoundland, which is a French possession. Not really geared to adults.

MCGILL GEOGRAPHY SUMMER SCHOOL

Stanstead College, Stanstead, Quebec

McGill's summer courses in such subjects as circumpolar lands, cartography, and air-photo interpretation are held in a small Quebec town in beautiful country less than a mile from the Vermont border. July through mid-August. For information, write the Director, Geography Summer School, Department of Geography, McGill University, Montreal, Quebec.

TROIS PISTOLES SUMMER SCHOOL

Trois Pistoles, Quebec

The University of Western Ontario conducts a variety of French courses for English-speaking students and adults who live with French families in the scenic little Quebec town. Inquiries should be directed to the Trois Pistoles Summer School Department, University of Western Ontario, London, Ontario.

JEUNESSES MUSICALES

Mt. Orford (near Magog), Quebec

This summer music camp for young people was established in 1949 by Gilles Lefevre, a French-Canadian musician. About 250 students between the ages of fourteen and thirty who aspire to professional careers are accepted for three-week training periods from the end of June to early September. Courses cover most branches of music and have recently been extended to include the theatre, sculpture, and painting. For information write: Jeunesses Musicales, 430 St. Joseph Boulevard West, Montreal, or Centre d'Art du Mont Orford, Magog, Quebec.

SUMMER COURSES IN FRENCH

Université Laval, Quebec City, Quebec

At this distinguished French-Canadian university, French is taught by audio-visual methods and in language laboratories. Students may live on campus or with French-speaking families in town. Business and professional men are particularly welcome, as well as anyone interested in French culture. For details, write Cours d'Été de Français, Université Laval, Pavillon De Koninck, Quebec 10, Quebec.

ARCTIC TOURS FOR STUDENTS

Butterfield and Robinson Travel, Essex House, 185 Bay Street, Toronto, Ontario

Inaugurated in 1969, these three-week summer tours promise a small group of students hard travel, discomfort, and excitement at a stiff price. Some of the travel is by Eskimo boat, some by charter plane. For excitement, an Eskimo hunt on the ice for walrus or polar bears is scheduled.

INTERNATIONAL MUSIC CAMP

International Peace Garden, on the border between Manitoba and North Dakota

Seven-week courses for young people in art, music—particularly band, chorus, and chamber music—ballet, modern dance, and drama. Inquiries should be sent to International Music Camp, Bottineau, North Dakota, 58318, by June 1.

INSTITUTE OF NORTHERN STUDIES

University of Saskatchewan, Rankin Inlet, Northwest Territories

A summer course in applied anthropology is given from early July to early August at the university's Arctic Research and Training Center. For further information, write the university's Registrar at Saskatoon, Saskatchewan.

BANFF SCHOOL OF THE FINE ARTS

University of Calgary, Banff, Alberta

During the summer session (from July 1 to August 10) courses are offered in painting, ballet, music, theatre arts, creative writing, modern languages, photography, ceramics, and even figure skating. Some courses may be taken for college credit. There are also short painting courses in early June and late August. Situated in the heart of the Rockies.

Festivals and Seasonal Events

ART FESTIVALS

SUMMER FESTIVAL

Confederation Centre, Charlottetown, Prince Edward Island

July and August. This festival stresses Canadian musicals and revues, and its big annual hit is Anne of Green Gables.

SHAW FESTIVAL

Queen Street Office, Niagara-on-the-Lake, Ontario

Distinguished visiting actors in plays by George Bernard Shaw and his contem-

poraries—*from late June to September 1. Also seminar, mime theatre, and film series.*

NATIONAL ARTS CENTRE

Confederation Square, Ottawa, Ontario

At the National Centre, productions from all the other festivals are usually scheduled at some time during the year, as well as concerts, ballet, experimental theatre, rock groups, folk dancers, and film revivals. There are three theatres of varying size to handle the variety of events, and a salon for chamber music.

STRATFORD FESTIVAL

Stratford, Ontario

The summer-long performances of Shakespeare given here in the Festival Theatre are so popular that ticket reservations are a must. In the town's Avon Theatre, the Festival organization stages modern plays as well. Write for the season's program in spring.

SUMMER REPERTORY SEASON

Talbot Theater, University of Western Ontario, London, Ontario

July to mid-August. A top professional company performs six times a week in the university's intimate theatre. Stratford is only forty miles away and the Shaw Festival at Niagara-on-the-Lake is not too distant. All this has created a first-rate dramatic circuit for visitors to southwestern Ontario.

FOLK FESTIVALS

NOVA SCOTIA GAELIC MOD

St. Anns, Nova Scotia

Held at the Gaelic College on Cape Breton in mid-July.

GATHERING OF THE CLANS AND FISHERMAN'S REGATTA

Pugwash, Nova Scotia

Early July.

LOBSTER CARNIVAL

Pictou, Nova Scotia

Early July. Lobster boat races and lobster feasts.

HIGHLAND GAMES

Antigonish, Nova Scotia

Mid-July. Caber tossing and pipe bands.

BLESSING OF THE FLEET

At Caraquet or Shippegan, New Brunswick

For the Acadian fishing community this is a significant event, though it may look merely gay and colorful to visitors. The two villages alternate as the site for the big event. Early summer.

SHEDIAC LOBSTER FESTIVAL

Shediac Beach, New Brunswick

Middle of August.

MAPLE SYRUP FESTIVAL

Plessisville, Quebec

In the maple-sugar capital of Quebec. Sugaring parties, French-Canadian food, and dances. Early spring.

SIX NATIONS INDIAN PAGEANT

Brantford, Ontario

Mid-August.

MAPLE SUGAR FESTIVAL

Elmira, Ontario

End of March. Hay wagons carry visitors to the sugar bush.

HIGHLAND GAMES

Maxville, Ontario

First Saturday in August.

NATIONAL HIGHLAND DANCING

Canadian National Exhibition, Exhibition Park, Toronto, Ontario

End of August.

THRESHERMEN'S REUNION

Agricultural Memorial Museum, Austin, Manitoba

In wheat country, late July. Includes a parade of old steam farm machines and sheaf-tying, bag-tying, and plowing contests.

ICELANDIC FESTIVAL

Gimli, Manitoba

Early in August.

THE SCOTTISH HIGHLAND GAMES

Assiniboia Downs, Winnipeg, Manitoba

On July 1, Canada's birthday, the racing season is interrupted to allow other sports on the racetracks, tossing the caber for one. Dancing, bagpipes, and drumming competitions.

OTHER SEASONAL EVENTS

NOVA SCOTIA FISHERIES EXHIBITION
AND FISHERMEN'S REUNION

Lunenburg, Nova Scotia

A genuine Nova Scotian event, held in early September when most of the summer people have left. Dory races, scallop shucking, and fish-filleting contests.

ATLANTIC NATIONAL EXHIBITION

Saint John, New Brunswick

Late August. Reflects maritime life.

MAN AND HIS WORLD

Expo Grounds, Montreal, Quebec

A good part of Expo 67—on two of the islands and in most of the original buildings—can still be toured as long as the city of Montreal finds the money to keep it open. Several of the permanent exhibits (Man the Explorer, etc.) remain excellent. The changing exhibits, sponsored by participating countries, provinces, the City of Montreal, and comcial companies, vary in interest from year to year. But the minirail still rolls, the biosphere glitters in the sun, and it is worth a visit by anyone who missed the big excitement. Early June to early September.

ICE-FISHING FESTIVAL

Ste. Anne de la Pérade, Quebec

At the end of December usually, though they can arrive as late as the middle of February, tomcod coming to spawn in the Rivière Ste. Anne where it enters the St. Lawrence turn this charming old village into a winter-carnival town visited by thousands of fishermen.

WINTER CARNIVAL

Quebec City, Quebec

A genuine ice carnival in which Québecois are even more involved than the visitors. Night after night the crowds are out, bundled to the ears except for the hardy beauties who decorate the parade floats. Even the weatherman seems to co-operate. A pre-Lenten gala, its dates are determined by the date of Easter.

The ice palace at Quebec's
annual Winter Carnival

THE CHANGING OF THE GUARD

Parliament Hill, Ottawa, Ontario

Ten o'clock daily from the last week in June to Labor Day. A colorful show. A piquet is also changed daily at Government House and can be seen when the governor general is not in residence.

CANADIAN NATIONAL EXHIBITION

Exhibition Grounds, Toronto, Ontario

Last half of August. An overgrown state fair with some big time aspects.

CALGARY STAMPEDE

Calgary, Alberta

Early July. Canada's big Wild West show seems to get bigger every year.

THE BIG "M" (MANITOBA STAMPEDE)

Morris, Manitoba

Mid-July. The second-largest such event in Canada.

The Scottish Festival at Cape Breton, Nova Scotia

INDIAN POWWOWS

Brocket, Gleichen, and Calgary, Alberta

Regular powwows are held throughout the summer. At many, champion dancers are chosen. These are genuine events, arranged not for tourists but for the Indians themselves.

INDIAN POWWOWS

Battleford, Fort Qu'Appelle, and Sturgeon Lake, Saskatchewan

Held regularly in summer for the Indians themselves to enjoy. A troop of dancers, including Sioux, Cree, Salteaux, and Blackfoot Indians, who regularly perform at such powwows recently toured Europe.

BRANDING PARTY AND STAMPEDE

Medicine Hat, Alberta

Late July.

KLONDIKE DAYS

Edmonton, Alberta

Last half of July. The Yukon resents this "southern" snatching of the Klondike's history, but it's an amiable event with everyone in town turning out in Gay 90's dress.

ABBOTSFORD INTERNATIONAL AIR SHOW

Abbotsford Airport, British Columbia

For three days in early August this combined air show and aviation trade fair draws aviation buffs from all over (more than 300,000 of them) to this town near the United States-Canadian border.

MOUNT CURRIE RODEO

Mount Currie
Near Pemberton, British Columbia

In this rodeo the cowboys are Indians. The rodeo grounds are on the Indian Reserve five miles from the village.

PACIFIC NATIONAL EXHIBITION

Vancouver, British Columbia

Last half of August. Pacific oriented.

YULE LOG CEREMONY

Empress Hotel, Victoria,
British Columbia

On Christmas Day, while carolers in Elizabethan dress sing, the yule log is brought in to one of the hotel's massive fireplaces. Nearby, the Provincial Parliament Building is illuminated with thousands of light bulbs.

Whitehorse, Yukon

At the end of February, the whole Yukon pours into town for a winter carnival few tourists have seen. It's a real celebration of the end of winter's worst, with dog-sled races, snowshoe races, and pack-carrying contests waged by men who do that sort of thing for a living. Whitehorse has fifteen hotels, but a reservation is a must.

TRAIL OF '98 CARNIVAL

Whitehorse, Yukon

Mid-July. Here they know what really happened in those great but hectic days.

Gardening

Its climate accounts to a degree for Canada's paucity, with a few notable exceptions, of fine gardens, though lack of interest has been equally responsible. The British influence in Canada has not generally expressed itself in the very English passion for gardening. So Ottawa, after its spring burst of tulips, is in summer unhappily overrun with petunias and marigolds.

But wild flowers abound in many areas, showing that the climate is not entirely to blame. There are whole fields of lupines on Prince Edward Island. Delicate numbers of minute flowers crowd around the historic lighthouse near the fortress of Louisbourg on Cape Breton Island. Trilliums in late spring are thick in Gatineau Park, Quebec, across the river from Ottawa. And thousands of tiny floral stars turn the tundra into a patterned carpet in the Northwest Territories. Every province has its official wild flower.

The gardens that have been developed reflect certain aspects of Canada's history, as the following list indicates.

GARDENS

MONTREAL BOTANICAL GARDEN

4101 Sherbrooke Street, Montreal, Quebec

Fine French formal gardens under glass, in addition to other styles. Said to be the third largest in the world, surpassed only by Paris and Vienna.

ROYAL BOTANICAL GARDENS

Hamilton, Ontario

Eighteen hundred acres of blooms. The spring garden is outstanding, and the rock garden features three seasonal displays. The Centennial Rose Garden is a recent addition. The English influence is evident here.

CENTRAL EXPERIMENTAL FARM
AND ARBORETUM

Route 16, Ottawa, Ontario

The gardens here vary with the seasons. Flowers are tested for bloom in Canada.

THE MAZE

Centre Island, Toronto, Ontario

This intricate puzzle garden, its cedar dividing walls now a good five feet high, was given to Toronto in the 1967 centennial year by the Dutch community.

HILLSIDE GARDENS

High Park, Toronto, Ontario

Toronto, once a bastion of the Empire, still has gardens that date from that era.

CASCADE GARDENS

Banff National Park, Alberta

The foundation rocks here represent successive geological periods.

NIKKA YUKO CENTENNIAL GARDEN

Lethbridge, Alberta

This Alberta town decided to develop a

Japanese garden as its centennial project. It covers four acres and is completely authentic.

PEACE ARCH PARK

International Boundary at Blaine, Washington, and Douglas, British Columbia

Famous formal gardens. Not English and not really American.

BLOEDEL FLORAL CONSERVATORY

Queen Elizabeth Park, Vancouver, British Columbia

The world's first triodetic dome conservatory, with its related covered walkways, provides a year-round garden of tropical and seasonal blooms. The park also has a fine arboretum and rock quarry gardens.

PARK AND TILFORD GARDENS

North Vancouver, British Columbia

A well-known distillery is developing a seven-garden complex, to be completed in 1971. Unusual are the colonnade garden and the games garden.

JAPANESE GARDEN

University of British Columbia, Vancouver, British Columbia

Designed by a leading Japanese architect, Professor Kannosuke Mori, in honor of Dr. Nitobe, a distinguished educator.

650 HANGING FLOWER BASKETS ON STREET LIGHT STANDARDS

Victoria, British Columbia

For thirty years, British Columbia's capital has been noted for this display of constant delicate blooms from June to October.

FLORAL EVENT

TULIP FESTIVAL (LATE MAY)

National Capital Commission parks and driveways, Ottawa, Ontario

The Queen of the Netherlands, in gratitude for the haven Canada provided her during World War II, gave its capital one million of the finest tulip bulbs, thereby starting in Ottawa a festival comparable to the Cherry Blossom Festival in Washington, D.C.

History

For a peaceable people, Canadians seem oddly obsessed with their historic forts. At last count, more than seventy of them had been preserved intact, restored, or entirely rebuilt. Some of the most interesting are listed here. It was around these forts, some of them not so much military posts as fur-trading centers, that many of Canada's cities and towns grew up. Most of the strictly military establishments were built to defend the country from American aggression. They can provide visiting Americans with new insights into the past of their own country.

HALIFAX CITADEL

Halifax, Nova Scotia

There has been a hilltop fortress on this height since 1749. The present one was developed over the years from 1828 to 1856. There are a military museum and a provincial museum within the walls. In summer, the junior Bengal Lancers patrol the grounds.

FORTRESS OF LOUISBOURG

Louisbourg National Historic Park, Cape Breton Island, Nova Scotia

Archaeological buffs will be interested, too, in the continuing dig behind Canada's major "rebuilt"—the greatest fort in North America north of Mexico. Outstanding array of French furnishings.

PORT ROYAL HABITATION

Port Royal National Historic Park, Nova Scotia

A handsomely atmospheric "rebuilt" of Champlain's 1605 stockaded settlement. The buildings are arranged around a courtyard like those in sixteenth-century French farms.

FORT CHAMBLY

Chambly, Quebec

Since the Richelieu River served as a short cut between Lake Champlain and the St. Lawrence River, it has always had protection. A fort built here in 1665 was captured and burned by the Americans in 1775; it was rebuilt in 1777. After serving as a Canadian base in 1812, it fell into ruins, but has been partially restored. An oddly pastoral spot.

FORT LENNOX

Ile-aux-Noix, twelve miles south of St. Jean, Quebec

Not a "rebuilt," but the original fortifications built in 1782, with additions made in 1812.

THE CITADEL

Quebec City, Quebec

This massive old stone fort high above the St. Lawrence is still a military installation, though it is also the summer residence of Canada's governor general. The changing of the guard may be viewed in summer at 10 A.M. daily. At 7:30 P.M. from May 15 to August 15, and at 6 P.M. from August 16 to September 15, the retreat ceremony is performed.

FORT HENRY

Kingston, Ontario

Guides in period uniforms, daily drills, and a perfectly performed retreat ceremony each Wednesday at sunset during July and August.

THE ESTABLISHMENTS

Penetanguishene, Ontario

The British naval and military "Establishments" (1814–1856); a recent restoration.

FORT WELLINGTON

Prescott, Ontario

A splendid display of portable military furniture.

FORT YORK

Toronto, Ontario

The first fort, built in 1793, was destroyed by invading American forces in 1813 and rebuilt in time to defeat another American force in 1814. Today, Toronto has grown up around it. Eight of the 1813–1815 buildings have been restored and are open the year round. In summer a fort guard, uniformed and armed as in 1813, performs drills of the period. The invading Americans now are all tourists.

LOWER FORT GARRY

Nineteen miles north of Winnipeg, Manitoba

This relic of the fur-trading days, given to the nation by the Hudson's Bay Company, has been scrupulously restored, even to the smell of tanned hides. The governor's spinet and fine china and silver were a flourish in the wilderness.

FORT BATTLEFORD NATIONAL PARK

Battleford, Saskatchewan

This reconstructed early North West Mounted Police post figured in the second Riel rising. Here, a handful of men represented law and order over a half million square miles. An early sod house is one of many exhibits.

EDMONTON HOUSE

12040 104th Avenue, Edmonton, Alberta

A replica of the chief factor's house, with blockhouses and stockade, originally part of Fort Edmonton, a Hudson's Bay post built in 1796.

FORT "WHOOP-UP"

Southwest of Lethbridge, Alberta

This is a reconstruction of the most notorious of the American trading posts set up to compete with the Hudson's Bay Company. All too often whisky and repeating rifles were traded to the Indians for furs. The Mounties closed this fort in 1874.

FORT MACLEOD MUSEUM

Macleod, Alberta

Not far from Lethbridge is a palisaded museum that preserves the history of the first R.C.M.P. post in Alberta. The unit, under Colonel J. F. Macleod, had marched a thousand miles to bring law and order to the wild country.

FORT LANGELEY

Langeley, British Columbia

A Hudson's Bay post as far up the Fraser as ocean-going vessels could reach. British Columbia was proclaimed a crown colony here, and the premier and his cabinet annually meet in the Big House to commemorate the event. A major restoration.

HISTORIC CHURCHES

There are innumerable old churches in Canada, scores of them in Quebec alone. We list a few that relate to our text or have a distinctively Canadian aspect.

ST. PAUL'S CHURCH

Barrington Street, Halifax, Nova Scotia

The oldest Protestant church in Canada (c. 1750). Captain James Lawrence ("Don't Give Up the Ship"), American

St. Paul's Church
at Brantford, Ontario

naval hero of the War of 1812 who died aboard his ship, was buried from St. Paul's. So was the English general Robert Ross, who burned Washington in the same war.

CHAPEL AT CHAPEL ISLAND

Near Soldiers Cove, Nova Scotia

Built in 1792 by the Micmac chiefs.

ST. ANDREW'S CHURCH

Berthierville, Quebec

The first Protestant chapel in Canada was built in 1786 on the seigneury that Wolfe's aide-de-camp purchased. It is now a provincial historic monument.

CHAPEL DE NOTRE-DAME-DU-ROSAIRE

Cap de la Madeleine, Quebec

This small chapel (1714) is a fine example of New France architecture. It was dedicated to the Virgin by the curé when by a quick freeze an ice bridge formed over the St. Lawrence so that stone could be transported across the river for the building of the church.

NOTRE DAME DE BON SECOURS

400 St. Paul East, Montreal, Quebec

The "sailors' church" (1657); its Virgin is a harbor landmark.

NOTRE DAME DES VICTOIRES

Place Royale, Quebec City, Quebec

Built in 1688 and restored in 1759 after Wolfe's bombardment.

THE WOOD CHAPEL

Tadoussac, Quebec

The chapel bell at this famous resort has summoned the faithful since 1647. Its Child Jesus in wax was a gift from Louis XIV to the Indians. The Child's robes are said to have been made by Queen Anne of Austria. The little chapel itself dates from 1747.

THE ANGLICAN CHURCH

East of Notre Dame Street,
Trois Rivières, Quebec

Formerly the Recollet Monastery, this is where Montgomery and Arnold planned the attack on Quebec City.

ST. PAUL'S CHURCH, HER MAJESTY'S CHAPEL OF THE MOHAWKS

Brantford, Ontario

The only Chapel Royal outside of the United Kingdom was built to serve the Mohawks. Fine communion service.

ST. ANDREWS ANGLICAN CHURCH

New Lockport, twelve miles north of Winnipeg, Manitoba

The oldest stone church in western Canada still in use. Its kneeling benches are covered in buffalo hides with the woolly side up. The parishioners replace worn-out covers by cutting up the discarded winter coats of the Winnipeg police, who again use buffalo hides for their greatcoats after experimenting with not-as-warm modern materials.

CHRIST CHURCH

The Pas, Manitoba

The pews, altars, and carvings here were made by ship carpenters during a winter hiatus in the search for the missing Arctic explorer Sir John Franklin.

ST. ANTOINE DE PADOUE CHURCH

Near Batouche National Historic Park, twenty miles west of Domremy, Saskatchewan

The park is the scene of the decisive battle ending the Riel Rebellion of 1885. The Church of St. Antoine de Padoue was Riel's headquarters. The rectory now houses a historical display.

ST. CHARLES MISSION

Dunvegan, Alberta

In 1884 Father Grouard cut, hewed, and sawed the logs for this little church with his own hands. Inside, he painted the ornate decorations. Restored by the government, the church is maintained as a museum by the Oblate Fathers.

HISTORICAL DRAMATIZATION

"THE TRIAL OF LOUIS RIEL"

Saskatchewan House, Regina, Saskatchewan

On Wednesdays, Fridays, and Saturdays, from early July to mid-September, the trial of the famous métis (French-Indian) rebel is re-enacted in Saskatchewan House, formerly the official residence of the lieutenant governor. Though Riel was hanged, he is today a Canadian folk hero.

HOUSES

ROOSEVELT SUMMER HOME

Campobello Island, New Brunswick

From boyhood, this was F.D.R.'s "beloved island." Islanders made his summer home here the first memorial to his memory. Accessible by bridge from Lubec, Maine, from May 15 to September 15.

PERKINS HOUSE MUSEUM

Main Street, Liverpool, Nova Scotia

Colonel Simeon Perkins was an eighteenth-century American, sympathetic to his countrymen until their raids on Liverpool drove him into opposition.

PRINCE'S LODGE

Route 2 near Rockingham, Nova Scotia

This eighteenth-century rotunda is all that is left of the Duke of Kent's country house during his stay in Halifax from 1794 to 1800. Queen Victoria's father used this structure as a music room. Recently restored as a historic site.

CHÂTEAU DE RAMESAY

290 rue Notre-Dame East, Montreal, Quebec

This shabby, old-fashioned museum was the American headquarters during the occupation of Quebec in 1775. Franklin and other Revolutionary notables were here. The portraits of early French inhabitants are also well worth viewing.

MAISON MAILLOU

17 St. Louis Street, Quebec City, Quebec

This eighteenth-century town house has been restored by the Chamber of Commerce, which has its headquarters here.

BRANT HOUSE MUSEUM

Burlington, Ontario

A replica of the Georgian house that was the residence of Chief Joseph Brant, the great Mohawk Indian who fought for the British in the American Revolution.

"UNCLE TOM'S" CABIN AND GRAVE

Dresden, Ontario

This was the home of the Rev. Josiah Henson, an escaped slave and leader

of the blacks in the area. *Harriet Beecher Stowe is believed to have modeled "Uncle Tom" after his character.*

DUNDURN CASTLE

From Toronto or Buffalo, take Queen Elizabeth Highway, exit at Highway 403, and follow signs. Ontario

Perhaps the best house restoration in Canada. A restaurant in the castle features Scottish dishes. Sound-and-light performances on evenings in fine weather between July 1 and Labor Day. The Dundurn Repertory Theatre performs nearby in summer.

MCQUESTEN HOUSE

Business district, Hamilton, Ontario

This unique Victorian (1840–1850) house, coach house, summerhouse, and garden on an acre of land contains all the original furnishings and other possessions of one prominent family, even to the clothes in the closets.

BELLEVUE HOUSE

Centre Street, Kingston, Ontario

The home of Canada's first prime minister, John A. Macdonald. He called it "The Tea Caddy." Restored in 1967 as a centennial project and charmingly furnished in period.

EARNSCLIFFE

Sussex Drive near Macdonald-Cartier Bridge, Ottawa, Ontario

The Victorian Ottawa residence of Sir John A. Macdonald. Not open, but lighted at night. Official residence of the British High Commissioner.

COLBORNE LODGE

High Park, Toronto, Ontario

This Regency house and coach house in Toronto's favorite park are open to tourists.

THE GRANGE

On the grounds of The Art Gallery of Ontario, Toronto, Ontario

The renovation of this 1820 mansion is a major project for Torontonians.

WILLIAM LYON MACKENZIE HOUSE

82 Bond Street, Toronto, Ontario

The leader of the ill-fated 1837 Rebellion spent his last years here. Old-fashioned tea served between 2 and 5 P.M.

THE OLD STONE HOUSE

North bank of St. Mary's River, Sault Ste. Marie, Ontario

This mansion, begun in 1814 by Charles Ermatinger of the North West Company when the town was a small fur-trading post, became a center of business and social life for a vast area. Visited by many notables. Recently restored.

THE JOHN WALTER SITE

Edmonton, Alberta

There are three early log houses in this exhibit. The Walter cabin is the oldest house in Edmonton. In its time it served as a ferryhouse, and an original ferry is moored there. So is a replica of a York boat, the boat Canadians developed to carry settlers, soldiers, freight, and animals over the prairie rivers.

RIEL HOMESTEAD

St. Vital, Manitoba

Louis Riel, the rebel leader, is recognized in this national museum as one of the founders of Manitoba.

THE ROBERT SERVICE CABIN

8th Avenue, Dawson City, Yukon

In this log cabin on a hillside, a visitor hears "the ghost of Service" recite his ballads, if the "ghost" isn't out to lunch.

MUSEUMS

Dozens of towns and cities across Canada have local historical museums, some elaborate, some modest indeed. Many were centennial projects opened in 1967. They are, in simple fact, "too numerous to mention." So we have selected a few that are of particular interest. Historic

House Museums are listed under "Houses" on pages 367–68.

NEW BRUNSWICK MUSEUM

Douglas Avenue, Saint John,
New Brunswick

An attractive historical museum, featuring memorabilia of General Wolfe. An extensive collection of Micmac and Maliseet handicrafts is also displayed.

MUSÉE DU FORT

Opposite the Château Frontenac,
Quebec City, Quebec

An intricate electronic system makes guns flash on the Plains of Abraham and ships clash in the St. Lawrence on a dioramic map of the old city and its environs two hundred years ago. A dramatic narration joins the flashing lights to explain all the famous battles in Quebec's history.

MUSÉE DES URSULINES

Quebec City, Quebec

Memorabilia of the oldest (1639) girls' school in America. Montcalm's skull is preserved in the chapel.

JEANNE MANSE MUSEUM

3840 St.-Urbain, Montreal, Quebec

Contains the furnishings of a hospital founded in 1642.

MILL OF KINTAIL MUSEUM

Route 29 near Almonte, Ontario

In an old gristmill, there are casts of medals and monuments done by Canada's surgeon-sculptor, R. Tait MacKenzie.

SIGMUND SAMUEL CANADIANA BUILDING

Royal Ontario Museum,
14 Queen's Park Crescent,
Toronto, Ontario

The early prints and paintings are exceptional.

MUSEUM OF THE UPPER LAKES

Nancy Island, Wasaga Beach, Ontario

When the Canadian schooner Nancy *was sunk in shallow water by three U.S. warships in the War of 1812, sand and silt piling around her hull created an island. Later the hull was raised, and a striking modern museum has been built around it and other Great Lakes historic relics.*

ROYAL CANADIAN MOUNTED POLICE MUSEUM

R.C.M.P. Training Headquarters,
Dewdney Avenue West, Regina,
Saskatchewan

Exhibits concerned with the Mounties' history and many famous cases handled by them. Open daily. Tours of the training area can also be arranged.

WESTERN DEVELOPMENT MUSEUMS

Saskatoon, North Battleford, and
Yorkton, Saskatchewan

The largest of these three museums is at Saskatoon. Featured are pioneer relics, including antique cars and farm machinery, all in working order. During Saskatoon's Pion-Era in early July, the machines come to life as the city relives the past.

OLD LOG CHURCH MUSEUM

302 Ellion Street, Whitehorse, Yukon

The building itself, as well as its colorful contents, is real Canadiana.

NATIONAL PARK

NOOTKA PARK

Nootka Reservation, Vancouver Island,
British Columbia

A main feature planned for this unusual park is an interpretation center that explains not only the west-coast Indian culture but also the early history of the island, where the Spanish built the first white settlement. The visits of the early English explorers, Captain James Cook and Captain George Vancouver, are also featured in displays.

PIONEER VILLAGES

In Canada, Pioneer Villages are next in popularity to forts for preserving local history. In conception, most of these more closely resemble Sturbridge and Dearborn villages in the United States than they do Williamsburg.

At Upper Canada Village, near Morrisburg, Ontario, a loom is demonstrated.

Historic structures and vehicles from several periods are moved to a convenient area and set up on rambling village streets. Eventually, everything that works—planing mill, cheese factory, steamboat—is put into operation. Where products are made on the site—fresh bread, cheese, ironwork from the forge—these are often sold directly to the public. School children arrive by the busload to cluck at the roving chickens, ride the early steam train, and otherwise learn a bit of history painlessly. These assemblies can give visitors a sense of both the differences and the similarities between Canadian and American life during successive periods.

There are notable exceptions to

this general pattern. Saint-Marie-among-the-Hurons is a careful reconstruction of the palisaded village built on that spot in 1639 by Jesuit missionaries. Nearby, a Huron Indian village has been re-created after equally scholarly study. Another exception is an ethnic re-creation, the Mennonite Village near Steinbach, Manitoba. In effect, the French-Canadian pioneer villages are "ethnic," too, quite unlike either the western Canadian or the American examples. Since most early habitant houses that survive are still occupied, these villages offer almost the only opportunity a casual visitor has to see the inside of a seventeenth-century French-Canadian cottage.

JACQUES DE CHAMBLY HISTORICAL VILLAGE

Route 1, fifteen miles south of Montreal, Quebec

Original French-Canadian buildings, dating from 1675 to 1825.

VILLAGE DE SERAPHIN

Ste. Adèle, Quebec

Another re-created French-Canadian village, privately operated. June through October.

GHOST TOWN

Val-Jalbert, Route 54A, Quebec

This town has now been converted into a tourist park with a hotel and camping grounds. Some of the old houses are open to the curious. There's a 236-foot waterfall as an added natural attraction.

SAINTE-MARIE-AMONG-THE-HURONS

Route 12 near Midland, Ontario

An important Canadian restoration of a palisaded village built by Jesuit missionaries in 1639. The archaeological work that preceded every step of the building is documented in the museum.

UPPER CANADA VILLAGE

Route 401 near Morrisburg, Ontario

The buildings here were moved when the development of the St. Lawrence Seaway threatened to inundate them. This restoration—one of the best—preserves the natural shabbiness and disorder of a nevertheless warm and appealing village.

BLACK CREEK VILLAGE

Toronto, Ontario

DOON ROAD VILLAGE

Near Kitchener, Ontario

FANSHAWE PIONEER VILLAGE

Near London, Ontario

WESTFIELD PIONEER VILLAGE

Near Hamilton, Ontario

HURON INDIAN VILLAGE

Route 12 near Midland, Ontario

Full-scale replica of a seventeenth-century native community. The Huronia Museum is nearby.

1910 LOGGING CAMP

Thunder Bay, Ontario

Visitors to this very complete reconstruction can also eat a logger's meal.

MENNONITE VILLAGE

Off Route 12, Steinbach, Manitoba

A simple but true ethnic recreation.

HERITAGE PARK

82nd Avenue Southwest and 14th Street West, Calgary, Alberta

This one has a steam locomotive in action and also offers rides on an old river boat.

GREAT NORTHWEST PIONEER VILLAGE

Route 16, twenty miles west of Edmonton, Alberta

BARKERVILLE HISTORIC PARK

Fifty miles off Route 97, British Columbia

A re-created gold-rush town with lots of live action. The most extensive in the west.

FORT STEELE HISTORIC PARK

On Route 93 near Cranbrook, British Columbia

A "ghost" mining village on the Kootenay River has been restored to bustling life. Outside the stockade one can take a train ride behind a steam engine inscribed with the names of former passengers: Kaiser Wilhelm, King Alphonso of Spain, and Edward VII of England.

PIONEER VILLAGE
Three Valley Gap, British Columbia

OTHER STRUCTURES

180 COVERED BRIDGES ACROSS NEW BRUNSWICK

The province has a long-range plan to restore to their original state its many existing covered bridges. A booklet on the most noted of these can be obtained from the provincial Department of Tourism at Fredericton, New Brunswick.

THE OLD TOWN CLOCK
Citadel Hill, Halifax, Nova Scotia

Erected by Queen Victoria's father, who was commander in chief at Halifax during the Napoleonic Wars. He had a mania for punctuality, and with the clock made sure Haligonians would have no excuse for being late at his functions.

TALON VAULTS
15 St. Nicholas Street, Lower Town, Quebec City, Quebec

In 1668 Intendant Jean Talon established the first brewery in Canada—largely so that beer might reduce the mounting consumption of brandy in the old city. These seven vaults were built into its foundation. Equipped today with antique relics of the brewing business, it is a favorite tourist attraction. Owned by Dow Brewery.

PALACE GRAND THEATRE
Dawson City, Yukon

See the "Gaslight Follies," a girlie show under sober official sponsorship, any night except Monday. This once raucous music hall was restored by federal money. Now Ottawa is planning to restore several more Gold Rush relics here and to set up a historic park on Bonanza Creek.

See also PUBLIC BUILDINGS under ARCHITECTURE.

TRAILS AND WALKING TOURS

WALKING TOUR OF OLD QUEBEC
Start from Municipal Tourist Bureau, D'Anteuil Street, Quebec City, Quebec

Get the local walking-tour map of the historic old city, much of which has been, and is being, restored with municipal and provincial monies.

ILE D'ORLEANS
Take bridge off Route 15 for island

Sixty miles round trip from Quebec City, Quebec. Old stone houses and churches in a compact area.

WALKING TOUR OF TROIS RIVIÈRES
Quebec

This St. Lawrence River town was a nursery for many of the famous coureurs de bois, explorers, and missionaries. In its oldest area there are houses dating from 1690. The Franciscan rectory (1699) was Montgomery's headquarters for a time in 1775. In the Ursuline Convent, sick and wounded Americans were cared for by the nuns.

WALKING TOUR OF OLD MONTREAL
Leaves from 440 Place Jacques Cartier, Montreal, Quebec

An hour-and-a-quarter walk with well-trained guides. Not free since it is run by a tour agency rather than the city.

VACATION TRAIL NO. I
Southeast Saskatchewan

The province of Saskatchewan has laid out several vacation trails of interest to visitors. The Cannington-Souris Trail around an area south of Moose Mountain Provincial Park has markers showing the trails of early explorers, Mounties, General Custer in pursuit of the Sioux, etc. For details, write the Tourist Development Branch, Power Building, Regina.

GASTOWN
Vancouver, British Columbia

Restoration of the city's oldest area has begun. At the Antique and Flea Market on Water Street everything from junk to rare Chinese art can be found on Sundays.

BASTION SQUARE

Victoria, British Columbia

This comparatively early square on the waterfront has been handsomely restored to its original Victorian British style. Shops and restaurants and a Maritime Museum in the Law Courts Building.

VESSELS

THE HUDSON'S BAY COMPANY'S *Nonsuch*

Museum of Man and Nature, Winnipeg, Manitoba

As part of its tricentenary celebration, "the Bay" built a reproduction of the little fifty-foot square-rigged ketch that sailed into Hudson Bay in 1668. Its crew set up the first of the forts that were to mark "the Bay's" history. After the return of the Nonsuch *with a rich load of furs, Charles II gave the Company its charter on May 2, 1670.*

THE SCHOONER *St. Roch*

In a shelter near The Marine Museum, Vancouver, British Columbia

This little wooden R.C.M.P. Arctic patrol ship was the first to travel the Northwest Passage from west to east and the only ship to cover the whole route in both directions.

S.S. *Keno*

Dawson City, Yukon

The old stern-wheeler that pioneered the Yukon travels nowhere these days, but is open as a museum.

Industry

Most Canadian industrial plants welcome visitors. Many have regular tours, particularly in the summer months. The local chambers of commerce will supply information about them, or when there are no scheduled tours at a specific plant, arrange one on request. We list only a few out of thousands, either because of their size, their convenient locations, or their oddity.

SMITH & RHULAND LTD.

Lunenberg, Nova Scotia

This shipyard is still turning out Nova Scotia schooners. It built the replica of H.M.S. Bounty *for the film* Mutiny on the Bounty.

NATIONAL SEA PRODUCTS, LTD.

Lunenberg, Nova Scotia

Said to be the largest fish plant in North America. Tours arranged.

CONLEY'S LOBSTER POUND

Northern Harbor, Deer Island, New Brunswick

The largest of its kind in the world, the pound may be reached by ferry from L'Etete, New Brunswick. It may be visited in summer and fall.

ALCAN ALUMINUM SMELTER

Arvida, Quebec

A co-ordinator of visitors handles reservations for the bus that takes guests on a two-hour tour of one of the world's largest aluminum-smelting plants. Bilingual guides. Nearby is the Shipsaw Power Plant, which provides the energy for this and other operations.

McCORMICK MONUMENT

Baie Comeau, Quebec

What is now a thriving industrial town in the northern Quebec wilderness grew up around the paper-pulp newsprint mill built in 1936 for the Chicago Tribune. Then, there was no overland communication with the settled world. Today it has a deepwater port, ferries, an aviation base for the whole region, a big aluminum refinery, huge grain elevators, fine churches, a sports arena, a ski tow, and a statue of the Tribune's Colonel Robert McCormick, fondateur de Baie Comeau, depicted paddling a canoe.

E. B. EDDY CO.

Hull, Quebec

Across the Ottawa River from Parliament. Morning tours of this paper factory are scheduled year-round.

CASAVANT FRÈRES, PIPE-ORGAN BUILDERS

St. Hyacinthe, Quebec

This unusual factory, founded in 1880, is listed by the town as one of its major "Places of Interest" for visitors.

CHISHOLM LACROSSE FACTORY

Cornwall Island, Ontario

In a factory on this island, part of the St. Regis Reserve, skilled Mohawk Indians manufacture 97 per cent of the lacrosse sticks used by players around the world. Since field lacrosse and box lacrosse are two different games, and since a team may use four different types of sticks, the plant produces a wide variety of styles. Orders for some eighty-five thousand sticks are received each year.

INTERNATIONAL NICKEL COMPANY OF CANADA LTD.

Four miles west on Route 17, Sudbury, Ontario

Daily tours of the world's largest nickel smelter and refinery are held from May 15 to September 15. Children are not admitted.

GREAT LAKES PAPER COMPANY

Thunder Bay, Ontario

The largest paper machine in the world turns out nearly 400,000 tons of newsprint a year.

ALCAN WORKS

Kitimat, British Columbia

Third-largest aluminum smelting plant in North America. Tours daily.

Mining and Mineralogy

MINES

Canada's underground riches are still keeping prospectors busy, although in these comparatively easy times they explore by bush plane. Working mines of all sorts can usually be toured on request. In the gold-silver-uranium mining area of northeastern Ontario, for example, the chambers of commerce of Cobalt, Kirkland Lake, Timmins, and Elliot Lake will quickly arrange visits. Where the gold is in streams and rivers rather than underground, visitors are often allowed to pan it for themselves. This is the case at the Fraser and Quesnal rivers near Quesnal, British Columbia, for instance. Tourists won't strike it rich, but a day's healthful work could provide them with unusual souvenirs. Here is a list of a few of the really big operations:

NORANDA MINES

Noranda, Quebec

This copper-and-gold complex is the center for some thirty mines in this far northwestern area of Quebec. The ore body at Noranda was discovered by an English-Canadian prospector who tried in vain to interest businessmen in his find. In 1920 he formed a syndicate with a capital of $225. Noranda's production is now worth $200 million annually. Surface installations can be toured with a guide.

ASBESTOS CORPORATION

Pie XI and S. Notre Dame Streets, Thetford Mines, Quebec

Tours of this asbestos mine and its processing plant are held daily. The innumerable tips now crowd up against the houses in the little town in frightening fashion, but the townsfolk are reluctant to leave.

STEEP ROCK IRON MINES

Three and one-half miles north of Atikokan, Ontario

An observation platform offers a view

of the open-pit workings of Ontario's largest iron mine. Tours arranged for this and other mines in the vicinity.

RANWICK URANIUM MINES

Montreal River Harbor, Route 17, north of Sault Ste. Marie, Ontario

Tours of the tunnel are conducted, but no collecting is permitted on the site. Some of the rarest minerals are found here.

FALCONBRIDGE NICKEL MINES

Sudbury, Ontario

Daily tours offered in July and August. No children admitted. One of the world's major nickel producers.

SULLIVAN MINE

Kimberley, British Columbia

"World's largest lead-zinc mine." Tours.

CRAIGMONT MINES

Merritt, British Columbia

From its 700-foot open pit, 50 million tons of copper were extracted from 1963 to 1969, and the operation is still going strong. Copper-colored Stetsons are for sale in Merritt, the province's copper capital.

CONSOLIDATED MINING & SMELTING COMPANY

Yellowknife, Northwest Territories

Tourists are welcome in summer at this big gold mine in the gold-rush town that has become the capital of the Northwest Territories.

MINING MUSEUMS

MINERS MUSEUM

Quarry Point, Glace Bay, Nova Scotia

COBALT MINING MUSEUM

Silver Street, Cobalt, Ontario

A fine museum where information on tours of local silver mines are available.

SILVER ISLET MINE

Sibley Provincial Park, Route 11 near Thunder Bay, Ontario

Off this park peninsula is the tiny dot of land, often washed over by waves, that was the site in 1872–1884 of one of the world's richest silver mines. Only resourceful engineering and extensive

cribworks, some still visible, made the operation possible. The park opens on the first Friday in June and closes on the second Sunday in September.

ROCK-COLLECTING SITES

Canada boasts more bonanza sites for rock hunters than we have space for in this single volume. We recommend that interested visitors send for one or more of the authoritative publications that Ann P. Sabina has compiled under federal auspices. Prepaid orders should be sent to The Director, Geological Survey of Canada, 601 Booth Street, Ottawa, Canada, with the check or money order made out to the Receiver General of Canada. The first series by Miss Sabina covers major areas, telling what can be found and where. The appendixes include addresses of Canadian mineral clubs. Each is a valuable handbook. The second series is a continuing project, each "paper" providing a detailed study of a specific small area. So far seven of these have been completed. The listing below indicates the area covered. Prices vary with the numbers of pages and location maps in each booklet.

Rock and Mineral Collecting in Canada, by Ann P. Sabina. Vol. I: Western Canada, starting with Manitoba and including the Yukon and the Northwest Territories. 147 pp. 23 location maps; 9 photos. $1.30

Vol. II: Ontario and Quebec. 252 pp. 47 location maps; 9 photos. $2.00

Vol. III: The Maritime Provinces and Newfoundland. 103 pp. 13 location maps; 8 photos. $1.00

Rocks and Minerals for the Collector, by Ann P. Sabina. Paper 63–18: Sudbury, Ontario to Winnipeg, Manitoba. 69 pp. Table, maps. .75

Paper 64–10: Bay of Fundy area, Nova Scotia, and New Brunswick. 96 pp. Figure and 8 plates. .75

Paper 65–10: Northeastern Nova Scotia, Cape Breton, and Prince Edward Island. 76 pp. Figure, 4 location maps, and 12 plates.   .75

Paper 66–51: Eastern Townships and Gaspé, Quebec. and parts of New Brunswick. 170 pp. Figure, 12 location maps, and 16 plates. $2.00

Paper 67–51: Kingston, Ontario to Lac St.-Jean, Quebec. 147 pp. Figure, 7 location maps, and 14 plates. $2.00

Paper 68–51: Buckingham-Mont Laurier-Granville, Quebec; Hawkesbury, Ontario. 107 pp. $2.00

Paper 69–50: Hull-Maniwaki. Quebec; Ottawa-Peterborough, Ontario. $2.00

Also available from the director is David M. Baird's series on the geology and scenery of Canada's national parks. There are twelve of them, ranging in price from seventy-five cents for the booklet on Cape Breton Highlands Park in Nova Scotia to three dollars for the 307-page volume on Banff National Park. For the collector who is expert enough to know what geological processes produce what rocks and minerals, they would be helpful, but they are not focused as directly as Miss Sabina's work on the rock-hunter's field. Most provincial tourist departments have some information available on rock sites, which they will send free on request. Many of them may quote Miss Sabina's first series as a reference. The information provided may be only a mimeographed sheet or it may be a handsome booklet like the Ontario Department's "Minerals and Rocks." As might be expected, mine dumps and disused mines will prove rich sources of minerals, but permission to explore them should always be asked. Courtesy requires it, but the safety of the rock hunter demands it. A

mine manager or property owner is the person best informed of hazards on a site.

MINERALOGICAL MISCELLANY

"SEVEN DAYS WORK" CLIFF
Whale Cove, Grand Manan Island, New Brunswick

This cliff, in which seven graduated strata of the earth's crust are plainly seen, was named from the Biblical account of creation. May be reached by passenger boat from either Saint John or St. Andrews.

JOGGINS FOSSIL CLIFFS
Joggins, Nova Scotia

Cliffs 150 feet high imbedded with fossilized plants.

ROCKHOUND ROUND-UP
Parrsboro, Nova Scotia

Mid-August. Tours of nearby rock and fossil areas.

GEM-BOREE
Bancroft, Ontario

Held in August, under the sponsorship of the Bancroft Chamber of Commerce, in a rock-rich area. Seventy minerals found here are displayed in the Royal Ontario Museum's Inco Gallery.

INCO MINERAL GALLERY
Royal Ontario Museum, Toronto, Ontario
One of the world's finest collections.

ROCK FINISHING PLANT
Golden, British Columbia
Chairs and tables made of boulders.

FRASER RIVER ROCK DISPLAY
Hope Tourist Bureau, Hope, British Columbia

Science
and
Engineering

CANALS

RIDEAU CANAL

Ottawa to Kingston, Ontario

Below Parliament Hill in Ottawa a notable series of eight locks lowers pleasure craft eighty feet to the Ottawa River. Other locks along the Rideau— whose 124-mile length is partly hand-hewn stone and partly natural water-way—are kept in their original 1832 condition, with locks manually operated.

See BOAT TRIPS *for:* Lift Lock Tours at Peterborough, Ontario. Soo Lock Tours at Sault Ste. Marie, Ontario. St. Lawrence Seaway Tours from Long Sault, Ontario.

DAMS AND POWER PLANTS

MANIC V

135 miles north of Baie Comeau, Quebec

This is the biggest of the five dams Quebec Hydro will eventually build on the Manicouagan River. When the multiple-vault system was proposed for a dam this size and height (705 feet), there were doubters, but they seem to have been silenced by the impressive reality. Québecois designed and constructed this one.

BERSIMIS I HYDRO PLANT

Labrieville, Quebec

This point on the Bersimis River was known as Grand-Remous (great whirl-pool). There, a big generating plant has been built into a mountain. The water carried to it comes through a tunnel seven and a half miles long, also carved out of rock. Tours are offered. This is one of several interesting dams along Quebec's North Shore.

ROBERT H. SAUNDERS–ST. LAWERENCE GENERATING STATION

Cornwall, Ontario

This giant powerhouse and dam across the St. Lawrence River is the key to Canadian-American Seaway power and development. Tours are scheduled from mid-May to mid-October.

SIR ADAM BECK–NIAGARA STATION No. 2

Niagara Falls, Ontario

Guides of daily tours explain how the power of the Falls is transformed into four million kilowatts of electrical energy.

DES JOACHIMS GENERATING STATION

Off Highway 11, Rolphton, Ontario

This nuclear power plant can be toured daily in July and August.

GARDINER DAM

Cutbank, Saskatchewan

Northwest of Moose Jaw, this is the largest earth-fill dam in Canada, rising 210 feet above the South Saskatchewan River. It has created Lake Diefenbaker, 140 miles long. Qu'Appelle Dam to the southeast controls the flow into Qu' Appelle Valley. Because the dam is situated on the major waterfowl flyway, there are huge concentrations of ducks and geese every fall. There is a display dealing with the development, operation, and usefulness of the project.

PEACE RIVER DAM

Hudson's Hope, British Columbia

This gigantic dam and power project can be toured while it is being built and after it is completed. The "new town" is worth examining, too. It is one of six already established under the aegis of the provincial government, some in remote regions. All are built around a key industry, but none are "company towns." They are independent munici-palities with all the amenities needed to attract workers.

WANETA POWER PLANT

Trail, British Columbia

A 950-foot dam with a spillway water-fall 45 feet higher than Niagara.

MEDICAL MISSION

GRENFELL MISSION

St. Anthony, Newfoundland

This is the headquarters of the world-famous Grenfell Mission that for decades has brought medical help to the isolated poor of northern New-foundland and Labrador, white fisher-men and Eskimo hunters alike. To serve a huge bleak area, it now has four hospitals, fourteen nursing stations, a hospital ship, and three planes (two from the Department of Health). St. Anthony, its center and most flourishing

Manic V, a huge dam on the Manicougan River in Quebec

community, can be toured informally.

MUSEUMS

ALEXANDER GRAHAM BELL MUSEUM

Baddeck, Nova Scotia

On display are working models of many of Bell's experiments and inventions, including not only the telephone but also hydrofoil boats, an early plane, and an iron lung.

THE BELL HOMESTEAD

Tutela Heights, Brantford, Ontario

While visiting his father here, Bell first conceived the idea of the telephone in 1874. Two summers later, the first long-distance call was made from this house, now a museum of telephone history.

NUCLEAR ENERGY MUSEUM

Public Information Centre,
Chalk River, Ontario

Displays on the development of the peaceful uses of atomic energy.

WOOD HOUSE

Cornwall, Ontario

Among its chiefly historical displays, this museum has the electrical equipment that Thomas Edison installed in the old Stormont Mill. Open daily 10–5; Sunday 2–5.

NATIONAL MUSEUM OF SCIENCE AND TECHNOLOGY

St. Laurent Boulevard and Russell Road, Ottawa, Ontario

A lively heterogeneous display.

NUCLEAR POWER DEMONSTRATION CENTRE

Rolphton, Ontario

Daily from mid-June to Labor Day.

ONTARIO SCIENCE CENTRE

770 Don Mills Road, Toronto, Ontario

An exceptional new science museum— the Province of Ontario's centennial project—provides space-age learning experiences for people of all ages.

Sports

ARCHERY

Some Canadian provinces set aside a special season in certain areas for hunting with a bow and arrow. Quebec's Rimouski Park, thirty miles south of the town of Rimouski, has such a season for deer hunting, which attracts large numbers of expert archers each year. For information on specific provincial arrangements, write to the various provincial departments of tourism. See Fishing and Hunting, page 380, for the addresses of all departments.

Archery Events
INDIAN MEMORIAL SHOOT

Onandaga, near Brantford, Ontario

The shoot is held in mid-July in Mohawk country

BICYCLE RACE

TOUR DE LA NOUVELLE FRANCE

Quebec

Starting in the townships south of the St. Lawrence, the grueling course takes the racers a thousand miles around the Province of Quebec to Qubec City, La Tuque, and Trois Rivières. It ends at St. Jérôme. The ten-day race takes place in the first half of July.

BOATING

With Canada's thousands of lakes and endless miles of rivers, boating of all sorts is a leading summer sport. Sailboats, powerboats, yachts of all sizes, houseboats, and canoes dot the highways as well, as they are towed or toted to a favorite stretch of water. National, provincial, and local authorities have naturally responded to this demand by setting up a variety of facilities.

British Columbia, for example, has ten marine parks. Established on a spit here or an island there along the province's beautiful coast, they have been designed for the convenience of vacationers who travel by water.

Nova Scotia publishes an informative "Cruising Guide," which includes in a back pocket a map showing the number of the Canadian nautical chart pertaining to each area. Copies of the guide available from the Nova Scotia Travel Bureau, Department of Trade and Industry, Halifax, Nova Scotia.

Ontario's Department of Tourism distributes a thick pamphlet, "Marine Facilities," which is a very complete compendium of the facilities, services, and supplies available on Ontario's lakes and waterways. Ontario also rebates the provincial gas tax on all fuel for visiting boats from the United States. The visitor obtains form GT-1001 from the Provincial Treasury Department and sends it, plus all gas receipts, to the Inspector of Gasoline Refunds, Treasury Department, Parliament Buildings, Toronto 5, Ontario, within eight months of purchase.

Along the St. Lawrence and at some points on Georgian Bay, Lake Huron, the most popular marine facilities are in national parks. Anyone interested in them should write the Canadian Government Travel Bureau in Ottawa. Wherever one intends to set out, he has only to pick his route and write the departments concerned (see under Hunting and Fishing for all addresses) to be overwhelmed with helpful material. In some of the big national parks, practical canoe routes have been mapped out for visitors. Guides and outfitters are subject to licensing, and lists of approved guides are available.

In the Northwest Territories, Hudson's Bay Company has set up a Rent-a-Canoe service for sportsmen. For details, write Hudson's Bay House, Winnipeg, Manitoba.

Houseboats for Rent
RICHELIEU RIVER AREA

Southern Quebec

> Contact the Quebec Department of Tourism for information on rentals along this placid, historic river.

CHIPPEWA

On the Niagara Parkway, Ontario

> Chippewa bills itself as the Houseboat Capital of Canada. Prices range from $150 to $300 a week, gas extra. Write the local tourist office for a list of dealers.

SHUSHWAP LAKE

Sicamous, British Columbia

> Currently there are thirty-one houseboats available for rent on this big, quiet lake. Prices as above. Twin Anchors Houseboats; Galaxy Houseboats Ltd., Box 69; and Shandy Cove Houseboats, Box 289, are all members of the Sicamous Houseboat Assocation.

Boating Events
NOVA SCOTIA SCHOONER RACES

Halifax, Nova Scotia

> Early July.

MARBLEHEAD-HALIFAX OCEAN YACHT RACE

Finishes at Halifax, Nova Scotia

> Mid-July.

REGATTA WEEK

Saint John, New Brunswick

> Second week in July.

HUNDRED-MILE INTERNATIONAL CANOE RACE

La Tuque to Trois Rivières, Quebec

> Along the Saint Maurice River on Labor Day weekend.

ROYAL CANADIAN HENLEY REGATTA

Henley Course, St. Catharines, Ontario

> Early July.

SEA FESTIVAL

Vancouver, British Columbia

> Last half of July.

FISHING AND HUNTING

There was a time when Americans came to Canada *only* to hunt and fish. Many still do, since the country's wealth of fish and game constitute a major attraction.

For a handy summing up of the hundreds of kinds of fish and the thousands of points across the country where they may be caught, write the Canadian Government Travel Bureau, Ottawa, Canada, for its pamphlet "Where to Fish in Canada." Then, for information on any specific area for a holiday, contact the provincial office concerned. They are listed below:

THE NEWFOUNDLAND TOURIST DEVELOPMENT OFFICE
Confederation Building, St. John's, Newfoundland

PRINCE EDWARD ISLAND TRAVEL BUREAU
Charlottetown, Prince Edward Island

NOVA SCOTIA TRAVEL BUREAU
Provincial Building, Halifax, Nova Scotia

NEW BRUNSWICK TRAVEL BUREAU
Fredericton, New Brunswick

DEPARTMENT OF TOURISM, FISH AND GAME
930 Chemin Ste. Foy, Quebec City.

ONTARIO DEPARTMENT OF TOURISM & INFORMATION
185 Bloor Street East, Toronto, Ontario

DEPARTMENT OF TOURISM &
RECREATION
408 Norquay Building, 401 York Street,
Winnipeg, Manitoba
SASKATCHEWAN TRAVEL BUREAU
Saskatchewan Power Building, Regina,
Saskatchewan
ALBERTA GOVERNMENT TRAVEL BUREAU
1629 Centennial Building, Edmonton,
Alberta
DEPARTMENT OF TRAVEL INDUSTRY
Victoria, British Columbia
TRAVELARCTIC
Tourist Development Section,
Yellowknife, Northwest Territories
DEPARTMENT OF TRAVEL &
INFORMATION
Box 2703, Lynn Building, Whitehorse,
Yukon Territory

The same course should be pursued in finding out about bird- and game-hunting opportunities and regulations across the country, since these vary.

In the Northwest Territories, for instance, sports hunters can go after seals, beluga whales, and for a stiff price, polar bears. Until 1970, only Eskimos were allowed to hunt them, and their bag is still limited to four a year; but now an Eskimo community can allow a white hunter to bag one of the bears in its quota—for a fee of two thousand dollars plus the hire of a guide and outfit. In the territories a hunter is required to use an indigenous guide. In De la Verendrye Provincial Park in northwest Quebec, fishing is open to anyone, but only Québecois are licensed to hunt the limited game. Given these regional differences, a hunter's best plan would be to write for full information before he begins to dream.

Fishing Events

THE SPORTSMEN'S MEET

Sherbrooke, Nova Scotia

Late July. Fly-casting contests.

TUNA CUP MATCH

Wedgport and Cape St. Mary,
Nova Scotia

Mid-September.

ANNUAL TROUT FESTIVAL

Phantom Lake, Flin Flon, Manitoba

One thousand dollars for the largest lake trout landed by line in this five-day festival. Must be more than twenty pounds to qualify. There is also a Gold Rush Canoe Derby run in two sections, amateur and professional.

HARNESS RACES

CHARLOTTETOWN DRIVING PARK

Charlottetown, Prince Edward Island

From June to October there are racing cards each night here and at the Summerside, Prince Edward Island, track. Sulky racing is found at many other points in Canada, but on "the Island" it's the major sport.

HOCKEY

The visitor who can lay his hands on a ticket for one of the home games at either the Maple Leaf Gardens in Toronto or the Forum at Montreal will witness Canadians really involved in their national sport.

HORSE RACES

Summer Meets

FORT ERIE JOCKEY CLUB

Fort Erie, Ontario

Mid-July through August. Some of the stake races have purses as high as $30,000.

WOODBINE RACE COURSE

Malton, Ontario

June 1 to mid-July. A big one is the

Queen's Plate on the Saturday nearest the Queen's Birthday holiday, June 24. This is Canada's Derby; it is fifteen years older than the Kentucky event. The $75,000 Woodbine Stakes is run in late October.

HORSE SHOWS

ATLANTIC WINTER FAIR

Halifax, Nova Scotia

First week in November.

CANADIAN NATIONAL EXHIBITION

Exhibition Park, Toronto, Ontario

National Horse Show, third week in August.

MOTORCYCLE RACES

INTERNATIONAL GRAND PRIX

Mosport Park, Orono, Ontario

Late June.

SKIING

Canada, a rugged country enjoying ample snow, has in recent years become intensely ski-minded. The largest ski club in the world is at Camp Fortune, Quebec, just across the river from Ottawa, where as many as fifty thousand men, women, and children use the slopes on a good weekend. At Revelstoke, British Columbia, skiing is a subject included in the standard school curriculum.

The Canadian Government Travel Bureau at Ottawa publishes a detailed booklet, "Ski Canada," listing more than fifty major resort areas, giving such data as vertical rise, longest run, numbers of trails, night skiing, snow-making, and accommodations, as well as the duration of the season.

Not listed is Bugaloo Lodge in British Columbia, which can only be reached by helicopter from Windermere, British Columbia. Its clients are also flown by helicopter to a virgin slope each morning.

SNOWMOBILE RACES

INTERNATIONAL SNOWMOBILE MEET

Mosport Park, Orono, Ontario

Late January.

Curling is a popular winter sport in Canada.

SPORTS CAR RACES

CANADIAN-AMERICAN CHALLENGE CUP

L'autodrome-du-Mont Tremblant,
St. Jovite, Quebec

One of the nine races in this series is run here, the date depending upon the yearly schedule. From June to October there are a variety of stock-car and motorcycle races at Mont Tremblant.

CANADIAN GRAND PRIX

Mosport Park, Orono, Ontario

This is the big racing-car event in Canada. Late summer. Another of the Canadian-American Challenge Cup races is held here, the date depending upon the schedule for that series.

Train Rides

For rail buffs, Canada still offers some exciting runs, though their numbers have sadly diminished. The legendary Newfie Bullet, which once wound at a snail's pace across Newfoundland ("Bullet" was said with affectionate irony) has been replaced by buses! But the White Pass & Yukon R. R. is reportedly making money, and the famous transcontinental trains still light up the snows in western passes when planes are grounded.

TRANS-CANADIAN

CANADIAN PACIFIC'S THE CANADIAN

Montreal, Quebec, to Vancouver,
British Columbia

One of the last great train rides. (The other is also trans-Canadian, and both are splendid in summer or winter.) Leaves Montreal at 1:30 P.M. daily, arriving at Vancouver 2,879 miles later at 11 A.M. of the third day. Crosses the Rockies at Banff and travels the

magnificent Fraser River country by daylight. Meals are free with all first-class-accommodations.

CANADIAN NATIONAL'S
SUPERCONTINENTAL

Montreal, Quebec, to Vancouver,
British Columbia

The other great transcontinental train ride. Leaves Montreal at 5:05 P.M., and while traveling thirty-five miles farther than the Canadian, shaves more than three hours off its rival's running time. Crosses the Rockies at Jasper.

REGIONAL

AGAWA CANYON TOUR, ALGOMA
CENTRAL R. R.

Sault Ste. Marie, Ontario

Daily train to the spectacular canyon cut by the Agawa River. Particularly popular at the end of September, when the autumn colors of the trees are as beautiful as the several waterfalls along the way. There is a two-hour stopover at the canyon.

THE POLAR BEAR EXPRESS, ONTARIO
NORTHLAND R. R.

Transportation Commission, North Bay,
Ontario

From Cochrane to Moosonee, one-day rail trips to the Arctic tidewater. On Monday, Wednesday, and Friday, June 15 to September 15. Allows five hours of sightseeing with photo stops during train run, or a visitor with a reservation at the Moosonee Lodge can stay over a day or more and take a later train south. Some years there are special Sunday trips in summer. Write for schedule.

DAILY TRAIN, WHITE PASS & YUKON
R. R.

Skagway, Alaska, to Whitehorse, Yukon

Built during the Gold Rush days of '98, this little narrow-gauge railway with only 110.7 miles of line still provides one of the world's most spectacular runs, at points reaching an elevation of nearly three thousand feet. The crew tries to keep to its five-hour, forty-minute schedule, but a bull moose or a grizzly can cause delay. One year the train was snowbound for thirty-one days. Recommended for mid-summer!

INDEX

Italic numbers indicate pages on which illustrations appear.

398